Kennedy in Ber¹'

Kennedy in Berlin examines one of the most spectacul&
eth century. This book tells the story of the enthusiast
president John F. Kennedy paid to Berlin, the "fronth
June 1963. The president's tour triggered the greatest pc   ...nan
history and resonated around the world, not least on ac   ...nedy's famous
declaration – "*Ich bin ein Berliner.*" Andreas W. Daum sets Kennedy's visit against
the background of the special relationship that had developed between the United
States and West Berlin in the wake of World War II. "America's Berlin" became the
place for staging politics as theatrical performance. Political performances helped
create a sense of transatlantic community and emotional closeness between the
United States and Germany that has now itself become history. *Kennedy in Berlin*
is an innovative contribution to the study of transatlantic relations, the Cold War,
and the conduct of diplomacy in the age of mass media. Using a broad range of
sources, this book sheds new light on the interplay between politics and culture in
the modern era.

Andreas W. Daum is a professor of modern history at the State University of New
York at Buffalo. He has taught at the University of Munich, where he earned
his doctorate, and has been a Research Fellow at the German Historical Institute,
Washington, D.C., and a John F. Kennedy Memorial Fellow at Harvard University.
He is the author of *Wissenschaftspopularisierung im 19. Jahrhundert* and the coeditor
of *America, the Vietnam War, and the World*, with Lloyd C. Gardner and Wilfried
Mausbach, and, with Christof Mauch, of *Berlin – Washington: Capital Cities, Cultural
Representations, and National Identities*, both published by Cambridge University
Press.

PUBLICATIONS OF THE GERMAN HISTORICAL INSTITUTE
WASHINGTON, D.C.

Edited by Christof Mauch
with the assistance of David Lazar

The German Historical Institute is a center for advanced study and research whose purpose is to provide a permanent basis for scholarly cooperation among historians from the Federal Republic of Germany and the United States. The Institute conducts, promotes, and supports research into both American and German political, social, economic, and cultural history; into transatlantic migration, especially in the nineteenth and twentieth centuries; and into the history of international relations, with special emphasis on the roles played by the United States and Germany.

Recent books in the series

Marc Flandreau, Carl-Ludwig Holtfrerich, and Harold James, editors, *International Financial History in the Twentieth Century: System and Anarchy*

Andreas W. Daum, Lloyd C. Gardner, and Wilfried Mausbach, editors, *America, the Vietnam War, and the World: International and Comparative Perspectives*

Detlef Junker, editor, *The United States and Germany in the Era of the Cold War: A Handbook*, 2 volumes

Roger Chickering, Stig Förster, and Bernd Greiner, editors, *A World at Total War: Global Conflict and the Politics of Destruction, 1937–1945*

Kiran Klaus Patel, *Soldiers of Labor: Labor Service in Nazi Germany and New Deal America, 1933–1945*

Andreas Daum and Christof Mauch, editors, *Berlin – Washington, 1800–2000: Capital Cities, Representation, and National Identities*

Peter Becker and Richard F. Wetzell, editors, *Criminals and Their Scientists: The History of Ciminology in International Perspective*

Michelle Mouton, *From Nurturing the Nation to Purifying the Volk: Weimar and Nazi Family Policy, 1918–1945*

Jonathan R. Zatlin, *The Currency of Socialism: Money and Political Culture in East Germany*

Kennedy in Berlin

ANDREAS W. DAUM
State University of New York at Buffalo

TRANSLATED BY DONA GEYER

GERMAN HISTORICAL INSTITUTE
Washington, D.C.
and

 CAMBRIDGE
UNIVERSITY PRESS

CAMBRIDGE UNIVERSITY PRESS
Cambridge, New York, Melbourne, Madrid, Cape Town, Singapore, São Paulo, Delhi

Cambridge University Press
32 Avenue of the Americas, New York, NY 10013-2473, USA

www.cambridge.org
Information on this title: www.cambridge.org/9780521858243

GERMAN HISTORICAL INSTITUTE
1607 New Hampshire Avenue, N.W., Washington, DC 20009, USA

© Verlag Ferdinand Schöningh 2003
© German Historical Institute 2008

First published in German by Verlag Ferdinand Schöningh 2003
English edition 2008

Printed in the United States of America

A catalog record for this publication is available from the British Library.

Library of Congress Cataloging in Publication Data

Daum, Andreas W.
[Kennedy in Berlin. English]
Kennedy in Berlin / Andreas W. Daum ; translated by Dona Geyer.
p. cm. – (Publications of the German Historical Institute)
Includes bibliographical references and index.
ISBN 978-0-521-85824-3 (hardback) – ISBN 978-0-521-67497-3 (pbk.)
1. Kennedy, John F. (John Fitzgerald), 1917–1963. 2. Berlin (Germany) – Politics and government –
1945–1990. 3. Berlin Wall, Berlin, Germany, 1961–1989. 4. United States – Foreign relations –
Soviet Union. 5. Soviet Union – Foreign relations – United States. I. Title. II. Series.
E841.D3513 2007
327.7304309'046-dc22 2006100006

ISBN 978-0-521-85824-3 hardback
ISBN 978-0-521-67497-3 paperback

Contents

Contents

Illustrations

Acknowledgments

I would like to express my sincere gratitude to those institutions and individuals who, over the course of many years, have made the research for this book enjoyable and its writing possible.

I am grateful to each of the archives and libraries listed in the bibliography, particularly those in Berlin; Bonn; Washington, D.C.; and Boston and Cambridge, Massachusetts, for allowing me to study their archival material extensively. At the archives of the Friedrich-Ebert-Stiftung, I received generous help from Gertrud Lenz, Harry Scholz, and Wolfgang Sterke. During my visits to the Landesarchiv Berlin and in our transatlantic correspondence, Dr. Christiane Schuchard, Monika Bartzsch, and Barbara Schäche were repeatedly very helpful. At the archives of the Free University Berlin, Dr. Wolfgang Engel advised me cordially, as did James Leyerzapf at the Dwight D. Eisenhower Library in Abilene, Kansas; Allan Goodrich and James Hill at the John F. Kennedy Library near Boston; and Elena Danielson at the Hoover Institution Archives.

The suggestions I received from Dirk Bönker and David E. Barclay from the very start of my project enriched it greatly. Harold Hurwitz, Carl Kaysen, Tom Johnson, Gerald D. Livingston, Martha Mautner, and Fritz Stern, as well as the late Gordon A. Craig, Horst Hartwich, Melvin J. Lasky, and Karl Mautner, deserve my sincerest gratitude for their gracious willingness to talk with me and provide me with important insights from their personal recollections. I was fortunate to be able to speak with two men who participated in Kennedy's procession through Berlin: Robert H. Lochner and Heinz Weber. I am also grateful for the valuable advice given to me by Peter Becker, Marion Deshmukh, Anselm Doering-Manteuffel, Martin H. Geyer, Robert Grathwol, Vernon Lidtke, Alf Lüdtke, Wolfgang Schivelbusch, James F. Tent, and Richard F. Wetzell. Jens Beckert, Georg Nicolaus

Knauer, Elfriede R. Knauer, Ulrich Krotz, and Wilfried Mausbach are to be thanked for their friendship and for reading parts of the manuscript.

I thank the Minda de Gunzburg Center for European Studies at Harvard University and the German Academic Exchange Service for the John F. Kennedy Memorial Fellowship that I was awarded for the academic year 2001/2002, during which the original manuscript was written. The Center for European Studies provided me exceptionally favorable conditions for this task; special thanks go to Abby Collins, Patricia Craig, Peter Hall, and Lisa Eschenbach. The German Historical Institute in Washington, D.C., a vitally important hinge in opening the doors of transatlantic exchange in academia, gave me a thoroughly stimulating environment for more than five years prior to 2001. I am also indebted to the College of Arts and Sciences at SUNY Buffalo for its support in defraying the cost of permission fees for using copyrighted materials.

Egon Bahr, former advisor to Willy Brandt and politically active far beyond the years on which my study focuses, kindly presented the original German version of this book to the public in June 2003 at the Schöneberg City Hall, in front of which John F. Kennedy delivered his famous speech to Berliners forty years earlier. My thanks go to Michael Werner, editor-in-chief at Schöningh Verlag, who agreed to a translation, and to the German Historical Institute, Washington, D.C., for its support of this project, which David Lazar handled with much care. I thank Cambridge University Press for including my book in its program in history and Dona Geyer, who translated it. The text profited from Dona's talent of combining accuracy with ingenuity; it was a pleasure to collaborate with her.

My sincere thanks are extended to those individuals who have supported me with their expertise and continual encouragement throughout the years of my transatlantic existence: Volker R. Berghahn, David Blackbourn, Rüdiger vom Bruch, Roger Chickering, Kathleen Conzen, Wolfgang Hardtwig, Martina Kessel, Johannes Paulmann, Gerhard A. Ritter, James J. Sheehan, and Margit Szöllösi-Janze.

Evis Daum supported me during the final writing phase and while I was working on the translation in her own uniquely generous way. Evis's belief in the value of both writing and reading books has always been encouraging; her kind reminders that there is much to discover beyond them, and her love, more than anything else, are essential for our life together. In the meantime, our son Nicholas has begun to draw his parents' attention to a very different genre of books, and I am happy to admit that the pictures in his are much nicer than those in mine, not to mention the absence of notes.

Once again, I wish to express my gratitude to my parents for all the support and affection they have given me throughout my life. The American edition of this book is dedicated to the memory of my father, Gerhard Daum. I have always admired his boundless curiosity and broad intellectual interests, and I continue to value the virtues he exemplified – his sincerity, his reliability, and his positive outlook on life.

August 2007

Preface to the English Edition

Kennedy in Berlin invites the reader to explore how politics has been staged in the twentieth century. This book wants to demonstrate how statesmen, diplomats, media, and people in the streets have contributed to dramatizing politics and how this drama has been used as a political argument for domestic and international purposes. Closely choreographed as they may be, political performances develop a dynamic of their own, as *Kennedy in Berlin* demonstrates, and their meaning changes over time in our collective memory. Political performances feature actors who follow predetermined roles, but they are equally constituted by those who watch the stage, articulate their reactions, and interfere in the script.

One specific moment in time stands in the center of the book, as its title indicates. On June 26, 1963, one of the most charismatic American presidents ever traveled to one of the most embattled sites of recent history, a city with highly ambiguous symbolical notions. John F. Kennedy toured Berlin – to be more precise: he toured America's Berlin. The president visited the western part of a city that had been, in previous times, the capital of Prussia and Imperial Germany, the metropolis of Weimar Germany, and the center of Hitler's Nazi dictatorship. But the Berlin Kennedy went to had begun to establish a special relationship with America in the late 1940s at the latest, in the early years of what contemporaries already called the Cold War. Kennedy's stay in Berlin, at that time sharply divided between East and West, triggered the greatest happening in German history prior to the fall of the Berlin Wall in 1989. In fact, it generated one of the most spectacular events of the modern era.

For sure, any moment in time is unique and, as in this prominent case, worth being appreciated. Surprisingly enough, we have been lacking so far not only a precise account of what happened on that June day along the Cold War's most dramatic dividing line, but also an explanation of why things occurred as they did. Any moment in time reflects the epoch at large. It is the result of multiple factors and only possible due to circumstances and developments that both precede and transcend the specific setting. A microperspective, that is, a close examination of a particular moment, may therefore allow new macroperspectives, meaning insights into the era in which the moment was embedded. Yet, as Carlo Ginzburg has rightly argued, the "reconciliation between macro- and microhistory" needs to be pursued consciously by the historian.[1] Using a microhistory to reveal larger issues at stake requires one to read the specific point in time closely as well as to frame this reading in broad terms, provided by general questions and today's knowledge, and to keep an eye on the historicity of the moment itself. *Kennedy in Berlin* undertakes such an attempt.

By looking at John F. Kennedy's trip to Berlin, this book identifies major features of the twentieth century and especially the era of the Cold War that have so far received little attention. It highlights symbolic politics, performative action, and emotions as constitutive for transatlantic and especially German-American relations. It emphasizes the tendency to dramatize politics in order to gain legitimacy for specific policies, a technique that characterized not only, as we often read, authoritarian regimes, but also democracies and relations among democratic states. *Kennedy in Berlin* focuses on what I would like to call the politics of visibility, a concern with visual imagery that became essential for gaining consensus in the twentieth century. Last, but not least, this book wants to explain why West Germans, even more so than people in America, cheered an American president so enthusiastically that he appeared almost as a divine sign promising a bright future – certainly a phenomenon that is hard to believe for today's generation.

My hope is to draw readers interested in American and German history, international relations, and the Cold War era, as well as, more generally, in the interactions between politics and culture. My arguments are meant to contribute specifically to the ongoing debates about the history and future of transatlantic and in particular German-American relations. We keep discussing whether the United States created a "consensual hegemony" (Charles S. Maier) or an "empire by invitation" (Geir Lundestad) in Europe following the Second World War. We continue debating to what degree the United States' "soft power" (Joseph S. Nye), that is, its ability to attract others by the legitimacy of its policies and the values that underlie them, affected domestic and international politics during the Cold War era. We want to know more about the potential and the limits of "cooperation among democracies" (Thomas Risse). We still ask why some European societies aligned themselves so closely with a hegemonic power located across the Atlantic. And we need to consider why they ultimately began disassociating themselves from this power and thus raised the challenge of defining a new European-American partnership as "one of equals, of real partners" (Stephen F. Szabo). As the reader will see, the chapters of this book offer a set of nuanced arguments about these and related questions.

Kennedy in Berlin is a piece of historical research, but it has profited immensely from dialogue with neighboring disciplines. It wants to show that source-based diplomatic history and a cultural history concerned with ideas, symbols, and emotions are mutually enriching and share common ground. I am indebted especially to works in the fields of political science and international relations inspired by Karl W. Deutsch. Clifford Geertz's anthropology and recent historical anthropology have greatly informed my approach to the topic, especially my attempt to provide a thick description of an event in which all action bore symbolic character and deserves to be explained in its historical context. Max Weber's sociology of community and society provided an important stimulus, as did modern art history with its emphasis on the interplay of images, media, and society. Finally, my analysis of a Cold War event would not have been possible without taking into account historical research that has dealt with very different epochs, especially works on the history of civil society and the emergence of nation states in the eighteenth and nineteenth centuries.

The city of Berlin – "the hottest spot in the world" as Scarlet, the daughter of a Coca-Cola manager, exclaimed in Billy Wilder's legendary movie *One, Two, Three* – was, indeed, a Cold War theater in two senses: as an arena of strategic contest and as a stage on which to perform politics. This dual character of Berlin has led me to experiment with the arrangement of the story. *Kennedy in Berlin* is structured along the sequence of a theater performance. Following an introduction that highlights the main analytical interests, the first chapter describes the story of America's Berlin, its protagonists and transformations over time. The second chapter looks at Kennedy's actual visit to Germany and its staging in 1963. The third chapter deals with the dramatic climax of Kennedy's trip, his tour of Berlin on June 26, 1963; it solves the many puzzles and myths surrounding Kennedy's sentence *"Ich bin ein Berliner."* The fourth chapter collects the audience's responses after the curtain fell, including a look at a counterperformance, the visit of Soviet leader Nikita Khrushchev to East Berlin only a few days after John F. Kennedy had triumphantly toured West Berlin. Finally, the epilogue describes how the show went on – from the staging of America's Berlin as part of a heroic postwar story to the turbulence of the succeeding decades, during which American presidents received a much more mixed reception in

Berlin, and to the redefinition of Berlin as the capital of unified Germany after 1990.

The translation differs slightly from the German original. I have shortened the text and only occasionally added a half sentence to explain a particular detail. The notes and bibliography have been updated; many references to literature in German have been replaced by ones to more recent works written in English.

Abbreviations

AA	Auswärtiges Amt
AAP	*Akten zur Auswärtigen Politik der Bundesrepublik Deutschland*
AFES	Archiv der sozialen Demokratie der Friedrich-Ebert-Stiftung, Bonn
AFL-CIO	American Federation of Labor–Congress of Industrial Organizations
ARD	Arbeitsgemeinschaft der Rundfunkanstalten Deutschlands
CBS	Columbia Broadcasting System
CDU	Christian Democratic Union
CIA	Central Intelligence Agency
CSU	Christian Social Union of Bavaria
DDEL	Dwight D. Eisenhower Library, Abilene, Kansas
EEC	European Economic Community
FDJ	Freie Deutsche Jugend
FRUS	*Foreign Relations of the United States of America*
FU	Freie Universität Berlin/Free University Berlin
FU Archiv	Universitätsarchiv der Freien Universität Berlin
GDR	German Democratic Republic
GML	George C. Marshall Library, Lexington, Virginia
GMMA	George Meany Memorial Archives, Silver Spring, Maryland
HIA	Hoover Institution Archives, Stanford, California
JFKL	John F. Kennedy Library, Boston, Massachusetts
LBJL	Lyndon B. Johnson Library, Austin, Texas
LAB	Landesarchiv Berlin, Berlin
LoC	Library of Congress, Manuscript Division, Washington, D.C.
MLF	Multilateral nuclear force
NA	National Archives II, College Park, Maryland
NBC	National Broadcasting Company

NSF	National Security Files
NSF, T & C	National Security Files, Trips & Conferences
PAAA	Politisches Archiv des Auswärtigen Amtes, Berlin
PK 1963	*Präsident Kennedy in Deutschland. Sonderdruck aus dem Bulletin des Presse- und Informationsamtes der Bundesregierung, nos. 108, 109, 110, 111, 112, 113/1963 (Bonn, 1963).*
PPP	*Public Papers of the Presidents of the United States*
RFK Papers	Robert F. Kennedy Papers, John F. Kennedy Library
RIAS	Rundfunk im Amerikanischen Sektor
SALT	Strategic Arms Limitation Talks
SDI	Strategic Defense Initiative
SFB	Sender Freies Berlin
SPD	Social Democratic Party
T & C	Trips & Conferences
UAW	United Automobile Workers Union
USIA	United States Information Agency
USIS	United States Information Service
WBA	Willy-Brandt-Archiv im Archiv der sozialen Demokratie der Friedrich-Ebert-Stiftung, Bonn
WH	White House
ZDF	Zweites Deutsches Fernsehen

Introduction

America's Berlin and John F. Kennedy

In the summer of 1963, President John F. Kennedy visited the Federal Republic of Germany for four days, from June 23 to 26. On the last day of this trip, he flew to the divided city of Berlin. The eight hours Kennedy spent in the western sector of the city became "one of the great spectacles" of the Cold War.[1] Hundreds of thousands of enthusiastic spectators lined the streets of the motorcade route to watch Kennedy, West German chancellor Konrad Adenauer, and Willy Brandt, then the mayor of West Berlin, drive by in an open car, covered with confetti and flowers, engulfed in cheers and jubilation, and followed by television cameras broadcasting the event to numerous countries. The pictures of this triumphal procession circled the globe, as did the president's rousing speech before the Schöneberg City Hall, the administrative headquarters of West Berlin at the time. Kennedy's speech culminated in a sentence that was destined to become one of the most famous statements ever made in the history of political rhetoric and one engraved forever upon the memories of people on both sides of the Atlantic: "*Ich bin ein Berliner.*"

John F. Kennedy's trip to Berlin represents one of the most electrifying events of Cold War history and marks a highpoint in German-American relations. Never before had Germans felt so close to an American president, nor would they ever again, except during the public mourning after the president's assassination five months later. Following Kennedy's death, his "*Ich bin ein Berliner*" became a mythic part of collective memory in the United States and West Germany alike. Now that the Cold War is over, we have the unique chance to reevaluate Kennedy's seminal visit to Germany and its historical importance. For the first time, this book makes use of the large pool of source material that is accessible today and thus aims to rediscover the fascination of this event.[2]

1

By reexamining Kennedy's Berlin visit in the context of the Cold War era, we are also able to take a new approach to the study of transatlantic relations in the twentieth century. As this book argues, cultural and emotional factors had a significant impact on these relations. So too did the social networks that spanned the Atlantic and certain ideas that appealed in equal measure to the historical awareness of many people in the United States and Germany. Furthermore, international Cold War politics was played out before a global audience. This was one reason why Kennedy's visit was choreographed and conducted much like a stage production: it was not only useful but also imperative that politics become visible and strike an emotional chord in everyone involved.

All of these moments helped create political and emotional links between the West German and American societies following the Second World War. I suggest that we are speaking here of a process of transnational community building, which was expressed most spectacularly by the Kennedy visit in June 1963. The experience of American support for West Berlin after 1948, the year in which the famous Berlin Airlift began, was the most important catalyst in making this process possible. West Berlin was more heavily influenced by the United States than any other part of Germany and developed a "special relationship" with America. The Soviet blockade and the Airlift opened the way for the incorporation of Berlin in the heroic reading of American history. In the eyes of many Americans, the defense of Berlin was a glowing example of the country fulfilling its mission to advance freedom worldwide. During the Cold War, West Berlin became the embodiment of America's "city on a hill" and thus helped perpetuate the old myth of American society as the promising new societal order once envisioned by seventeenth-century pilgrim settlers.[3]

For this reason the significance of West Berlin during the Cold War resonated through both German and American history. To call the city "America's Berlin," as I do in this book, is the most succinct way to state that the relationship between West Berlin and the United States during the Cold War intensified and became a close cultural and emotional bond.[4] Kennedy's *"Ich bin ein Berliner"* marked the symbolic highpoint of this bond, which began to weaken after 1963. The account of why the special relationship between Berlin and America both intensified and waned during the Cold War is an integral part of understanding the history of Kennedy's visit. The story of America's Berlin thus demonstrates that the development of West Germany after 1945 was deeply influenced by the politics and ideologies of other countries, especially the United States. Therefore, one aim of this book is to argue in favor of extending the scope and evaluation of both American and German history to the transnational level.[5]

Kennedy's trip to Berlin in June 1963 was an event unparalleled in Germany's postwar history prior to the fall of the Berlin Wall in 1989. Crowds of people gathered in the streets in what were then unprecedented numbers to celebrate the presence of a single politician. The media provided uninterrupted coverage. The mood in the city alternated between enthusiastic jubilation, Carnival revelry, and respectful silence. Never again in the history of the Federal Republic would the charisma of a politician mobilize such emotions and instill such devotion in the population. At the same time, Kennedy was walking a political tightrope in coming to Germany. The trip was risky with regard to alliance politics, proved controversial in the United States, and took place during a serious transatlantic crisis.[6]

Following the erection of the Berlin Wall in 1961, massive criticism was directed at the United States' involvement with West Berlin. The Federal Republic and other Western European countries were highly skeptical of the strategic reorientation undertaken by the Kennedy administration. Likewise, the United States exerted massive pressure on the Europeans in matters of fiscal policy. Moreover, the American government feared that the Franco-German friendship treaty of January 1963 and the nationalism of French president Charles de Gaulle would undermine both the transatlantic alliance and American hegemony in Western Europe. In addition, the Kennedy visit prompted power struggles among political forces within West Germany, namely, between Bonn and Berlin, between the Christian Democratic Union (CDU) and the Social Democratic Party (SPD), between the so-called Gaullists and Atlanticists, and between Konrad Adenauer and Willy Brandt.

More than the ritualized commemoration of Kennedy's famous statement "*Ich bin ein Berliner*" reveals, the visit of the American president was an event of considerable drama not only with regard to its impact on society but also in the way it influenced domestic and foreign policies. This book seeks to unravel the multiple dimensions of Kennedy's visit by choosing three main foci. First, I seek to decode, through a thick description, the various aspects of the event as a microhistory of the Cold War in order to reveal the macrohistorical conditions of the era.[7] The events of June 1963 help us understand the larger issues at stake in transatlantic relations during the Cold War era. This emphasis explains why this book does not simply start with the arrival of Air Force One at the Cologne-Bonn Airport on June 23, 1963, but discusses the preceding decades as well as Kennedy's assassination and the staging of transatlantic politics that followed. My hope is to help give new meaning to a history of events that does justice to the specific moment and, at the same time, links it to broader issues and long-term developments.

An accurate evaluation of Kennedy's trip is only possible if we examine the entire spectrum of historical sources. These sources include unpublished files and private papers found in German and American archives, the comprehensive press and television coverage on both sides of the Atlantic, and the memoirs of contemporaries.[8] Only comparative and multiarchival research brings to light much of what has been forgotten or unknown until now and can help lay more than one legend to rest. Such an approach can also elucidate the surprising origin of Kennedy's statement "*Ich bin ein Berliner,*" so often quoted and so often misunderstood. Moreover, source-based analysis is not a privilege of diplomatic history alone but creates a broad and solid foundation for issues of cultural history. A close look at the sources explains the motivations and mind-sets of the actors involved and enables us to recognize the political and ideological frameworks and the emotional impact of the event with which we are dealing.

Second, I will use the Kennedy visit to examine the close interplay between politics, culture, and public opinion in the second half of the twentieth century. These three factors certainly do not exist independently of one another. Political decisions are shaped by culture and public opinion, which are in turn influenced by politics. Likewise, the realms of culture and public opinion are influenced by political decisions and thereby become political themselves.[9] An increasing number of attempts have been made recently to overcome the long-standing absence of dialogue between political and cultural historians. At least in the discipline of international relations history, we see a growing willingness to crawl out of old disciplinary trenches, abandon fruitless debates about the primacy of either foreign policy or domestic policy, and expand political history to include the history of culture and the history of society.[10]

Third, I would therefore like to emphasize the societal and cultural dimensions of transatlantic relations in particular. States, nations, and societies communicate with one another via governments and state institutions. This is why we usually speak of *international* relations. However, researchers in political science as well as in the historical sciences are increasingly recognizing that nongovernmental actors — for example, societal organizations, media, social networks, and lobbies — also contribute to these relations. International action at the governmental level and the action of actors originating from other societal contexts often mutually influence each other, as Thomas Risse has rightly argued. This is what is meant by the term *transnational.*[11] In relations between the United States and the Federal Republic of Germany after 1945 and especially in the story of America's Berlin, both the German and American peoples played just as important a role as the governments involved; so too did certain individuals who were the embodiment of political clout, social engagement, and symbolic power, such as Lucius D. Clay, the acclaimed hero of the Berlin Airlift.

"ONE OF THE GREATEST DRAMAS": POLITICS AS THEATER

The reconstruction of the event as a microhistory of the era; the interplay of politics, culture, and public opinion; and the transnational relations among West Berlin, the Federal Republic of Germany, and the United States – these three foci of this book are bound together by one underlying theme. I will present Kennedy's trip to Germany as a political performance aimed at winning public consensus through symbolic acts. The nature of this trip can be best understood if we compare it to the way a stage play is prepared, produced, and ultimately received by the public. Such a comparison is not meant to suggest that the script for the trip had been written out in concrete detail years before, merely awaiting performance at the hands of some almighty director. No such director ever existed, and it is certainly not the place of the historian to assume such a role. Instead, this book attempts to present and to invite discussion about the idea that theater should not be understood merely as a metaphor for politics, but as an elementary form of politics in the era of mass public opinion.

Politics has always meant performance. Politics is a constant state of performance because the actions and statements that constitute politics only become political once they are presented and communicated to others in a social context. The study of social interaction, as conducted by Erving Goffman, has demonstrated how everyday social interactions are, to varying degrees, performances. Social actions portray a topic or issue by way of people performing on a stage before an audience that reacts to what it sees happening on that stage.[12] The theater analogy helps us understand the nature of the performance that influenced Kennedy's visit and was inherent to Berlin politics following the blockade of the city's western sectors in 1948 and 1949. The effort to stage events, script sequences, set political sceneries, and establish rapport with the audience permeated the Kennedy trip of 1963 and even at times dominated it.

To call politics a form of theater is certainly not unusual but often leaves a negative aftertaste, especially when politicians are referred to as actors. However, the analogy to the theatrical world is anything but a later invention of historians. After the Second World War, the world viewed Berlin as a political stage. Contemporaries often used theatrical metaphors, referring to the Berlin situation as a "drama," the city as a "showcase," and the East-West border as the "Iron Curtain." At the latest by 1948, when the Soviet Union started to blockade the city, West Berlin entered the spotlight of world attention. The city visibly symbolized the emerging East-West confrontation that was becoming known as the Cold War.[13] In 1963, an American president made his way to Berlin for the first time since Harry S. Truman had met with the wartime allies in Potsdam in 1945 to discuss the postwar order. Thus the city was particularly vulnerable to being seen as a political stage. Even before Kennedy's departure, the *New York Times* reported that a "ceremonial spectacle" awaited the president. A year before his visit to the divided city, a major American industrialist had maintained that Berlin represented "the scene of one of the greatest dramas ever played by humans."[14]

The interplay between theater and politics is in no way new. Even in Greek antiquity, politics not only developed out of public assemblies and theoretical reflection but also arose as a "political art" within the realm of classic theater.[15] The peripatetic visitations and rituals of kings in the Middle Ages were established as acts of symbolic politics for the benefit of the polity. In early modern France, the court life and self-aggrandizement of Louis XIV reflected and reinforced the concept of state. Later, the modern concept of the nation was symbolized and celebrated by rituals and festivities connected to the French Revolution and by commemorations of the storming of the Bastille. Spontaneous gatherings and hunger protests by the lower classes of Europe in the late eighteenth and nineteenth centuries were forms of political "street theater," as were, for example, parades in the towns and cities of the expanding American republic.[16] Thomas Nipperdey pointed out quite some time ago that, particularly in Germany, political architecture, civic celebrations, and the construction of national memorials in the nineteenth century established claims of political power. They formulated modes through which the connection between nationalism and civic culture could be understood and interpreted.[17] Moreover, political language in Germany had been imbued with metaphors from the theatrical world since the mid-nineteenth century. Politics was understood as stage-acting before a large audience, as David Blackbourn has shown. These ideas have stimulated very recent studies. Johannes Paulmann has underscored the importance of ritual appearances for the nineteenth century and deciphered monarchial trips and meetings between royal heads of state as the mirrors of systemic changes in the international system. Edgar Wolfrum has recently demonstrated how important public performances were for the political use of national history in the German postwar period.[18]

In 1963, however, any continuation of theatrical politics faced an enormous dilemma, especially in Germany. National Socialism had carried the use of rituals, theatrical practices, and certain symbols to an extreme. With Mussolini's Fascist Italy having already paved the way,[19] the totalitarian regime in Germany aestheticized politics by a range of means that extended from encouraging a fetish for uniforms and the swastika to organizing cult celebrations for youth and staging grandiose events such as the Reich Party Congress. Such performances and symbols helped generate enormous pressure to conform and created the "alluring appearance of the Third Reich."[20] Furthermore, the Nazi dictatorship elevated such practices to cult acts of consecration – its "political liturgies" – and used them to propagate a form of "political religion" that provided the ideological foundation for its genocidal policies.[21] Klaus Vondung, Hans-Ulrich Thamer, Wolfgang Hardtwig, and Hans Maier have emphasized the connection between mass rituals, politics, and the production of meaning in creating a sense of identity for both dictatorships and democracies.[22] As a consequence of Nazi practices, the staging of large-scale public events and the use of symbolic forms were fully discredited in the Federal Republic. They might prompt direct associations with the Nazi dictatorship at home and abroad and thus appear as writing on the wall with regard to the development of postwar Germany. Herein lay both the problem and the challenge facing any attempt to stage politics on German soil.

This book adopts the theater analogy even in its structure. The first chapter describes how the story line of America's Berlin took shape following World War II. It identifies the main actors and describes the political context, giving particular attention to the development of American policy on Berlin in the years following the Airlift and to the international situation in the early 1960s. America's special relationship with Berlin was sustained by a transnational culture of memory, this chapter demonstrates, and was promoted by a network of Berlin supporters in the United States. This network eventually counted Vice President Lyndon B. Johnson and Attorney General Robert F. Kennedy among its members, and their visits to West Berlin in 1961 and 1962, respectively, were the prologue for John F. Kennedy's visit in 1963.

The second chapter describes the actual script for the president's trip to Germany and its staging. The spotlight here is on Kennedy's first days in West Germany and the haggling over politically sensitive points of protocol, the stage setting, and the itinerary of the trip. The dramaturgy of the visit was heavily influenced by the West German media and public. I will therefore pay special attention to the way the political actors balanced both the wish to mobilize the public and the need to discipline it.

The third chapter of the book leads to the dramatic climax of the play. It describes Kennedy's triumphant motorcade through West Berlin and demonstrates that the political topography of his itinerary was highly laden with symbolism. This chapter also traces the surprising deviation Kennedy made from the script during his appearance in front of the Schöneberg City Hall and reveals the secret of the famous words "*Ich bin ein Berliner.*"

The fourth chapter discusses what happened after "the curtain fell," both in the immediate aftermath and from a long-term historical perspective. It examines the reactions of the public in America and Europe, especially in the German Democratic Republic (GDR), as the way in which the public handled such a highly emotionalized spectacle. This chapter therefore includes the trip undertaken by Soviet party leader and head of state Nikita Khrushchev to East Berlin in answer to the Kennedy visit. Last but certainly not least, the chapter presents the reactions of Germans to the assassination of President Kennedy.

The fifth chapter explores why memories of the Kennedy visit have been reduced to only a few scenes. This epilogue then brings us back to the present by reviewing Robert F. Kennedy's visit to Berlin in 1964 and subsequent presidential visits, which throw light on the the changes that have occurred in German-American relations.

"BEACON FOR FREEDOM": SYMBOLS AND POWER

Symbolic acts become increasingly important in relation to the degree that politics constitutes itself as a performance. Political symbols are sensory, metaphoric, and demonstrative acts and statements that aim to express a political message. They can include language uses; gestures; images; architectural styles, especially for edifices like monuments; or social events such as festivities, commemorations, anniversary and ceremonial rituals, as well as official visits. Therefore, symbolic acts are themselves political acts and can occur in connection with other acts – such as state formations, elections, governmental decisions, military actions, and treaty signings – in order to support and legitimize them.[23] Symbolic acts fulfill these tasks by creating opportunities for social experience, by appealing to popular sentiments, and by mobilizing approval among the population. This also holds true of memorial services for political figures, such as those held in West Germany on the occasion of Kennedy's assassination. Even Ronald Reagan's 1987 declaration, in outmoded Cold War rhetoric, that Berlin represented a "beacon for freedom" was an attempt to mobilize public approval.[24]

Particularly in the social and cultural sciences, recent research on social constructions of reality has clearly shown that political symbols play a major role in our societies. They make it possible to produce and experience internal unity, coherence, and continuity in social relations. However, both social scientists and historians recognize that the character of such constructions is dependent on the period and context in which they exist.[25] Therefore, scholars use the term *invention* to clarify that symbols and ideas are not natural phenomena but originate in human acts and imaginations.[26] Still, political symbols are more than just a means to present or represent politics that are formulated and decided elsewhere. The use of political symbols can evolve into symbolic politics and divorce itself from the function of reinforcing other politics.

Symbolic politics is similar to other forms of politics in that it aims to increase power, prestige, and approval. It selects primarily symbolic acts to achieve concrete political ends.[27] Consequently, symbolic politics is more than illusion or mere show. It can be used in conjunction with other political forms to offer an independent decision-making option and an alternative type of action. The advantage of such politics is that it offers an array of instruments to impart meaning to political and social contexts.[28] With this book, I would like to show that the use of symbolic politics was a decisive factor at critical moments in German-American relations in overcoming crises and maintaining the transatlantic bond between the United States and the Federal Republic. Symbolic politics was also deployed to attack the East and isolate the GDR, which had been quick to emphasize political symbols after its founding. Parades of youth marching in the uniforms of East Germany's Freie Deutsche Jugend (FDJ, the official communist youth organization) and waving red flags were interpreted in the West as an echo of Nazi practices. For good reasons, the West German government adopted, in its own words, a "position of moderation" toward such practices when representing itself.[29] Faced with the mass spectacle that Kennedy's visit promised to be, the government found this very policy being put to the test in two ways. Would it be possible to find democratic forms of political theater to celebrate Kennedy that would free West Germany from Hitler's shadow and at the same time disassociate the Federal Republic from the GDR?

"LOOK UPON THIS CITY": THE POLITICS OF VISIBILITY

Political theater and symbolic acts are not the prerogatives of dictators alone, even if that often appears to be the case.[30] Both are basic political forms applicable to modern societies in the age of public opinion amplified by mass media. Nontotalitarian states and democratic nations alike are faced with the question about how best to stage politics and evoke – via architecture, images, or the form and tone of language – a sense of political aesthetics that makes valid statements about their own societies. The planners of Kennedy's trip spent a major portion of their time on these aspects. They were supported by the mass media, which sought to keep an eye on every detail of the president's trip.

The idea of keeping an eye on things actually became a maxim for all participants. To have the American president "see – and be seen"[31] as much as possible was more than just one of the aims of Kennedy's trip to Germany: it was the main purpose. I would argue that the principle of seeing and being seen was part of a larger trend in the age of mass media, namely, a politics of visibility that wove together political action and appeals to the eye. In 1963, the politics of visibility became so important that we can even speak of the primacy of visibility.[32] Above all, the *politics of visibility* means to seek and achieve the visibility of actions, actors, and objects in order to articulate and strengthen political statements. The image of Kennedy in the Paulskirche, a former church in Frankfurt that has become the outstanding symbol of the German revolutionary movement of 1848, was juxtaposed with the image of the president at the Berlin Wall, the symbol of the deprivation of freedom for the people living in the communist state on the opposite side. Both of these images were deliberately sought for their political import. They were "public images" in which political statements and symbols often amalgamated into what Aby Warburg termed *Schlagbilder*, images that take on an iconic nature.[33]

The politics of visibility interprets the mutual process of seeing and being seen as a political statement. It aims to influence not only this process but also the people's perspective and attempts to use media coverage to publicize both the process and perspective. Actors are to be seen as observers as well as the objects of observation. They are allowed to see; indeed they should see. At the same time, the public should see them in the process of observing certain places or objects. Kennedy was not merely to stand next to or in front of the Berlin Wall: he was to look at the Wall and beyond it into East Berlin. In turn, the entire world was to see the picture of Kennedy looking eastward. In order to make the politics of visibility succeed, it is necessary to supply the requisite props – for example, binoculars, speaker podium, press stand – to help actors see as well as to document their viewing process and communicate this as a symbolic or allegoric public act. Thus, we can speak of a "political optic" that brings forth certain "visual strategies."[34]

Such an optic was not specific to the twentieth century, but it did become particularly important then. During the Cold War, most actors, spectators, and those whose job it was to convey images viewed the world through specially tinted eyeglasses that led them to interpret events in terms of good and evil. The fact that this Manichaean optic of the Cold War remained effective for so long can be attributed yet again to the comprehensive process of communicating realities through the media, as had been occurring since the end of the nineteenth century. Over the course of time, forms of political communication became increasingly constitutive for politics, and images were particularly effective in achieving such communication. One consequence of the media's influence on politics, argues art historian Michael Diers, is that "the 'actors' on the public stage design their roles more and more to enhance their image and that, in staging politics, much is conceived as image to the point that the image is prefigured in the arrangement of political ceremony."[35]

The Kennedy trip strongly exhibited the character of a stage production. In West Berlin, the fixation on producing positive images had already played a role far more pronounced than elsewhere when the blockade and ensuing air transports began in 1948. To watch Berlin, meaning to focus deliberately on visual documentation of the blockade, became a political statement, one aimed at inspiring solidarity with West Berliners and condemning the Soviet Union, the instigator of the blockade. The iconography of the widely publicized photos from the Berlin Airlift focuses on images of need and on gestures of German-American solidarity: we see landing transport aircraft being greeted by waving West Berliners who thereby constitute "seeing" actors against the backdrop of the ruins of their city (Illustration 1). These West Berliners are represented just as prominently as the men unloading sacks of coal from the planes and the people who sit by candlelight in poorly furnished apartments with no electricity.[36]

To keep an encircled West Berlin in the limelight was not only politically important, it was at times essential to the city's survival. Like no other German politician, West Berlin Mayor Ernst Reuter understood the importance of visibility. In September 1948, he declared before hundreds of thousands of people gathered in front of the Reichstag, Germany's nineteenth-century parliamentary building that had been bombed to ruins during the Second World War: "Look upon this city . . . people of the world, look upon Berlin!"[37] (Illustration 2). The primacy of visibility continued. "The whole world is watching Berlin," reported Vice President Lyndon B. Johnson in August 1961 following his visit to the city.[38] When John F. Kennedy flew to Berlin nearly two years later, it was clear to everyone involved in the preparation for the visit that the act of seeing-and-being-seen would play and indeed had to play an overriding role.

Illustration 1. America's Berlin becomes visible: West Berlin children watch a plane land at Tempelhof in 1948 during the Airlift. Source: Landesarchiv Berlin.

This act was political insofar as its occurrence created a sense of community. The visual presence of Kennedy was tantamount to his political presence. An American president only appears where he wants to appear. The decisions he makes regarding places to visit immediately become political decisions, for in doing so he is granting his immediate surroundings and – via the media – a larger public the privilege of seeing him and therefore of being associated with a specific place. Since a president does not go where he does not want to go, this choice and the privileges attached to it have a fundamentally affirmative character.[39]

"THE GUEST WHO MAKES THE GERMANS ECSTATIC": EMOTIONS

In an article published in the *Süddeutsche Zeitung*, one of West Germany's major newspapers, on June 28, 1963, star reporter Hans Ulrich Kempski came to a remarkable conclusion in reviewing Kennedy's visit to Germany. Kennedy was the guest who "makes the Germans ecstatic." In the whirlwind of the "four-day mass frenzy," indeed a "German spectacle," masses of humanity, at times "robbed of all sense," had reveled "uninhibitedly" to the

Illustration 2. "Look upon this city": Ernst Reuter, the Social Democratic mayor of Berlin and soon-to-become anticommunist hero in the United States, outside the Reichstag building on September 9, 1948. Source: Landesarchiv Berlin.

point of "hysteria."[40] Was the American president the person who could uncork the bottled-up emotions of postwar Germans? These were strong words indeed from an experienced journalist, but they were representative of the mood at the time. The media coverage, innumerable comments from the public, and the language of high-level politicians involved were permeated with metaphors of warmth and emotionality. According to these sources, Germans reacted to Kennedy in a way that made the thermometer of public sentiment rise rapidly: "Hearts beat" themselves into a "Kennedy fever" that hit the public much "like a tropical heat wave," as the employees in the payroll department of a Berlin electrical firm wrote to Kennedy in July, apparently once they had cooled off somewhat.[41]

Compared to their counterparts in the United States and in France, German historians have been late in discovering the history of emotions.[42] With regard to international relations, emotions and moods have almost never been taken into consideration as decisive factors. Only very recently do we find the first forays into this area. These studies concentrate on the relations between individual political actors and their emotional states.[43] A look at Kennedy's visit to Germany, however, can clearly demonstrate that emotions appear in various roles with respect to relations between societies and that they influence the history of these relations in a number of different ways. To start, we should understand emotionality to be statements made by subjects about themselves and others, statements that describe their inner state and identify the factors influencing their feelings, perceptions, and behavior, in addition to other factors such as rational considerations or constraints. It is hard to know whether such statements are authentic or are being used for instrumental purposes. Usually we historians are dealing with a combination of both. Therefore it is better first to ask whether emotionality was being articulated, by whom, what the nature of the expressed emotionality was, and how it defined social reality. With regard to transnational relations, four dimensions can be discerned.

One dimension is the emotionality of each individual actor and the emotions permeating their relations to others. Diplomats, politicians, and heads of state are not simply rational actors who think only in terms of opportunity costs and act strictly out of calculated expediency.[44] They are people with emotions, and as such, they are receptive to the feelings of their counterparts and the public in general. In turn, their own moods and personal behavior in dealing with others can influence not only perceptions, but also the course of decision-making processes and actions. We can speak here of a "personalized foreign policy," also in an emotional sense.[45] This book will capture such individual emotionality, particularly in the three-way relationship between Kennedy, Adenauer, and Brandt, as well as in the experiences of these three politicians during the presidential trip. Trust and mistrust, sincerity and doubt, anger and reconciliation, intimacy and distance are categories that these politicians and those observing them repeatedly attempt to use in order to determine reality.

Another dimension involves the emotionality fundamental to the behavior and perceptions of collective actors, such as nations, states, societies, and the populations of a region or a city. This should not be taken to mean the attribution of a static psychology to an entire people, as much as we may enjoy or are offended by the idea of serious Germans, hot-blooded Brazilians, melancholic Portuguese, and reserved Englishmen. It is more productive to ask when, from whom, and with what intent emotional attributes are given to societies and peoples and whether these groups have actually experienced or exhibited collective moods and sentiments. How could it happen during Kennedy's four-day visit to West Germany and Berlin in June 1963 that serious, somber, and workaholic West Germans turned into relaxed, disorderly, boisterous – or at any rate enthusiastic – people, to whom employers in Berlin even granted time off from work in order to join the celebrations? How could this happen when disappointment with the United States had been widespread among these same Germans just two years before in the wake of the erection of the Berlin Wall? As I will argue in this book, this transformation occurred primarily through the experience of symbolic politics.

A third dimension of emotionality in relations between societies involves another collective actor: the enthusiastic crowd that turned out to see Kennedy. No other event in the history of the Federal Republic before the fall of the Berlin Wall in November 1989 mobilized such a large number of people as did the visit by Kennedy. This effect was looked upon with favor by many in the West, but it also presented a problem. Cultural assumptions about the behavior and psyche of the masses now came into play. The gathering of hundreds of thousands of people harbored risks for the president's security and for the political purpose of the visit. The authorities involved in planning the trip had the dual tasks of simultaneously keeping the crowd both in high spirits and under control. In 1963, planners designed "street politics" to maintain a balance between the control and mobilization of the public.[46] Still, they were not able to circumvent this challenge, which had a specific meaning on German soil. Over every mass gathering in Germany, especially when held in such a historically significant place as Berlin, loomed the dark shadow of National Socialism.

Collective actors act and define themselves not only in relation to themselves, but also often in relation to other major collective actors. This helps us identify a fourth dimension: the role of emotions as ascriptions in international relations. For example, such ascriptions can be used to cement the idea of a historical friendship (for example, between the United States and Great Britain in the twentieth century) or a historical animosity (for example, between Germany and France before and during the First World War) and to accentuate the many shades of gray found in international relations. A great deal of emotion was projected upon German–American relations during the events leading up to and including those days in late June 1963 when Kennedy visited West Germany. As had been the case when the Berlin Wall was built in 1961, such emotion became a powerful factor in these relations and, in turn, demanded an emotional response on the part of the governments involved.

America's Berlin reflected such projections of emotion. Kennedy represented the United States, the key defender of West Berlin, the city in which enemy armies and ideologies stood face to face. Therefore, in the eyes of West Berliners, his visit became a test of American resolve to support their city. The United States had to prove to the people of West Berlin that it trusted them and took their emotions seriously. The Americans, too, had concerns about German-American relations and likewise looked upon the president's trip as a test. How was morale among the West Berliners? Did West Germans trust the United States sufficiently? The experience of the Berlin Wall had taught both sides that it was not possible, as Adenauer emphasized in August 1961, to dismiss emotional and psychological factors as a *quantité négligeable*. These factors were themselves elements of political action.[47] Moreover, there was "a great deal of theology" inherent in Berlin policy, as Secretary of State Dean Rusk observed shortly before Kennedy arrived in West Germany.[48] Berlin policy was always a matter of faith. Thus, Kennedy's tasks were to win over public opinion, to deter destructive emotionality, and to awaken positive feelings of solidarity.

"THE FEELING OF CLOSENESS": COMMUNITY BUILDING AND CHARISMA

Following the second day of Kennedy's trip to Germany, the *New York Times* informed its readers not only of the enthusiastic reception that cheering Rhinelanders had given the American president; the newspaper also mentioned in its front-page report that Kennedy and the elderly Konrad Adenauer had discovered an "unexpected personal intimacy." The chancellor had emphasized this "feeling of closeness in an emotional toast."[49] The expressions of trust and the metaphors of affection were not used exclusively to describe the personal relationship between the statesmen. With each passing day of the visit, they were found more frequently in descriptions of relations between the United States and Germany. Did this language merely constitute empty, situationally determined rhetoric or even a manipulative tactic by the press speakers and media? I would like to take a different tack in answering this question. It is my intention to show that in June 1963 a temporary and never completely harmonious process of transnational community building reached its highpoint.

In Max Weber's categorizataion of social relationships, a "communal relationship" (*Vergemeinschaftung*) exists if and in so far as the "orientation of social action – whether in the individual case, on the average, or in the pure type – is based on a subjective feeling of the parties, whether affectual or traditional, that they belong together." An "associative relationship"

(*Vergesellschaftung*), on the other hand, is the product of "rationally motivated adjustment of interests or a similarly motivated agreement." Most
social relationships, as Weber pointed out, are of a mixed character and
develop from both communal and associative relationships.[50] Such a combination was characteristic not only of Kennedy's visit in particular but of
German-American relations in general during the Cold War.

However, it is important to differentiate between two concepts of community that can overlap but are not identical. On the one hand, there was
the concept of the North Atlantic community, a term that had been common in political vocabulary since the 1950s. This concept offered a mental
map meant to underscore the membership of countries in NATO, their
anti-Soviet orientation (West against East), and an adherence to the values
of their Christian cultural heritage. John F. Kennedy tried to redefine this
community by introducing his concept of the Atlantic community.[51] On the
other hand, the concept of community has also been analytically applied –
as is done in this book – in the manner used by Weber and in the theory
of political communications developed by Karl W. Deutsch. As Deutsch
demonstrated two generations ago, political communities are complex structures. They are just as dependent on dense social communication and the
fulfillment of mutual expectations between the members of the community
as they are on personnel networking, shared values, and identity-endowing
symbols.[52] So far, Deutsch's approach has been used to study developments
within nation states; however, it can also explain relations between societies
and states. Just as a political system requires legitimacy within the borders of
a nation-state, international relations also need the willingness to seek consensus. In order to develop into a political community, international relations
require the experience and the sensation of an emotional and transcendent
community.

Another factor played into the process of transnational community building in 1963. The television images and press photographs of West Germans
cheering the president show people of all ages, their arms and hands stretched
out toward Kennedy in the hopes of touching him. Women are seen faint-
ing out of both physical exhaustion and excitement. Crowds of spectators
are shown surrounding the president and his motorcade. In June 1963,
West Germans yearned to be physically near the guest from the United
States in the same way they had with Lyndon B. Johnson and Robert
F. Kennedy previously. For many West Germans, the leading personali-
ties of the American government embodied a salvation-bringing, super-
natural power. Particularly for the people of West Berlin, this fixation on
American leaders contributed to the development of an "emotional form of

communal relationship" (*emotionale Vergemeinschaftung*), which was held together by the devotion to the exceptional qualities of an "individual person, and of the normative patterns or order revealed or ordained by him," to quote Max Weber again.[53]

Two sources generate both the legitimacy and the emotional resonance of this community experience. One is the leader's charisma, which Weber described as possessing qualities such as sanctity (*Heiligkeit*), heroism (*Heldenkraft*), and exemplary character (*Vorbildlichkeit*). The quality of such charisma thus exceeds the recognition of rational competence and cannot be merely derived from a traditional form of authority (*Herrschaftstradition*).[54] The aura radiating from John F. Kennedy was that of a politically powerful, intellectually brilliant, seemingly youthful, rhetorically gifted, and sexually attractive man. Germans had come to be charmed by Kennedy's charisma at the latest by 1960. His election demonstrated that a new generation of politicians, one diametrically different from the preceding generation of Dwight D. Eisenhower and Konrad Adenauer, had stepped up to the plate. Corresponding to this effect was the other source of legitimacy: the direct support of the public in West Germany. The crowds expressed jubilation, respect, and devotion. People were willing to overcome whatever doubts they may have held about the alliance guarantees of the United States and the anger they had often felt over the behavior of the American government. They were ready to declare their allegiance to Kennedy. One of the president's advisors remembers Kennedy admitting with some horror after his speech at the Schöneberg City Hall that he could have convinced the enthusiastic crowd to storm the Wall and tear it down, had he wanted.[55] A key to the success of Kennedy's declaration "*Ich bin ein Berliner*" is that these words seemed to confirm rhetorically and therefore substantiate the belief in a mutually felt bond of solidarity between Berliners and Americans.

As the enthusiastic spectators in the squares and streets of the city pressed hard to get close to the president, even to touch him, they were demonstrating a hunger for salvation analogous to that expressed in religious ritual. In the modern era, political rituals have embraced many religious practices and the hope for salvation; they have transferred both into the political arena. This transference from the sacral to the political realm becomes even stronger in the followings of charismatic figures.[56] Inspired by the devout desire for salvation, people willing to follow a charismatic leader can even go as far as to seek oneness with this person and to see their own identity mirrored in that of the other. West Berlin Deputy Mayor Heinrich Albertz summarized this hope in the eulogy for Kennedy he delivered in front of Schöneberg City Hall in November 1963. Kennedy had appeared there as a "brother, in whom we saw a reflection of ourselves, our worries, our tasks, our hopes, our goals."[57]

None of these effects are untypical for the age of nation-states and mass politics since the French Revolution. The past two centuries have witnessed situations in both dictatorships and democracies in which symbolic politics and mass emotionality have been linked to the charisma of an individual and to a ritualistic acquiescence, often shaped by religious anticipation and fervor, on the part of the public. The remarkable aspect of the communal relationships described in this book is that they occurred between a people and the representative of a foreign state, thereby taking place on a transnational level. Both in this respect and chronologically, Charles de Gaulle's 1962 visit to Germany preceded Kennedy's. Both of these events became experiences that, by conveying a sense of purpose and community, created a subjective bond between the Federal Republic and the West. In these experiences, the transnational communal relationship between West Germans and the West was made manifest.

Such an interpretation has an impact on the interpretation of West Germany's postwar history, which Heinrich August Winkler has described as the last stretch of a "long road west."[58] For some time, historians have emphasized the multifaceted American influence on postwar Germany. The "Americanization" and "Westernization" of West Germans have been analyzed primarily as a process of societal and intellectual orientation toward the values and behavior of American culture. According to this approach, the process manifested itself in consumption patterns, popular culture, business practices, and the transmission of the political concepts characteristic of the democratic-liberal order that had developed in the United States out of philosophical pragmatism, totalitarian theory, and postwar sociology.[59] These interpretations have revealed important aspects pertaining to the integration of the Federal Republic into the West and have emphasized in particular the processes involved in associative relationships. In this book, I include the forms of communal relationships as an additional set of factors – one largely ignored until now. The integration of West German society into the Western societal model, particularly the North American one, did not come about merely because politics and economics, intellectual pursuits, and popular culture began to converge. This integration was also strengthened because social communication, emotional solidarity, and the experience of political community intensified.

The process of community building and the stability of communal relationships require consensus, but they do not occur only through consensus. Max Weber was careful to point out that conflict, rivalry, and force occur in all types of communities and that social relationships and their meanings can change.[60] This also holds true for German–American relations. Transatlantic community building did not at all contradict American hegemony in Western Europe after 1945. Community building does not preclude misunderstandings, controversy, or emotional disappointment. Political communities are not always harmonious, and they are also not necessarily permanent. Should the charisma disappear, so too does the opportunity for emotional engagement. Should the interests of the participants start to diverge, then the commonality becomes weaker and faces the danger of falling apart or being reduced to matters of expediency. The political differences and the mutual estrangement existing between the United States and Germany in the early years of the twenty-first century attest to this situation.

However, before we commit to a scenario of decline, we should recognize that every social reality evolves from the active participation of those involved in defining it. Social reality can be influenced by a multitude of factors and can change in a variety of directions. The unpredictability and the potential for influence and change, combined with the uniqueness of each moment in time, are evident in the staging of politics and in symbolic acts. This will become clearer the more this topic is explored – an exploration this book invites the reader to embark upon.

1

The Story and Its Protagonists

John F. Kennedy's visit to Germany took place more than two and a half years after the 43-year-old Democrat from Boston was elected to be the thirty-fifth president of the United States. The election results had been close and not completely free from irregularities. Still, the Republican candidate, Vice President Richard M. Nixon, conceded. After eight years of Republican leadership spearheaded by the war hero Dwight D. Eisenhower, the pinnacle of Western leadership changed in several respects. Once again, the Democrats were in charge of the White House. The new president brought a fresh, new team with him when he assumed office, which meant that a much younger elite had now taken over the helm of politics. No less significant was the fact that the United States had elected a Catholic to the presidency for the first time in the country's history.

The first two years of the new Kennedy administration proved to be dramatic ones as it faced an array of domestic and foreign crises. Thus the political communities on both sides of the Atlantic were all the more surprised in January 1963 when the first reports of Kennedy's plans to visit Germany were leaked. This occurred just as the Franco-German friendship treaty was being signed, much to the displeasure of the American government. The news of the planned trip attracted even greater attention the moment Berlin was mentioned as a possible stop on Kennedy's itinerary. Kennedy in the Federal Republic and in Berlin – that would not be an easy event to organize. It would demand a masterpiece of staging in which the existing policy toward Berlin would have to be weighed as well as the experience gained in previous visits by American dignitaries.

POWERS AT PLAY: THE UNITED STATES, EUROPE, AND GERMANY

When Kennedy took office in January 1961, he knew that he faced a world experiencing much upheaval.[1] Relations between the Soviet Union and the

People's Republic of China were tense. National independence movements and centrifugal forces were gaining momentum in the Congo, Vietnam, and other former European colonies. The countries of the so-called Third World were demanding more and more attention from the West. Cuban leader Fidel Castro was offering Latin America an alternative to America's dominance and threatened to place the Soviet Union at America's doorstep. At the same time, the Cold War issues Kennedy inherited from Eisenhower had not at all diminished in relevance. Would America be able to maintain its lead in the arms race in light of the speed with which the Soviet Union was catching up in technology, especially in the area of rocket science? The launch of the Soviet satellite *Sputnik* in 1957 came as a shock and a wake-up call to Americans. Suddenly there was talk in the United States about a threatening missile gap.[2] What should be done about Berlin? Khrushchev made the first of a series of ultimatums in November 1958 and continued to push for an end to the city's Four-Power status even after the failure of the 1959 Geneva Summit. Could the transatlantic alliance be maintained if the new French president, Charles de Gaulle, was seriously working at uncoupling Western Europe – including the Federal Republic – from the United States? It was also unclear what course West Germany would pursue after the elderly Konrad Adenauer retired, as he was soon expected to do.

Among the many pressing challenges was an economic policy issue that had an immediate impact on America's international relations.[3] Since 1958, the United States had been experiencing a growing deficit in its balance of payments. Too much capital was flowing abroad, particularly to Europe, and the country's gold reserves were declining. American expenditures for military operations abroad (including the stationing of troops in Germany), for development aid, and for the financial support of foreign governments were indeed important in guaranteeing the powerful political presence of the United States abroad. But they were expensive. The problematic economic issue strained German-American relations once the Federal Republic ceased contributing financially toward the costs incurred by the United States in stationing its troops in West Germany. In the United States, a debate ensued over a possible reduction of American troops in Europe. Even the Eisenhower administration had openly threatened to use such a measure in 1960, but had met with bitter resistance in the Federal Republic. The monetary issue was closely intertwined with that of security. The Federal Republic feared that a reduction of American troops in Europe would undermine the American guarantee of protection. Yet at the same time, West Germany was not willing to compensate the Americans for their foreign currency expenses.[4]

The Kennedy administration had to try to ward off harm to the domestic economy and simultaneously keep its allies toeing the line. Therefore, the allies were strongly urged to increase their defense budgets, to take some of the burden of foreign aid off the United States, and to help compensate the deficit in the American balance of payments. The United States needed to get more money flowing back into the country. One possible approach to solving the problem was to convince Europeans to buy American arms. In this way, the costs of stationing American troops in Europe could be compensated; thus this matter became the focus of the so-called offset negotiations. Starting in 1961, the Federal Republic played a particularly prominent role in these negotiations, not without economic and domestic repercussions that would eventually contribute to the fall of Chancellor Ludwig Erhard in 1966.[5]

Another problem surfaced in America's relations to its European allies. Already under the Eisenhower administration, the United States had begun to rethink its existing military policy and the strategic concept of massive retaliation. Could the American people themselves believe or even accept the threat to respond to any attack against the West with a catastrophic nuclear strike? The new administration felt it more sensible to have an array of "flexible responses" at its disposal. By relying on a graduated range of options – from conventional defense to selective atomic strikes to all-out nuclear retaliation – the escalation of a possible war would have to occur more deliberately and therefore, at least theoretically, could be more easily halted. The seriousness with which such considerations were pondered increased because the strategy of massive retaliation left the United States vulnerable to a destructive counterstrike regardless of how far away the threat of conflict was from the North American continent. For the Europeans, conversely, the willingness of the United States to assume the risks inherent in the strategy of massive retaliation offered the best guarantee that America could be counted on to fulfill its obligations to its allies.[6] Not only did the older generation of leading European politicians sense a danger in the new strategy of flexible response, so too did the West European public. The two superpowers could come to an arrangement over the heads of their allies that would keep nuclear destruction at arm's length from their own soil. Accordingly, the concept of flexible response found few adherents in Western Europe, and certainly not in Konrad Adenauer. Still, the Germans could not be spared from hearing that, especially with regard to Berlin, it was "not always possible to wave an atomic bomb whenever one wants to ensure autobahn access" to the city.[7]

A paradoxical situation arose in connection with the fiscal policy problems. Under Kennedy, the United States was willing to maintain its nuclear arsenal and even to modernize it. Furthermore, Kennedy upgraded conventional armament in order to expand the range of military options should conflict arise. In his very first year in office, the young president significantly increased the defense budget. All of these measures satisfied the European expectation that the United States would remain committed to the Old World. At the same time, however, Kennedy exerted even greater pressure on his European allies to do more themselves for defense within the framework of a strategic reorientation in which they did not want to participate.

The Berlin question had interested Kennedy for a long time. He devoted a great deal of attention to it as he prepared to assume the responsibilities of the Oval Office. The outgoing administration hoped Kennedy would adopt Eisenhower's stance and state unequivocally that America would fight for Berlin should hostilities break out. Indeed, this is just what the senator from Boston had announced during the presidential election campaign.[8] At the same time, Kennedy's foreign policy advisors, including the experienced diplomat Paul H. Nitze, complained that the West had gone too far in the recent negotiations over Berlin. They feared that too many concessions had been offered to the Soviet Union. In their evaluation, even Adenauer did not fare well: "Adenauer doesn't appear to have any idea as to what to do, other than to remain intransigent in opposing any change in regard to Berlin."[9]

At the beginning of 1961, Kennedy was therefore not expected to be more conciliatory on Berlin than Eisenhower and his secretaries of state, John Foster Dulles and Christian Herter, had been. Indeed, continuity was the hallmark of the Berlin policy pursued by the new administration during its first few months in power. However, Kennedy would soon find a way to link political resolve with receptiveness to a change in strategy. The new administration invested much time and attention to contingency planning. One memorandum after another was written in an effort to work out a position and evaluate the possibilities open to the United States in the eventuality of a political and military emergency. Moreover, Kennedy brought additional expertise into the White House by calling upon the help of former Secretary of State Dean Acheson and the up-and-coming Harvard security policy expert Henry Kissinger.

In the summer of 1961, the president began to spell out the American commitment to Berlin and at the same time embed it in a new political strategy. This strategy was not the "grand design"[10] that many had hoped for and that the administration declared it to be in 1962; yet it sought to achieve three aims. First, it managed to redress the balance between the interests of Germany and those of the Soviet Union. Second, Kennedy saved the North Atlantic alliance from drifting apart by thwarting France's European policy. Third, he was able to defuse the Berlin problem by incorporating it into a policy of détente between the superpowers. At first, this complicated initiative was criticized from all sides, particularly by Adenauer and the so-called Gaullists in Germany, the advocates of a close alliance with France under President Charles de Gaulle. Kennedy broke several taboos of conventional policy toward Germany and at times triggered outrage and shock among Berliners – particularly following the erection of the Berlin Wall in August 1961 and the death of Peter Fechter at the Wall a year later.

In the meantime, historians have come to evaluate Kennedy's actions more positively.[11] There is much evidence to substantiate the argument that Kennedy had begun to pursue his new strategy determinedly by the summer of 1961 and that his was also an appropriate strategy in light of the realities of world politics, for it guaranteed the survival of West Berlin until 1963 and afterward. Kennedy's "*Ich bin ein Berliner*" declaration in June 1963 was meant to reconcile Germans – especially those in West Berlin – with the American president, even though he was not deviating from his new political course in the least. Kennedy was able to pull this off because the statement "*Ich bin ein Berliner*" tended to camouflage rhetorically the abandonment of long-held illusions and thus made the change easier to swallow. Kennedy would act in their best interest, Germans could reason. After all, he was one of them!

Kennedy's course provoked controversy even within his own administration. It soon became quite clear that serious differences of opinion had arisen among his advisors.[12] Supporting a hard line on the question of Berlin and therefore toward the Soviet Union was a small group associated with Acheson and the deputy security advisor Walt W. Rostow. These men favored military mobilization and, if necessary, escalation. From July 1961 on, they were even ready to declare a state of emergency in the United States. Opposing this approach were Secretary of State Dean Rusk and the younger advisors Henry Kissinger, Arthur M. Schlesinger, and Theodore C. Sorensen, who sought a diplomatic and political solution instead. Such a solution was conceived as part of a new approach toward the Soviet Union in which the legitimate security interests of the opposing superpower were to be acknowledged to a greater extent than they had been under Eisenhower. But this solution could succeed only if the reorientation from massive retaliation to flexible response was actually implemented. Above all, actors on both sides of the political divide were no longer allowed to fixate on the questions of Berlin and Germany. The point was to understand these issues as part of a more comprehensive course of détente and thus to strip them of their potential as a constant source of conflict.

Specifically, this approach meant an acknowledgment of the Oder-Neisse line, the post-1945 line of demarcation between Polish and German territory. Even the de facto recognition of the German Democratic Republic (GDR) would become not only possible but advantageous. This did not mean, however, that the United States was abandoning the Four-Power status of Berlin. This status not only guaranteed the presence of the Western powers in Berlin but also offered them a twofold source of leverage. The Four-Power status was used time and again to get the Soviet Union to take its share of the responsibility for Berlin. The status also guaranteed the United States special Allied rights in the city and thus blocked the efforts by West Germany and a few Berlin politicians simply to declare West Berlin a *Bundesland* – a constituent state of the Federal Republic – a status the city could not have according to the legal standpoint of the Western Allies.[13] Still, the liberal advisors at the White House now struck German reunification from the political agenda. It was thought that the pragmatism of acknowledging the division of Germany and handing over the sole responsibility of the eastern sector of Berlin de facto, though not de jure, to the Soviet Union and the GDR would create more leeway for both of the superpowers to communicate outside the narrow confines of bloc politics.

The United States began, on the one hand, to restrict its interests and limit its protective functions to the western sectors of the city. This restriction was accompanied, on the other hand, by a step-up in military strength and a more explicit specification of the U.S. guarantee to protect West Berlin. Both measures irritated Germans, who at first did not understand the link between the two aims. It required an – occasionally painful – learning process to concede that the two-track policy would eventually guarantee the safety of West Berlin. Nikita Khrushchev provided the catalyst that prompted widespread adherence to this policy. On June 3, 1961, Khrushchev and Kennedy opened a two-day summit conference in Vienna. The Soviet leader brandished his "tools of torture,"[14] the plan for Germany he had first proposed in 1958. The superpowers, Khrushchev contended, should sign a peace treaty with the GDR. If the United States was not willing to do so, the Soviet Union would proceed on its own by the end of 1961. Under the treaty Khrushchev envisioned, West Berlin would become a free city and Western troops were to be pulled out, except for a symbolic contingent.

The West was to recognize the sovereign rights of the GDR, in whose territory Berlin was located.

In the weeks following Khrushchev's threat of unilateral action, the White House worked feverishly on its position. The representatives of the various schools of thought were at odds. In the end, Kennedy made concessions to Acheson's group of hardliners by emphasizing the military components of deterrence and strengthening conventional forces. But the concept Kennedy decided on was the flexible, two-track policy proposed by his younger advisors. The United States now defined three vital interests in its policy for Germany and Berlin. If necessary, the United States was willing to fight for these "essentials" – as they were soon referred to even in German – but only for them. The essentials comprised, first, the presence and security of Western troops in West Berlin; second, the security and viability of West Berlin; and third, Western access to West Berlin. The eastern sector of the city and American access to it were no longer considered to be vital to American interests. In a television broadcast on July 25, 1961, Kennedy presented this definition of the country's interests to the world in a subdued tone. He linked the announcement of a strengthened U.S. military commitment with an offer to enter into negotiations with the Soviet Union.[15] The president did not mention the unification of the two German states, nor did he declare a national state of emergency or send additional troops to Europe.

Despite these efforts, the situation in Berlin escalated. The flow of refugees from East to West Berlin, which had long hobbled the GDR, grew dramatically. On the last weekend in July 1961, nearly four thousand East German citizens reported to the provisional refugee camp Berlin-Marienfelde.[16] Two weeks later came the turning point. In the early morning hours of August 13, 1961, the GDR began to block off access to the western sectors of the city. In the weeks that followed, barbed wire fence gave way to the infamous concrete structure known as the Berlin Wall. Within only a few days, the outrage of West Berliners over this measure took a surprising turn. The reaction of the United States and Great Britain to the Wall had been guarded, even tepid. It became clear that the Anglo-American defenders were willing to accept the action taken by the East and, moreover, that they viewed this action as a solution to the refugee crisis and therefore a chance to defuse the Berlin problem. The popular tabloid *Bild* summed up the mood in Germany in its oversized headline: "The West does NOTHING!"[17]

West Berlin's mayor now felt the time had come to remind the friendly superpower of its responsibilities to the city. On August 15, Willy Brandt sent Kennedy a long letter; Adenauer received a copy as well. Brandt's press secretary Egon Bahr had drawn up the draft, which the mayor then revised. Brandt did not mince words. He criticized the ineffectual reaction of the Western commanders. The SPD politician predicted a severe "crisis of confidence" between Berliners and the Western powers should the latter continue to remain "inert and strictly on the defensive." Then the mayor went a step further and proposed what he thought to be the best steps for the United States to take: to proclaim a "Three Power" status for West Berlin; to repeat the guarantee of security until reunification was achieved and to have this confirmed by popular referendum in West Berlin, if necessary; to bring the Berlin problem before the United Nations; and to strengthen demonstratively the American garrison in West Berlin.[18]

Kennedy was furious. No one dictated to the United States what it should do. Brandt had overstepped – greatly overstepped – his position. He had presumed an undue familiarity with the president at a moment when he should have limited himself to a straightforward report on the situation. To make matters worse, the letter was published in the *Frankfurter Allgemeine Zeitung*, one of Germany's leading newspapers. The publication of this letter was particularly aggravating because it redirected public outrage away from those responsible for building the Wall and toward the Western powers. As Vice President Lyndon B. Johnson pointed out to Brandt a few days later, the letter "had shifted the propaganda effect" of building the Wall to the West's disadvantage. There was no greater political disaster conceivable. Kennedy's written response to Brandt was courteous but distant.[19] Except for the step to strengthen the garrison, he categorically rejected all of Brandt's proposals. Kennedy emphasized once again that only West Berlin, not the entire city, was under American protection. The president placed the symbolic value of West Berlin as an outpost of freedom in an even more glaring spotlight. During this crisis in German-American relations, created in part by external events and in part by the two countries themselves, symbolic politics now emerged as a plausible and promising option for political action.

Shortly afterward, Kennedy sent Vice President Lyndon B. Johnson and Airlift hero Lucius D. Clay on a trip to Bonn and Berlin. In addition, he deployed a contingent of American soldiers to reinforce the garrison in West Berlin. These measures could not and were not intended to stop the work to make the Wall permanent. The United States took a symbolic stand and thus was able to dampen West German outrage. The Johnson-Clay trip, which we will examine more closely in the third section of this chapter, served to create solidarity between America and Berlin and to regenerate public trust in the United States on the part of the West Germans. Yet, the public show of solidarity actually concealed the fact that, behind the curtains, the visit was seen as an opportunity to discipline Brandt. Kennedy sent his representatives to Germany with the explicit instructions "to speak frankly with Mayor Brandt" and "to make it clear to him" that he should cease his criticism of the United States.[20] Adenauer, whose office had leaked Brandt's letter to the press, could rub his hands in glee and express the same view to Johnson in order to score against his domestic opponent.

The crisis caused by the construction of the Wall reached another critical point in October 1961. By that time, Clay was residing in Berlin as Kennedy's special envoy. The situation escalated when the GDR refused to let the nominal American mission chief, Allan E. Lightner, enter the city's eastern sector. Clay sent tanks to Checkpoint Charlie; the Soviet Union did the same. For the first and only time during the Cold War, the armed forces of the two superpowers faced off against one another, prepared for combat. The Cold War did not boil over into a hot war, but Clay had forced the Soviet Union to reveal itself as the dominant actor in the eastern sector of Berlin. This too was an exercise in the politics of visibility. Clay had the American tanks positioned at the checkpoint in a manner that enabled the photographers in the surrounding area to take good pictures (Illustration 3).[21] Although Clay's position faced growing opposition from Washington, he staunchly defended his ideas into the winter months: "We cannot succeed unless we take the lead. . . . [W]e should seek the confrontation sooner rather than later."[22]

Clay made few friends in Washington with his eagerness to act and unrelenting attitude toward the Soviet Union. Both ran contrary to the new course U.S. foreign policy had taken since July. In American leadership circles, Clay was viewed as an "old warhorse returned to the scene" of his former glory.[23] Frustrated by the lack of clarity over his role and by the fight with State Department diplomats over his responsibilities, Clay complained to Secretary of State Dean Rusk: "Here in Berlin without authority or influence, I serve only as a symbol and I am not sure as a symbol of what."[24] Nevertheless, Clay remained in Berlin until the spring of 1962, when he was removed, at his own request, from the special Berlin mission. When it came to the Berlin issue, using individuals as political symbols was a form of poltical action. But there was a tension between those individuals, the symbolic value attributed to them, and the political purposes they were supposed to be serving.

Between September 1961 and March 1962, direct talks were held at various locations between high-ranking representatives from the United States and the Soviet Union. The Kennedy administration was determined to

Illustration 3. A dramatic event in the world spotlight: American tanks at Checkpoint Charlie, October 27–28, 1961. Source: Bildarchiv Preußischer Kulturbesitz, Berlin (Art Resource Inc., New York).

realize its strategy of integrating the issues of Berlin and Germany into a global policy of détente. Adenauer rejected this strategy flat out. The chancellor blocked all American attempts to draw concessions from him on the question of Germany. Foreign Minister Gerhard Schröder, a few other so-called Atlanticists within the CDU, and Willy Brandt were more receptive to the U.S. position. Brandt himself began to adjust to the realities of the Berlin Wall. Historian Diethelm Prowe is certainly correct to emphasize that the building of the Berlin Wall became an important inspiration for Brandt's own policy of détente a decade later. More recently, Wolfgang Schmidt has argued that the origins for Brandt's ideas about détente can even be traced back to the mid-1950s.[25]

In February 1962, the Soviet Union once again pushed the Berlin question to the fore by interfering in the air traffic to the western half of the city. This action infringed upon the three American essentials. The United States government did not back down, although it did not follow Clay's suggestion that very provocative countermeasures be undertaken. Kennedy in particular demonstrated a willingness to recognize the security interests of the

Soviet Union. At the end of February, the United States even proposed the establishment of an international body to regulate travel to West Berlin. In March, Secretary of State Rusk officially signaled to his Soviet counterpart, Andrej Gromyko, that, on the basis of the American-defined essentials, the superpowers could agree to demand more détente from the two German states, to prevent them from possessing nuclear arms, and to guarantee the postwar borders. Rusk's overture roiled German-American relations. Adenauer demanded that the United States break off the negotiations. Within the German political parties, opinions differed. Then the American position was leaked to the press. Although the source of this leak was not clear, the United States held the German ambassador, Wilhelm G. Grewe, responsible. On account of the pressure exerted by the Kennedy administration, Grewe asked Bonn to be released from his position in Washington. Adenauer, in turn, publicly exposed the superpower negotiations on Berlin and undermined any chance of their success. German-American relations were at a postwar low.[26]

In the months between this controversy and Kennedy's trip to Germany, relations between the United States, the Soviet Union, and Europe, including the Federal Republic and West Berlin, were influenced by four developments:

- The shock wave following the death of Peter Fechter at the Berlin Wall in August 1962
- The Cuban Missile Crisis of October 1962, which led the superpowers to the brink of a nuclear war
- French efforts to remove Western Europe from the alliance with the United States, to isolate Great Britain, and to create an axis with West Germany
- The successful American effort to prevent the Federal Republic from acquiring nuclear weapons and to encourage détente with the Soviet Union

Just over a year after the Berlin Wall went up, an 18-year-old German named Peter Fechter was shot and wounded by East German border guards in his attempt to flee from the Soviet sector of Berlin to the American side. He was left to bleed to death. American soldiers did not believe they were in a position to rescue him. Eventually, he was carried off by East German police and border guards. Pictures of the episode circled the globe. Fechter was by no means the first person to die while attempting to escape. By June 1962, the death toll had already reached thirty-two.[27] But like the appearance of the Wall itself, Fechter's horrendous death on August 17 spurred disillusionment with the United States. His death underscored how helpless the Western powers seemed and how uncoordinated their

Illustration 4. "Pot of repressed anger": The death of Peter Fechter on August 17, 1962, at the Berlin Wall sparks anti-American demonstrations in West Berlin. Scene outside of Schöneberg City Hall on August 19. Source: Landesarchiv Berlin.

operations were in the city where the opposing political blocs confronted one another. Kennedy immediately recognized this dilemma and insisted on being briefed personally as events unfolded.[28]

From the perspective of both the United States and the Berlin Senate (the executive branch of West Berlin's government), the dynamics of the situation became increasingly dangerous. At first, the outrage of West Berliners was directed clearly against the GDR and the Soviet Union, as the demolition of a Soviet bus in West Berlin so graphically demonstrated. The West Berlin police had to use water cannons against demonstrators to prevent them from storming Checkpoint Charlie. This meant that the Wall was now being protected against mounting emotions in the western sectors of the city. Yet more was to come. The "pot of repressed anger...boiled over" (Illustration 4). In some places, the search for the guilty parties turned into a "stunning indictment of American occupation forces."[29] Suddenly it was American vehicles that were being attacked. Some West Berliners exhibited their anger by driving by U.S. mission headquarters loudly honking their horns. At spontaneously occurring protest gatherings, a poster was seen that read "Allied protectors: tolerators and abettors of murder"

(*Schutzmächte: Morddulder, Mordhelfer*). In the newspaper *Die Welt*, Sebastian Haffner expressed his criticism in harsh language and argued that such slogans were justified. Something had to be done where the "Gorgon's grimace of smirking cruelty" was found, he said, even if it meant jeopardizing peace – as crossing the border into the Soviet sector would mean.[30] The press now spoke bluntly about anti-American sentiments in West Berlin. Washington reacted cautiously to this development, although the Kennedy administration suspected that instigators from the East had infiltrated the crowds of demonstrators. After all, the United States was deploying its own people to protect Berliners. German journalist Jan Reifenberg attempted to compare these developments to a "stab in the back" in order to illustrate the concerns of the United States.[31]

Once again, Brandt was tempted to turn directly to the American president and thus prepared several letter drafts. However, the blunder of August 1961 had made him cautious. Following the advice of Adenauer and the Foreign Office, he did not send the emotionally laden letter. Instead, Brandt used Lucius D. Clay in his effort to dispel the impression in the United States that anti-Americanism was spreading in Berlin. He argued that the Wall should not again be allowed to divide the allies.[32] The main objective was to control popular emotions, which from a political viewpoint could head in any direction – even against the West itself. Too much anger directed against the GDR on account of Fechter's death would be just as destabilizing as indignation undermining the moral and political authority of the United States.

Such considerations were not found solely in government circles in Berlin and the Federal Republic. Kennedy confided to West German president Heinrich Lübke that the feelings of anger expressed in West Berlin were "completely understandable." However, the political course that needed to be taken was clear. In "a situation so potentially explosive," everything had to be done to ensure that "reason can prevail." Kennedy thanked Lübke for his efforts "to persuade the people of the city to maintain their coolness as well as their customary courage under heavy provocation."[33] Yet in the end it was Willy Brandt himself who succeeded in containing the threat. He called upon the citizens of Berlin to demonstrate moderation, addressed demonstrators at the Schöneberg City Hall on August 19, and even took measures to have the Wall protected. If any political figure emerged from the crisis in a stronger position and with the ability to re-instill public confidence in the United States, it was the mayor of West Berlin.

Besides the situation in Germany, the most dangerous moments of 1962 resulted from the attempt of the Soviet Union to station missile launchers and atomic warheads in Cuba. After a dramatic thirteen days[34] and an intensive yet cautious weighing of the risks involved, Kennedy was able to bring the Soviet Union to remove the weapons systems. In doing so, he made several concessions to the Soviet Union, but the public did not learn about them until later. This episode reestablished the reputation of the United States as the tougher and eventually more successful partner in negotiations, a development that could only enhance the security of West Berlin. In his decisive television broadcast about the Cuban Missile Crisis on October 22, 1962, Kennedy explicitly emphasized America's commitment to "the brave people of West Berlin."[35] The Cuban Missile Crisis brought the United States and Berlin closer together and reinstated the confidence in one another that had been so damaged in the wake of the tumultuous August weeks of 1961 and 1962. This reconciliation particularly affected the relationship between Willy Brandt and John F. Kennedy. In early October, Kennedy invited the mayor to the White House and granted Brandt the privilege of a private meeting, as he had in earlier visits. The two men got along well together.[36]

In his talks with Brandt, Kennedy made no secret of his disappointment over the West German intransigence with regard to the Berlin issue. The American president was growing tired, on the one hand, of being reminded repeatedly by the Federal Republic and particularly by Adenauer of America's commitments to Germany, and on the other, of being permanently suspected of not really standing up for West Berlin.[37] Brandt was quite receptive to such complaints. The SPD politician was very willing to assume the role of a true confidant in Germany. At the peak of the Cuban Missile Crisis, Kennedy put Brandt on equal footing with the most important Western heads of state and government and kept him directly informed of what was happening. The mayor appreciated this. For his part, Brandt was now able to use this newly acquired frankness to inject his own ideas, such as that of a popular referendum in West Berlin, into his correspondence with the American president.[38] At the end of 1962, Brandt and Kennedy found themselves on the same wavelength more often than they had ever been before, whereas Chancellor Adenauer was pushed more and more to the sidelines.

It was not solely generational and personal factors that created a growing distance between Adenauer and the United States. Much more serious causes for American concern were Adenauer's maneuvering with the Western alliance and the policies of Charles de Gaulle. Immediately after the Berlin Wall was built, de Gaulle refused to support any form of compromise with the East and thus appeared even "to out-German the Germans" in his intransigence.[39] Starting in the spring of 1962, the rapport between the

Federal Republic and France became so strong and so apparent that their rapprochement could be interpreted as a step toward decoupling continental Western Europe from America. Adenauer's visit to France in July 1962 and de Gaulle's trip to Germany in September of that year were used to celebrate this new Franco-German friendship with symbolic gestures and great cordiality, as will be discussed in detail later in this chapter. In mid-January 1963, de Gaulle finally turned down the American offer of cooperation in the area of nuclear weapons.

On January 22, 1963, Franco-German rapprochement reached its zenith with the signing of the Élysée Treaty in Paris.[40] This treaty appeared to the United States to be the culmination of a dangerous decoupling policy, particularly since de Gaulle concurrently broke off negotiations with Great Britain over admittance into the European Economic Community (EEC). Kennedy was extremely angry. For his advisor Acheson, the former secretary of state, the signing of the treaty was simply "one of the darkest days of the postwar period." Another friend of Berlin, former American High Commissioner in Germany John McCloy, complained bitterly to Adenauer: "I am more deeply disturbed about the turn of events [in Europe] than I have been at any time since the end of the war." Furthermore, "many Americans who . . . see in Berlin a symbol of the common destiny of Germany and the United States are now disquieted."[41]

Outside observers did not always realize that ultimately Adenauer neither could accept nor sought to embrace de Gaulle's vision of a Franco-German bilateral alliance decoupled from the United States. What became evident was the formation of the Atlanticists as a pro-American group within the West German political establishment. Supporters were recruited from all political parties and included Foreign Minister Schröder and the future chancellor Ludwig Erhard. The Atlanticists worked hard to thwart the plans of those proposing a Franco-German axis – namely, the German Gaullists grouped around Franz Josef Strauß, the leader of Bavaria's conservative party, the Christian Social Union – and to maintain good relations with the United States. Thanks to their efforts, the West German parliament did not ratify the Franco-German friendship treaty until May 1963, once a preamble had been included that underscored West Germany's allegiance to the North Atlantic alliance.

The debate on the feasibility and desirability of a Franco-German alliance took place at the exact same time as Kennedy's trip to Germany was being planned. This coincidence made the planning all the more important because the trip was intended to send an unambiguous message: with Kennedy's visit, West Germany and the United States would be affirming their commitment to the transatlantic alliance. Kennedy and his concept of an Atlantic community thus prevailed over de Gaulle without placing in question the political and moral value of the Franco–German reconciliation.

One reason the United States disapproved of Franco–German bilateralism was the fear that West Germany could use this relationship to gain possession of nuclear weapons. The United States sought to prevent that while at the same time compensating West Germany by giving it an alternative nuclear option. Here too, the American government followed a two-track approach. First, it invited its most important Western European allies to participate in a "multilateral nuclear force" (MLF). This offer was not much more than political window dressing because the United States would have retained the exclusive right to decide on the deployment of nuclear weapons had the MLF been established, which it was not. Moreover, such a force was to be based on a fleet of ships and would have been very vulnerable. Second, the United States pushed hard, against Adenauer's advice, to complete negotiations on a treaty to limit nuclear testing.

The Nuclear Test Ban Treaty was eventually signed in August 1963 and went into effect in October of that year. This first arms control treaty of the Cold War was signed by both German states and prohibited them de facto from having access to nuclear weapons, which was in complete accord with the interests of both the United States and the Soviet Union. The GDR acted as a sovereign entity just as the Federal Republic did. Thus Kennedy achieved what Adenauer had always fought to prevent and what Brandt had come to accept: the German question became subordinate to negotiation between the two superpowers and was thereby divested of much of the particular dynamic that had made this issue so disruptive for so long in world politics. For this reason, it is correct to refer to the Nuclear Test Ban Treaty as a "disguised agreement on the Berlin and German questions."[42]

A SPECIAL RELATIONSHIP: NETWORKS AND THE POLITICS OF MEMORY

During the critical months of the Berlin crisis between the Vienna summit and the armed face-off between the United States and the Soviet Union at Checkpoint Charlie in 1961, the new American administration experienced something astonishing. The White House was outpaced by the American citizenry in the demand to remain steadfast in Berlin and, if necessary, to risk war. The State Department, which followed public opinion closely, had already noted this trend in the late 1950s.[43] The results of the Gallup polls taken in the United States in 1961 spoke volumes. In mid-July, 85 percent of those polled were in favor of keeping American troops in West Berlin, even if it meant the possibility of war. Should West Berlin be subjected to another blockade, 67 percent believed force should be used to secure access to the city. Should the Soviet Union continue its hard-line approach, 59 percent of those questioned considered war probable and 40 percent thought this would again mean world war.[44] At the end of August, 90 percent of those polled said they had heard or read about the situation in Berlin. Sixty-four percent wanted to engage in war in order to secure access to Berlin; a month later this figure rose to 70 percent.[45]

The White House was flooded by letters and telegrams from citizens from all walks of life who wanted to express their views on the Berlin crisis. Some were critical. They warned of the risk of war or against linking the fate of the United States to that of Berlin. Others recommended pragmatic solutions: a corridor of territory leading from West Germany to West Berlin could be purchased from the GDR; the city could be exchanged for cash; better yet, the city could even be rebuilt in another, far less dangerous place. The overwhelming majority of those expressing their opinion to the White House, however, urged the president to remain steadfast in his dealings with the Soviet Union and to ensure the freedom of West Berlin. Some, holding to the basic anticommunist position, invoked the domino theory: if Berlin were to fall to the communists, the rest of Western Europe would follow ("As Berlin goes, so will the free world"). Others argued that a firm stand would serve American interests or that the country had a special commitment to Berlin. Nearly all supporters of unconditional American commitment to West Berlin felt that such support reflected the moral position of the United States and West Berlin. By promising to keep Berlin "a bastion of freedom," argued Senator Robert C. Byrd, Americans "have not only a moral commitment to the people of West Berlin but we have a prior moral commitment to ourselves." In Berlin, America was not only providing protection to others but was maintaining a moral and political presence as well. "Berlin is the place for us to make our stand," wrote one industrialist from Illinois in a letter to the president.[46]

Undoubtedly, the American public was highly involved in the Berlin issue. Many in the United States sympathized with Berliners and saw the future of New York and Chicago at risk in Berlin. Berlin became the urban symbol of the Cold War struggle that American society was fighting. Berlin was thought of as America's city. In a concerted action in September 1961, the mayors of numerous American cities announced their solidarity with Berlin.[47] As Ernest May explains, "the experiences of America's allies were not the experiences of colonial subjects . . . they were, rather, the experiences of Americans." This was particularly true in the case of Berlin. Americans identified with the sacrifices, the dangerous position, and the hopes of West Berliners more than with those of any other ally.[48] The United States had already established its presence in Berlin through its military and civilian personnel, but Americans at home were also spellbound by the city and its fate. They behaved like the enraptured viewers of a political drama, following it passionately and participating in it through their commitment. The American government was well aware of this fascination and its political import.

From at least the time of the Berlin Airlift, Berlin was a political issue in the United States. A politician or official who appeared soft on the question of Berlin was courting trouble. Every administration since President Truman's used the American position on Berlin to gain the support of not only the Germans and Western Europeans but also of the American public. In turn, the political elite in West Berlin were aware that their city had a strong effect on America. This effect was deliberately enhanced by advertising agents in the United States. Starting in the spring of 1963, Harold Hurwitz, an American living in Berlin and a friend of Willy Brandt, published his *Berlin Briefing* for American leaders. Hurwitz's take on events and the public mood reflected Brandt's view of the political situation. Brandt did not hesitate to include the president and Robert F. Kennedy on the mailing list.[49]

Many West Berliners and the Berlin Senate viewed the close relationship between Berlin and the United States more positively than other West Germans. Egon Bahr, who became press secretary for the Berlin Senate in 1960 and was soon one of Willy Brandt's closest advisors, was very aware of this disparity. Shortly after assuming his post, he informed the publisher Axel Springer about the success of an advertising campaign ("Message from Berlin") running in the United States. Bahr emphasized that the campaign had prompted a tremendous response, particularly from "average Americans." The Senate, he reported, had received a mountain of mail

including moving lines from people who were once in Berlin themselves. But also from people in the Midwest and the West of the United States. These are addressed to the mayor and express an almost enthusiastic appreciation for the necessity to maintain Berlin's freedom under all circumstances. They encourage him to remain vigilant in his position. I remember one piece of mail in which a farmer inquired what he could do to support this good cause. As you . . . will draw from this, the success of the ad series is unfortunately far grander, with regard to the emotions and reactions of the Americans, than anything we have experienced here at city hall from the Federal Republic in this respect.[50]

The Cold War created the conditions that made the Federal Republic an ally of the United States. This was formally recognized by West Germany's acceptance into NATO in 1955. At the same time, the United States also had a special ally within West Germany that appealed strongly to the emotions of the Americans, namely, West Berlin. The unusually close relationship between Berlin and the Americans – one may speak of a "special relationship"[51] – began at the end of the nineteenth century. From then on, Berlin was seen on both sides of the Atlantic as a city that exhibited the characteristics of American society and urbanity. Berlin developed into a multiethnic city. The population increased and industrialization took place at a breathtaking pace; at least that is how it was perceived.[52] The dynamics propelling the city manifested themselves in a building boom and the concentration of scientific and cultural establishments. Moreover, the city featured a broad spectrum of popular mass culture, publications and press, entertainment establishments, and avant-garde art. Berlin's cabarets were no less legendary than the editorials of Alfred Kerr or Kurt Tucholsky.[53] Mark Twain once referred to Berlin as the "European Chicago"; Walther Rathenau dubbed it the "Chicago on the Spree"; and Hermann Walden called it "America in a microcosm."[54] During the Weimar Republic, analogies to New York were more popular. Berlin was Germany's only metropolis, an often chaotically strange jumble of streets, ethnicities, and activities.

When Adolf Hitler seized power in 1933, Berlin became the national capital of the Nazi dictatorship. The city became the place where the Enabling Act was passed and the Reichstag burned, where the Wannsee Conference to plan the genocide of the European Jews took place, and where the final desperate commands of the Nazi regime to hold out to the last echoed from the Führer bunker. Few in America had forgotten these events. However, the onset of the Cold War made the public believe that West Berlin represented a bastion of freedom and democracy not only for West Germans but for Americans as well. The crucial military operations of the British and American armed forces, spurred on by Military Governor Lucius D. Clay, were the reason why Berlin survived the Soviet blockade between June 1948 and May 1949. The Airlift represented the psychostrategic turning point of the postwar period. Enemies became friends,[55] and Hitler's Berlin became America's Berlin, which – although German – still became more American than anywhere else in Germany (Illustration 5). During the decade and a half following the Airlift, Americans viewed events in Berlin as a drama, as the story of the imperiled frontline city of the Cold War bravely standing up to the Soviet threat. This story enabled West Berlin to reinterpret its role and reestablish a connection to its cosmopolitan, pre-Nazi past.

Berlin's place in American popular culture was helped a great deal by the movies and novels set in Berlin that dramatized the various facets of the city in the postwar world. Billy Wilder's film *A Foreign Affair* (1948), with

Illustration 5. The end of Hitler's Berlin: President Harry S. Truman, sitting in the backseat of the car between Secretary of State James Byrnes and Navy admiral William D. Leahy, in August 1945, at the ruins of the Reich Chancellery. Source: Harry S. Truman Library (U.S. Army Signal Corps).

Marlene Dietrich and Jean Arthur, deals with the black market milieu and American occupation, which produced a mixture of control, consumption, and new entertainments. George Seaton brought the heroic story of the Airlift to the big screen in *The Big Lift* (1950). Wilder's satire *One, Two, Three* (1961), starring James Cagney, Pamela Tiffin, and Horst Buchholz, makes fun of the confrontation between the superpowers and the Coca-Cola expansionism of the Americans. Lastly, numerous spy stories took place in Berlin. Particularly popular in the United States was John le Carré's novel *The Spy Who Came in from the Cold*. The British film adaptation of Carré's thriller begins and ends with a view of the barbed wire on top of the Berlin Wall. Richard Burton received an Oscar in 1966 for his portrayal of the main character, who dies at the end after being shot in the back at the Wall. In that same year, Leon Uris published his novel *Armageddon*, which describes Berlin as the battlefield of the two opposing superpowers.[56]

The long-term impact of the Airlift and other memories of Berlin did not simply happen on their own. They required public presentation and a certain degree of nurturing. The transatlantic culture of memory was cultivated and expanded by an ever-growing network of people and institutions in America and West Berlin. It extended far beyond the interaction of governmental actors. The American-Berlin network illustrates that transnational relations between societies are not limited to state interactions. Governmental actors shared the political stage with individuals and institutions outside the ranks of officialdom – for example, interest groups, cultural exchange institutions, and "alliance managers."[57] Relations between Berlin and the United States in the early 1960s were conducted on multiple levels and through multiple channels, and power politics, public opinion, economic interests, and cultural assumptions all had a shaping influence.

Berlin received massive economic aid from the United States and the Marshall Plan. The amount of this aid surpassed that of the subsidies coming from the Federal Republic until the second half of the 1950s. Moreover, the American aid was publicized through exhibits and posters, making it even more popular among the people of Berlin and useful as propaganda against the GDR.[58] During the course of the 1950s, many American observers noticed that the level of consumption in West Berlin was approaching that of the United States. The International Film Festival was started in 1951, bringing some of the glamour of Hollywood into the city each year and helping West Berlin present itself as the "showcase of the West" and as a center of culture and entertainment up to American standards. Some observers referred to the Kurfürstendamm, the city's famous main avenue, as Berlin's Broadway. In contrast, life in East Berlin appeared all the more "dreary," "desolate," and "colorless."[59]

The United States left a strong imprint not only on the business world and consumption patterns of West Berlin but also on the academic life and landscape of the city. With the energetic assistance of the American commanders Frank L. Howley and General Clay, the Americans helped to

Illustration 6. A revival of modernism and a projection of a liberal society: The Congress Hall in West Berlin's Tiergarten, dedicated in 1957. Source: Landesarchiv Berlin.

establish the Free University (FU) in 1948. In the years to follow, the FU received generous contributions from the Ford Foundation in New York. Clay's former colleague Shepard Stone ensured that the interest in Berlin at the Foundation did not diminish over the years. The Henry Ford Building at the FU became the architectural symbol of this aid. In addition, American social scientists introduced the ideas of American pragmatism and modern social research to the university, while German professors were given the opportunity to become acquainted with the American university system.[60]

The two conferences of the supranational Congress for Cultural Freedom held in Berlin in 1950 and 1960 helped to introduce to West Berlin various liberal-democratic social theories, including the anticommunist theory of totalitarianism.[61] Finally, in September 1957, the stylistically progressive Congress Hall in the Tiergarten, a large park in the heart of the city bordering on the Soviet sector, was dedicated (Illustration 6). Eleanor Lansing Dulles, the sister of Secretary of State John Foster Dulles and CIA chief Allan Dulles, was particularly active in this project. A diplomat herself, Eleanor Dulles had been responsible for Berlin affairs for years in the State Department. She helped raise the funds to build the Congress Hall, to establish the Benjamin Franklin Foundation as its official sponsor, and to get

Illustration 7. Transatlantic culture of memory: The Airlift Memorial at Tempelhof Airport in West Berlin, 1951. Source: Landesarchiv Berlin.

the American star architect Hugh Stubbins for the planning. As Jeffrey M. Diefendorf has pointed out, the Congress Hall brought everything together: Cold War politics, modern architecture, the myths of liberty, and the incorporation of West Berlin into modern urban planning.[62]

At the same time, memory was being cultivated. The intensive coverage of the Airlift had kept Americans in great suspense. In this situation, the politics of visibility played a large role. The pictures of the American photographer and native-born Berliner Henry Ries were seen throughout the world. Often these photographs showed transport planes flying low over the rooftops of Berlin as people, especially women and children, watched and waved.[63] Not only Berliners but also Americans now found themselves in the role of spectator. In July 1951, a monument to the Berlin Airlift was dedicated at Tempelhof Airport and a companion piece was installed at Rhein-Main Air Base in Frankfurt. The *"Hungerharke"* (hunger rake), as the Berliners christened the monument, rose high in the Berlin sky in commemoration of an experience shared by Americans and Berliners (Illustration 7). The names of the American servicemen who lost their lives during the Airlift were engraved on the monument. It thus represented the transnational relationship between Berlin and the United States as a partnership "between those who are living, those who are dead, and those who are to be born."[64] That one partner was willing to risk the lives of its troops in making common cause with the other was proof of the seriousness of their relationship. The future of that relationship would rest on remembering the shared past. In August 1959, the Berlin Senate created the Stiftung Luftbrückendank (Airlift Gratitude Foundation) to aid the survivors of those who died in the Airlift, and the British, French, and American military commanders in the city founded the Luftbrücken-Gedenkfond (Airlift Memorial Fund). Over time, both organizations developed into student scholarship funds.[65]

The melding of past, present, and future as a shared political experience did not occur on its own. The process had to be actively promoted and sustained. The celebrations and ceremonies that took place when high-ranking Americans visited Berlin and numerous commemorative rituals appealing to Germans and Americans alike played a crucial part in that process. Nearly a year after the dedication of the Airlift Memorial, Berlin Mayor Ernst Reuter and Secretary of State Dean Acheson laid the cornerstone for the America Memorial Library. The construction of this facility was financed by contributions from the United States; the library opened in 1954. Four years earlier, the so-called Freedom Bell had been dedicated at the Schöneberg City Hall on October 24, 1950. This ceremony and its preparation formed a spectacular chain of events. In the weeks preceding its arrival in Berlin, the bell had toured the United States from New York to Los Angeles and back again. The Freedom Bell was reminiscent of the Liberty Bell in Philadelphia, which eternalized the moment in which the British colonies in America had unified to declare themselves an independent political entity. The inscription engraved on the ten-ton Freedom Bell read: "That This World Under God Shall Have A New Birth of Freedom." This was a line taken from Lincoln's Gettysburg Address, in which the president had sworn at the height of the Civil War in 1863 to uphold the unity and peaceful future of the United States.

The Freedom Bell was brought to Berlin in October 1950 by Lucius D. Clay, who had retired from military service a year and a half earlier. He was accompanied by a delegation from the self-named Crusade for Freedom, which had been financed, unbeknownst to the public, by the CIA. The crusade organizers had collected nearly sixteen million signatures in the United States endorsing a so-called declaration of freedom, which made a great impression on the public. Clay himself described the transport of the bell from the United States to Berlin as a "spiritual airlift."[66] It endowed the Schöneberg City Hall with a special allure. In the ceremony itself, the bell

Illustration 8. A transatlantic symbol of West Berlin: Willy Brandt presents Kennedy with a model of the Freedom Bell at the White House on March 13, 1961. Source: John F. Kennedy Library (Audiovisual Archives, no. AR 6423-C, Abbie Rowe).

was treated with religious reverence, as was the daily chiming transmitted by the popular American radio broadcaster RIAS (Rundfunk im Amerikanischen Sektor). West Berlin's city hall in Schöneberg, previously little known in the United States, became a transnational commemorative site, a symbolic place recognized in both Germany and the United States. Later, both the city hall and the Freedom Bell would help create the visual backdrop – and in the case of the bell, also the acoustic accompaniment – for John F. Kennedy's enthusiastically celebrated speech on June 26, 1963.

The Freedom Bell was soon ritualized and popularized. Models of the bell became more popular as souvenirs and a miniature symbol of Berlin than those of the traditional Berlin Bear. Ernst Reuter was as willing to have himself photographed with a miniature copy of the bell in the United States as was Willy Brandt (Illustration 8). Many times in the 1950s and 1960s, the resounding chimes of the Freedom Bell were heard on American radio broadcasts. The propagandistic purpose was to remind the world that West Berlin remained free and thereby to link the fate of the city with those of other nations in the noncommunist world. In 1960, the rumor that President Eisenhower might be persuaded to come to Berlin for the tenth anniversary celebration of the bell spread through the city. In the end, Eisenhower stayed in Washington.[67] But an official delegation from the United States did turn up for the anniversary, and many American mayors sent telegrams. Berlin Deputy Mayor Franz Amrehm used the occasion to point out that the Freedom Bell introduced a transnational dimension to complement the Brandenburg Gate, the symbol for German reunification. The bell had become a "supranational symbol of solidarity" with the friends of Berlin. Once again it became clear that Berlin's symbolism in the Cold War was twofold. Amrehm maintained that the relevance of the bell within Germany was coupled significantly with the resonance it found in the United States: "It is not yet widely known in Germany just how much support this bell has mobilized for us in America. . . . We could sense that the Americans are a bit proud of this Freedom Bell and of their own commitment to Berlin. . . . Freedom Bell Day has shown how much we can depend not only on the government but on the American people and that they can also depend on us."[68]

Amrehm's words captured the essence of a decisive moment much as had Egon Bahr's in the above-quoted letter he wrote to Axel Springer in 1960. As symbols of the West's determination to guarantee liberty, the Freedom Bell in particular and Berlin in general were galvanizing Americans. The mobilization of such emotional and political support injected an additional and unique dynamic into Berlin policy that the governments involved on both sides of the Atlantic had to take into consideration in their political strategies. This dynamic affected far more than the interaction between governments alone. It could be instrumentalized to build American popular support for West Berlin and for maintaining the American military presence there. However, the impact of mobilizing this emotional and political potential had to be contained when the danger appeared acute that the dynamic behind it could itself lead to renewed conflict. Such a development certainly did not lie in the interests of those in power in Washington, Bonn, and the West Berlin Senate. The interaction between the desire to mobilize support from the American people for West Berlin and the necessity to keep the enthusiasm for Berlin under control was shown clearly on the first anniversary marking the erection of the Berlin Wall.

In the summer of 1962, several American nongovernmental organizations launched a campaign to mark the anniversary of the erection of the Berlin Wall. The purpose of the planned event was to remind the American and European publics once again of the fate of the people living under communist regimes. The Free Europe Committee, the American Friends of the Captive Nations, and the American Council on Germany systematically contacted politicians and government officials, members of the press, representatives of various associations, and, above all, the mayors of cities across the United States. Their aim was to have August 13, 1962, the first anniversary of the Berlin Wall, declared "Remember Berlin Day." A proclamation of solidarity was drafted and sent to nearly 900 cities. The organizers of the campaign arranged for a broadcast of the ringing of the Freedom Bell in Berlin and the Liberty Bell in Philadelphia, accompanied by short speeches by Willy Brandt and Lucius D. Clay, at noon on the day of the anniversary. That evening, Attorney General Robert F. Kennedy and AFL-CIO head George Meany read statements of solidarity with Berlin on television. Meany and Clay had also served as the honorary chairmen of the campaign. They urged churches and synagogues to participate by holding worship services as "symbolic acts" of solidarity with West Berlin.[69] Ceremonial proclamations by nearly ninety cities – from Honolulu to New Orleans and from San Francisco to Orlando, Florida – used similarly strong language.

The passionate rhetoric of the campaign raised a problem. The organizers had planned to hand their Berlin proclamations to Willy Brandt in West Berlin in a highly publicized ceremony. Yet they had been warned in advance by Edward R. Murrow, head of the United States Information Agency (USIA), that the Western Allies were not interested in using a commemoration of the Berlin Wall as a major propaganda event.[70] Although the organizers had already approached Egon Bahr about their plans, the Berlin Senate began to have second thoughts. The protocol department asked that plans for a public presentation of the proclamations to Willy Brandt, especially if scheduled for August 13, be canceled. The Senate wanted to avoid providing occasion for public demonstrations in West Berlin that could heighten tensions in the divided city. In the end, the solidarity proclamations were indeed presented to Brandt, albeit in a ceremony closed to the public at the Schöneberg City Hall. Joseph Kovago, the last freely elected mayor of Budapest, served as the official courier of the proclamations. His impressions of the Wall only confirmed that the atmosphere in Berlin could easily lead to "volcanic eruptions" should an "emotional volunteer speaker" address the crowds or a shot be fired.[71] Such a scenario was precisely what those concerned about the event in both the United States and Berlin wanted to avoid.

The history of the Freedom Bell and the commemorative rituals for West Berlin attest to the enormous evocative power that symbols possessed in the relations between Berlin and the United States. These examples show how powerfully symbols could mobilize West Berliners and Americans alike. This history also demonstrates that symbols were created and events organized for the specific purpose of mobilizing support and forging an anticommunist consensus. Such efforts required mediators in the form of institutions and individuals. On the American side, several liberal anticommunist organizations took up the Berlin cause. In addition to the Free Europe Committee, the American Friends of the Captive Nations, and the American Council on Germany, there were the National League of Cities, the Americans for Democratic Action (ADA), the United Automobile Workers (UAW), the Congress of Industrial Organizations (CIO), and – after the latter merged with the American Federation of Labor (AFL) in 1955 – the AFL–CIO. Moreover, many of these organizations were linked through interlocking directorships.

During the course of the 1950s, many of America's top labor union leaders were extremely excited about Berlin. Their enthusiasm was caused in large part by the pronounced anticommunist course they were pursuing. In their eyes, German Social Democrats who were not dogmatic but pro-American and antitotalitarian, such as the Berlin mayors Ernst Reuter and Willy Brandt, were ideal partners. This ideological convergence also explains why John F. Kennedy chose to make the side trip to Berlin to attend the labor union congress there in June 1963. The friendship between Berlin and the unions represented solidarity among the anticommunist left.[72] George Meany of the AFL–CIO and the brothers Walter and Victor G. Reuther played key roles. The latter two had their support base in the automobile workers union, but both exerted a great deal of influence within the CIO and later the AFL–CIO. Walther Reuther even made an appearance at the gigantic May Day demonstration held by West Berlin labor unions in 1959.[73]

Meany and the Reuther brothers represented the left wing, as it were, of that informal Berlin alliance in the United States that people at the time already referred to as the Berlin lobby. The members of this informal lobby included Democratic senator Hubert Humphrey, the diplomats Robert Murphy and Eleanor L. Dulles, former high commissioner for Germany John McCloy, and the former American liaison officer to the Berlin Senate, Karl Mautner. The Berlin veterans Frank L. Howley and Lucius D. Clay, journalist Marguerite Higgins, Shepard Stone of the Ford Foundation, advertising expert Roy Blumenthal, and Leo Cherne, who worked in several anticommunist organizations, also supported the cause of West Berlin and participated in this network.[74] It was no accident that many of them were involved directly or indirectly in planning and preparing Kennedy's trip. They all knew Berlin well and had become American Berliners after

1948. When Maxwell D. Taylor left his post as the U.S. commander in Berlin in 1950, he summarized the key experience of this group. In Berlin one felt "the spirit of the frontline, which brings a solidarity found nowhere in Germany, perhaps nowhere else in Europe." The general made a simple prediction about his successor: "He will be another American who came to occupy Berlin, stayed to defend it, and left as a Berliner."[75]

Four years after Maxwell's departure, former president Herbert Hoover visited West Berlin. Hoover was ceremonially welcomed by the Berlin Senate and invited to sign the city's honorary guest book. It has now been long forgotten that on this occasion, the Republican Hoover closed his speech to the political representatives of West Berlin by articulating the idea that Kennedy would later so poignantly express in 1963: "You face an enemy who lives just across the street. You have seen your duty and have performed it well. Thanks to the spirit and courage of men under the leadership of two great mayors, you can, like the men of ancient Athens, hold your heads high and say: 'I am a Berliner.'" Hoover's speech, including this last sentence, was given completely in English, and it is interesting to note that this quote was not picked up by either the German or American press.[76]

Since the days when Ernst Reuter was mayor, the existence of the Berlin lobby in the United States had not only reassured the West Berlin leadership that the city could depend on favorable public opinion in that country; it could also be used as a means to advance the aims of the Berlin municipal leadership in America. Both sides harbored the desire and willingness to cooperate. After a discussion with Lucius D. Clay in May 1962, Willy Brandt noted that Clay had stressed his willingness always to come to the aid of the city, should he be needed. In New York, John McCloy, Shepard Stone, and Clay constituted a "Berlin club on which we can rely."[77]

The counterparts to the pro-Berlin Americans in the United States were the pro-American Berliners in the divided city itself. They were led by Ernst Reuter and his political crown prince, Willy Brandt. When the Federal Republic was founded, these two men represented the weak but growing Western-oriented, anti-neutralist, and pro-American wing of the SPD. This position stemmed from the experience of direct confrontation with the Soviet system. Unlike Kurt Schumacher, the first SPD party chairman in West Germany, Reuter and Brandt developed an unequivocally positive attitude toward the United States from this experience. They joined the ranks of those who willingly sought to understand and accept American society.[78] This willingness was reflected in an open-mindedness toward Western political theories and ideas about government. It went hand in hand with the intention to make use of the institutional and personal networks between Berlin and America described earlier.

During their tenures as mayor, Reuter and Brandt brought a dynamic to West Berlin's relations with the United States that neither of the men who served in the period between Reuter's death in 1953 and Brandt's election in 1957 – Walther Schreiber (CDU, 1953–55) and Otto Suhr (SPD, 1955–57) – could duplicate. Reuter laid a solid foundation for Berlin-American relations by visiting the United States three times between 1949 and 1953. He was recognized as America's "Number One German"[79] before Chancellor Konrad Adenauer had set foot upon American soil for the first time. Willy Brandt's trips to the United States in 1958 and 1959 represented a continuation of Reuter's policies and catapulted his popularity to new heights. In February 1959, Brandt – whose trip was part of a worldwide Berlin campaign sponsored by the West German government – was celebrated in the United States as a charismatic, anticommunist personality. He gave a speech commemorating the 150th birthday of Abraham Lincoln in Springfield, Illinois. Brandt was also the center of attraction at a tickertape parade in New York, met Eisenhower in Washington, and was photographed in Los Angeles with Hollywood stars.[80] After that, a trip to the White House was always a part of Brandt's itinerary when he came to the United States. The experience gained through such trips belongs to the prehistory of Kennedy's visit to Berlin. The Americanized Berliners in the divided city, such as Brandt, and the pro-Berlin Americans in the United States could look back on a history of being welcomed in each other's country long before the American president flew to Berlin in June 1963.

LBJ AND BOBBY: PROLOGUE AND THE JOHNSON TACTIC

The highest ranking members of the American government to visit Berlin in the decade and a half following the Potsdam Conference were the secretaries of state Dean Acheson, John Foster Dulles, and Christian Herter. Nothing came of rumors that Eisenhower or his vice president, Richard Nixon, would visit the city.[81] In late July 1961, Edward R. Murrow proposed that former president Truman be sent to Berlin; that proposal fell by the wayside when Vice President Johnson traveled to the city the following month.[82]

Christian Herter's vist in July 1959 is particularly illuminating. The West Berliners welcomed him in a style that would reach a highpoint between 1961 and 1963. The form their welcome to the visiting foreign dignitary took can be described in terms of street politics, emotion, and theater.[83] Masses of West Berliners filled the streets – under the careful surveillance of the police – and sought direct contact with the arriving visitor. They did not hesitate to express their exuberance, and this articulation of emotion had an effect, in turn, on the guests. The event was perceived by everyone involved as a spectacular experience; it was like a one-time theatrical performance in which all participants were members of both the audience and the cast simultaneously. The American ambassador to Germany, David K. E. Bruce, noted his impressions of the drive with Herter from Tempelhof Airport to the Spechtstrasse in his journal: "I have never seen so enthusiastic a crowd. The people lined the streets from the airport almost to our house, waving handkerchiefs and applauding. It was an extremely hot day, but there were tens of thousands of Berliners along the route. It was really a touching spectacle."[84] The Berlin police estimated that 130,000 people were on the streets that day.

There was no guarantee of a repeat of the welcome Herter had received when Johnson traveled to Berlin in August 1961. The building of the Berlin Wall had undermined many West Berliners' confidence in the United States. President Kennedy had to pull out all the stops. He and his advisors had quickly realized that the policy of demonstrative calm after the events of August 13 was not being well received in Berlin; it was actually being used against the United States. That needed to be countered to avert a potentially severe crisis within the Western alliance. Therefore, Kennedy decided to send no less a representative than his vice president to Bonn and Berlin. In the hopes of enhancing the political effect, the administration immediately decided to include another American figure of leadership. The list of candidates was limited to men who were "extremely positive symbols" in Germany: Lucius D. Clay, the hero of the Berlin Airlift; John McCloy, the former U.S. high commissioner in West Germany; and Maxwell D. Taylor, the former U.S. commander for West Berlin. The decision was quickly made in favor of Clay,[85] who had actually proposed himself. On August 15, Clay had contacted Taylor, whom Kennedy had coaxed out of retirement to serve as a White House advisor. Clay was confident that his name would mean something to both Berliners and "the Russians" and that his involvement would mean a "propaganda plus" for the U.S. government. After all, he was "still a soldier, always wholly and immediately available."[86] Clay was not able to take over command in Berlin immediately, as he had hoped. Not until September did he receive the authorization to act as the president's special envoy and to make use of the American forces in the city.

The decision to send Clay to Berlin with Johnson turned out to be ingenious. The delegation first headed to Bonn to visit Adenauer on August 19 in the company of Charles Bohlen, one of America's top diplomats and an expert on Soviet affairs. That very afternoon the Americans continued on to Berlin in order to spend the next day there. Johnson refused to let the chancellor fly to the divided city in the same airplane. This refusal angered Adenauer tremendously for it threw a brighter, more flattering light on Brandt as Berlin's mayor and the Social Democratic candidate for chancellorship.[87] However, the American government was not willing to use the current situation to undermine the special rights enjoyed by the Americans and the restrictions on official representatives of the Federal Republic with respect to Berlin.[88]

The Johnson visit had two central aims: to underscore American solidarity with West Berlin, where morale needed to be lifted if the United States did not want to lose its most loyal ally in Europe, and to discipline Brandt. The second aim was handled diplomatically behind closed doors in Bonn and Berlin. With all due respect to protocol, Johnson made it very clear that differences in opinion were to be handled confidentially, not by going public, as Brandt had done. He reminded Brandt that the United States had strengthened its military presence under Kennedy and that most of Brandt's proposals were therefore inappropriate. The mayor was understanding and cooperative.[89] Before the eyes of the watching world, the first and more important aim of the trip took center stage. Johnson's arrival in Berlin and his public appearances were not merely appreciated by the people of West Berlin: they were jubilantly celebrated. The real "drama of the day," newspaper readers in America learned, did not take place on the Rhine, but on the Spree. The vice president himself later compared his reception in Berlin to a "triumphant procession."[90]

Seven tanks fired a salute as the delegation arrived at Tempelhof Airport to the welcome of Mayor Brandt and U.S. Ambassador Walter C. Dowling. American troops and West Berlin police stood in parade formation. It was a stirring welcome, and Johnson's first public remarks were resonant with meaning. He praised West Berlin as a "fortress of the free" and "home of the brave."[91] In quoting from the American national anthem, Johnson paid the city a special honor. Tens of thousands of spectators lined the streets taken by the motorcade from Tempelhof to Potsdamer Platz. Johnson and Brandt even walked a stretch of the route; it was Johnson's habit to mingle directly with people. In Berlin, he encountered an enthusiastic public. People elbowed their way past each other in the hopes of getting close and perhaps even shaking the hands of the visitor. "Men and women stretched out their arms to the vice president. Some had tears in their eyes and many cried openly."[92]

At Potsdamer Platz, the once busy square at the heart of the city, West Berlin Minister of the Interior Joachim Lipschitz showed the vice president

Illustration 9. Symbolic politics and the Johnson tactic: Lucius D. Clay, Robert H. Lochner, Lyndon B. Johnson, and Willy Brandt outside Schöneberg City Hall on August 19, 1961. Source: Landesarchiv Berlin.

the Wall. Then the delegation proceeded to Schöneberg City Hall, where Johnson addressed the city's parliament as well as a huge crowd gathered outside on Rudolph Wilde Platz (Illustration 9). Estimates of the size of this crowd vary. As many as 150,000 people may have lined the streets along the route of the motorcade, and another 300,000 are thought to have gathered in front of the city hall. Some estimates put the total number of spectators as high as one million.[93] A collage of memorable moments created an impressive performance: Johnson signing the honorary guest book, cheers and ovations for Clay, Johnson holding a Berlin boy on his right arm and a floral bouquet in his left hand in front of the RIAS microphones, the chiming of the Freedom Bell, posters with slogans of solidarity, chants from the crowd successfully calling for Johnson to appear once again on the balcony of the city hall after the official banquet. The press reported this as being an "emotion-filled day" in which Berlin experienced "joyous bedlam" that had an "electric effect on the city." Johnson himself described a "chord of deep emotion" mixed with "noble tears."[94] Expressions of emotionality could not have been any more prevalent, and small gestures reflecting amicable human nature did indeed fit well into the picture. For

Illustration 10. Soldiers as political symbols: An American convoy bringing 1,500 additional GIs to West Berlin arrives at the border of the American sector, Checkpoint Dreilinden, on August 20, 1961, amid the cheers of West Berliners. Source: Landesarchiv Berlin.

example, the shoes Willy Brandt was wearing impressed Johnson so much that he bought himself a pair while in Berlin.[95]

The following day, August 20, 1961, Johnson and Clay greeted the 1,500 American soldiers arriving in Berlin to reinforce the garrison there (Illustration 10). Once again, the enthusiasm of the West Berliners bubbled over. A U.S. government official who had helped organize the trip later compared this display of enthusiasm to that of the French following the liberation of Paris.[96] Several times that day spectators broke through the security barriers, encircled jeeps, handed soldiers flowers, and yelled "bravo." These breaches of regulation were gladly overlooked, particularly because the press was watching attentively and such incidents enhanced the purpose of the trip. The morale of the Berliners was being lifted by the Americans. Within a single day, the mood of the city had turned around 180 degrees in a positive direction. Johnson's itinerary then took him to the American headquarters and the camp in Marienfelde for East German refugees. Once again, in the words of the *New York Times*, "the same dramatic effect" occurred. "People wanted just to touch him," and the diplomats present watched such scenes in disbelief.[97] The guest from America radiated a charisma reminiscent of religious exaltation. People were drawn to Johnson by their desire to come into direct contact with him as a bringer of redemption, as their hope of salvation, and to ensure their salvation through physical proximity. Johnson and his advisors recognized this need and struck just the right chord with the crowds. "I have just seen the soul of a city," the vice president reassured the Berliners in his farewell. The success of this "evangelistic approach" to the people of Berlin was noted positively in the United States.[98]

Moreover, the images of the trip clearly pointed out the primacy of visibility, something that was evident during this visit and could not be overlooked two years later when John F. Kennedy arrived in the city. On August 20, Johnson did not pass up the chance to take a good swig from a bottle of *Berliner Weiße*, a beer specialty of Berlin, offered to him by a man standing on a street curb. Johnson as a man of the people – such pictures made a big impression. Johnson was furious to discover at one point during his visit that he was not being given an open limousine for a certain stretch of travel through Berlin. He wanted to be seen. Once underway, Johnson suddenly opened his car door for a distance of several miles and, instructing Walter C. Dowling to get down on his knees and hold onto his left leg, he swung his right leg out of the car and leaned out of the vehicle as far as he could. Now he could be seen.[99]

At home, the Texan Johnson had been known for many years as a skilled tactician and strategist. As Democratic whip in the Senate, he had proven himself to be a clever operator and mobilizer of votes. Now, a new stage had opened up unexpectedly for him in Berlin, one from which his words and actions resonated politically in the United States no less than in Europe. The vice president was suddenly in a position to present himself as a charismatic leader and talented speaker.[100] In light of the purpose of this trip, the rhetoric used could not have been more cleverly selected. I would like to describe it as the "Johnson tactic." Two years later in front of Schöneberg City Hall, John F. Kennedy would follow the example set by his vice president. Johnson's rhetoric was laden with historical references, rich in emphatic wording, and sympathetic to the emotions expressed by Berliners: "I understand the pain and outrage you feel."[101] The language used not only appealed to the listeners' reason but was aimed at their hearts and was thus appropriate to the situation. Even if it was not immediately clear to everyone listening, Johnson's words, although emphatic, remained noncommittal in detail and did not delineate any concrete policy measures. But this is precisely why his rhetoric was an effective political instrument. Walt W. Rostow, who had drafted the text of the speech, described the foreign policy message of the Johnson tactic by saying that the United States "had to wrap the American flag around Berlin. That was the only way to break up Khrushchev's nuclear blackmail technique."[102]

Johnson conveyed a very human and very personal sense of solidarity. In his rhetoric, he sought to weave Berlin's fate into the tapestry of American national mythology. Upon his arrival at Tempelhof, Johnson picked up this theme and expressed it dramatically yet succinctly in the climax of his speech before Berlin's elected representatives. Just as eighteenth-century Americans had fought for independence in 1776, so too would twentieth-century Americans pledge "our lives, our fortunes and our sacred honor" to assure the survival of Berlin. The fact that Johnson applied the famous closing of the American Declaration of Independence to the context of Berlin with Kennedy's expressed approval was a symbolic act without equal. On both sides of the Atlantic, it made a huge impression on public opinion.[103]

Nevertheless, close observers noted in the days that followed, as the "emotional hangovers" began to wear off,[104] that this expression of solidarity had left many questions open. It had not outlined any concrete policy for the United States nor had it indicated what the United States would do to protect the city should a new crisis arise. Had Johnson's assurances been nothing more than rhetoric? Following this line of argument would lead to an explanatory dead end. It would overlook the interplay of rhetoric, theater, and politics. The Johnson trip was primarily a symbolic gesture. However, the administration realized that this trip, precisely because of its symbolic nature, was the only political step that made sense if the situation in Berlin was to be stabilized. The theatrical aspect of the event was necessary to make the presence of American power in Berlin visible and credible – more credible, in fact, than the existence of the American nuclear arsenal in Western Europe could make it. By means of Johnson's charisma, the religious echoes in his public comments, and the pledge of transatlantic community, the visit created an important social effect at a time of political crisis.

The American newspaper *Sunday Star* succinctly made the point. Cynics could argue that the entire trip was "a good deal of play acting. . . . And yet, at this time and in this place, the most absurdly theatrical gestures can be of the greatest importance."[105] The communism expert William E. Griffith was of the same opinion. The entire trip was a "brilliant stroke – *Gestalt* psychology at is best." Public opinion and Western diplomats agreed: they celebrated the trip as a triumph.[106] The opinion polls from Germany confirmed that the American strategy had been successful: 83 percent of West Berliners approved of the Johnson trip (67 percent in West Germany), and 63 percent of those polled in West Berlin (39 percent in West Germany) said the visit had convinced them of the seriousness of American commitment to the city.[107]

The propaganda effect of this coup was invaluable. In August 1961, discussion within the Kennedy administration focused increasingly on the question of how to use symbolic politics with more precision and on a larger scale to avoid losing ground on the issue of Berlin vis-à-vis the Eastern bloc, within the Western alliance, or in the eyes of the world at large. Many measures were considered, including increasing travel contacts, sending prominent Americans to visit Berlin, mobilizing the American public through solidarity campaigns (e.g., encouraging half a million American children to write letters to Berlin pen pals), working with labor leaders associated with Walther Reuther and George Meany known to be friends of Berlin, intensifying and expanding academic contact with the Free University, and streamlining foreign propaganda policy. Having taken a political beating during the initial months of the Berlin Wall's existence, the United States could not afford to let this sudden opportunity slip by: "We have been handed a propaganda victory of tremendous dimensions on a silver platter and we are just not taking advantage of it."[108] The author of this message to the president was none other than Robert F. Kennedy.

Robert F. (Bobby) Kennedy knew Berlin from two visits to the city, the first in 1948 during the blockade and the second in 1955. In Berlin, he was correctly thought to be one of the city's most loyal friends.[109] Willy Brandt knew this. So, when the journalist Marguerite Higgins indicated to him that Bobby Kennedy was planning a world trip for February 1962, the mayor did not hesitate to invite the attorney general to Berlin to give a lecture at the Free University. The Kennedy administration sought to advance U.S. policy objectives by having the program "capitalize on" the psychological advantage of a trip to Berlin.[110] Likewise, Higgins and the responsible authorities on both the German and American sides were aware that the itinerary and the visibility of the visit were of the utmost importance in achieving the desired effect of promoting solidarity. Early in the planning, Clay insisted that the attorney general spend two nights in the city. Every detail needed to be carefully planned. The question was even raised whether Robert Kennedy's scheduled arrival might be too late in the day to maximize the visibility of the event because of the early hour at which the sun set.[111]

There was yet another reason why so much energy was expended in planning the trip. As mentioned earlier, tension was growing between Clay and administration officials. In the eyes of many in Washington, Clay was an incorrigible Cold War warrior. Frustration and misunderstanding increased

on both sides.[112] Robert Kennedy's visit was thus also supposed to demonstrate unanimity and patch up relations with Clay. Both parties did indeed
make a great effort. The attorney general, for instance, voiced strong support
for Clay's "Viability Program," an initiative to attract American investors and
businesses to Berlin.

It was cold in Berlin and the clouds were heavy with snow when Robert
F. Kennedy landed at Tempelhof Airport on February 22, 1962. Despite the
unfriendly weather, the delegation drove in open cars – as had Johnson –
to Potsdamer Platz and then to the city hall. Once again, tens of thousands
of people, young and old, lined the streets to cheer the visitor; many had
tears in their eyes.[113] More than 100,000 people (some estimates speak of
180,000) were waiting on the square in front of the city hall and in the
side streets. Kennedy was so cold that he had difficulty starting his speech.
Still, the weather did not stop him from paying his respects to the people of
Berlin. He told them that the "warmth of your greetings" outweighed the
cold weather. Nothing on his trip around the world so far had moved him
as much as this reception. Kennedy stressed the differences between the two
halves of the city. The Berlin Wall "lies like a snake across the heart of your
city." Yet this was but proof that communism had failed. A military attack
on Berlin would be comparable to one on Chicago, New York, London,
or Paris, Kennedy said to reassure his audience of America's commitment –
something Berliners could never hear often enough. "You are our brothers."
That declaration, Willy Brandt noted, demonstrated that Americans "fully
identified" with the people of Berlin. Johnson had already employed this
rhetorical tactic, and now Robert F. Kennedy was repeating it, dressed in the
metaphor of family.[114] The crowds cheered. During Kennedy's appearance,
red balloons were sent floating from East Berlin into the West to shower the
city with little red flags. Kennedy welcomed this opportunity to criticize
the communist rulers amid thunderous applause.

Departing from the itinerary, Robert Kennedy and his wife, Ethel,
climbed the city hall tower to see the Freedom Bell. Kennedy had already
received a model of the bell as a welcoming gift. That evening, the attorney
general held his lecture in the auditorium of the Free University. He began
with a reference to the legendary postwar mayor for whom the lecture series
was named, Ernst Reuter. Kennedy drew an analogy between Reuter and
the first American president, George Washington. The lecture expanded on
ideas presented in his speech at the city hall earlier that day and outlined the
"New Frontier" his brother envisioned for America. He also emphasized
America's "essentials" on West Berlin.[115] Kennedy's first scheduled event
on the second day of his visit was to breakfast with church representatives

Illustration 11. "Personal outrage and contempt": Robert F. and Ethel Kennedy, Rut and Willy Brandt, Edward Kennedy, and Egon Bahr at the Brandenburg Gate on February 23, 1962. Source: Landesarchiv Berlin.

and Wilhelm W. Schütz from the Kuratorium Freies Deutschland (Committee for a Free Germany), an organization that had been championing the idea of Berlin as the capital of a united Germany for a number of years.[116] Then Kennedy met Brandt and his wife at the Brandenburg Gate (Illustration 11). This was Kennedy's second viewing of the Berlin Wall. Seldom, Brandt would maintain later, had he ever seen a visitor stare at the Wall "with so much personal outrage and contempt."[117]

Up to this point, Kennedy's trip had closely resembled Johnson's. However, the attorney general also set a new tone, which made his itinerary considerably more politically charged. For one, he broadened the scope of the politics of commemoration. The attorney general laid a wreath at the spot on Bernauer Straße where an East German woman, Ida Siekmann, had jumped to her death the previous September in an attempt to escape the eastern sector of the city. The now walled-up windows of the buildings on the side of the street belonging to East Berlin dramatically symbolized the division of the city. For another wreath-laying ceremony, Kennedy drove to the Plötzensee Memorial to those who died resisting National Socialism. There he met Annedore Leber, the widow of the murdered Nazi opponent

Julius Leber, whom Willy Brandt esteemed highly. By explicitly drawing a comparison between the victims of communism and National Socialism, Kennedy echoed West Germans' own understanding of the recent German past. He emphasized the continuity of totalitarian rule in Germany from the Nazi dictatorship to the German Democratic Republic. With this statement, the attorney general underscored that antitotalitarianism belonged to the common values of the transatlantic community.

Kennedy also set a new tone by incorporating a visit to the world of business and labor in his tour of the city. He visited a factory of the Auer Company, a manufacturer of safety devices that had had a subsidiary in the United States since 1901. This excursion not only acknowledged the German economic miracle, it pointed to the success of German-American economic cooperation. Moreover, union representatives were given the chance for the first time to hold talks with one of America's most powerful politicians. This meeting reflected the long-standing triangular relationship between unions, Americans, and Berliners.

Bobby Kennedy was more aware of the importance of the media than any other American visitor before him had been. As part of his public relations campaign, he made appearances on German radio and television and had coffee with the editors-in-chief of the Berlin press. Nor did he neglect to give his visit a more populist touch. Kennedy could not be dissuaded from walking amid the throngs of well-wishers from the Amerika Haus to the Zoological Garden. Once there, the attorney general presented the zoo director with an American bald eagle, which Kennedy had named Willy Brandt. Unfortunately, the bird's age had been substantially underestimated, and Willy died only two years later.[118] Still, Berlin had been lucky; for a while the politicians in Washington had seriously considered presenting the zoo with a somewhat less magnificent animal – an opossum.

This trip also introduced, for the first time, a special program for the dignitaries' wives. Ethel Kennedy visited the Kaufhaus des Westens, an enormous department store with a magnificent display of goods. She also went to the German-American school, the Free University, and the refugee camp at Marienfelde. In this way, the spectrum of symbolic signs became broader than ever before. An excursion into East Berlin remained one of these important symbols. Just as Lucius D. Clay had done on August 19, 1961, during Johnson's trip, Edward Kennedy, the younger brother of John and Robert, used the opportunity of Robert's trip to visit East Berlin. The fact that Edward Kennedy was required to show his passport when crossing into East Berlin was presented by the GDR as evidence of its sovereignty;

however, such a practice was no more than long-standing diplomatic custom among the Allied powers.[119]

Bobby Kennedy's trip to Berlin was seen in the West as a complete success, just as the trip by Johnson and Clay in 1961 had been. Once again, there was an interplay of street politics, emotion, and theater. Once again, the aspects of warmth, enthusiasm, and cordiality ranked very high in the evaluation of the press and other participants.[120] Once again, Berliners had sought physical contact with the visitor and representative of their protector. Back in Washington, the attorney general received fan mail. Women and girls in particular seem to have been thrilled by seeing or shaking hands with Kennedy and his wife. "You have taken the hearts of all Berliners by storm with your open, casual manner," wrote two women from Berlin.[121] In spurring metaphors of conquest, in raising hopes of political salvation, and in employing a particular set of symbols, the visits by Johnson and Kennedy to Berlin served as a prelude to John F. Kennedy's visit in 1963. Another, more problematic prelude came in September 1962 when President Charles de Gaulle of France visited the Federal Republic of Germany.

DE GAULLE: SYMBOLIC PRECEDENT AND STRATEGIC COMPETITION

John F. Kennedy was the first leader of one of the Western Allied powers to visit West Berlin after the Potsdam Conference of 1945. His visit was not, however, entirely without precedent, at least as far as the competition for West German public opinion was concerned. In September 1962, French President Charles de Gaulle had traveled to Germany, but Berlin had not been included on his itinerary. De Gaulle's visit and Adenauer's earlier visit to France (July 2–8, 1962) had met with enormous public approval and set high standards for symbolic politics. As soon as it was decided that Kennedy would be traveling to Germany, it was clear that his visit would have to match de Gaulle's *tour d'Allemagne* in public impact.[122]

Both Franco-German encounters, particularly de Gaulle's trip to Germany, served to underscore a political concept that ran counter to American policy on Europe and the Atlantic alliance. From the American point of view, these encounters were creating symbolic forms and sending a political message that threatened the cohesion of the Western alliance. The higher the "wave of emotion" crested during de Gaulle's September trip to Germany and the fiercer the "storm of enthusiasm" among Germans raged,[123] the greater this danger appeared. As during Johnson's and Robert Kennedy's trips to Germany, the combination of appeals to emotion and staged performances with declarations of commitment to the alliance created a highly charged situation.

Indeed, the meetings between Adenauer and de Gaulle in 1962 fueled speculation that France and Germany sought to decouple themselves from the United States. Neither statesman hesitated to emphasize the positive concept of a Franco-German union by criticizing U.S. national interests and American efforts to dominate NATO. From their point of view, the United States was chiefly interested in reducing its balance-of-payments deficit, preserving its nuclear predominance within NATO, and backing out of its military commitment through the new strategic concept of flexible response without calling American hegemony in Western Europe into question. Nothing placed the alternative vision of a Franco-German union more into the limelight than the staging of Franco-German state visits and the visual images they produced. When Adenauer arrived in Paris, de Gaulle showered his guest with much pomp and ceremony. Motorcades through the city in open cars provided the desired visibility, even if the applause of the crowd was more friendly than enthusiastic.

The highpoint of Adenauer's visit to France came outside the capital city at two memorials, whose historic and symbolic significance was nearly unsurpassable. In the heart of Champagne, where the battles between German and French soldiers had once soaked the fields with blood, de Gaulle and Adenauer stood shoulder-to-shoulder to watch German and French troops parading at the training grounds of Mourmelon. Afterward, a church service was held in the Gothic cathedral of Reims, the site where numerous French kings had been coronated. Allusions to French national history, demonstrations of the new Franco-German friendship, and an implicit concept of a Christian Occident, personified by the Catholics de Gaulle and Adenauer, mingled together here.[124] The pictures of the two statesmen in dark suits, their faces somber and their hands folded in prayer (Illustration 12), stand along with those of Kennedy in front of Schöneberg City Hall (1963), Willy Brandt kneeling in Warsaw (1970), and Helmut Kohl and François Mitterand holding hands in Verdun (1984) as iconic images of West German history. "Never before and never again in the history of the Federal Republic," writes Hans-Peter Schwarz of the scenes in Champagne and Reims, "has the power of historical memory and images been applied with such sovereignty in order to gain public opinion approval for a fundamental direction in foreign policy."[125]

In fact, however, the staging of Kennedy's visit to Berlin was just as masterful in the use of historical imagery and just as successful in shaping public opinion as Adenauer and de Gaulle's visit to Champagne. There were

Illustration 12. Symbolic precedent and strategic competition: Konrad Adenauer and Charles de Gaulle in the Reims Cathedral, July 8, 1962. Source: Bundesarchiv Koblenz (no. 183/A 0710/64/1).

two very important differences between these two events. First, Kennedy's 1963 performance was staged not only on German soil but also against the politically charged backdrop of Berlin, an urban landscape that represented better than any other the vicissitudes of German history. Second, Kennedy's performance demonstrated the suggestive power of an opposing foreign policy option. Due in large part to Kennedy's own efforts and his sense of history, the option he offered would eventually incorporate the Franco-German friendship within a transatlantic framework.

Still, in early September 1962, there was no indication that the idea of an Atlantic alliance led by the United States might eventually prevail over the idea of a Franco-German alliance. The French president's visit had turned into a triumphal procession. He was received by the West Germans in much the same way Johnson and Robert Kennedy had been. The German people were interested in, even enthusiastic about, de Gaulle. They displayed intense, at times "explosive" emotion. The visit was marked by strong "out-pourings of warmth" noted the dispassionate *Frankfurter Allgemeine Zeitung*. For his part, de Gaulle did not shy away from embracing "everyone to his French heart." Particularly impressive was that he repeatedly addressed his audience in German. The program itself appeared to be a "masterpiece in applied psychology."[126]

De Gaulle scheduled events that were gracious gestures to the German chancellor – a visit to the Cologne cathedral and a dinner in Cologne's late medieval banquet hall, the *Gürzenich*; a trip on the Rhine; and excursions to Adenauer's private home in Rhöndorf and to the nearby Petersberg, the former seat of the Allied High Commission in Germany located on top of one of the hills lining the east bank of the Rhine near Bonn. The French president also spoke to large crowds in Düsseldorf, Bonn, Munich, and Ludwigsburg. The military dimension of the trip was fulfilled with a ceremonial tattoo and a visit to the Bundeswehr's military academy in Hamburg. A meeting was also scheduled between de Gaulle and steelworkers at the Thyssen works in Duisburg, although the site was associated with the sensitive issues of defense and economic policy; there, too, the French president was greeted with enthusiastic cheers. De Gaulle wanted to mingle with the crowds, and, like Johnson and Robert Kennedy, he sought constant visibility. Even rain did not prevent him from driving in an open limousine.

One important difference between de Gaulle's trip and those of Johnson and Robert Kennedy cannot be overlooked: Berlin was not on de Gaulle's itinerary. Later, de Gaulle would justify excluding Berlin by arguing that the risk of an "emotional explosion" in the city had been too great. A visit to Berlin had, however, probably seemed too tricky a diplomatic challenge in the eyes of French officials. Willy Brandt reacted prudently. In a speech before the West Berlin parliament, he thanked de Gaulle for the ongoing French support of Berlin and held open the possibility of a visit in the future.[127] Overall, the political resonance in West Germany was positive. Only in the months that followed did the Atlanticists consolidate their strength to counter the Gaullists. Abroad, the reaction to de Gaulle's trip ranged from awe to amazement to skepticism. The American press reported extensively on the visit, but it described the jubilation as "spooky."[128]

It was obvious to everyone that the enthusiastic emphasis placed on the Franco-German friendship was linked to the troubled state of German-American relations. At the same time that de Gaulle was visiting West Germany, Ambassador Grewe was taking leave of his post in Washington. In an interview, the dismissed diplomat acknowledged the difficulties in German-American relations.[129] However, when the Cuban Missile Crisis erupted just a few weeks later, communication between Bonn, Berlin, and Washington improved once again. That autumn, two leading foreign policy experts in the Kennedy administration, McGeorge Bundy and Walt W. Rostow, visited Berlin. Rostow gave a highly celebrated foreign policy speech at the Free University in which he emphasized the hopes placed on West Berlin as an attractive location for business.[130]

As soon as an invitation was extended to the American president to visit West Germany, the Kennedy administration interpreted the Franco-German state visits of 1962 as both a challenge and an opportunity in three respects. First, such a trip would have to adopt a strategy that would best emphasize the necessity of a U.S. presence in Western Europe, particularly in West Germany. The ultimate aim was to deflect the danger posed by the possibility that West Germany and France might form an alliance of their own. Second, the decision had to be made whether Kennedy should travel to Berlin. This question remained unanswered for quite a while because the idea met considerable resistance at home. De Gaulle's refusal to go to the city provided proponents of such a visit with a powerful argument. Furthermore, Soviet leader Nikita Khrushchev had already visited East Berlin several times. A quick trip to the city by Kennedy could therefore be used to take a dig at de Gaulle and to win a round in the East-West political competition simultaneously. Since de Gaulle had not gone to Berlin, the American president now had the "opportunity for a little one-upmanship."[131] Third, de Gaulle's trip to the Federal Republic had shown that the symbolically laden theatricalization of politics was not the sole prerogative of the Americans. West Germans were attracted not only to American politicians: they were just as willing to cheer non-American leaders and be captivated by their charisma. The visits by Eisenhower to Bonn[132] and Secretary of State Herter to Berlin in 1959 as well as those of Johnson in 1961 and Robert F. Kennedy in 1962 had been highly celebrated. De Gaulle's triumphant trip expanded the scope of West German political emotion and made positive emotions an element in Franco-German relations. Franco-German friendship now thrived alongside the German-American community of shared experience.

From the American point of view, the latter should not be allowed to lag behind the former in importance. Most importantly, a visit by the American president would have to be "a demonstration of popular support of the President personally." Kennedy would also have to reach the crowds. Even if the administration did not want to admit it, particularly publicly, this trip was to be a "popularity contest with de Gaulle."[133] In the end, the image of the youthful American president standing before Schöneberg City Hall, where a cheering crowd of hundreds of thousands of people had gathered, would take its place alongside that of Adenauer and de Gaulle in the Reims cathedral as a political icon of its era.

THE CAST COMES TOGETHER

International relations are not determined solely by national leaders' intentions and their interactions with one another. But these factors and the public profiles of leading politicians do play an important part in international relations. Can leaders communicate with one another? Can they find a common political language? Do they share common experiences that facilitate understanding? Can they trust one another and take one another at their word? Following the American presidential election in November 1960, such questions became crucial for the three key actors in the triangular relations between the United States, West Germany, and Berlin: John F. Kennedy, Konrad Adenauer, and Willy Brandt. Questions of personality and compatibility became acute as Kennedy's trip to Berlin was being planned and during the trip itself. There was a huge generational gap separating Adenauer from Kennedy and Brandt. Moreover, the rivalry between Adenauer's Christian Democratic Union and Brandt's Social Democratic Party could not be ignored.[134] The association of certain security policy proposals with particular individuals contributed to the politicization of individual behavior. Last but not least, the weight of influence shifted within the triad of Kennedy, Adenauer, and Brandt because the participants distributed their trust and mistrust differently.

Kennedy was 46 years old when he visited Berlin, only four years older than Willy Brandt. Robert F. Kennedy was eight years younger than his brother. Two generations separated these three men from the chancellor. Adenauer, often referred to as "the Old Man" (*Der Alte*), had celebrated his eighty-seventh birthday in January 1963. The Kennedy brothers and West Berlin's mayor were clearly not part of the political elite who had shaped American, European, and Soviet politics in the immediate postwar period. Dwight Eisenhower, John Foster Dulles, Charles de Gaulle, Nikita Khrushchev, Walter Ulbricht, Harold Macmillan, Robert Schuman, and Jean Monnet had all been born around 1890. Even Adenauer's successor, Ludwig Erhard, belonged to this generation.[135] They all had experienced the First World War, the crises of the interwar period, and the National Socialist dictatorship. Many of them had held positions of power for decades; the most prominent example was Adenauer, who had been mayor of Cologne from 1917 to 1933 and the president of the Prussian State Council for twelve years preceding Hitler's seizure of power.[136]

The old guard of leading Western European politicians and the Young Turks associated with Kennedy and Brandt were united in their opposition to totalitarianism, even if their antitotalitarianism took very different forms.

John F. Kennedy had taken a sharply critical view of the policy of appeasement in a widely acclaimed book he wrote as a student.[137] Adenauer, opting for "internal emigration," dropped out of political life during the Nazi period, and his conservative and Christian values spurred his commitment to the West after 1945. With regard to both lifestyle and political outlook, the contrast between Adenauer and Brandt could hardly have been greater. Brandt had emigrated to Scandinavia in 1933 and worked for the underground anti-Nazi resistance. After his return to Germany as an employee of the Norwegian government in 1946, Brandt became active in the Berlin SPD and eventually caught the eye of Ernst Reuter.[138]

The antitotalitarian consensus remained firmly anti-Soviet as long as the front lines of the Cold War were hard and fixed. Beginning in the late 1950s, the international political situation became increasingly complex. The rise of the non-aligned movement, the challenges of the Third World, and the realization that the question of the future of Germany and Berlin could not be resolved with the old strategies transformed generational differences into fundamental differences of political outlook. This transformation also pertained to the domestic challenges of race equality, educational opportunity, and the transition to a consumer-oriented, middle-class society. Willy Brandt agreed with Kennedy that domestic politics and international relations required new ideas and new political instruments. Herein lay the real political break with the Adenauer generation.

Throughout the world, special emphasis was placed on the youth and the sense of a new start associated with the new American president. Both were interpreted as either an opportunity or a handicap. Adenauer chose to see it as the latter. In the words of his most important biographer, Adenauer was "a very old man" who "found himself an alien in a new era" when Kennedy was elected. The chancellor had eyed Kennedy with considerable skepticism during the presidential campaign, and the fact that the Democrat from Boston had already announced in 1957 that the Adenauer era was coming to a close did not make Kennedy any more appealing to the Rhinelander.[139] Brandt, who was the Social Democrats' candidate for the chancellorship in 1961, came to the opposite conclusion. He worked at becoming familiar with Kennedy's thinking and political aims. Increasingly, he tried to cultivate a conceptual proximity to the American president and to make this outwardly visible. Brandt had read closely the famous New Frontier speech that Kennedy had given when he accepted his party's nomination for the presidency in July 1960, and he cleverly applied this same theme to West Germany.[140] Brandt also adopted other rhetorical formulations used by Kennedy in his speeches. In 1960, the SPD executive committee sent

Alex Möller and Klaus Schütz to the United States to study the campaign practices and techniques of both presidential candidates for possible adaptation. Brandt's campaign trip across West Germany in 1961 was modeled on the Kennedy campaign. The relative youth of both Kennedy and Brandt and their good looks also encouraged an association between the two. Klaus Schütz later described this effect:

All the top SPD leaders understood that Kennedy was a winner. The association with Brandt practically imposed itself. . . . It was simply so obvious to draw parallels to Kennedy. In Brandt, the SPD also had a candidate who was good-looking and seemed intelligent. The opportunity to let a bit of the Kennedy magic rub off on Brandt just seemed to offer itself. For Brandt, the essence of his politics was his desire to create something like a great brotherhood with the young, progressive leaders in the world. . . . The familiarity between Brandt and Kennedy that we emphasized in the campaign was not merely an advertising gag. The times were like that; something truly international was in the air, a departure from nationalistic outlooks.[141]

The parallels between Kennedy and Brandt were reinforced in the public's mind by the fact that each campaigned with his young, attractive wife at his side. "Willy's charm and Rut's chic"[142] were typical attributes journalists used to describe the political roles each Brandt was thought to play. This was also true for John F. Kennedy and Jacqueline Bouvier Kennedy. Furthermore, Kennedy had a distinctly positive effect on the West German public, just as Brandt did on the American. Kennedy's public approval in the Federal Republic remained high in the period following his election, considering the Berlin crisis, and would reach its highpoint in 1963. Fascination with the glamorous couple in the White House and the elegance radiated by Jacqueline Kennedy contributed to this effect.[143] Likewise, Brandt's position in the United States had been quite good for some time. He had first become widely noticed in November 1956, when he managed to prevent West Berlin street demonstrations against the Soviet invasion of Hungary from getting out of control.[144] From that point on, the American press and internal governmental memoranda spoke of Brandt's leadership, tactical skill, and charisma. These attributes were supplemented by body-language metaphors that painted a picture of an open-minded, attractive, dynamic leader who, at the same time, was wholesomely pragmatic and still had both feet planted firmly on the ground. This man represented American ideals. In press accounts, Americans could read that the "energetic, open-faced, trim" Brandt could easily be "taken for the spark plug of a midwestern Junior Chamber of Commerce."[145]

Two lectures that Brandt held at Harvard University in early October 1962 also received considerable attention in the United States. They took up Kennedy's idea of a new policy of coexistence with the Eastern bloc.[146] Brandt also met with important cabinet members and the president during this visit. It again became clear in these talks that Kennedy's patience with the inflexibility demonstrated by Bonn and Paris was running out. The president demanded that Western leaders discard outdated mind-sets and approaches in order to prevent the West from ever again being in a situation in which its leaders found themselves conceptually at a loss and faced with a Soviet fait accompli.[147]

Adenauer's public image in the United States was no match for Brandt's. When he assumed the chancellorship in 1949, the elderly politician recalled from retirement was widely seen as formal, authoritarian, and conservative in his politics, character, and lifestyle. That view was soon tempered, however, by acknowledgment of his achievements in building the Federal Republic. Secretary of State Dulles in particular had a great deal of faith in Adenauer. Opinion about Adenauer in Washington had begun to change by the time Kennedy arrived in the White House. Appreciation of Adenauer's political accomplishments was increasingly coupled with skepticism about him. Many in the new administration thought him obstinate, inflexible, and difficult to deal with.

Adenauer was not anti-American, but he was not very familiar with U.S. history and society and therefore rarely deviated from long-held stereotypes of the country, such as the view that the United States was not fully democratic. Adenauer radiated mistrust. His constant doubting of the U.S. commitment to its allies and constant admonishments annoyed the Kennedy administration; it chose to place its trust in Brandt instead, despite Brandt's ill-fated attempt to intervene on the international scene immediately following the building of the Berlin Wall. Brandt and Kennedy found themselves on the same wavelength, whereas Adenauer and Kennedy did not. Adenauer and Kennedy communicated with one another, but this communication was often inadequate. Such, in brief, was the state of the personal relations between these key actors before Kennedy set out on his trip to West Germany.[148]

The personal relations between these three political leaders were important because each was associated with specific foreign policy objectives. For many observers, Adenauer and Brandt personified the choice between Franco-German alliance, on the one hand, and American-led Atlantic alliance, on the other. From this perspective, Adenauer represented the Gaullist wing of the CDU, and Brandt the pro-American Berlin wing of the SPD. Adenauer's political career was clearly coming to an end, but the Americans were neither willing nor able to disregard him, especially since he had never turned his back on the United States. In the months before and after the Kennedy visit, Adenauer remained the driving force behind the West German government. The American political leadership nonetheless considered Brandt to be the more dynamic politician and welcomed the statements in favor of a policy of coexistence with the Soviet Union that he had made while campaigning for the chancellorship. But Washington could not openly court Brandt because that would be interpreted as intervention in West German domestic politics. This was precisely what Adenauer feared. He was aware of the political and personal connection between Kennedy and Brandt. Between 1961 and 1963, the chancellor continuously suspected that the Social Democrats might try to exploit their proximity to Kennedy for domestic political advantage.

It was against this backdrop that Kennedy was invited to visit West Germany. Brandt himself later gave a very condensed account of events that suggested his personal relationship with Kennedy lay behind the invitation.[149] The initiative that led to the invitation actually came, however, from another, in hindsight rather surprising, source. The political factors leading to the invitation had a complicated prehistory and were part of the domestic struggle for power within the Federal Republic. The invitation also became a controversial issue in the United States.

During his first visit to the White House in March 1961, Brandt did indeed issue an invitation to the president. Henry Kissinger, an advisor to the new administration at the time, recommended that serious and careful consideration be given to the idea of a stop in Berlin during Kennedy's planned trip to Paris. But a delicate problem was already evident. Because national elections in Germany were scheduled for the autumn of that year, the American government could not afford to exclude Adenauer. It would be necessary to divide American attention equally between Brandt and the chancellor.[150] In the weeks that followed, the Berlin lobby in the United States intervened. Harold Hurwitz was the pipeline to labor leader Walter Reuther. He had lobbied hard but unsuccessfully to have Kennedy stop in Berlin on his way to the summit with Khrushchev in Vienna.[151] To travel to Berlin amid an escalating crisis there would have been political suicide. Travel plans were shelved during 1961 and 1962, not least on account of Johnson's and Robert Kennedy's trips to West Germany in this period.

In January 1963, just as preparations to celebrate the signing of the Elysée Treaty were underway, this issue gained new momentum. De Gaulle had just taken aim at the United States at a press conference in Paris and refused to cooperate with the Kennedy administration on nuclear weapons. Now it was Adenauer himself who took the initiative. On January 18, he sent

Kennedy a short letter stating that he had learned of the president's intentions to travel to Rome. The chancellor expressed his hope that Kennedy could "come to Bonn for a few days for a working visit."[152] Unpretentious in form, this invitation was a small stroke of genius. Adenauer was signaling German solidarity with the United States during the most serious crisis within the alliance since 1949 and associating that solidarity with Bonn, that is, with his own government. He was more cautious in issuing this invitation than he had been when he invited de Gaulle to West Germany, and he ignored Berlin and the pro-American wing of the SPD.

The proposed visit would have been a coup for Adenauer. It would have served all of his foreign and domestic policy interests. In particular, a working visit in Bonn would have excluded Willy Brandt, his most important political rival. For a while, it looked as if this scenario would become reality. Kennedy answered Adenauer the very next day that he would be pleased to have an opportunity to come to West Germany. The State Department instructed the U.S. mission in Berlin to be guarded in answering Brandt, who was facing a municipal election on February 17, should he inquire about the possibility of welcoming the president to Berlin.[153] In early February, Adenauer sent Foreign Office State Secretary Karl Carstens to Washington to dispel any doubts about the Franco-German treaty. Although he could not find out anything about the possibility of Kennedy visiting Berlin, Carstens did learn that the president still intended to visit West Germany despite his vexation over Franco-German bilateralism.[154]

Things did not go as easily as expected, however. Kennedy's plans to travel to Bonn became known before the Franco-German treaty was signed. As a result, Brandt himself implemented a strategy to bring Kennedy to Berlin, in part because the mayor had suffered a noticeable political setback on January 17. At the time, Khrushchev had been in East Berlin attending a party congress and had made a highly publicized point of visiting the Wall. He had offered to meet Brandt while in East Berlin. Brandt had wanted to consult Adenauer and the Western allies about accepting. But Brandt's coalition partner, the Berlin CDU, forced him to turn down the offer.[155] At this point, it became widely known that Kennedy was considering a trip to West Germany. Much to Brandt's consternation, a nongovernmental interest group suddenly intervened in an attempt to promote the best interests of the city. On January 28, Wilhelm W. Schütz from the Kuratorium Unteilbares Deutschland addressed a letter directly to the president in which he asked Kennedy to include Berlin in his travel plans.[156]

Brandt was angry. To launch such a sensitive initiative outside of the official channels without even consulting him beforehand contradicted diplomatic custom. Transnational contacts could not and should not simply replace the international relations between governmental actors. Such actions could cause a great deal of damage should Kennedy feel himself under pressure.[157] Once before, Brandt had been forced to deal with a similarly unprofessional action. While drinking beer with Bobby Kennedy during his visit to Berlin in February 1962, German trade unionists had given the attorney general a letter addressed to the president, inviting him to their traditional May 1 celebrations.[158] At that time Brandt had just let the action run its unsuccessful course; this time, he was more careful, and more clever, in handling the matter. He used both his direct contact to Kennedy and his contacts to the Berlin lobby in America. Brandt let the U.S. mission in Berlin know how greatly all Berliners would welcome a visit by Kennedy. At the same time, he signaled his understanding for a wait-and-see approach on the part of the United States. After all, this was indeed a highly complicated matter, which Brandt said was the reason he had not formally invited Kennedy to Berlin. But Brandt also subtly mentioned all the arguments in favor of such a trip. For one, he noted, it would demonstrate Western unity. For another, the people of Berlin would be particularly encouraged by a visit at a moment when there was no immediate need to strengthen their morale. Likewise, they would find it hard to understand why Kennedy's trip should be limited only to Bonn. Brandt did not forget to mention Khrushchev's recent trip to East Berlin in this context.[159]

The mayor remained composed and confident. He was not about to court the president's favor zealously. Instead, he emphasized that his overriding concern was to keep the larger foreign policy framework in mind. In a personal note written a few days later, Brandt assured the American president of the enduring friendship of Berliners and of their continued support for the "Atlantic partnership" – the prime political objective. In doing so, he was also playing on the news of France's refusal to approve Great Britain's membership in the European Economic Community (EEC). Brandt acknowledged in his note that only the president himself could decide whether or not to visit Berlin.[160] In his reply, Kennedy did not respond directly to Brandt's overture. He congratulated the mayor on his party's excellent showing in the Berlin election (61.9 percent of the vote) and emphasized the link between Berlin's freedom and the Atlantic community. The administration now began to examine the possibility of a presidential visit to Berlin.

On March 12, Brandt took his next step. He repeated his arguments more emphatically while at the same time cleverly signaling that he was distancing himself from Bonn. Morale in the city was good, he maintained. It was not necessary to compete with Khrushchev's visits. However, in light of the difficulties among the Western powers, he suggested, a visit to Berlin with the joint appearance of all three Western Allies would go far in visibly demonstrating the unity of the West.[161] Meanwhile, Brandt asked the American friends of Berlin, including Shepard Stone, Harold Hurwitz, Melvin Lasky, and Lucius D. Clay, to help facilitate communication between the governmental bodies involved and create an atmosphere favorable to a Berlin trip.[162]

The White House hesitated. Brandt's invitation sparked intense debate not only within the Kennedy administration but also in Bonn and among the European members of the Atlantic alliance. Any decision would be controversial.

2

The Script and the Staging

Following the diplomatic exchanges of January 1963, President Kennedy's trip to West Germany entered a phase of serious planning. Adenauer had initiated the idea of the trip; Kennedy seemed to be basically open to it; and Brandt had positioned himself well to represent the interests of West Berlin. Everything pointed to an interplay of theater, emotion, and political symbolism comparable to that displayed in the trips made by Johnson and Robert F. Kennedy. It remained to be seen whether John F. Kennedy would try to duplicate the Johnson tactic, that is, whether he would combine emphatic rhetoric with political elusiveness. The public was curious what the American president would do about Berlin. Would he visit the divided city, or would he turn his back on it, as Charles de Gaulle had in 1962?

It quickly became clear that West Germany would only be one stop on a sweeping tour of Western Europe. This did not make things any easier for the Germans; instead, diplomatic activity behind the scenes now began in earnest. Bonn, Washington, and Berlin each subjected every detail of the trip to scrutiny, weighing the political implications and potential political utility. Furthermore, the president's journey was causing controversy in America. On the eve of the trip, some in the United States were still strongly advising against it although he had not been to Europe in more than a year. Kennedy had already taken nine trips abroad since taking office.[1] Why should he now crisscross Europe when there were serious problems at home demanding solutions?

CONTROVERSIES OVER THE EUROPEAN ITINERARY

The preparation and execution of Kennedy's visit to Europe in 1963 made one thing clear: American hegemony in Western Europe depended upon the effective use of both political power and political symbolism. "A trip abroad nowadays is nothing if it is not symbolic of interest and power," wrote the *New York Times* upon Kennedy's departure for West Germany.[2] Yet many observers were not sure which interests should be expressed with which political symbols. The political situation within the alliance was rather complicated on account of the signing of the Élysée Treaty between France and West Germany, American and Soviet efforts at détente, and de Gaulle's Anglophobic behavior. In addition, four of the five countries chosen for the visit were in periods of transition or struggling with domestic difficulties. Some of those difficulties had been predictable in January 1963; others arose unexpectedly that summer.

Adenauer had used the occasion of Kennedy's meeting with Italian Prime Minister Amintore Fanfani on January 16, 1963, in Washington to issue his invitation. Fanfani had arranged with Kennedy that the American president would travel to Italy in the summer. To have gone back on this promise when the political situation in Italy took a startling bad turn for the United States that spring would have been a foreign policy affront. In the Italian parliamentary elections held at the end of April, the communists, who had long opposed the presence of NATO and its missile sites in their country, won 25 percent of the vote. On May 16, Fanfani resigned as head of the coalition government but he continued to lead a minority cabinet until June 21. Not until a week before Kennedy's departure did anyone know who the prime minister welcoming the president to Italy would be. The program for Italy remained uncertain up to the last minute. Eighteen days after the death of Pope John XXIII on June 3, 1963, the College of Cardinals elected Giovanni Cardinal Montini as pope, Paul VI; an audience for Kennedy with the newly elected pope was arranged on short notice. All of these improvised arrangements fueled criticism of the president's travel plans in the American press.

The political situation in West Germany, which was slated as the first stop on the trip, was also unclear. Adenauer's days as chancellor were numbered. Everyone knew this, even though it did not become official until April. Still, Adenauer was to remain in office through the summer. As the counterpart to the youthful, forward-looking Kennedy, the elderly chancellor cut a poor profile. His party did not appear to have much chance of winning the next election, and it was divided on foreign policy between Gaullists and Atlanticists. American vexation over the Élysée Treaty was well known. Under the circumstances, critics had reason to question the wisdom of including West Germany on Kennedy's itinerary. The case for a stop in Great Britain was much stronger. It certainly seemed logical to the administration to have Kennedy visit the country's closest ally, and planning for this visit was started in January. Then Defense Minister John Profumo caused a major uproar and turmoil throughout the British Isles as the world watched. A sex scandal exposed Profumo to accusations of having betrayed state secrets to the Soviet Union by way of his mistress. To make matters worse, Profumo lied to Parliament. He was forced to resign in early June. The entire affair undermined the authority of Prime Minister Harold Macmillan even within his own Conservative Party. Suddenly England did not seem to be an ideal place for a visit. Kennedy's short side trip to Macmillan's private home in Birch Grove, Sussex, was arranged very late in the planning.

The only safe haven for Kennedy was Ireland, the land of his forebears. In April, the White House announced that Kennedy would travel there. It was a personal decision that Kennedy made contrary to the advice of some of his staff. The administration sought to maintain the impression outwardly that this was "not merely a sentimental journey." At one point, however, Kennedy's advisor Theodore C. Sorensen commented that any reporter who did not know why the president was visiting Ireland should turn in his typewriter.[3]

The *New York Times* and columnist Walter Lippmann took the lead in questioning the utility of a European trip. Why, asked the *Times*, should the president travel to a politically turbulent continent at a time of change to countries where his political counterparts were not secure in their authority and thus could not negotiate anything concrete during their meetings?[4] The Republicans did not pass up this opportunity to criticize the president. As late as June 16, several demanded that Kennedy cancel the entire trip. In addition to the foreign policy arguments against the trip, there were domestic problems to consider. Trouble was brewing in the South. The issue of racial segregation and discrimination was becoming more pressing by the day. Demonstrators protesting the denial of basic civil rights to the country's African-American minority were subject to brutal attack by mobs and police alike. In the spring of 1963, during a campaign led by Martin Luther King, Jr., police in Birmingham, Alabama, viciously broke up a peaceful civil rights march. Television coverage of this event, broadcast nationwide, helped to place the issue of civil rights on the political agenda in Washington. Up to this point, neither the president nor the attorney general had spoken out on this issue. In a televised speech on June 11, two weeks before he was scheduled to leave for Europe, the president finally condemned racial discrimination for the first time and announced legislation to abolish it. Republican Senator Hugh Scott linked domestic and foreign policy to attack Kennedy on both fronts: "I'd rather see him go to Birmingham than to Berlin just now."[5]

The trip to Europe took place despite the problems at home. Noteworthy was the country Kennedy excluded from his travel plans and whose airspace Air Force One even made a point of avoiding: France. Officially, Washington played down this exclusion by stating that the president had not been invited. Yet it was obvious to all involved that Kennedy wished to send a clear signal of his displeasure with de Gaulle's European policy and French-German bilateralism while simultaneously emphasizing his support for the Atlantic community. Otherwise, said Walt W. Rostow, who had meanwhile been promoted to chairman of the planning staff in the State Department, the danger of a "full-scale Atlantic crisis" threatened.[6] In this regard, Brandt had proved to be far-sighted by casting the proposed Berlin visit as a demonstration of transatlantic solidarity. His aims corresponded perfectly with the interests of the American government. The Americans realized that the timing and execution of the presidential trip to Europe would be problematic. Therefore, U.S. officials long deliberated how the trip should be justified and, in the process, drew up language-usage rules for public relations work. Kennedy's spokesman Pierre Salinger had a great deal of convincing to do.

Three main objectives emerged. The first and most important was to bypass de Gaulle and demonstrate the unity of the transatlantic community, under American leadership, to both the Soviet Union and the Western allies. The Western Europeans needed to be convinced that the United States was serious about its commitment to its allies and that it was "not about to make a deal with the Soviet Union behind their back or at their expense."[7] For this reason, the president would visit the Southern European NATO headquarters in Italy to promote the MLF. He nonetheless also sought to remind the Europeans that they also needed to step up their own defense efforts. The second objective was to win Western Europe over to the concept of peaceful coexistence between the antagonistic political blocs. This meant facilitating efforts at détente and showing clearly that the ongoing American-Soviet negotiations on a nuclear test ban treaty would help ensure international peace.

The administration's third objective concerned economic policy. The United States had to make a serious effort to reduce its balance-of-payments deficit. As part of this effort, negotiations were underway on tariff cuts in American-European trade, the so-called Kennedy Roundtable. These needed to be accelerated. Any initiative to liberalize trade between the most important industrial nations would have to include Great Britain, whose entrance into the EEC had been blocked by de Gaulle in January. The period of major foreign policy decisions à la Woodrow Wilson, Franklin Delano Roosevelt, and Harry S. Truman – Kennedy's three immediate Democratic predecessors in the White House – was over, wrote Rostow to Kennedy. Today progress could only be made in small steps. All Western European nations found themselves in a transitional period and a "somewhat adolescent mood." The United States was in a position to demonstrate its leadership. "We are still the leaders of this boy scout troop; and we must continue to be, if their interests and ours are to be protected for the next decade at least."[8]

There was yet another dimension. Washington wished to use Kennedy's personal charisma to shine a positive light on America and to win a "vote of confidence" against the opposing "candidate," de Gaulle. Even Kennedy's critics in the press admitted that his personality was the country's "supreme political weapon abroad."[9] Few American observers doubted his charisma would affect the people in the countries he had selected to visit, especially since the planned route reflected very much the personal preferences of the Catholic president of Irish descent. It would be an emotionally laden trip. The question thus arose whether appealing to the emotions of Kennedy's European audiences would serve American interests. Following the enthusiastic welcome Kennedy received upon arrival at the Cologne-Bonn airport, the *New York Times* pointed to the potential drawbacks of bringing emotion into politics. The "outpouring of sentiment is genuine," the paper reported, but it also posed the danger that Kennedy would be "carried away by the enthusiasm of his audiences into making promises that cannot be kept."[10]

Everyone knew that the emotional and political expectations on Kennedy would be higher in Berlin than anywhere else in Europe. But at the end of March 1963 it had by no means been settled that the president would be traveling to the divided city. Adenauer, the CDU national party leadership, and the Foreign Office made sure that the question remained open. Quite a few people in the West German government were not interested in seeing the president fly to the stronghold of the once and – quite certainly – future Social Democratic candidate for the chancellorship. By accompanying the president on a triumphant parade through the streets of Berlin, Willy Brandt could profit from Kennedy's glamour and capture the attention of the entire world. Adenauer had only mentioned Bonn when suggesting a visit to Kennedy in January. In the two months that followed, the Foreign Office acted on these instructions exclusively. It planned a "working visit" that excluded Berlin and used Eisenhower's 1959 stop in Bonn as a model.[11] By early March, this strategy looked as if it would succeed. The American press reported that the president had decided against including Berlin in his European trip so as to avoid heightening tension unnecessarily between the two superpowers. Officials in West Berlin remained calm and sought further information. As mentioned previously, Brandt contacted Kennedy directly on March 12.[12] Furthermore, a great deal of trust was placed in the Berlin lobby in America. John McCloy, Walther Reuther, and George Meany had joined Shepard Stone and Lucius Clay in encouraging the administration to include Berlin on the president's European itinerary.[13]

Beginning in February, the White House had been canvassing officials in Washington and at American embassies for their views on the political and psychological desirability of a stop in Berlin. There were some notable opponents to the idea. One was Edward R. Murrow, the head of the U.S. Information Agency. He turned Brandt's original argument on its head. Since Brandt himself had adduced the lack of an acute crisis and the good "morale" of Berlin's population, Murrow argued that a presidential trip would be interpreted by the Soviet Union as a loss of trust in Berlin. In his opinion, it would be better to wait until the situation actually required such a trip to strengthen the U.S. position in negotiations. In other words, he advised the administration to keep a Berlin trip hidden like a "weapon in reserve."[14] Meanwhile, advocates of the trip, including Robert Kennedy, were pressing their arguments more strongly. One State Department official put the matter bluntly in a memorandum: this was not a time to wait but to cash in on the existing political advantage because the pressure exerted on the president from outside sources would only become greater. "He must go to Berlin." This sentence was underlined. Others argued along similar lines. Kennedy would win an immense measure of public support by such a demonstration of Western unity. The West Germans could get over the fact that de Gaulle and Macmillan had not yet been in the divided city, but if the representative of the most powerful guarantor of Berlin's freedom also did not appear, there would be no end to the "howling."[15]

Finally, in the second half of March, the matter was settled. The White House announced that the president would visit Berlin. Behind closed doors, the administration quietly kept open the option of canceling the trip should another Berlin crisis arise. The German press was jubilant. The Foreign Office began to expand protocol plans to include West Berlin.[16] It was still not clear which other cities would be included in the president's itinerary. De Gaulle had traveled to Hamburg and Munich during his visit to the Federal Republic in September 1962. Munich wanted to play host again. On March 21, Mayor Hans-Jochen Vogel issued Kennedy an invitation to visit the Bavarian capital. Washington had to consider the city's symbolic and political utility. Without a doubt, Munich was an important regional center. A visit would give the United States a chance to counterbalance the traditionally strong ties between Bavaria and France, which de Gaulle had reinforced with his visit. If West Berlin seemed very American in American eyes, Munich was the prototypical, postcard-perfect German city.[17]

The disadvantage of Munich was the danger of playing into the hands of Franz Josef Strauß, the notoriously Gaullist leader of the Christian Social Union (CSU). Besides, Kennedy's schedule was already full with visits to the Rhine-Main region and Berlin. Despite the recommendations of such prominent figures as John McCloy, Jean Monnet, Karl Carstens, and Ambassador Walter C. Dowling, the Kennedy administration decided against Munich. Nor were Heidelberg and the Ruhr region, two other proposals, selected.[18] In choosing the cities and settling the issues of protocol connected to each stop, the Americans were forced to deal with rivalries between West German parties and politicians as well as within the parties: Gaullists and Atlanticists; pro-Americans and America skeptics; Berlin's SPD government and the Christian Democratic–Liberal (CDU-CSU-FDP) coalition in Bonn; Adenauer and Brandt; Adenauer and Erhard. Everyone was "jockeying for position."[19] Granted, this infighting among the West Germans was never fierce enough to endanger the trip seriously. But the Americans had to be careful to avoid taking sides.

The haggling within the Federal Republic intensified during the planning for the Berlin visit. Before I turn to the debates over protocol, however, it would be useful to look first at the opening of Kennedy's trip. To give a sense of immediacy, I will use the present tense in narrating the course of events while Kennedy was in Germany.

ACT ONE: KENNEDY IN WEST GERMANY

As the president enters Air Force One on the evening of June 22, 1963, its turbines already droning loudly in preparation for the flight to West Germany, he cannot know that he will also find his ears drumming with noise while he is on German soil. From the first stop in Cologne to the last in Berlin, cheering crowds of West Germans will repeatedly chant three syllables in loud staccato: "Ken-Ne-Dy! Ken-Ne-Dy!" The acoustics of the trip are political. They convey to the entire world the dramatic experiences that bond West Germans and Americans. American journalists are particularly surprised and impressed. The chant will become the slogan of a trip that commentators are already calling a "rousing triumphal procession" by the end of the first day.[20]

The political acoustics of "Ken-Ne-Dy" echo the rhythm of the political drumbeats pounded out by the two most powerful statesmen in the West, Kennedy and de Gaulle, in the days leading up to this trip. On June 10,

Kennedy had used the occasion of the commencement ceremony at American University in Washington, D.C., to deliver a landmark speech. In his commencement address, he outlined what he called a "strategy of peace" that broke with long-held assumptions about the Cold War. The president, emphasizing the innovative aspects of his administration's foreign policy, linked what had been rather scattered ideas into a cohesive plan. Peace, Kennedy had told the audience at American University, should not be defined as a Pax Americana alone. It must be a global, "genuine" peace that would make "life on earth worth living" – a peace to be striven for and enjoyed by all nations. Toward that end, Americans would have to examine their attitudes and assumptions about peace, the Cold War, and relations with the Soviet Union. Kennedy then called for concrete actions and enforceable agreements with the communist countries to overcome the ideological stalemate. It is important not to condemn the Russian people, but to acknowledge and respect their sacrifices and achievements. It is important to emphasize that the two superpowers share the common interest of survival in the nuclear age, for they are in "the most danger of devastation." The "vicious and dangerous cycle" of mutual distrust, Kennedy had insisted, must be broken. The time had come to abandon the bipolar mind-set of the Cold War and to seek new strategies to solve conflict, such as strengthening the United Nations, ensuring self-determination for all peoples, and strengthening international law.[21]

Never before had such ideas, combined with such self-criticism, been heard coming from the mouth of an American president. Mention of America's continued commitment to the defense of Western Europe and West Berlin and of the U.S. refusal to make any deal at the expense of its European allies had been squeezed in toward the end of the speech. Those skeptical toward Kennedy in Western Europe and West Germany took notice. Five days later, Charles de Gaulle announced that he would withdraw France's Atlantic fleet from NATO command. The Americans, in response, tried to downplay speculation that the Western alliance might collapse. Tensions within the alliance had eased in recent months, administration officials noted, and the Bundestag had agreed to ratify the Élysée Treaty only after an Atlanticist preamble was added.

Sunday, June 23. After a seven-hour flight, Air Force One lands at 9:42 a.m. at the Cologne-Bonn Airport and slowly comes to a stop. The red carpet is rolled out. The president, dressed in a gray suit and dark tie and holding a summer hat, descends the gangway (Illustration 13). His manner is relaxed and unpretentious; a 21-gun howitzer salute by a Bundeswehr honor guard serves as a reminder that this is an extraordinary event. Then

Illustration 13. June 23, 1963 – A trip despite all opposition: Kennedy is welcomed by Chancellor Adenauer at Cologne-Bonn Airport; behind them stand Defense Minister Kai-Uwe von Hassel (left) and the inspector general of the German Armed Forces, Friedrich Foertsch (right). Source: John F. Kennedy Library (Audiovisual Archives, no. KN-C 29221, Robert Knudsen).

Kennedy shakes hands with Adenauer. Although officially this trip is not a state visit, which explains the absence of President Heinrich Lübke, Kennedy is welcomed with full honors. Flags are flying, and the national anthems of the United States and the Federal Republic are played. Adenauer and Kennedy inspect the honor guard, and the chancellor presents his cabinet to the guest.

Anyone expecting Adenauer to indulge in innocuous formalities now is proven wrong. To the surprise of everyone, the chancellor takes the offensive in his welcoming speech. He calls Kennedy's trip to Germany "a political act" and offers his own interpretation of Kennedy's June 10 speech. Adenauer focuses exclusively on the few comments made by the president about America's commitment to its allies. This is typical of what one has come to expect from "the Old Man," who has repeatedly caused the Kennedy administration many headaches with his Cold War mind-set. However, the president remains unperturbed, both here at the airport and during a press conference in Bonn the next day when he is asked about the shift in emphasis in Adenauer's welcoming speech.[22] Kennedy himself uses the moment at the airport to pledge America's backing for West Germany in terms highly reminiscent of the comments made by Vice President Lyndon Johnson two years earlier: "Your safety is our safety, your liberty is our liberty, and any attack on your soil is an attack upon our own."[23]

From Kennedy's arrival on June 23 to his departure on June 26, a common thread runs through all of the speeches and public remarks while he is in Germany. He repeatedly expresses his respect for the chancellor, who will soon be leaving office, and his achievements as a statesman. To do this may not be very risky, politically speaking, but it is noble, creates a friendly atmosphere, and helps to improve relations between the two men in the coming days. The gestures by the younger but more powerful politician to the elder, whose power is already waning, are simultaneously enhanced by and overlaid with a visual image quite apparent from the moment Kennedy arrives. The welcoming ceremony and the subsequent drive together in an open car place Adenauer and Kennedy in unprecedented physical proximity to one another. The body language of the two men as they are side by side conveys a peculiar nearness yet distance. The visibility of the event, thanks to extensive television coverage and countless photos in the press, sends biographical and political messages. Not for a moment does the body language of these men reveal any discord. Kennedy and Adenauer get along well and laugh together. However, they are dependent on a translator to communicate. The joint appearance of the two leaders calls attention to the generation gap and, in the eyes of many observers, the political gap between them. On one side is the elderly, frowning Adenauer. Loose skin hangs from his neck. His narrow eyes are accentuated by his high forehead. His few remaining strands of hair are severely combed back and plastered to his head. On the other side is Kennedy. His wrinkle-free face is lightly tanned. His expressive eyes seem to be looking into the future. His abundant brown hair is fashionably styled. The photographs juxtaposing these two distinguished-looking, strong-willed men in profile make an especially strong impression.

At 10:16 a.m., Adenauer and Kennedy leave the airport in an open-roofed Mercedes, the same car Eisenhower used during his trip to West Germany in 1959. Along an autobahn bisecting the surrounding villages and fields, their motorcade drives toward the center of Cologne. With each passing mile, Kennedy's visit becomes increasingly important as a communal experience. Responsibility for this aspect of the visit lies with another actor in the drama: the countless people who, individually and in small groups, stream into the streets to get a look at Kennedy everywhere he goes. Even on the outskirts of Cologne tens of thousands of people turn out, all of them waving, yelling, cheering: "Ken–Ne–Dy! Ken–Ne–Dy!" The president can hardly wave enough. Escorted by fifteen motorcycles, the famous Mercedes crosses the Rhine. The bells of the Cologne cathedral ring out. The size of the crowds along the route forces the motorcade to slow down to a crawl.

At Cologne City Hall, the president is welcomed by Mayor Theo Burauen (SPD). On the front wall of the great hall hangs the seal of the United States. Kennedy signs the city's guest book. A simple podium has been set up in front of the building. Kennedy approaches it but finds it impossible at first to start his speech. "Ken–Ne–Dy! Ken–Ne–Dy!" Kennedy smiles and attempts to quiet the crowd, eventually with some success. He then gives a cleverly worded speech in which he extends greetings from the citizens of three American municipalities named Cologne and injects a little humor as he mentions the chancellor. He has heard, he says, that the name Adenauer is again to be reckoned with in local politics. This is a reference to Max Adenauer, the chancellor's son, who is the most senior official in the city government. "In my own country it is sometimes said that there are too many Kennedys in American public life. But I am certain that no one has made that complaint here about the Adenauers in the city of Cologne."[24] The crowd rewards such statements with loud cheers. Yet it is the last sentence that unleashes "a veritable storm of enthusiasm." Kennedy closes his remarks with the traditional Cologne carnival greeting "*Kölle Alaaf.*" (He actually says "*Köln Alaaf*" but no one is being picky.) Now even the chancellor is swept up by the magic of the moment. Ignoring planned protocol, Adenauer climbs onto the podium and thanks the president. He jokes about the persistence of the "*Kölner Klüngel*" (Cologne old boys' network) and then himself leads another round of "*Kölle Alaaf.*"[25]

A mass is scheduled for twelve o'clock in the Cologne cathedral. It is the pendant to the high mass celebrated by Adenauer and de Gaulle in Reims the previous September. That the most powerful politicians in West Germany, France, and the United States are Catholic is unique (and remains so to this day). Even though thousands of invited guests fill the Cologne cathedral, the service retains a rather intimate character. There are no pictures of the event, only speculation on the part of some observers that the kneeling during the mass has caused the president back pain.[26] Afterward, the politicians drive in the open car on the autobahn to Bonn. Running a good thirty minutes late, Adenauer and Kennedy arrive at the Bonn City Hall at 1:45 p.m. They are greeted by Mayor Wilhelm Daniels. On the outside stairway of the city hall's baroque façade, Kennedy praises Bonn as the "capital of the Free World." It is meant as a polite gesture but is quickly forgotten.

Something else proves far more interesting politically. The president refers to the "great half-circle, stretching from Berlin to Saigon" of free countries that could expect American support.[27] In the years to come, this phrase will be heard more often as the United States sends growing numbers of troops to Vietnam and becomes fully engaged in the war there. Under Kennedy's successor, the U.S. government will use the Berlin-Saigon analogy to define a political front linking the defense of the two widely separated cities. Critics of the Vietnam War will consider this link not as credible but as dangerous, and they will question the purpose of American engagement in Asia and Europe. As Kennedy makes the Berlin-Saigon analogy, nobody except the editors at the East Berlin newspaper *Neues Deutschland* suggests that the president is likening Brandt to the notoriously corrupt South Vietnamese leader Ngo Dinh Diem.[28]

The president then drives to Bad Godesberg to spend the afternoon at the theater in Plittersdorf, where he expresses his gratitude to the personnel of the U.S. embassy for their service and further encourages them in their work. The embassy is receiving congratulatory notes from many Germans who have assumed that June 26 is the president's name day. Kennedy will spend the night in Plittersdorf at the home of the envoy Martin J. Hillenbrand, who will later become the American ambassador to the Federal Republic.[29] In honor of Kennedy, the city of Godesberg has installed a special red-white-and-blue light show on the banks of the Rhine. The first day of Kennedy's visit does not end until midnight, following a black-tie banquet in Schaumburg Palace at Adenauer's invitation. The chancellor himself has chosen the wines. At this event, Kennedy and Brandt meet for the first time on German soil. The large number of politicians invited to the dinner indicates that this is not just a social event. Political talks are planned for the next day.

Monday, June 24. The public sees far less of Kennedy today. The program concentrates on pivotal political contacts in Bonn. In the morning, Kennedy meets Adenauer at the Palais Schaumburg for an exchange of views. Attending this meeting are just the two leaders and their interpreters. Such secretiveness has long been one of Adenauer's tactics to keep his cabinet at arm's length and to maintain his control over West German foreign policy. Kennedy has been extensively briefed in advance by his advisors on Adenauer's persistent doubts about American foreign policy.[30] It is therefore surprising when this topic does not arise during the meeting. Adenauer abstains entirely from criticizing the United States.

The conversation deals in large part with another strictly confidential matter.[31] The chancellor informs Kennedy in detail about his relations with the Soviet leader Khrushchev. He says that the summer of 1962 was the first time he proposed to the Soviet Union the idea of a ten-year *Burgfrieden* (truce) during which the status quo of divided Germany would be respected and bilateral relations normalized. He proposed Hans Kroll, the former German ambassador to the Soviet Union, serve as the middleman for this extremely secret, private mission. Kennedy does not think much of the idea of a truce, but he does not want to stand in the way of a cautious attempt on a personal level to scout out the possibilities. His own middleman, Averell Harriman, is undertaking a similar effort.

During this private conversation with Adenauer, Kennedy's actual concern is de Gaulle, the withdrawal of the French Atlantic fleet from NATO command, and the nationalism of the *Grande Nation*. Adenauer indicates that he sympathizes with the president's concerns. At the same time, he emphasizes the importance of Franco-German reconciliation for Europe. Kennedy, too, acknowledges the importance of Franco-German relations. Overall, the president seems quite happy with the state of German-American relations, particularly regarding recent German arms purchases and the MLF plan. Something else is remarkable about this meeting. Adenauer brings up the sensitive issue of the Oder-Neisse line, the border between East Germany and Poland. For domestic reasons, he cannot and will not go so far as to recognize Poland's western border officially, but he accepts it in practice. Although Kennedy urges him to go a step further and take a firmer position, the two men are not really at odds on the issue. The chancellor and the president avoid open disagreement, and the icy mistrust between them begins to melt. The public will notice this change later that evening.

While Adenauer and Kennedy are talking, high-level officials of the two governments are also meeting behind closed doors.[32] Two topics dominate the talks: the chances of creating the multilateral nuclear force proposed by the United States and the handling of the reunification issue. Both sides agree that the MLF idea is important politically and psychologically for the cohesion of the Western alliance. Yet no substantial results come from the discussion of whether and how to entice the British and Italians to join and how the French nuclear forces can be fit in. Erhard dares to pose the question of whether the MLF is perhaps only camouflage. Foreign Minister Gerhard Schröder brings up the topic of German reunification. The differences in the two delegations' perspectives quickly become apparent. Berlin plays a role here. The German foreign minister indirectly expresses his criticism of the United States for rarely mentioning reunification. The Berlin issue can only be considered in this context. Secretary of State Rusk takes the opposite stance. He reminds the Germans that one of the declared political aims of

Illustration 14. June 24, 1963 – Among presidents: Kennedy on the front steps of the Villa Hammerschmidt in Bonn with German president Heinrich Lübke and Chancellor Konrad Adenauer. Source: Bundesarchiv Koblenz (no. 146/2003/1/7A).

the United States is to ensure the self-determination of peoples worldwide, meaning universally and not just in the specific case of Germany. The first step is to achieve a few concrete improvements in the situation. Schröder's concern that the GDR will earn increasing international recognition does not bother Rusk. Surprisingly it is Erhard who agrees with the American position and expresses his sympathy for the legitimate concerns regarding status coming from the East.

The consultations are adjourned at this point because Kennedy is scheduled to visit President Heinrich Lübke, his only political equal according to political protocol, at the Villa Hammerschmidt, the official residence of the West German presidents (Illustration 14). The political justification for the visit coincides neatly with Kennedy's foreign policy course. The American president talks about establishing a West German foreign development aid service. The Federal Republic wants to use this agency to send young aid workers to Asia, Africa, and Latin America. Kennedy explicitly proposes the U.S. Peace Corps, which he initiated in 1961, as a model. One of the favorite topics of the American president has long been social justice in the Third World. Kennedy wants to use his trip to encourage the Europeans to view the Third World countries as part of the international political and economic order. Behind this plea are hard budget facts. The United States seeks greater participation from Germany in shouldering the costs of foreign aid. Kennedy also urges this in his talk with Lübke, particularly with an eye on Latin America and India. The West German president also proves to be well prepared to discuss the economic strength of the Soviet Union. The Americans fear that the Soviets might be in a position to buy influence in the Third World. The Germans, by contrast, take a more skeptical view of Soviet economic power.[33]

Following a lunch hosted by Lübke, the German and American delegations meet for another round of consultations, joined this time by Adenauer and Kennedy.[34] Once again, talk focuses on the MLF, particularly on the problem that only two countries, the United States and West Germany, have so far shown any interest in participating; opposition to the plan is growing in Great Britain and the political situation in Italy remains unstable. For this reason, Adenauer suggests Washington as the location of the coming round of negotiations. Kennedy readily accepts this proposal. At the same time, he indicates cautiously that he is distancing himself from the MLF project. Then the president brings up the topic of the nuclear test ban treaty. In an apparent effort to quiet German concerns that the superpowers might make a deal at their allies' expense, he plays down the chances of coming to an agreement with the Soviet Union.

Finally, attention turns to the most pressing item on the agenda: economic, fiscal, and trade issues. Kennedy makes it very clear that these issues are high priority and that they cannot be left to technocrats to solve. The United States wants to correct the deficits in its payment and trade balances. The Germans welcome this but place the American interests in a slightly different light. Even the Federal Republic has deficits. After all, a substantial portion of its reserves are in U.S. dollars. Erhard argues that it is necessary to establish international regulations, not bilateral ones. He expressly asks the Americans to show "more open-mindedness." Adenauer then lists the various political problems involved. They are dealing here with German farmers whose interests, in turn, would not be accepted by the French. The German unions are also a problem; there is no one leader of the German labor movement with authority comparable to the AFL–CIO's George Meany.[35] One of the remarkable aspects about the political talks held on June 24 is the moderation displayed by the American officials in dealing with the West Germans. They often praise and compliment them, and they do not raise very controversial issues or make demands the Germans would find hard to accept. They are intent on maintaining harmony.

At a wide-ranging press conference at the Foreign Office afterward, Kennedy addresses the entire spectrum of foreign policy issues. He remains at ease throughout the questioning. Asked about German reunification, an issue of central concern to the West German government, he gives a minimalist response. For many years, he explains, it has been the official policy of the United States "not to recognize in the juridical sense the division of Germany." There is "no immediate solution" to this problem. By taking this stance, Kennedy holds to his advisors' recommendation that the United States commit itself as little as possible on the issue of reunification.[36]

Before a gala dinner at the American embassy club in Bad Godesberg, Willy Brandt is permitted his first political appearance. This is meant as an honor to him personally and to West Berlin as a whole. Brandt and his closest advisors, Egon Bahr and Klaus Schütz, meet with Secretary of State Rusk, Assistant Secretary William R. Tyler, and Martin J. Hillenbrand. The talks focus on bringing American firms to Berlin within the framework of the Viability Program, which Lucius D. Clay has been promoting since the winter of 1961–62, and on possible tax breaks for American investors. Above all, they discuss access to Berlin. The GDR has opened a new Wall crossing that would link West Berlin to East Berlin's Schönefeld Airport. Should this new crossing be blocked? Brandt and Rusk agree that, in Brandt's words, a "Counter-Wall" should not be built despite public opposition to the East German initiative and that international air traffic to East Berlin should not be hindered. The American secretary of state explicitly expresses his agreement with Brandt's policy of trying to "punch holes in the Wall."[37]

During the course of the meeting, Rusk underscores two points regarding Berlin. The presence of the United States in the city is "based on the right of victory, not on agreement" with anyone – in the East or in the West. This is a position that the American government has long held, and it distances the United States from the idea repeatedly suggested by Brandt of replacing the Four-Power status still legally valid for Berlin as a whole with a Three-Power status agreement among the Western Allies applicable to West Berlin. The American position is that the World War II Allies should retain their occupation rights in the city.[38] If the United States were to pull out of Berlin, it would do so on its own volition. "We won't be pushed out or negotiated out," Rusk insists. "Of course we might consider leaving if we heard the West Berliners shouting 'Yanks go home.'" Rusk cannot know at this point that such shouts will indeed be heard in Berlin only a few years later; no one can imagine that. Rusk finds it very important to keep an eye on ensuring the "confidence of the population" and on "public opinion" in the city as a guarantee for its security.[39]

At the dinner in Bad Godesberg that evening, the chancellor once again uses exceptionally warmhearted words in his toast. He emphasizes his deep respect for the way the United States "as the victorious people extended a hand to the vanquished" after the war. Adenauer is obviously moved. His view of German-American relations is reinforced by having witnessed the outpouring of emotion on the part of the German citizens who had lined the road as he and Kennedy drove to Cologne and Bonn. Adenauer takes up the emotions displayed and employs them for his own political purposes. Two mutually reinforcing processes are at work here: the crowds have impressed the main actors with their expression of emotion, and the main actors, in turn, convey emotion before the public. The visual impact made by the cheering audience is evident in the political language of the protagonists on the stage. Several times that evening, Adenauer tells the assembled guests what a great impression it made on Kennedy and him to look into the eyes of the enthusiastic crowds lining the streets. The "sense of a great presence of emotion" in the crowd left its mark on Adenauer. He interprets what he saw to be proof of German-American solidarity.[40] The American press picks up right away on the emotionality of the chancellor's remarks and his new personal solidarity with Kennedy. It is reported that "an unexpected personal intimacy achieved by the two Government heads" became apparent when "Adenauer expressed the feeling of closeness in an emotional toast."[41]

Adenauer even swallows what has long been the bitterest pill of all: the subordination of the German question to the pursuit of East-West détente. He does not repeat his usual call for German reunification in his toast. After two long years, the ice is finally breaking between the president and the chancellor as a result of Kennedy's presence in West Germany and the public enthusiasm it generates. In his own toast, Kennedy is not to be outdone by Adenauer. He is also mightily moved by the "opportunity to come face to face" with the German people. His delegation is "very much warmed, heartened, encouraged, strengthened by the generosity of the reception."[42] He praises the chancellor as a historical figure. Kennedy does prove to have a problem with dates, however. In the toast he gave the evening before, he wanted to be anecdotal and historical. Kennedy mentions that Adenauer was born two years before the Battle of the Little Bighorn (1876). He was close. The chancellor actually entered this world the same year as the famous battle.[43]

Tuesday, June 25. Shortly after eight o'clock in the morning, Willy Brandt is again granted a privilege. This time Brandt has been invited to breakfast alone with the president. Among other things, the two discuss the situation

Illustration 15. June 25, 1963 – Demonstrating power in Hanau: Kennedy inspects a tank formation at the American air force base. Source: John F. Kennedy Library (Audiovisual Archives, no. ST-C230–28–63, Cecil W. Stoughton).

in Berlin, the transition from Adenauer to Erhard, the MFL, and de Gaulle.[44] Then Kennedy is flown by helicopter to an American Air Force base in Hanau, near Frankfurt, where he views troops from four NATO member states (Illustration 15). In addition to the German and American national anthems, the military band plays those of Canada and France. This symbolic act is the first including Western nations other than West Germany and the United States. Considering the recent friction with de Gaulle, the inclusion of France in the symbolic military event can be interpreted as a conciliatory signal. Another sign of harmony stands out. Ludwig Erhard is accompanying the president on his trip today. The future chancellor is enjoying the honor of being in Kennedy's immediate company. The two politicians want to get to know one another better and to communicate directly. Still, Adenauer, who thinks Erhard a poor choice for the chancellorship, keeps a close eye on them.[45]

A motorcycle squad escorts Kennedy and Erhard to Frankfurt City Hall. The crowd in Frankfurt is estimated at one million people. Accompanied by Minister President Georg August Zinn of Hessen, one of West Germany's most senior politicians, Kennedy addresses the cheering crowd at the Römerberg, the square in front of Frankfurt's city hall. This imposing backdrop notwithstanding, the president displays his trademark humor. He tells the crowd that, on their way to the Römerberg, Zinn pointed out the SPD supporters he saw in the crowd and Erhard directed his attention to all the Christian Democrats. Kennedy, however, could not see a difference: "In any case, I see friends."[46] Like many of the short speeches he gave the day before, Kennedy's brief remarks include many references to German-American history and the German immigrants in the United States. A prominent role is played by the forty-eighters, the political refugees who left Germany after the suppression of the Revolution of 1848. Kennedy mentions figures such as Gottfried Kinkel and Carl Schurz. The president also quotes Abraham Lincoln, who enjoyed strong backing from liberal German-Americans.[47]

The most important commemorative gesture made during the trip before Kennedy departs for Berlin is the speech he delivers in Frankfurt Paulskirche. He is the first foreign politician to have been asked to speak in this church, where the delegates of the German National Assembly had met from 1848 to 1849 before the assembly was forcefully disbanded in May 1849. The *New York Times* describes the Paulskirche to its readers as a "shrine of German democracy."[48] By accepting the offer to give the first political speech of his visit in the Paulskirche, Kennedy associates himself with the tradition of liberalism and democracy in Germany. In this way, what Kennedy says on the afternoon of June 25 sends a historical and political signal to Germans and the world at large to accept the Federal Republic of Germany as a free and democratic nation. The selection of this site for Kennedy's speech also serves another purpose. Earlier the German government had considered asking Kennedy to address the Bundestag, West Germany's national parliament. No foreign head of state had yet been offered that honor. There was concern, however, that such an unprecedented step would raise expectations for the speech even further. The politically adroit Adenauer recognized back in May that a speech by Kennedy posed a problem of rhetorical and therefore political balance, especially with regard to the German question. Should Kennedy speak in terms "hard enough" to please the West German members of parliament, he would endanger the dialogue with the Russians. However, should he speak "too softly" in order to satisfy the Soviet Union, he would disappoint the West German parliament.[49] Therefore, the selection of the Paulskirche for Kennedy's policy speech is also a compromise solution, especially since many members of parliament are in the audience, and Kennedy is welcomed by the president of the parliament, Eugen Gerstenmaier.

Kennedy gives a landmark speech. He espouses the ideas presented in his American University speech of June 10 and concentrates on imparting his vision of the "Atlantic partnership" and the "Atlantic community" – both terms are mentioned at key junctures. He outlines an Atlantic partnership that is based on three things: first, on the desire for a common military defense and "not by turning the clock backward to separate nuclear deterrents." Naturally, this is interpreted as a sideswipe aimed at de Gaulle. Yet Kennedy is not interested in scoring political points against his opponent but in painting a larger picture, and so he does not forget to mention Franco-German reconciliation. Second, the Atlantic community should become a free trade zone, establish common industrial and agricultural policies, and resolve the currency disequilibrium among the member states. Third, this partnership is a joint effort to create an integrated and strong Europe, to defuse Cold War tensions, and to stop the arms race. The Germans are particularly pleased to hear the president explicitly urge the allies to practice the "art of consultation" within the alliance more than they have in the past. The speech, in sum, is an appeal to the Western nations to look beyond their own invidivual national problems and to recognize that all nations in the world, including the Third World countries, are now living in an "age of interdependence as well as independence." Kennedy wants to pursue a "great new mission," and Europe should have an important role in it.[50] The strong emphasis on Europe in this speech was in large part the doing of Undersecretary of State George W. Ball, who had discussed the speech beforehand with Jean Monnet.[51]

Kennedy receives a great round of applause upon concluding the speech, and not only because his speechwriters had worked in a number of quotations from Goethe and, to the particular delight of the classicist Gerstenmaier, Thucydides.[52] Afterward, Kennedy flies by helicopter from Frankfurt to Wiesbaden, where he meets Erhard in the Hotel Steuben for a private meeting; the only other people present are their interpreters. This discussion focuses on two key topics: the U.S. balance of payments and its fiscal policy. Erhard, a former economics professor, lectures. He expounds the ideas behind the Federal Republic's social market economy, in particular its vision of an active role for the state in regulating the economy. Erhard cannot accept the premises of American economic policy. He argues that economic growth cannot be achieved with the strategy used by the United States, namely, to rely solely on tax cuts to increase spending power. Erhard recommends that the discount and interest rates be raised and a more active fiscal policy be pursued. The future chancellor even detects a conspiracy with American industrial and business circles to keep unemployment at a high level for their own benefit. There is not much that Kennedy can say to this.[53]

At a reception that evening, the president speaks highly of his first three days in Germany. Kennedy has already referred to his time in Frankfurt as the "most heartwarming days" he has experienced during his political career. When his term of office comes to an end, he says, he will leave an envelope behind in the Oval Office, for his successor to open when nothing seems to be going his way. The note inside will read: "Go visit Germany."[54] Who would have thought that the most powerful man in the world would find visiting Germany so uplifting and emotionally rewarding? Those inclined to think that Kennedy was just being polite are proven wrong the very next day. On the morning of June 26, Kennedy flies to Berlin. There, he experiences an outpouring of emotion that could hardly be surpassed. And although spontaneous, this outpouring accompanies a staged performance that is the product of months of detailed planning.

STAGE DIRECTIONS: PLANNING THE PROTOCOL FOR BERLIN

As soon as Kennedy had decided he would visit Berlin, a new conflict developed behind the scenes. Bonn and West Berlin, personified by Chancellor Adenauer and Mayor Brandt, began to negotiate the agenda for the Berlin visit. Both sides blatantly pursued their own interests and consequently found themselves skating on thin ice, legally and politically. The Four-Power status in Berlin placed protocol in a tight corset, and a visit to the divided city by an Allied head of state represented a first for diplomatic protocol. There were no precedents to fall back on; what was called for was ceremonial innovation. Cooperation among the Germans, as Brandt later acknowledged, was impeded by the "clash of egos."[55] In the end, the Western Allies, particularly the United States, had to take on the "anomalous role" as "arbiters of protocol in Berlin."[56]

The final word in all questions of protocol was left neither to the West German government nor to the West Berlin Senate but to the Western Allies, owing to their special legal status in Berlin. As if the entire situation was not complicated enough, France, Great Britain, and the United States had to agree among themselves on the protocol while avoiding any violation of the Four-Power status that could possibly provoke the Soviet Union. Because of its ability to interfere in travel between West Berlin and West Germany, the Soviet Union loomed menacingly in the background. Surprisingly, the Kremlin did not create any hurdles to block Kennedy's visit to Berlin. It criticized the trip as a provocation, but it nonetheless signaled its assurance that the American president would be allowed to fly to and from West Berlin without problem.[57]

In deciding on the protocol for the visit, German and American officials
had to contend with the dense tangle of legal, political, and symbolic claims
put forward by the different political entitites with a stake in Berlin. International law, national law, constitutional law, and occupation agreements all
had a bearing on the issue of Berlin. Another complication was the differing
views among the Western Allies and among the West Germans themselves
on whether Berlin should be regarded as the capital of Germany and what
that might mean while Germany and the city itself remained divided.[58]
Secretary of State Dean Rusk summed up the American position succinctly
while speaking in Bonn on June 24, 1963. The United States' presence and
rights in Berlin derived from its victory over National Socialist Germany
and the agreements the Allies made in 1944 – that is, during war – in anticipation of victory. The United States, Great Britain, and the Soviet Union
agreed in 1944 to govern Berlin together through an Allied command, the
so-called Kommandantura, following Germany's surrender. Each country
would receive a sector of the city to occupy, and each sector would be
governed by a military commander from this occupying nation. The sector commands were subordinate to the Allied Control Council, which was
responsible for the occupation of Germany as a whole.[59] Even before the
war ended, France became the fourth Allied power to receive an occupation
zone in Germany and its own sector of Berlin in the northwestern part of
the city, the part that Kennedy would happen to fly into upon his arrival on
June 26, 1963. One oversight in these agreements was that the free use of
access roads leading to West Berlin was not specified in writing before the
end of the war.

As the East-West conflict intensified, the Soviet Union withdrew from
the Allied Control Council in March 1948 and from the Kommandantura
three months later. Even without Soviet participation, the Western powers
decided to continue the functions of the Kommandantura. They did not
relinquish the Four-Power status and its legitimation through the occupation statutes imposed following Germany's surrender, but in practice they
increasingly limited the exercise of their rights to the territory of West
Berlin. Some aspects of the original joint military government continued to
function, such as the incarceration of Nazi leaders in Spandau Prison, the
air traffic control over Berlin, and the acknowledged privilege of Western
Allied military to travel to East Berlin in uniform without having to present
a passport. The Western powers found themselves fighting a battle on two
fronts. On the one hand, they rejected the Soviet Union's interpretation of
the legal situation, which justified the Soviet presence in Berlin solely by the
postwar agreements. The Soviets supported this position with two major

arguments: first, Berlin was geographically located in their occupation zone and after 1949 in the GDR; and second, Berlin had been conquered by the Red Army. The Western Allies did not accept this interpretation, nor did they accept the GDR's appropriation of the name "Berlin" for the eastern half of the city or East Berlin's status as the GDR's capital.

On the other hand, the three Western Allies blocked all attempts by the Federal Republic and West Berlin to declare the western sectors of the city as the twelfth *Land* (state) of the Federal Republic and to integrate it constitutionally into the Federal Republic. Although the United States, Great Britain, and France encouraged close relations between West Berlin and West Germany, they limited the extent of these links even after the occupation status of the Federal Republic formally came to an end in 1955. According to their interpretation of the law, West Berlin was not a *Land* and had to pass special regulations to adopt West German laws. West Berlin sent representatives to the Bundestag, but they were not selected by popular election and could not vote on the most important parliamentary issues. At the same time, the mandatory military service required of young men in West Germany beginning in 1956 did not apply to residents of West Berlin. In fact, the Bundeswehr was not allowed to be present in the city. Nor was West Berlin considered NATO territory, even though NATO had committed itself to the defense of the city. The Bundesgrenzschutz (Federal Border Police) was not to be seen in West Berlin. Public order was put in the hands of the West Berlin police force, which was subordinate to the supervision of the Western commanders. Even this detail played a role in the reception organized for Kennedy.

Between 1954 and 1957, several groups in West Germany and West Berlin made great strides in their attempts to make West Berlin an integral part of the Federal Republic and to declare it the nation's capital. The Federal Assembly (Bundesversammlung) met in West Berlin to elect the country's president (a practice continued until 1969), and the parliament met there for the first time in 1955. There was an architectural competition to design "Capital City Berlin." The publisher and CDU parliamentarian Gerd Bucerius drummed up popular support for an initiative to designate Berlin as the Federal Republic's capital. The same cause was also advocated by Wilhelm W. Schütz from the Kuratorium Unteilbares Deutschland (Committee for an Indivisible Germany), "a type of manager for German reunification illusions."[60] In February 1957, the Bundestag did indeed decide by unanimous vote to declare Berlin the capital of Germany. Three months later, the Constitutional Court (Bundesverfassungsgericht) handed down a decision that made Berlin a *Land* in the Federal Republic.

Berlin's champions were, however, exerting effort for nothing. Adenauer and the foreign policy experts in Bonn knew they would get nowhere with the Western Allies.

Despite the differences in their interpretation of law, the West Germans and the three Western powers were faced with a common challenge in planning Kennedy's visit.[61] No serving American president had visited Berlin since Harry S. Truman participated in the Potsdam Conference in the summer of 1945. Herbert Hoover had gone to West Berlin in 1954, but he had been out of office for twenty-one years by then. Nor had the head of state of any of the other Western powers been in the divided city. In short, no precedence in protocol existed. To complicate matters further, Adenauer was forcing a situation on the planners for which established protocol also offered no guidelines. The chancellor wanted the president to be greeted in West Berlin by both Brandt and himself, even though the West German government was being urged to keep a low profile in Berlin for legal reasons. The planners were faced with a serious problem. They needed to achieve two things. Like those in charge of planning the protocol for the royal visits of the nineteenth century, a topic historian Johannes Paulmann has explored in depth, planners in 1963 found it necessary, for one, to "reduce risk. The actors and their aides wanted to do everything in their power to prevent anything from going wrong." The protocol departments also strove to "control the interpretation" of the visit by carefully organizing the program. The unity of the West must be on display, and there could be no sign of the allies' differing positions on Berlin's legal status.[62]

Beginning in April, Bonn and Berlin each attempted to influence the protocol for the Kennedy visit for its own advantage. There was a tug-of-war over every question of status, every symbolic gesture, and every event on the program. Each side hoped that victory on a particular point would serve its domestic and foreign policies. Thus, even the smallest details of protocol became immensely significant. Three issues dominated the discussion. The first was the route Kennedy would travel and thus the political topography of the trip. Which places in the city should the president visit? How much time should he spend at each? What political message should be communicated? The second was the order of events from Kennedy's arrival until his departure. Who should address the president publicly and when, where, and with what words? The third was the stage directions and props. Who should stand where and in what proximity to Kennedy? Who should drive with him in an open car through the city? How should the classic symbols of nation-states – national anthems, flags, and uniforms – be handled? How should the public platforms and podiums be decorated?

Negotiations on these issues began in mid-April and continued right up to the last minute before the president arrived. The two offices responsible for these negotiations were the protocol departments of the Foreign Office and the West Berlin Senate. However, both Adenauer and Brandt became personally involved. On June 9, the two men met in Cologne but were unable to come to terms on the divisive issues.[63] The chancellor and the mayor each had his own channels of communication with the Americans through which he tried to influence the planning. Adenauer's was the U.S. embassy in Bonn, Brandt's, the U.S. mission in Berlin. The Americans, meanwhile, were also taking the planning very seriously. On May 9, Pierre Salinger, Kennedy's press secretary, and Kenneth O'Donnell, a presidential advisor, arrived in Berlin to inspect all of the sites that might be on the program for the visit.[64]

The Americans soon realized that Bonn and West Berlin were pursuing different interests and therefore made the wise decision to keep both actors at arm's length and to let them decide as much as possible between themselves. The proposals submitted by the Germans would then be measured against the Allied interpretation of Berlin's legal status. The Americans proved to be generous toward the Germans. The main German actors were given precedence over the Allied commanders when it came to the question of who should greet Kennedy and when. This was remarkable because, according to the protocol of the Western Allies, the ambassadors of the United States, Great Britain, and France were the legal successors to the Allied High Commissioner and therefore the highest authorities in West Berlin. Strictly speaking, they had priority in protocol, followed by the Allied commanders, the mission chiefs, and only then the city's mayor.[65]

Berlin had last hosted an Allied head of government from the West eighteen years earlier under very different political circumstances. In the summer of 1945, the Allies met in Potsdam, just outside the ruins of the German capital. Allied leaders made their way through the rubble of Berlin and visited the remnants of the symbols of the Nazi dictatorship. The Cold War had not yet begun. By June 1963, the situation had changed entirely. The spatial and communicative parameters were completely different, as were the symbolic and commemorative signposts. Kennedy would be traveling through a political topography quite unlike the one Harry Truman had experienced.[66]

From the outset, American officials made it clear that Kennedy would only visit the Western sectors of the city and would not cross into the East, even though he had the right to do so. Kennedy confirmed this again at the press conference held in Bonn: "I don't think that any gesture, however spectacular, of this kind would materially improve the lot of the people of East Berlin."[67] Two fundamental differences from 1945 became immediately apparent from this self-imposed restriction. First, the eastern half of the city could no longer be viewed from within, only from without. Whatever opinion a person had about the East, it could no longer be confirmed or corrected by firsthand experience and observation. This highlighted the second difference. A trip to Berlin was a trip to the edge, to a border – not the open, unexplored, promising kind of border that Kennedy liked to evoke when he talked of the New Frontier. This trip was a confrontation with a closed border. The Wall gave physical expression to the basic fact of West Berlin's Cold War existence: its encirclement. It was the border Kennedy would see, and it limited the possible routes through the city for his motorcade. Moreover, the Wall was not to be simply one sight that the president would be seeing during his visit. It was to be the focal point of the trip. The Wall epitomized the moral inferiority and inhumanity of the Eastern bloc's communist system, and Kennedy's trip was meant to highlight that point.[68] West Berlin's new political and commemorative landmarks would serve as a positive counterpoint to the Wall. Sites demonstrating American solidarity with the West Berliners during the Cold War would be especially important. The president would be coming to a city that has long since cleared away the rubble of war, even if gaps in the cityscape could still be seen. The president would drive through densely populated neighborhoods and past symbols of West Berlin's reconstruction. This too was part of the positive symbolism of America's Berlin, the Berlin that Germans and Americans had created in the years following the Berlin Airlift.

Kennedy's arrival and departure points were clear. The president's jet required a long runway. It therefore had to land at Tegel Airport in northwestern West Berlin. This technical necessity meant Kennedy's visit would have a different political topography from that of other American dignitaries' visits. He would not be arriving in and departing from the American sector. Tegel lay in the French sector, a somewhat ironic twist, given the headaches France's president had been causing in Washington. The northern sections of West Berlin had not previously been included in the official tour route for high-ranking American guests. It was soon decided that Kennedy would be visiting the Free University in Dahlem, a neighborhood in West Berlin's southwest that was in the American sector. Consequently, his path through the city would run along an extended north–south axis. It would cross through all three of the Western Allies' sectors of West Berlin and would run approximately 33 miles.[69]

At first, the West German government suggested places for the president to visit that were not associated with the Cold War. One was a symbol of the royal Prussian past – Charlottenburg Palace – and two others that represented religious life in the city – the Jewish community center that had opened in 1959 on Fasanen Strasse and the recently completed Regina Martyrum, a Catholic church on the Heckerdamm that was dedicated to the memory of the victims of National Socialism. The Regina Martyrum was located near the Plötzensee Memorial to political prisoners executed during the Nazi dictatorship.[70] The Americans did not follow up on any of these suggestions. Symbolism connected to the Cold War was more important. It was agreed that the president would make stops to view the Berlin Wall and the Brandenburg Gate. Cut off by the Wall, the Brandenburg Gate was for West Germans at once a potent symbol of Germany's division and a reminder of the existence of a single German nation. It was also quickly decided that Kennedy would visit Schöneberg City Hall, the seat of West Berlin's municipal government, and the American military headquarters in the southwestern corner of the American sector.

Planning became more complicated when choosing between sites meant having to choose between different political messages. With great tenacity, Willy Brandt kept proposing that Kennedy visit Bernauer Strasse to pay tribute to the individuals who had lost their lives trying to cross the Berlin Wall. Brandt had been able to convince Robert Kennedy and George Meany to go there during their visits to West Berlin in 1962.[71] Brandt wanted the president's itinerary to include a stop at the Wall in order to document the human tragedy that had occurred – and continued to occur – in the divided city; the memorial to Ida Siekmann, who had lept to her death trying to get across the Wall at Bernauer Strasse shortly after the Wall was erected, would represent that ongoing tragedy. The mayor especially wanted to take Kennedy to points along the Wall where the Eastern bloc would not have the opportunity to display its power. That, in hindsight, explains Brandt's surprising resistance to the planned stop at Checkpoint Charlie. He was not interested in dramatizing the standoff between the superpowers or in giving the GDR a chance to show off its military muscle with a parade of border troops. From a "public-relations viewpoint in [the] U.S.," however, the exclusion of the famous checkpoint on Friedrich Strasse was out of the question.[72] Thanks in no small part to the American tanks Lucius Clay had stationed there in October 1961, Checkpoint Charlie was one of the best-known points of confrontation between East and West.

In principle, the Kennedy administration was not against including Bernauer Strasse on the program. But, as planning for the visit progressed, time became an immense problem. Despite several intercessions by Brandt, the Americans ended up rejecting his suggestion. Plans were made, however, for an act of remembrance of those who had lost their lives at the Berlin Wall. Eunice Shriver, Kennedy's sister and a member of the delegation, was to stop on Bernauer Strasse to lay a wreath at the memorial for Ida Siekmann.

The American planners also turned down a proposal to visit a different sort of Western symbol linked to the Wall, the headquarters of the Springer publishing house. Axel Springer, the head of this successful firm, openly used his press publications to further the cause of German unification and to lambaste both the Wall and the "GDR" (the Springer stylebook dictated that all references to the German Democratic Republic be put in quotation marks). The company used its contacts to advisors close to Kennedy to try to convince the president to stop at the new press house Springer had built close to Wall near Checkpoint Charlie.[73] The Americans turned down Springer's offer with the explanation that time was short and they could not promote the interests of a commercial enterprise.

Another proposal that was eventually turned down was a tour of the AEG turbine factory. The proposal had been put forward by the U.S. mission in Berlin. American diplomats in the city were particularly interested in underscoring West Berlin's economic importance as a modern industrial center. Taking the president to a German workplace would also bolster relations with German trade unions. In the end, the AEG tour fell through not only because there was not enough time for it but also because the German unions approached Kennedy directly with another invitation. On April 25, Georg Leber, an SPD politician and the chairman of the Industrial Trade Union of Construction Workers, invited the president to attend the union's sixth national meeting, which would be taking place in Berlin at the time of Kennedy's visit.[74] This unusually direct overture would have quickly been side-stepped if not for the intervention of George Meany. The AFL-CIO head had direct contacts not only with West Berlin labor leaders but also with Brandt. In July 1961, during the Berlin crisis that followed on the heels of the Vienna summit, Brandt gratefully noted in a letter to Meany that "the American trade union movement was the first to lend our resistance [to pressure from the East] moral support from abroad and that American labour has, throughout the years, remained among our most consistent and most active friends."[75]

Meany had brought the International Federation of Free Trade Unions to Berlin for a congress in July 1962. Now, less than a year later, he intervened personally and persuaded the president to appear at the 1963 trade union congress with him.[76] This was not good news to either the German Foreign Office or Adenauer. On May 20, the chancellor used the first official visit from the new American ambassador in Bonn, George McGhee, to argue against such an unprecedented appearance. It was obvious that he wanted to keep the SPD-linked trade union movement off the stage.[77] Meany prevailed, however. His success meant that the president would be visiting a site that fit perfectly in the political topography of America's Berlin. The trade union convention would be taking place in the Congress Hall, the most prominent example of postwar American architecture in the city.

The Berlin lobby in the United States was also successful in setting up another item on the president's itinerary. Willy Brandt informed Shepard Stone early on that the president might come to Berlin. As the director of the international department of the Ford Foundation, Stone had supported the Free University for years through sponsorships, subsidies, and help with academic exchanges.[78] He cooperated closely with the director of the FU's foreign studies office, Horst Hartwich. In the spring of 1963, Stone used this connection to propose informally to the FU that it invite Kennedy to the campus during his visit and award him an honorary degree. The proposal fell on fertile soil. Very soon afterward, the FU senate approved the rector's petition to name Kennedy an honorary member of the university.[79]

Like the Congress Hall, the Free University was firmly established in the political topography of America's Berlin. No other German university had been established with such direct American support or enjoyed as much ongoing financial and intellectual support from American sources. No German university was closer to the United States ideologically than the FU. Like many American universities, the FU had a campus, spread out across extensive grounds, that had a suburban feel to it. The university was well known for its hospitality to visiting American professors and its openness to American developments in the social sciences.[80]

By the end of May, the main stops on Kennedy's route through West Berlin had been set. From Tegel, he would travel to the Congress Hall, located in the Tiergarten park, and Brandenburg Gate, then on to Checkpoint Charlie and Schöneberg City Hall. Afterward, the president and his entourage would continue to the southwest corner of the American sector to the FU and the American military headquarters, from which they would drive northward along a slightly curvy path back to Tegel Airport. Seven hours had been allotted for the president's visit, and the proposed program filled every minute. The planners had considered having him travel the stretch from Schöneberg to the FU by helicopter, but that idea was abandoned.[81] Flying Kennedy across Berlin would run counter to the idea of celebrating his visit as a triumphal procession cheered on by throngs of spectators. But despite the effort and politicking that had gone into putting this itinerary together, it quickly became clear that the plans for the president's visit would have to be revised. West Berliners spoke out loudly, just as they had following the construction of the Berlin Wall and the death of Peter Fechter. They were not willing to leave the arrangements for Kennedy's visit solely in the hands of the diplomats.

When the planned route became known in early June, the West Berlin media voiced strong criticism, and even some of the foreign correspondents based there joined in. The route had been mapped out using a stopwatch and not with an instinct for what was important to Berlin, a local television news show complained. Even if the president would be able to hear the voices of the Berlin crowd, he would "not see the heartbeat of the city." The clock should be forgotten and "Berlin presented to the American president as it really is."[82] What had caused such anger? The itinerary highlighted symbols of the Cold War (the Wall, the now inaccessible Brandenburg Gate, Checkpoint Charlie, the Airlift Memorial); it included stops for contact with the trade unions and academic community (the Congress Hall, the FU); and it gave prominent part to the centers of political power (Schöneberg City Hall, U.S. military headquarters). The itinerary did not, however, make provision for Kennedy to see what many West Berliners thought he should. The route for the drive from Brandenburg Gate to Checkpoint Charlie had been chosen to save time. It bypassed the heart of West Berlin and the symbols of its postwar reconstruction and its flourishing urban life: the area stretching from the Bahnhof Zoo, the Kaiser Wilhelm Memorial Church, and the Kurfürstendamm to Ernst Reuter Platz. This was the section of the city that West Berliners felt reflected Berlin's new postwar identity and simply could not be excluded.

Suddenly, the planners of the president's trip were faced with a challenge that illustrates a fundamental dimension of diplomatic visits in the age of public opinion. The public wants to have a say about the locations and sites that foreign dignitaries will be seeing when they come on diplomatic visits. It wants to have an opportunity to present itself. In other words, the public wants its identity to be reflected in the political topography of such visits. The protest in Berlin in early June 1963 made clear that two aspects of diplomatic visits – namely, the presentation of select sites to the visitor and the self-representation of those being visited – could not be decoupled. A gap between the two would be a source of conflict. In the itinerary prepared by the German and American officials, an important facet of the West Berliners' self-image was missing, and the public wanted that facet to be visible. It was important to the West Berliners that the city's postwar reconstruction and revival be displayed against the backdrop of its total destruction, which was represented above all by the Kaiser Wilhelm Memorial Church, a modern church constructed within the ruins of an older one. It was not simply local patriotism that spurred the public's attachment to the Kaiser Wilhelm Memorial Church and the area around the Kurfürstendamm, the section of West Berlin that most impressively attested to its postwar rebirth as a center of entertainment, consumption, and technology. For years, the city worked to create an image of itself to project toward the East and the West alike. One French journalist explained the shortcomings of the itinerary and West Berliners' dissatisfaction with it by offering a comparison: having Kennedy follow the program as was now planned would be like showing a visitor Paris without taking him to the Champs-Elysées.[83]

Brandt and his press secretary Bahr immediately realized that Kennedy's motorcade would in effect bypass the West Berlin public even as it was driving through jubilant crowds. They now began to pressure the American authorities to reconsider the route. The Americans gave in. The total length of the trip was extended by thirty minutes and the motorcade route lengthened considerably to include much of the heart of the city. As a result of these changes, the north-to-east diagonal leading from Tegel Airport to the Brandenburg Gate now bulged westward. The motorcade would travel west along the Strasse des 17. Juni, cross Ernst Reuter Platz, head toward the Zoological Garden, continue down the Kurfürstendamm in the direction of the Kaiser Wilhelm Memorial Church, and then make its way to the Congress Hall. This was a triumph for the people of West Berlin. Even before the visit had begun, they had made their mark upon the topography of the trip (Illustration 16).

Parallel to the debate on the motorcade route there was discussion in the planning meetings of the script to be followed at the official arrival ceremony and the speech outside Schöneberg City Hall. On May 14, the *Berliner Zeitung*, an East Berlin newspaper, commented, not inaccurately, that Adenauer and Brandt were jockeying for the privilege of being the first to shake hands with Kennedy in Berlin.[84] Officials in West Berlin had initially assumed Adenauer would not be present. If he was to participate at all, the protocol department of the Berlin Senate wanted to limit him to an appearance at the city hall. The chancellor refused flat out to be shunted aside that way.[85] During a television interview in April, the chancellor emphasized that he thought it absolutely necessary to have the West German government represented in Berlin when Kennedy arrived there. The State Department thereafter found it hard to dispel the impression that the United

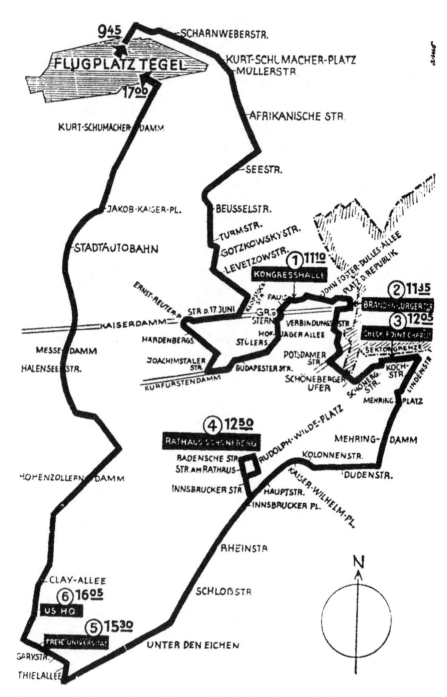

Illustration 16. Kennedy's route through West Berlin: Result of tedious negotiations and ultimately a triumphal procession from start to finish. Source: *Der Tagesspiegel*, Berlin, June 25, 1963.

States was against the participation of the chancellor.[86] Still, with Adenauer now planning to be at the airport to welcome Kennedy to Berlin, protocol for the arrival ceremony became truly tricky.

The legal question was whether the chancellor could greet the president on territory that, although closely tied to the Federal Republic, was not a part of the Federal Republic according to the Western Allies' and the Soviets' understanding of Berlin's legal status. This legal problem only added to the difficulties arising from the political issue of deciding whether the Christian Democratic chancellor or his Social Democratic rival should be singled out for attention. A decision in either's favor, both German camps assumed, would give his party a boost in the eyes of the public. The situation was still deadlocked just days before Kennedy's arrival. Neither Adenauer nor Brandt was willing to back down. The chancellor refused to be relegated to second place in the protocol. Adenauer instructed the Foreign Office to enter the protocol negotiations only on the firm assurance that he should be the first to greet Kennedy at Tegel Airport and the last to say farewell. Moreover, the chancellor wanted to address the planned rally at Schöneberg City Hall as the last and – in his mind – the most prominent speaker. He wanted to display the presence of the West German government in Berlin and thereby prove that West Berlin belonged to the Federal Republic. This is not to say that he held the same position as other conservatives who advocated making Berlin the capital of West Germany. Adenauer was not trying to reopen this entire issue and unseat Bonn as the capital.[87]

Adenauer was clearly trying to prevent the SPD from gaining prestige through Brandt's public appearances with Kennedy. With that objective in mind, strategists in Adenauer's CDU and its coalition partner, the Free Democratic Party (FDP), proposed that leaders of the two parties be sent to Berlin on June 26 in the company of the Bundestag president, Eugen Gerstenmaier. FDP head Erich Mende expressed his concern that Brandt might "steal the show" if the governing coalition were not more prominently represented in Berlin during Kennedy's visit.[88]

Brandt was not going to allow himself to be pushed aside. He was against Adenauer making any kind of public statement during the welcoming at Tegel and wanted to be the first to welcome the president. Like Adenauer, Brandt considered West Berlin a part of the Federal Republic, but he drew a very different conclusion from that premise than Adenauer. If West Berlin belonged to West Germany, he argued, it would be inconsistent to have the chancellor greet the president a second time. At the city hall, Adenauer should only be permitted to say a few words in closing. Brandt was willing, though, to entrust Adenauer with Kennedy's sendoff, since this would represent the official end of the president's trip to Germany as a whole.[89]

In the end, the thorny problems of protocol could only be worked out because the Western Allies stepped in to act subtly as "referees"[90] between Bonn and West Berlin. Their intervention provided a process for resolving problems of legality and status in international politics that could be applied beyond the specific case of Kennedy's visit. This process consisted of three elements: status flexibility, trust in compliance, and ceremonial innovation. The Western powers allowed the Germans to take precedence in matters of protocol without placing their special rights in Berlin in question. They granted the Federal Republic and West Berlin an unprecedented prominence on the political stage but did not depart from their interpretation of Berlin's Four-Power status. This required consultation among all participating actors and the confidence that all sides would comply with whatever was agreed upon and not try to exploit it as a legal precedent in the future. Agreement was facilitated, above all, by the extraordinary circumstances. The necessity of introducing ceremonial innovation was itself the solution. Only the acknowledgment that these were "unique and unprecedented circumstances," as the U.S. mission in Berlin wrote at the end of May, made it possible to bend existing rules and develop a new protocol.[91]

The agreements on the details of Kennedy's visit did more than just establish a protocol model that might prove useful in the future. The protocol the Western Allies and the West Germans settled upon brilliantly conveyed the main goals the Americans hoped to advance through Kennedy's visit. It demonstrated the solidarity within the Atlantic alliance and included France. It emphasized the transatlantic community and politically upgraded the West German partner without surrendering Allied claims in Berlin. One important factor behind the success of the new protocol was a change in the stage setting.

Even the spatial arrangements set out in the protocol were innovative, and they contributed to the resolution of the above-mentioned controversies (Illustration 17). Had the protocol officers arranged to have the Allied and German dignitaries stand in a row at the airport, as was customary, deciding

Illustration 17. A bird's-eye view of the arrangement drawn up by protocol planners for the arrival ceremony at the airport in West Berlin: As Kennedy descends the gangway, he is welcomed by German officials on his left and Allied dignitaries on his right – just as Willy Brandt suggested. At the end of the honor guard formation, which Kennedy inspects, stands a unit of West Berlin police. (Sketch found in Kennedy's travel papers.) Source: John F. Kennedy Library (John Fitzgerald Kennedy Papers, Presidential Papers, National Security Files, Trips & Conferences, Box 241, folder: President's Trip, Europe, 6/63–7/63, Germany, 6/11/63–7/12/63, folder 2 of 4).

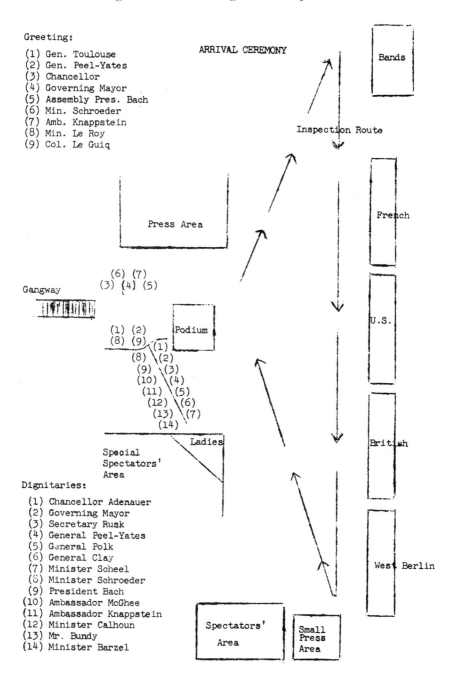

Greeting:

(1) Gen. Toulouse
(2) Gen. Peel-Yates
(3) Chancellor
(4) Governing Mayor
(5) Assembly Pres. Bach
(6) Min. Schroeder
(7) Amb. Knappstein
(8) Min. Le Roy
(9) Col. Le Guiq

ARRIVAL CEREMONY

Bands

Inspection Route

Press Area

French

(6) (7)
(3) (4) (5)

Gangway

U.S.

(1) (2)
(8) (9) (1)
(8) (2)
(9) (3)
(10) (4)
(11) (5)
(12) (6)
(13) (7)
(14)

Podium

Ladies

British

Special
Spectators'
Area

Dignitaries:

(1) Chancellor Adenauer
(2) Governing Mayor
(3) Secretary Rusk
(4) General Peel-Yates
(5) General Polk
(6) General Clay
(7) Minister Scheel
(8) Minister Schroeder
(9) President Bach
(10) Ambassador McGhee
(11) Ambassador Knappstein
(12) Minister Calhoun
(13) Mr. Bundy
(14) Minister Barzel

West Berlin

Spectators'
Area

Small
Press
Area

the precise order would have been much more difficult than usual. Brandt offered a simple yet ingenious solution: the German politicians would stand together in a small group to Kennedy's left as he came out of his plane and the Western military commanders would stand across from them to Kennedy's right. The order within each of these groups still had to be decided. In the end, Adenauer was the first in the German delegation to shake Kennedy's hand and the French commander the first of the Allied representatives. As a matter of fairness, Brandt was given the privilege of extending the official welcome to Kennedy instead of Adenauer. At Schöneberg City Hall, Kennedy was to be greeted by the president of the Berlin parliament, Otto Bach. Adenauer would be the second to speak, followed by the president. The last speaker would be Brandt. The official farewell at Tegel Airport was placed in Adenauer's hand: this detail had been uncontested from the outset of planning negotiations.

The placement of the protagonists on the Berlin stage was so important to Adenauer and Brandt that two matters of protocol preoccupied them for weeks. Kennedy was to tour Berlin, like the other German cities on his trip, in a convertible automobile. This is the clearest evidence that visibility, so important an aspect of Johnson's trip in 1961, was a primary concern in planning Kennedy's visit as well. It was assumed that the president would stand in the car so that he would be more visible to the crowds and could wave to them. Who would be allowed to accompany Kennedy in the car? How would they be positioned in the car? Such details would have been no more than curious footnotes to Kennedy's trip if those involved had not been so concerned about their practical political implications. The planners, consequently, had to deal with these details not as fine points of diplomatic etiquette but as political matters.

Several hours rubbing shoulders with the most powerful man on earth – that was political capital that Adenauer and Brandt were eager to exploit. Television and print coverage promised extensive public exposure. The way the two rivals were positioned in the car could possibly be interpreted as a reflection of each man's political importance. Let us turn straightaway to the results of the negotiations. The well-known image, taken from several angles, of confetti raining down on the president's car as it inches through the streets of Berlin has become iconic. In this image, both Brandt and Adenauer are standing next to Kennedy in the car, while the interpreter, Robert H. Lochner, sits in the back. The order of the politicians is surprising. The youngest of the three, Willy Brandt, is standing in the middle. The middle position is conventionally considered the most central and therefore the most important position. Since Brandt was also the tallest of the three, he automatically drew viewers' attention. Viewed head-on, the classic photo perspective, Adenauer stands on the right, which is considered the closing side according to art historian Heinrich Wölfflin.[92] Kennedy's position in the picture, the left, is generally considered a less prominent position, perhaps even the least prominent.

In planning the motorcade, the protocol department of the Berlin Senate first explored the possibility of excluding Adenauer completely, but the Foreign Office made it very clear that he would definitely be present. The diplomats proposed that Kennedy stand in the middle with the chancellor positioned on his left and Brandt on his right. Initially, Brandt wanted to have the position on the left. Deciding the placement was then complicated by a message from the Americans that Kennedy could not stand in the middle, but only on the right side of the car, where he would be able to brace himself during the strenuous drive. This was critical on account of his back problems. With that point settled, it then had to be decided who would stand in the middle. Brandt was very interested in being the central figure but made a point of not pressing the issue. He was, however, careful to point out that he spoke English and could explain things to Kennedy during the drive. Without actually saying so, Brandt was offering Bonn a deal: Adenauer could be the first in the German delegation to shake Kennedy's hand at Tegel if, in exchange, Brandt was given the middle spot in the presidential limousine. That arrangement was ultimately accepted by all sides.[93]

In addition to the stage directions for the sequence of the speakers and the positioning of the protagonists, there were other arrangements that needed to be made. Among them were the acoustic background, the backdrop and curtains, and the props. Each detail of the program was carefully planned because, on the one hand, the officials responsible were very sensitive to the possible political and legal nuances of such arrangements and, on the other, the public had high expectations for the visit. Particular attention was thus given to military uniforms, national anthems, and national flags, the classic symbols of national sovereignty.

The question of who would appear in uniform on stage was the easiest to answer. For legal reasons, the Bundeswehr was excluded. West Berlin was to be represented instead by its police force. The Western commanders would, of course, all appear in uniform. They commanded the troops stationed in the three western sectors and as such personified the military defense of the city. Their participation in Kennedy's visit was fully in keeping with the status quo in Berlin, where the British, French, and Americans regularly held military parades to celebrate their national holidays. Because Kennedy was to be welcomed with full honors even though he was not making an

Illustration 18. June 26, 1963 – A ceremonial innovation: Kennedy inspects the honor guard with French commander Edouard Toulouse (far left) during the military ceremony at Tegel Airport. West Berlin is represented by a police unit. Source: Landesarchiv Berlin.

official state visit, it was a matter of course that an honor guard of French, British, and American troops would await him at Tegel Airport. As a gesture of respect to Berlin, the honor guard included a unit of the municipal police at the end of the formation (Illustration 18).

The Berlin Senate was not interested, however, in playing up the Allied military presence. The West Berliners were not looking for Kennedy's visit to serve as a reminder of American military power, as Johnson's visit and Clay's appointment as special envoy had been. No one wanted to provoke the East. West Berlin had also become more self-confident in its dealings with the Western powers. The city wanted to be seen as a political actor in its own right and not merely as the needy beneficiary of Western protection. During the planning of Kennedy's visit, there was a suggestion to have troops march past Schöneberg City Hall during his stop there; the idea was quickly dropped.[94] The Allied commanders would, in any event, be readily visible throughout the visit on account of their protocolar status. The route to and from Tegel Airport provided the perfect means to give each his due. The French commander would inspect the honor guard at the airport with Kennedy; the British commander would accompany Kennedy to the

Congress Hall and the Brandenburg Gate; and the American commander would appear at Checkpoint Charlie. All three were to be present among the dignitaries next to Kennedy on the speakers' platform during his Schöneberg speech. Once again, the protocol arrangements would demonstrate Western unity.

Considerably more difficult to handle were the closely related problems of national anthems and flags, and they were resolved only days before Kennedy arrived. At first it was the French who insisted that national anthems be played during the arrival ceremony at Tegel. They knew that the "Marseillaise" would have to be played since Tegel was located in the French sector. The Americans and British could accept that. Brandt and Adenauer, in a rare instance of unity, insisted that if the Western Allies' anthems were played and their flags displayed at Tegel, the Federal Republic's anthem and flag would have to be included as well. The welcoming ceremony offered a rare opportunity for West Germany to display its new self-confidence. "We must insist on this in any case," asserted Dietrich Spangenberg, the head of the Berlin Senate chancery, following a meeting with the Foreign Offices' chief of protocol on May 9. At that point, it looked as if Bonn, Berlin, and the Western Allies were heading toward an agreement that would treat the anthem and flag of the Federal Republic on equal footing with those of Britain, France, and the United States.[95] From the German standpoint, that solution would have been the ultimate symbol that West Germany was a political equal of the Western powers. It would have represented yet another step on the path toward complete sovereignty. Moreover, it would have reinforced Bonn's position that West Berlin was part of the Federal Republic.

In the end, the legal experts in London, Paris, and Washington rejected the plan that had been drafted in Berlin. Instead of using the anthems and flags of all the states involved or playing only the French and American anthems,[96] the planners eventually decided that no national anthems would be played at the arrival ceremony. A band would instead strike up "Hail to the Chief." Kennedy would inspect an Allied honor guard and a formation of West Berlin police. The Federal Republic's flag would not appear on the policemen's uniforms. This protocol agreement was consistent with Berlin's special status, and, more importantly, it provided a way around the Allies' and the West Germans' differing interpretations of international law.

The last subject to be addressed was flags. Should the motorcade route be decorated with flags? Should the West Berlin government supply residents with German, American, and Berlin flags to wave as Kennedy drove by? The West Berlin Senate eventually decided against providing the public with flags. Its attitude was understandable given not only the city's status but also in light of the recent past.

The image of flag-waving crowds was all too familiar from the Nazi years as well as from present-day East Germany. The West Berlin planners shuddered at the thought of such a totalitarian touch. This was the main reason why the protocol planners opted for a policy of restraint and understatement in West Berlin. The Senate refrained from an extensive display of flags along Kennedy's route, except at Schöneberg City Hall. It did not urge city residents to wave or fly flags, as the Berlin CDU proposed in May. *Der Tagesspiegel*, a West Berlin daily, supported the Senate's restraint, contending that Germany suffered from a "flag complex." There was also the simple, practical problem, the paper added, that hardly anyone in Berlin owned a flag.[97] An interesting paradox thus arose. At the time, the U.S. mission was debating whether to order a large number of flags from a Berlin firm. The Americans wanted to see flags in the hands of cheering spectators and hanging in the streets and store windows, and they were willing to make them widely available. The Senate urgently requested them to abandon their plans, however, arguing that West Berliners wouldn't know what to make of such an unprecedented initiative. Several department stores and newspapers did end up selling or giving away paper flags; they went like hotcakes.[98]

The debate between the Germans and Americans over the display of flags clearly reflected the two countries' very different experiences with national symbols. In the United States, the public display of flags, particularly the national flag, was, and is, quite commonplace. It is encouraged by the government and educational institutions. The flag is considered an indubitable symbol of identification with the nation-state. In Germany, by contrast, flags long carried a totalitarian connotation in the post-Nazi period. National symbols were long used only sparingly in the Federal Republic. Foreign policy considerations prompted Bonn to limit the display of black-red-gold, the colors of the Federal Republic's flag, especially at large public events. Even domestically, the flag issue always provided occasion for critical debate on the import of symbols of collective identity. The fact that West Berliners waved to the American president with handkerchiefs more often than with flags was the result of a deliberate political decision and demonstrated the historical sensitivity of the responsible authorities in the Berlin Senate. Props say a great deal about a performance.

"TO SEE AND BE SEEN": VISIBILITY AND STREET POLITICS

All discussion of the plans for Kennedy's visit were ultimately concerned with one objective. Politicians in Germany and the United States realized that the visit of the American president would be a success only if it made the greatest possible public impact in Europe, the United States, and the world. None of the strategic calculations, none of the partisan wrangling for advantage, none of the symbolic gestures, and none of the staging would bear fruit if the public did not receive the intended message. In the age of mass media, with the rise of television in Germany, this meant that, above all, publicity had to be created by making the events and images of them highly visible. Indeed, the very reason for undertaking the trip in the first place was to enable the American president "to see – and be seen by as many Germans as possible."[99] This primacy of visibility had two important practical consequences. First, the planners had to provide the technical means to enable the actors to see and be seen. They had to rely on cooperation with the media, particularly with the television broadcasters. Second, the planners needed to create large public spaces in the city to accommodate all the Berliners who wanted to witness the event firsthand, to see for themselves. The streets of Berlin were the most important public space. Since the Berlin Senate and the American authorities found it politically advantageous to broadcast the picture of cheering crowds worldwide, they also had to control the crowds of spectators and impose certain security precautions for their own safety as well as the president's. A policy on managing the crowds was needed; we can call this policy street politics.

Three aims soon overrode all others during the planning phase of Kennedy's trip: to see, to be seen, and to publicize this visibility as much as possible throughout the world for the benefit of those not participating. These aims applied to all actors involved. The president was to see Berlin its people, its urban symbols, and its division by the Wall. He would peer into East Berlin from outside, having made the decision against seeing the eastern half of the city from inside. The people of Berlin were to see the president, the German politicians accompanying him, and symbolic gestures at critical spots in the city's topography, and they were to recognize themselves in the way the city was portrayed – at the Berlin Wall no less than on the Kurfürstendamm.

Moreover, the "ceremonial spectacle"[100] was to be made visible to everyone who could not be on the streets to watch the president drive by, an audience many times the size of the anticipated crowd. For the millions of people outside Berlin who were interested in the visit, the media coverage would be highly important. Since the Kennedy trip primarily conveyed itself in visual images, television and live coverage assumed a key role. The Kennedy trip is an early milestone in German television journalism, even if the black-and-white images seem unspectacular today. Americans were aware of the exceptional role played by television in the Old World. On

the very first day, the Associated Press reported that the greatest achievement of the trip would be Kennedy's appearance on television screens across
Europe.[101]

The days Kennedy spent in the Rhineland and Frankfurt attracted great
media attention. Nonetheless, the coverage of his day in Berlin on June
26 exceeded everything that had preceded it. More than 1,500 journalists,
local and foreign, were accredited to cover the event. Among them were
100 Washington-based White House correspondents. The White House
sent twenty of its own press staff.[102] Great effort to accommodate the press
was made at the Schöneberg City Hall. Its restaurant was transformed into a
state-of-the-art press center, fully equipped with modern typewriters (some
with American keyboards), carbon paper at all workstations, thirty telephone
booths, several teletype machines, television sets, and press kits. The guests
from the press were to be treated well: when the day was done, they had
worked their way through 4,540 sandwiches, 690 sausages, 987 bottles of
beer, 402 packs of cigarettes, and 23 bottles of whisky.[103]

Even through the haze of cigarette smoke and alcohol, the reporters in
the improvised press center could follow what was happening on Berlin's
streets thanks to the efforts of the television crews. During the second half
of the 1950s, West German television had developed into a mass medium
that offered viewers primarily a mix of variety shows, sports coverage, and
made-for-television dramas.[104] Kennedy's visit now gave the medium the
opportunity to score a coup in political news reporting. It broadcast the
whole of the event live with few interruptions. The presidential visit in
Berlin was so spectacular and promised such a large audience that the two
West German broadcasters, ARD and the recently established ZDF, decided
to broadcast jointly. More than 30 television cameras, including one portable
camera, were used. The multinational Eurovision agency provided coverage to fourteen countries. CBS provided the camera footage, moderated
by the sonorous voice of the journalist Daniel Schorr. CBS had more than
100 special correspondents, cameramen, and technicians working on the
Kennedy visit. Seventy million viewers in the United States could receive
the broadcast.[105] The guard towers at Checkpoint Charlie were structurally
reinforced so that cameras could be installed on their roofs. Several nonmedia
organizations were also filming the day's events. The United States Information Agency (USIA) put together a team of fifteen to record Kennedy's
visit on color film so that it could later be used for propaganda purposes.
The West Berlin police sent out more than a dozen officers armed with
cameras and hand-held film cameras to record any disturbances that might
occur.[106]

Illustration 19. The primacy of visibility – The observers being observed: Press photographers in front of Schöneberg City Hall. Source: Landesarchiv Berlin.

The primacy of visibility was most explicitly expressed in the intensive efforts of the protocol departments to provide the president a podium, in the literal sense of the word, on which to rise above the crowd at all major points along his route and whenever he got out of the car. Few technical matters received such attention from the very start as the construction of podiums, rostrums, and viewing platforms for Kennedy. The French authorities arranged for a small podium for the ceremony at Tegel Airport; the British erected a new viewing platform at the Brandenburg Gate; and the Americans built a new observation post at Checkpoint Charlie. An enormous speakers' platform was constructed directly in front of Schöneberg City Hall; the FU set up a rostrum in the courtyard of its Henry Ford Building; and a podium was set up at the American military headquarters. In addition, press platforms for camera crews were erected on Rudolph Wilde Platz opposite the speakers' platform in front of the city hall (Illustration 19).

Stands were not provided for the crowds along the motorcade route, so West Berliners created their own alternatives. Ladders were set up on the sidewalks, and construction cranes provided many spectators with good views. Balcony seats overlooking the street were highly sought after, just as at the opera. Clusters of people hung from balconies. It was reported that balcony spots were being offered for as much as DM 250.[107] When all else failed, people climbed up trees, flagpoles, and street signs or out onto the ledges and roofs of buildings. Like the specially built stands and platforms, these informal viewing spots attested that this was a day when everyone wanted to see everything. Everyone, including the reporters covering the visit, was simultaneously viewer and viewed. The cameras repeatedly scanned the crowds, and the spectators on the street watched the reporters and photographers in the motorcade passing by. But the participant who most impressively embodied the duality of seeing and being seen was the main figure, Kennedy himself. At the points where the GDR had set limits to visibility, the president was given binoculars to help him see or explanatory diagrams and pictures to show what he could not see.

On June 25, East German troops started to hang flags between the six large columns of the Brandenburg Gate. In the middle space, they hung the flag of the GDR between two solid red banners. The next day, huge signs in English were hastily erected in front of the Brandenburg Gate and Checkpoint Charlie that admonished Kennedy for allegedly failing to fulfill the promises made by his predecessors at the Yalta and Potsdam Conferences and that denounced Western militarism.[108] In response, the Berlin Senate briefly considered the idea of thwarting the GDR's propaganda efforts by having Kennedy view the Wall and East Berlin from one of the towers of the Reichstag. It was not possible, however, to change the program at such a late date.

East Berlin also filmed and photographed Kennedy whenever he was in the vicinity of the Wall. Paralleling the preparations underway on a larger scale in the western half of the city, a platform for camera crews was erected between the Brandenburg Gate and the Wall. Photographers and cameramen stood on the Brandenburg Gate and pointed their photo lenses westward. With its film teams, flags, and placards, the GDR was also engaging in the politics of visibility. The strategies the Cold War rivals employed in this competition for visibility mirrored their opposing political strategies. The West German and American governments strove to maximize visibility in all directions, but they did set some limits. Kennedy did not wish to see the Eastern half of the city from within. The press and information office of the West German government was adamantly opposed to accrediting any East German journalists to cover the president's visit.[109] The GDR also wanted to see and be seen, but, paradoxically, to be seen it had to block Kennedy's view of the East. It created additional limitations to visibility beyond those imposed by the Berlin Wall. When the president looked eastward, he would see the GDR's national symbols and its political declarations. The politics of visibility during Kennedy's visit was the Cold War in miniature.

The clearest symbol of the primacy of visibility during Kennedy's visit and of the visit's importance as a media event was the president's motorcade. The Lincoln convertible in which Kennedy, Brandt, and Adenauer rode was of critical importance. It epitomized the dual see-and-be-seen experience. The U.S. mission in Berlin had insisted before the visit that the president spend "as much of the day as possible" in Berlin driving through the city in order to "be seen by the maximum number of West Berliners . . . and to see for himself the actual situation in West Berlin."[110] The motorcade comprised thirty-eight vehicles. Nine cars chauffeured the political guests and their subordinates. They were followed by eight vehicles, mainly buses, filled with members of the press. The professional observers thereby became subjects of observation for the spectators. The photos of Kennedy, Brandt, and Adenauer in the open limousine attest to the conspicuous presence of the media. Behind the president's limousine and the Secret Service vehicle towered the first press bus, packed with American, West German, and West Berlin journalists.

The many head-on photos of the president's car were taken by the press photographers who were crowded together on a bleacher-like structure mounted on the cargo bed of a large trailer driving just ahead of the presidential limousine. So what did Kennedy, Brandt, and Adenauer see? To their right and left they saw the cheering crowds of West Berliners. Directly in front of them, they saw Berlin's broad avenues – but above all else, the lenses of the photographers and cameramen. These professional observers sought to capture on film each reaction of the curiously arranged trio and thereby fulfill the three leaders' express wish to be seen as well as to see.

During the planning phase there had never been a doubt that Kennedy would spend most of his visit being driven through the city. The streets along the motorcade's route thus became an important public arena. On the day of the visit, more than one million people filled this 33-mile-long public space. The streets Kennedy drove through constituted the largest political stage Germany had seen since the war. Likewise, the audience that gathered along them was the largest that had turned out for a political event since the founding of the Federal Republic. From the outset, government officials in Berlin and Washington had expected and hoped for a massive turnout. They worked to ensure that a "maximum number of Berliners" would see the president.[111] This created a massive problem. The city could not simply allow hundreds of thousands of people to stream into the streets, especially if many of them were in a highly emotional state.

The public was not just a passive backdrop to Kennedy's visit; it assumed an active role in the staging of the visit. The political parties and trade unions, in a rare case of unified action, called upon the public to give Kennedy a big reception. The unions even succeeded in getting workers and civil servants several hours off on June 26. Many department stores and businesses closed of their own accord to give their employees and customers the chance to go see the president. Even certain occupational groups, such as bakers and butchers guilds took the afternoon off. Schools were closed for the day. As the *Berliner Morgenpost*, summarized, Kennedy was to "see as much as possible and be seen by as many as possible."[112] It was precisely this effort that made it necessary to implement a policy of crowd control. For the planners, this meant the residents of Berlin were not only to be mobilized; they also had to be kept in check, and that would require the authority of the state. Mobilization of the public could not be undertaken without preventative disciplinary measures.

Kennedy's visit was by no means the first time the streets of Berlin served as a political arena. As Alf Lüdtke, Thomas Lindenberger, and Belinda Davis have shown, the streets of Berlin were a favored public space from the 1890s through the end of the First World War and beyond.[113] A multifold political and symbolic use of the streets developed that allowed both oppositional demonstrations by the working classes and displays of power by the crown and court. The government deemed it necessary to control and regulate life on the streets. Thomas Lindenberger has described these efforts as *Strassenpolitik*, street politics. According to Lindenberger, street politics includes both the perspective of the ruling class from above as well as that of the entire society from below. It can be defined as "the *prevention* initiated locally *by police* against what appears to the authorities to be a constantly lurking and ever-present danger to *public order*, while at the same time the preferentiality given to certain street spaces for the symbolic representation of estate-feudal elements in the state and societal order."[114]

Political and social circumstances in Berlin had changed considerably since the Imperial era. The West Berlin of 1963 was no longer home to either an emperor or an urban proletariat. Its police commissioner no longer sent his men off to do battle with rebelling workers and Social Democrats. We could continue to list the historical differences. The concept of street politics nonetheless helps us in analyzing and understanding how politics was orchestrated during the Cold War, how the ceremonial representation of state and the local population interacted, and how this interaction was directed and controlled. In 1963, the streets of Berlin presented themselves as a public space in which the presence of crowds mobilized for the event put pressure on the authorities to exercise a degree of control. The authorities aimed to strike a balance between the display of emotion and the maintenance of order at the very least and, if possible, to reconcile the two. For this purpose, the West Berlin police, in consultation with the Western powers, had to design a general plan of action and undertake its largest deployment of officers ever.

Over twenty-six days, a special team at police headquarters conducted a total of forty-eight meetings with representatives of all the agencies and organizations involved in maintaining public safety and security.[115] On June 26, Berlin was put on "major alert" (*Grosse Alarmstufe*). Seven thousand regular police officers were on duty, backed up by approximately 2,000 uniformed volunteers from police reserves. The Berlin Senate and the Western powers had specially authorized this expanded police mobilization. The immediate personal safety of the president was the responsibility of the Secret Service, and special security measures, too numerous to list in full, were also taken. For example, the number of vehicles escorting the motorcade was several times larger than that customarily prescribed by protocol. Along the motorcade route, 114 potentially dangerous points, such as bridges and abandoned buildings, were placed under special police guard. The police used more than ten miles of tape and three miles of barricades to cordon off sections of the motorcade route. There were also divers in the rivers and canals, and a helicopter kept watch overhead.

Prominent West Berliners and West German politicians joined in calling on the public to give Kennedy a warm welcome.[116] But the officials responsible for planning the visit recognized the risk posed by a large, highly emotional crowd. Their concern went beyond the usual consideration for maintaining public order and safety. Emotionally charged masses pose the danger of uncontrolled behavior. That was a political problem. Emotions were welcome if they expressed a positive attitude toward Kennedy. No one in West Berlin needed to worry about this. Of course, it was necessary to protect Kennedy. However, it was more important to protect him from the exuberant wave of positive emotion expressed by Berliners than from the danger of a negative reaction or even assassination. The overriding concern was that Kennedy would be "crushed by the far too ardent displays of friendship."[117] Indeed, the people who swarmed the presidential limousine as it drove by did not have weapons in their hands; they had bouquets and even, in one instance, a freshly baked cake (which ended up with Foreign Minister Schröder).[118]

Popular emotions are harmful not only when they result in injury to people or damage to property. They are also politically unwelcome when they spur the crowd to violence against political symbols, whether of their own state or of a rival state. In the case of Berlin, that effect could endanger the precarious status quo. An outbreak of violence would damage West Berlin's self-image as a peaceful outpost of the free world. It could only give the GDR an excuse to impose new repressive measures and to denounce the West for warmongering. The events following the erection of the Berlin Wall and the death of Peter Fechter had been warning signals. Another came just one week before Kennedy was to arrive in West Berlin. Following the official rally in front of Schöneberg City Hall commemorating the tenth anniversary of the June 17, 1953, uprising in the GDR, more than one thousand young people marched to the Friedrich Strasse checkpoint. There, they clashed with West Berlin police, who used water cannons to break up the demonstration and to prevent the marchers from storming the Wall.[119]

As after Peter Fechter's death in 1962, West Berlin officials faced a paradoxical situation: they had to take precautions to guard the Wall against attacks by residents of the western half of the city.[120] The danger inherent in this inversion of the Cold War status quo was glaringly clear to the leading advocate of a new policy of coexistence with the East. Mayor Willy Brandt had learned a lesson from the events of 1961–62. Enthusiasm had an important part in politics, but it had to be controlled, and responsibility for providing the necessary control fell to him. In the final days prior to Kennedy's arrival, Brandt warned the citizens of West Berlin repeatedly against "uncontrollable emotions" and "unrestrained advances."[121]

The politics of visibility needed to be reconciled with crowd control. Brandt expressly sought to prevent the crowd from displaying banners at the main rally in front of the city hall.[122] The municipal government, as the sponsor of the event, did not want to lose control over the way it was interpreted. The police chief went a step further and addressed himself directly to the public in an appeal that was also distributed as a leaflet. Kennedy's visit was to take a "dignified and undisturbed course." No one should allow strangers "asking for a place at the window" into their apartment. Suspicious "troublemakers" in the crowd were to be reported. Cars parked along the motorcade route would be towed away. Special regulations announced through the media were to be observed. Last but not least: no floral bouquets were to be thrown from windows.[123] The public did not fully comply with the bouquet ban, and, more importantly, it took advantage of a police oversight. The regulations said nothing about confetti, so on June 26 Kennedy and his motorcade were showered with paper.

In their attention to questions of security and crowd control, the officials planning the president's visit did not take into account West Berliners' *Eigensinn*.[124] Following Alf Lüdtke, I use *Eigensinn* to denote the self-reliant behavior of individuals and crowds, their use of body, language, and social action to pursue their needs and to express their wish to shape social relations. *Eigensinn* is not simply stubbornness or willfulness, although the term is often translated that way. During Kennedy's visit, West Berliners manifested their *Eigensinn* by disregarding the rules city officials had tried to impose, but they were not trying to express opposition or resistance to either their government or the American guest. Quite the contrary: as I will show in Chapter 4, West Berliners' determination to articulate their enthusiasm for Kennedy converged with the political aims of the governments involved. Their exercise of *Eigensinn* demonstrated that the audience had an active part in the political performance that was staged in Berlin and, in fact, contributed in an unexpected way to the creation of the lasting image of the jubilant crowd that received the visitor from America.

3

Dramatic Climax

At 9:40 on the morning of June 26, 1963, the Boeing 707 carrying the American president touches down on the runway at Tegel Airport,[1] and the final act of his trip to Germany begins. The date for the long-awaited performance has been set for three months. The stage has been undergoing preparation for weeks. Behind the scenes, there has been hard-nosed haggling over the script, the stage setting, and the props. The main actors have been briefed about their roles over and over again. Now the time has come for the performance. The curtain parts on the Berlin stage, and the spectators begin to watch the dramatic climax of the trip. They are seeing the final act of a political play. With each symbolic detail, this play dramatizes the division of Europe and the power politics of the Cold War. It reflects the situation within the Western alliance as well as the transnational community building that links the West Berliners and the Americans. At the end of the day, several journalists will describe this performance as the "greatest show on earth" and declare that it surpassed even the triumphal processions of ancient Rome.[2]

One of the subtle ironies of Kennedy's visit to West Berlin is that it begins and ends in the French sector. As a result, Kennedy is first welcomed to the city by the commander from the country that he deliberately flew around on his journey to Germany because the French president had been causing him so much trouble. The time and place of Kennedy's arrival have been selected for their own historical relevance: the Berlin Airlift began on this day fifteen years earlier, and Tegel Airport was built to accommodate the transport aircraft arriving in Berlin from the West. Today, June 26, 1963, three other airplanes, carrying reporters and the president's entourage, arrive in Berlin ahead of Air Force One. The members of the press do not want to miss anything. The performance begins punctually, and the actors carefully follow the stage directions that the planners have been working on almost until curtain time.

Kennedy is greeted next by Adenauer, who arrived the previous evening and now stands on the tarmac to the left, from Kennedy's perspective, of the gangway. Kennedy then greets Brandt and the president of the Berlin parliament, Otto Bach. Standing to the president's right, the Allied dignitaries await their turn to be presented. A salute is fired and a band begins to play the traditional presidential welcome "Hail to the Chief." The French commander, General Edouard Toulouse, accompanies Kennedy in his inspection of the honor guard, at the end of which stands a unit of Berlin police. There are no national anthems, and the welcoming speeches are kept short. RIAS director Robert H. Lochner is with the delegation on the small podium at the airport. He will act as translator for the president throughout the entire day, except for the speech given at the Schöneberg City Hall.[3]

Then it is Brandt's turn to say a few words of welcome. Like Adenauer's first words to Kennedy three days before, Brandt's opening lines include a political message more substantial than standard ceremonial rhetoric. Here in Berlin, the mayor says, no one expects to hear renewed reassurances of guarantees already given – "we trust our friends."[4] This is a sideswipe aimed at Adenauer and his persistent distrust of Washington. Brandt wants to emphasize instead the special role that West Berliners play as Americanized Germans and their close, direct relations to the United States.

In response, Kennedy repeats Brandt's reference to the joint appearance of all three Western powers. He then pays tribute, as he will do several times in the course of the day, to Lucius D. Clay as "an old veteran of this frontier" – meaning the border between West and East – and in so doing links West Berlin to American national myth and the promise of freedom associated with the idea of the frontier.[5] Fully aware of the extraordinary symbolic role Clay plays in Berlin, Kennedy himself had sent the general to the divided city as a special envoy in the autumn of 1961. He has now invited Clay and labor leader George Meany to accompany him to Berlin. It is a noble gesture and an absolute must in the eyes of West Berliners, for they revere Clay. As a symbol of American support for Berlin, Clay has an important part to play in the commemorative politics planned for June 26, 1963. In 1949, Berlin named a major avenue after Clay; in 1962, it made him an honorary citizen. Today, his presence in Berlin alongside Kennedy serves to link the first generation of American Berliners and the new guard in Washington associated with the president.

To some observers, the welcoming ceremony appears formal and businesslike.[6] Then, however, the delegation leaves the restricted area at the airport to the melody of the popular local song *"Berliner Luft"* and enters the public space of the Berlin streets. Kennedy sees an urban landscape very different from those he had seen on two short visits to Berlin many years before. The first visit took place in late August 1939, when the young John F. Kennedy stopped for a few days in Berlin after a trip to Prague. Hitler's army was preparing to invade Poland, and officials at the American embassy knew it. The chargé d'affaires gave Kennedy a secret message to pass on to his father, who was then serving as the U.S. ambassador to Great Britain, stating that war would break out within a week. Nearly six years later, in late July 1945, Kennedy was again in Berlin, this time as an American press correspondent. Berlin lay in ruins. The German attack on Poland had turned into a world war that American intervention had helped bring to an end. Surveying the destruction, Kennedy thought it unlikely Berlin would ever become a major metropolis again and predicted that "it will be many years before Berlin can clear the wreckage and get the material to rebuild."[7] Now, eighteen years later, Kennedy sees a thriving and almost entirely rebuilt city.

The car in which the president, Brandt, and Adenauer are riding is decorated with the banner flags of West Germany and the United States. As the motorcade leaves Tegel Airport, a "storm of enthusiasm" hits the lead automobile "like a wallop," as one newspaper reports.[8] People are tightly packed along the sides of the streets. They hang from trees, write Berlin journalists, "stand on flatbed trucks and gas station roofs and wave whatever they can to show their enthusiasm: flags, welcome signs, umbrellas, poster-size photos, and even snow-white bedsheets."[9] If they are fortunate enough to have garnered a good spot in the crowd or a safe place to stand on a balcony, the people see the bright white uniform jackets of the motorcycle police escort, the truck carrying the photographers, which nearly blocks the view of the president's limousine, and then – often only for seconds – the blue Lincoln convertible with Kennedy, Brandt, and Adenauer. The haggling over who would stand where is now forgotten. The spectators cheer and chant the now-famous chorus of "Ken-Ne-Dy."

The motorcade route crosses Kurt Schumacher Platz, passes the Westhafen docks, and proceeds through the industrial neighborhood of Moabit. At the dockyards, construction workers wave from a gigantic construction crane. Television viewers watching the live broadcast cannot follow the entire procession because contact with the relay stations is repeatedly interrupted despite the use of the most modern wireless cameras available, as commentators never tire of pointing out. Still, the people sitting in front of television sets, like the hundreds of thousands on the streets, see something that is entirely missing from the photos of Kennedy, Adenauer, and Brandt together in the limousine: they see the visual dominance of the press photographers massed on the truck driving directly in front of the limousine who are keeping their camera lenses trained on Kennedy.[10] The photographers themselves thus become a part of the procession and one of the attractions. The same holds true for the buses filled with reporters following the presidential limousine; like Kennedy, the reporters now wave to the people lining the streets.

As the crowd cheers without pause, the motorcade crosses the Spree River and turns into the Hansa Quarter. This side trip is a politically symbolic act in many respects. Kennedy is shown a West Berlin landmark that helps the city distance itself from National Socialism and East German socialism. The Hansa Quarter represents architecturally the integration of West Germany and West Berlin into the West. Most of the buildings had been built for the International Building Exhibition held in West Berlin in 1957. Several internationally renowned architects worked on the project, including Le Corbusier, Walter Gropius, Oscar Niemeyer, and Hans Scharoun. The quarter features modern housing blocks of various sizes and extensive green space. The buildings are not arranged along a central axis or around a fixed center point. The Hansa Quarter is an experimental development and a showcase of West Berlin's new architectural internationalism. It reconnects the Federal Republic and Berlin with pre-1933 German architectural traditions that were forced into exile, such as the Bauhaus. It also combines these traditions with new architectural developments coming from the United States, France, Finland, and other countries. At the same time, the quarter is a product of the Cold War. It is the liberal opposite of East Berlin's more monumental, more tightly organized Stalinallee.[11]

Once the motorcade has passed the Hansa Quarter, it does not head directly to the Congress Hall. It turns right onto the Strasse des 17. Juni, the boulevard named in commemoration of the insurrection in East Germany in 1953, circles around Ernst Reuter Platz, and drives to Bahnhof Zoo, West Berlin's main train station, thus making the loop West Berliners had demanded earlier in the month. In the political topography of the city, this loop represents the postwar Berlin exemplified by the modern glass and steel office buildings around Ernst Reuter Platz. Reflecting the optimism of city planners at the time, the press kit describes the square as a "point

Illustration 20. Politics of identity and triumphant Berliners: As a result of public pressure, the official route of the presidential motorcade includes a swing past the Kranzler-Eck via the Kurfürstendamm. Source: Landesarchiv Berlin.

of intersection generously dispersed with waterworks and green spaces."[12] Along the way, Kennedy also passes Amerika Haus, the U.S. information center in Berlin that opened in 1957.

The motorcade enters the heart of West Berlin, a section of the city that the planners of the visit, owing to public protest, could not exclude from Kennedy's itinerary. The column of cars turns right just beyond the tracks of the Bahnhof Zoo onto Joachimstaler Strasse and crosses the Kurfürstendamm – the long shopping street some Berliners think of as their Broadway – at the corner where the landmark Café Kranzler stands (Illustration 20). At this point, the press notes "great surges . . . of enthusiasm. . . . The old Kranzler corner has certainly never experienced anything like this in its long history."[13] Pink confetti rains down upon the motorcade as postwar Berlin, trying to recapture some of the bustle and glamour of the Weimar era, presents itself as a center of consumption and entertainment. Decorations for the just-ended thirteenth International Film Festival enhance the stage setting for Kennedy's visit. Turning left onto Kurfürstendamm, the motorcade heads to Breitscheidplatz, past the Kaiser Wilhelm Memorial Church.

It is one of only two memorial sites on Kennedy's route that explicitly recall the period of National Socialism and the Second World War. The historical emphasis of this trip is clearly another era, namely, the Cold War.

From Breitscheidplatz, the motorcade heads toward the intersection of avenues known as the Great Star, in the middle of which stands the Victory Column, a Prussian military memorial. It then proceeds down the John Foster Dulles Allee – named after Eisenhower's long-serving secretary of state – and arrives at the Congress Hall at eleven o'clock. The hall, a pendant to the Hansa Quarter, was also constructed as part of the Berlin International Building Exhibition of 1957. Eleanor Dulles, an enthusiastic supporter of Berlin, had been a particularly active advocate of this building. The daring, sweeping roof is meant to symbolize the liberality and cosmopolitanism of the West. As a meeting facility, the Congress Hall represents West Berlin's new role as a forum for intercultural communication. In 1960, the Congress for Cultural Freedom celebrated its tenth anniversary here.[14] With regard to its structural stability, even contemporaries noted that the prestressed-concrete construction was risky. Indeed, the roof of the Congress Hall collapsed in May 1980. The Congress Hall was subsequently rebuilt; the exterior design was preserved, but the roof was reengineered. Officially renamed the House of World Cultures, the building remains known to Berliners as the "pregnant oyster" (*Schwangere Auster*).

On the day of Kennedy's visit, the Congress Hall stands quite firm. The president is to appear before the sixth national congress of the Industrial Trade Union of Construction Workers (Illustration 21).[15] The efforts of George Meany have proven successful. For the first time, a Western head of state is officially visiting a German labor congress. By attending this event, Kennedy becomes part of the special relationship between the German and American labor movements in the city where those relations are closest. The slogan displayed on the front wall of the auditorium expresses faith in the capitalist promise of prosperity for all: "We build homes, factories, schools. We are also building a better future" (*Wir bauen Häuser Fabriken Schulen. Wir bauen auch an einer glücklichen Zukunft*). The slogan would not have been worded much differently in the GDR, but on this day no one in the Congress Hall takes note of this similarity. Quite the opposite: in his opening remarks, Georg Leber draws a sharp contrast between the independent unions in the West and the government-organized unions in the East. This contrast will be a recurring motif throughout the congress. Welcoming the special guest, Leber presents Kennedy with a bouquet of flowers that had been picked in East Berlin. This is hardly a spontaneous gesture: the bouquet had

Illustration 21. Success of the Berlin lobby: Kennedy addresses the trade union convention in the Congress Hall; George Meany sits to the right of Brandt. Source: Landesarchiv Berlin.

been procured well in advance and turned over to the Secret Service to be checked.[16]

The president cordially thanks his host and gives – without even a glance at the manuscript in front of him – a short and rhetorically polished speech. He praises the role of labor unions in the democratic world. One sentence in particular sticks with his audience: "West Berlin is my country." Naturally Kennedy is not talking about an "outright annexation" of the city by the United States, as the East German newspaper *Neues Deutschland* reports to its readership the next day.[17] Kennedy is merely using a personal declaration to reemphasize the message that his visit is meant to symbolize, a message with more weight than any of the political actions taken before or after this trip: West Berlin is America's Berlin. The city belongs to the liberal democratic order that the United States sees itself exemplifying and defending in the ideological competition of the Cold War. In making this declaration, the president is rewording a sentence taken from a longer quote by Benjamin Franklin that is on display in the Congress Hall.[18] *Neues Deutschland*'s commentary notwithstanding, this stop on Kennedy's program receives little attention and is quickly forgotten.

Kennedy makes no official statements from the time he leaves the stage at the Congress Hall until he appears at the city hall in Schöneberg. The script prohibits speeches. There is a political reason for this official silence. The main character is deliberately silent at the locations where he experiences "moments charged with drama."[19] During the ninety minutes between the two appearances, Kennedy goes to the Berlin Wall, the most charged point of contact between the Cold War adversaries. On this politically delicate stretch of his route, the president remains silent except for hushed conversations with the officials accompanying him. Yet his silence speaks volumes. The president knows that each syllable out of his mouth is being transmitted worldwide and could, counter to his intention, exacerbate the East-West conflict. It is one of the ironies of this trip that the president will abandon this caution as soon as he has left the Wall. While still under the emotional impact of experiencing the Wall, he will stray from the script during his most important speech in the city and thus make himself very vulnerable to all sorts of misunderstanding.

However, that is jumping ahead. At this point, the motorcade is moving from the Congress Hall, past the back of the Soviet War Memorial in the eastern section of the Tiergarten and past the Reichstag building. The Soviet War Memorial is dedicated to the Red Army soldiers who died during the extremely bloody battle for Berlin in April and May of 1945. A massive statue of a Red Army soldier towers over a curved row of columns flanked by two field cannons and two T34 tanks. The Soviet War Memorial is built of stone blocks taken from the ruins of Hitler's chancellery and was dedicated in November 1945. The posting of Soviet soldiers to guard the memorial is one of the few remaining vestiges of Four-Power governance. It would not have occurred to anyone involved in planning Kennedy's visit to suggest the president stop here. Not stopping is also an act of symbolic politics (Illustration 22). The Cold War mentality and the city's immediate postwar experiences with Soviet soldiers, who were responsible for many rapes, prevent the West from considering honoring the fallen Red Army soldiers.[20] Nor does the motorcade stop at the Reichstag. Evoking the Imperial era, the former parliament building has no symbolic value for postwar German-American relations.

At 11:45 a.m., the presidential limousine drives out of the Tiergarten and into the square in front of the Brandenburg Gate (Illustration 23). For the second time today, Kennedy gets out of the car. He climbs the stairs of the new observation platform built by the British. Brandt and Adenauer follow him. Now, for the very first time, Kennedy is faced with problems in seeing, with limits to visibility. As noted earlier, the East German government had

Illustration 22. A Cold War exclusion: The presidential motorcade drives by the Soviet War Memorial without stopping. Source: Landesarchiv Berlin.

Illustration 23. Limits to visibility: Kennedy appears in front of the curtained Brandenburg Gate within sight of cameras on both sides of the Wall. Source: Landesarchiv Berlin.

hung large flags between the columns of the Brandenburg Gate and thereby blocked the view of landmark boulevard Unter den Linden from the west. Using a diagram, General David Peel Yates, the commander of the British garrison, explains the topography to Kennedy. The president wants to know where the Hotel Adlon had stood; he spent a few nights there in 1939.[21] A swarm of journalists has gathered in the square by now. Their sole interest is to see how Kennedy reacts to the Wall and to hear what he says. Their curiosity goes unsatisfied, for the program planners have made sure there are no microphones on the platform. Everyone feels the "pregnant silence." Low voices are heard on the observation platform, and not a sound is heard from "over there," the East. A few journalists think they see Kennedy display the "typical aloofness" for which he is known.[22] Others describe his facial expression as "deadly serious."[23]

From the Brandenburg Gate, the motorcade drives again past the Soviet War Memorial, passing the front side this time, and turns left. The West Berlin Philharmonic, designed by Hans Scharoun, comes into view. Across Potsdamer Strasse, then along a stretch of the Landwehr Canal, again northeast past the ruins of the Anhalter Bahnhof, the motorcade follows a zigzag route dictated by the division of the city. Not far from the intersection of Koch Strasse and Friedrich Strasse, the visitors get out of the car and walk to Checkpoint Charlie past a large honor guard made up of American troops and West Berlin police. It is nearly noon. Kennedy stops just short of the white line demarcating the boundary between West and East Berlin. The American commander, General James H. Polk, now assumes the role of political tour guide. He accompanies Kennedy, Adenauer, Brandt, and several other political guests as they climb onto a new wooden platform constructed for the occasion.

The East German leadership has set up billboards at Checkpoint Charlie. Otherwise, the view into the East is unhindered. At a distance one can see small groups of East Berliners, and the echo of their calls of greeting can be heard. Reporters notice a sign on the eastern side of Lindenstrasse reading "We welcome Kennedy also on behalf of East Berliners."[24] The president is photographed and filmed by East German border guards. Unlike the face-off of October 1961, when Clay and his Soviet counterparts ranged their tanks barrel to barrel across the line of demarcation, it is now only camera lenses that take aim at each other. Despite the drama of this trip, this change marks a degree of de-escalation in the East-West confrontation. Other details make this clear as well. Shortly before Kennedy arrived at the checkpoint, the normal business of border-crossing had been fully underway. Just an hour before, an old man with a wheelbarrow had pulled weeds in the strip of Eastern territory between the Wall and the observation platform. The Americans had actually asked the East German authorities to have the area weeded so that even the sinister border would be telegenic.[25]

Again the journalists are anxious to see how the president will react to the Wall. Everyone agrees that the trip to Checkpoint Charlie makes a particularly strong impression on Kennedy. "The usual radiant smile has disappeared from Kennedy's face." Now "he suddenly seems completely different; his mouth is firmly shut and the lips are tightly pressed together."[26] The Wall marks a boundary to the liberal vision behind Kennedy's New Frontier. The unyieldingness of this border has an effect on him. Kennedy "was not smiling as he left the Wall," summarized an NBC television report; "It seemed obvious that the president had been emotionally aroused by what he had seen." Kennedy later says that he actually did not see much at the Wall. Still, observers feel that the trip to the Berlin Wall "moved him deeply."[27] His body language, speechlessness, and serious facial expression indicate that the president is now experiencing what his public has gone through the past three days and what Adenauer pointed out in his very first dinner speech in Bonn. Kennedy himself has been stirred emotionally. This emotional surge will discharge a little over an hour after Kennedy's stop at Checkpoint Charlie, during his speech at Schöneberg City Hall. Before that point comes, however, he must first travel several miles through cheering throngs. Much to the horror of the Secret Service agents, Kennedy does not immediately return to the car at the corner of Friedrich Strasse and Koch Strasse. Instead he spends a few minutes with the cheering crowd, shaking the hands of waiting West Berliners.

Shortly after 12:30, the presidential limousine continues southward through the neighborhood of Kreuzberg to Schöneberg, where West Berlin's city hall is located. On the way, it passes two other architectural symbols of American support for Berlin in the Cold War: the American Memorial Library and the Airlift Memorial at the northwest corner of Tempelhof Airport. The memorial, designed by Eduard Ludwig, features three cement ribs curving upward to the west that symbolize the air corridors through which life-sustaining goods were flown into the western sectors of Berlin between June 1948 and May 1949. On Dudenstrasse, the crowds can no longer be contained. "Just like in New York," confetti is thrown and "the entire parade stops," comments one television reporter (Illustration 24).[28] The crowd's enthusiasm knows no bounds. Many want to touch Kennedy, and the presidential limousine fills quickly with confetti and flowers. Finally, the delegation reaches the rear of the Schöneberg City Hall.

Illustration 24. "Just like in New York": Confetti and paper streamers rain down on the presidential motorcade during the triumphal procession through West Berlin. Source: Harry S. Truman Library.

STRAYING FROM THE SCRIPT: THE SPEECH AT
THE SCHÖNEBERG CITY HALL

In the mayor's office, the president enjoys his first short break since his arrival in Berlin three hours earlier. Refreshments are served. Adenauer entertains himself at Brandt's desk by reading *Neues Deutschland*, East Germany's party-line newspaper. Protocol officials and security agents, interpreters, and advisors mill around.[29] Excitement is mounting. Outside, in the absolutely packed Rudolph Wilde Platz, the square in front of the city hall, the "cheering and exuberant crowd" can be heard.[30] Kennedy confers one last time with his national security advisor, McGeorge Bundy, and both of his interpreters, Robert H. Lochner and Heinz Weber (Illustration 25). The president reads through the small index cards on which the text of his speech is typed. He makes a few final additions by hand, and they will turn out to be pivotal. The president and the rest of the delegation then head out the door toward the speaker's platform in front of the city hall.

Shortly after 1 p.m., Kennedy, Adenauer, and Brandt mount the platform. At the sight of the three men "a thunderous roar breaks out." The crowd

Illustration 25. Final consultation before "*Ich bin ein Berliner*": (Left to right) National Security Advisor McGeorge Bundy, interpreter Heinz Weber, and President John F. Kennedy. Source: Landesarchiv Berlin.

cheers, waves, and cries out "Ken-Ne-Dy!"[31] People have been waiting here for hours. Some had even camped out on the square the night before in order to secure a good view. The enormous crowd extends beyond the square far down the side streets. The live radio coverage of the day's events so far has been broadcast over speakers set up around the square. The political acoustics have thus been taken care of. Fourteen months earlier, when Robert F. Kennedy was in Berlin, several people in the crowd had called out: "Bobby, Johnny should come too!" Now Johnny is here, waving again and again to the crowd.[32] It is estimated that as many as 450,000 people are in the square. Beyond all doubt, Kennedy's appearance at Schöneberg City Hall is the highpoint of the Berlin program, if not of the entire trip to Germany.[33]

The public senses the significance of the moment. The crowd cheers repeatedly. The speeches – the only portion of the official program directed at the public – are held up by the cheering. Thousands of spectators wave handkerchiefs; very few have flags – just as the Berlin Senate wanted. Some Berliners have disregarded the ban on signs and posters. One sign reads "Welcome Jonny," enthusiasm getting the better of orthography. The Berlin public has again demonstrated its self-reliance and initiative – in other words,

Eigensinn – by not backing away from a confrontation with government officials in defending its interests. The previous evening, protest against the placement of the press platform in the middle of Rudolph Wilde Platz, which would have obstructed much of the audience's view, had been so vehement that the platform was moved farther back shortly before the event.

Meanwhile, the long, narrow speakers' platform fills with prominent political and military guests. From the spectators' perspective, the West German politicians are gathered to the left of the podium. Secretary of State Dean Rusk and a beaming Lucius D. Clay are standing with them. Behind the podium and to its right stand Willy Brandt, West Berlin parliament president Otto Bach, members of the U.S. mission in Berlin, and the Allied commanders. Also standing on the right side are the women who have accompanied Kennedy. Jacqueline Bouvier Kennedy, who is expecting their third child in August, has stayed home, much to the disappointment of the Berlin public. Instead, Kennedy's sister Eunice Shriver and his sister-in-law Princess Lee Bouvier Radziwill have joined him. Brandt attempts to stay near the president. He points out buildings around the square and calls attention to the people crowded in the side streets. It pays off politically to keep close to Kennedy.

Otto Bach is scheduled to speak first and to welcome Kennedy. However, the surges of cheering prevent him from starting his speech for several minutes. Adenauer looks at his watch; they are running behind schedule. Finally Bach can begin. The public's enthusiasm is an "expression of our gratitude," he says.[34] Bach mentions several of the historical symbols that Kennedy had just seen during his drive through the city, and he then points out the Freedom Bell hanging above them in the tower of the city hall. The obstacles the East Berlin authorities have set up, Bach notes, will not prevent reports of the day's events from being broadcast to the East. Like Robert F. Kennedy sixteen months earlier, Bach turns the GDR's propaganda efforts to the West's advantage.

Adenauer then approaches the podium. He also receives a warm welcome. Kennedy claps enthusiastically and smiles. The chancellor understands intuitively that he should take a backseat to Kennedy today, and the audience appreciates his attitude. "Dear friends," he says, using a familiar form of address common in his native Rhineland, "you have come here today to hear President Kennedy." The crowd cheers. "And therefore I will make but only a few remarks." Another round of cheering. Today, the chancellor continues, a "popular referendum" has taken place that the "entire world" will notice. He thanks Kennedy for coming "to this part of the Federal Republic." This seemingly matter-of-fact comment is actually a highly

Illustration 26. The star and his public: Kennedy on the platform in front of Schöneberg City Hall. Source: John F. Kennedy Library (Audiovisual Archives: KN-C 29248, Robert Knudsen).

charged political statement, skillfully put forward by a master tactician. The idea of a formal referendum in West Berlin on its association with the West has been discussed repeatedly in West Berlin, Bonn, and Washington for about two years. Conducting one would cause legal and political problems. The Western powers do not share the chancellor's view that Berlin is simply "a part of" the Federal Republic, as the chancellor has once again asserted. But amid the cheering, no one takes issue with him. After reminding the audience that this is the anniversary of the start of the Airlift, paying tribute to Clay, and praising the people of Berlin for their steadfastness, Adenauer makes good on his promise and turns the stage over to Kennedy.[35]

Chants of "Ken-Ne-Dy" echo across the square and countless spectators again begin waving their handkerchiefs as the celebrated guest rises to take his place at the slightly elevated wooden podium (Illustration 26). The enthusiastic cheering prevents him from starting his speech, but this does not seem to bother him in the least. The president smiles, sways slightly from right to left, arranges his index cards, appears almost a bit embarrassed. Kennedy runs his hand through his hair a few times. A strong breeze tosses the red-white-and-blue banner that Berlin officials have hung over the city hall balconies behind the platform. This decoration caused some misunderstanding at first because many thought it was the French Tricolor.

Surprisingly, it is Heinz Weber, the head interpreter from the Foreign Office in Bonn, whom the public sees standing to the left of the president instead of Robert Lochner, who acted as his interpreter at the airport and the Congress Hall. At the request of McGeorge Bundy, Lochner is letting Weber do the interpreting here since Weber has not yet had the opportunity.[36] The real surprise, however, unfolds over the next twenty minutes. The vivid, incisive speech the crowd and the millions of people following the event on television and radio hear is a political sensation that no one accompanying the president, least of all the protocol planners, has expected.

For months, political advisors and protocol planners on both sides of the Atlantic had debated whether it would be wise for the president to travel to Berlin. Despite the relative quiet there at the moment, the city was, after all, the most conspicuous trouble spot of the Cold War. Nothing had commanded more of the advisors' and planners' attention than the need to avoid provoking the Soviets or the other Western Allies on the thorny issues surrounding Berlin's legal status. The script for the trip attempted to balance the interests of all parties involved. It stipulated in minute detail every step and handshake so that none of the participants might take offense. The White House and the State Department went over draft after draft of the speech Kennedy would deliver at Schöneberg City Hall.[37] The final product of their efforts is typed on the index cards that the president now takes out of his jacket pocket and holds in his hands.

Now something unplanned and unexpected happens. It is not the emotionally worked up crowd or disruptive action by the Eastern authorities that prompts a departure from the script. Except for the officials and advisors who had a hand in planning this speech, no one realizes what is happening. Kennedy disregards the painstakingly formulated speech – an improvisation that few are aware of even decades after the event. He will only use a few passages of the text that he holds in his hands and deliver instead an unscripted speech. The star of the show disregards his lines and improvises. He says more than he should, something different from what his advisors had recommended, and is more provocative than he had intended to be. Consequently, he seems to contradict his previous pronouncements on coexistence with the Soviet bloc. Attentive observers and journalists are quick to note the apparent inconsistency.[38]

According to the script, the president was supposed to begin by recalling the dramatic events of postwar history: the Berlin blockade, the 1953 uprising in East Germany, Khrushchev's 1958 ultimatum, and the erection of the Berlin Wall. He was then to reiterate the position on Berlin that the United States had held since 1961, the American "essentials" regarding West Berlin. This is the "defensive minimum position," as Diethelm Prowe later termed it,[39] that the United States has held to since 1961 – initially to the vexation of the West Germans – in an attempt to defuse the Berlin issue and to embed it in an international framework of coexistence between the superpowers. Now Kennedy does just the opposite. He points an accusing finger at the communist world. He argues that the Berlin Wall proves how communism has failed and he refuses to accept the existence of the Wall as an opportunity by default to defuse tensions at a critical point of confrontation between East and West.

Kennedy speaks off the cuff for the most part during the first half of the speech, as he has done with increasing frequency during his visit to Germany. Not until the second half does he return to the basic ideas and formulations of the prepared text. (The text of his speech can be found in the appendix of this book, along with, for the first time, Weber's full translation.[40]) Kennedy interrupts his speech several times to give Weber the chance to translate his sentences into German. The crowd in the square and the broadcast audience thus hear the speech twice, once in English and once in German.

The first deviation from the prepared script comes at the very beginning. Kennedy drops the planned salutations. A "thank you" is drowned out by the crowd. The president smiles and does not seem to mind the interruption. Then he launches into his speech, speaking with his familiar, patrician Boston accent and exhibiting a few characteristic traits. Occasionally, he pauses in mid-sentence where normally a pause would not be expected. He is known to do this when he is concentrating and needs a second to find the right word.[41] In the first two sentences, Kennedy skillfully expresses his pride at being in Berlin; his respect for Brandt, Adenauer, and Clay; and his admiration for the city's "fighting spirit." From the start, the cheering crowd repeatedly interrupts Kennedy. It is especially loud and enthusiastic when Kennedy mentions Clay and beckons Clay to the podium after Weber has translated this passage. The two of them have broad smiles on their faces. Clay waves to the crowd. A number of spontaneous moments like this occur as Kennedy delivers his speech. They made the occasion much more relaxed and popular in tone than the film excerpts that became familiar in later years would suggest.

Then, for the first time, Kennedy says the sentence that will remain indelible in the memory of generations to come. He builds up to it by citing an ancient Roman. "Two thousand years ago the proudest boast was '*Civis Romanus sum*' [I am a Roman citizen]." He glances quickly at Weber, as if briefly seeking reassurance, then continues. "Today, in the world of freedom, the proudest boast is '*Ich bin ein Berliner.*'" The crowd cheers. With his right hand Kennedy then gestures left, turns to his right, steps back a bit, and takes his index cards again in his hands. The president is obviously relieved. Clay smiles contentedly and nods. Heinz Weber translates this passage into German and repeats Kennedy's own German sentence, "*Ich bin ein Berliner.*" Now everyone in the crowd at Rudolph Wilde Platz better understands what Kennedy has just said and enthusiastically cheers in response, rewarding him for his efforts in two foreign languages. Kennedy gestures to Weber and, with a smile, thanks him for improving his German; Weber also translates that compliment for the crowd.

Kennedy, who fiddles a bit with his suit jacket, is grinning like a boy who has just pulled off a coup. He has just delivered another memorable sentence that outshines his declaration "West Berlin is my country" earlier that day at the Congress Hall. He has once again used a personal declaration to make a political statement that expresses a sense of shared identity between Americans and West Berliners and that emphasizes the special relationship between the two. "*Ich bin ein Berliner,*" he has just announced to the world: not one word of this sentence is included in the typed manuscript he holds.

Another key passage ending with a sentence in German soon follows. It deviates unmistakably from the position Kennedy had outlined in his speech at American University on June 10. In that earlier speech, Kennedy had called upon the communist countries and liberal democracies to come to an understanding on vital issues despite their ideological differences. His experience in Berlin has, however, shown the president how insurmountable the border is between the democratic and communist societies. "There are many people in the world who really don't understand, or say they don't, what is the great issue between the free world and the Communist world. Let them come to Berlin." The crowd applauds. "There are some who say that Communism is the wave of the future. Let them come to Berlin." Boos and hisses. "And there are some who say in Europe and elsewhere we can work with the Communists. Let them come to Berlin." Applause. "And there are even a few who say that it's true that Communism is an evil system, but it permits us to make economic progress." Booing and hissing after the German translation. "*Laßt sie nach Berlin kommen!* Let them come to Berlin!" The president seems angry. Kennedy enhances the rhetorical effect of this challenge by rapping on the podium and using both German and English the third time he repeats the line.

After Weber has translated these words, Kennedy continues. "Freedom has many difficulties and democracy is not perfect," he says, "but we have never had to put a wall up to keep our people in, to prevent them" – the crowd almost instinctively begins to chant "Ken-Ne-Dy" at this point – "from leaving us." This sentence is the clearest evidence that the president is still greatly moved by just having seen the Berlin Wall for the first time. He speaks this sentence more spontaneously than all the others. At first there is no applause since most of the people in the audience have not understood the quickly spoken English sentence; they wait for the translation as the president looks at his index cards. When he resumes speaking, Kennedy repeats his previously expressed respect for the "vitality," "force," and "determination" of West Berlin. He then mentions the Wall again. He takes an idea from his manuscript but gives it a more pointed, more critical twist as he charges that the Wall is "an offense against humanity, separating families . . . and dividing a people who wish to be joined together." Here Kennedy balls his right hand into a fist, pounds the podium, and again delivers a powerful sentence that is not in his manuscript: the Berlin Wall "is the most obvious and vivid demonstration of the failures of the Communist system."

As he continues from this point, Kennedy closely follows the manuscript. That this passage is less spontaneous and less engaging is clear from the fact that the crowd does not interrupt him for several minutes. The president argues that true and lasting peace in Europe can only be achieved once all Germans are free and can exercise self-determination. West Berliners live "in a defended island of freedom" – one of the commonly heard expressions used in the West to describe the city since the Soviet blockade. Then, as in many of his speeches, Kennedy carefully steps up his rhetoric and gradually adopts a more visionary tone. He urges the people of Berlin "to lift your eyes beyond the dangers of today, to the hopes of tomorrow, beyond the freedom merely of . . . your country of Germany to the advance of freedom everywhere, beyond the wall to the day of peace with justice." This sentence is an excellent example of classic rhetoric. The construction of "beyond . . . to" acts as an anaphora; its repetition at the beginning of each phrase moves the line of argument from the specific to the general. Indeed, by calling on the Berliners to transcend the confines of their city's situation and to think of humankind at large, Kennedy follows, in brilliant manner, the line of thought he has articulated in public for the past two years, namely his attempt to defuse the Berlin issue by embedding it in the policy of East-West coexistence.

Kennedy concludes his speech with a final reference to the situation in Berlin, and again he departs from the script. The people of Berlin can be proud, he says, that they have endured nearly two decades on the front line. Once more, the president uses a Cold War metaphor. But the most ingenious move happens in the very last sentence. Kennedy links West Berlin's Cold War identity with the universal desire for freedom and with a personal declaration. He repeats the German sentence he used earlier in his speech. He enhances its impact by expressing it as his own, proudly asserted identity. "All free men, wherever they may live, are citizens of Berlin, and, therefore, as a free man, I take pride in the words: "*Ich bin ein Berliner!*" While delivering these concluding sentences, Kennedy has glanced twice at the manuscript in front of him. The sentence "*Ich bin ein Berliner*" is nowhere to be found in the carefully prepared text typed on the cards. During the pause in Brandt's office right before the speech, the president jotted down the line, spelling it phonetically so he could pronounce it correctly ("Ish bin ein Bearleener"). He had done the same in Cologne for the pronunciation of "*Kölle Alaaf*" and also in this speech for the Latin phrase "*Civis Romanus sum*" and the German sentence "*Laßt sie nach Berlin kommen.*"[42]

Kennedy's final words have barely resounded from the loudspeakers when the crowd begins to applaud and chant "Ken-Ne-Dy." The cheering turns into a roar of enthusiasm as soon as Heinz Weber finishes translating the last sentence into German and repeats the German line "*Ich bin ein Berliner.*" Despite the audience's roar of approval, the lead actor himself does not strike a triumphal pose. Visibly relieved, Kennedy turns from the podium almost abruptly, sticks his index cards in the left pocket of his jacket, and steps down. This expression of modesty is much more effective than heroic posturing would have been, and it wins Kennedy additional favor with the crowd and the dignitaries on the platform. The first to shake Kennedy's hand and congratulate him on his speech is Otto Bach; others follow. Kennedy smiles and walks from the podium to the other side of the speaker platform where Adenauer is standing.

The last speaker is Brandt: "This is a great day in the history of our city!" The mayor emphasizes Berlin's role as the midwife of German-American friendship following the Second World War and claims that "the heart of the German people" can be heard beating in Berlin, which Brandt calls "Germany's capital." Brandt pays special tribute to Lucius D. Clay and Ernst Reuter, and he does not forget to "speak on behalf of fellow countrymen on the other side of the wall." In fact, Brandt is the only person at this early afternoon rally to use the word *Wiedervereinigung* (reunification).[43] Even more conspicuous than his use of this word is the message being sent by his body language. Of the politicians gathered on the platform, Brandt is the tensest throughout the event.[44] His mood – mirrored in his facial expressions – appears to fluctuate between nervousness, tension, and paralysis. Even when Kennedy mentions Brandt during his speech as he condemns the Wall as an offense against humanity, the mayor remains stone-faced.

When Brandt takes the podium, he is repeatedly interrupted by the crowd. The disruptions are by no means directed against him. The great majority of West Berliners support the mayor and his party. The crowd's reaction is, rather, a spontaneous outburst of enthusiasm for the American president. Still, Brandt is irritated, even indignant. Almost angrily, he shakes his head and gestures dismissively as the crowd begins to chant "Ken-Ne-Dy!" and thus hinders Brandt from concluding his speech. At this point, it is the chancellor who invites Kennedy to step forward once more and wave to the jubilant crowd. Suddenly, Brandt and Adenauer have switched roles. On this afternoon, the young, aspiring, charismatic Brandt, who has been celebrated in the United States and West Germany so often as a dynamic, ambitious, and popular leader finds himself tense and irritated on his political home turf. He acts as if a heavy burden is weighing on his shoulders, unlike the other politicians there, young and old, who relish the cheering. In contrast to Brandt, Adenauer and Kennedy smile, and "Old Man" Adenauer waves to the spectators.

What happens then is almost beyond imagination. The crowd begins to cheer the chancellor – in the middle of a speech by his most important rival and directly in front of that rival's office. And of all people, it is Adenauer they are cheering, the man who had kept his distance from the West Berliners, who had such an emotionally detached relationship to the city, who had been so seemingly nonchalant when the Wall was built and had hesitated several days before traveling to West Berlin to see it for himself. But it is indeed Adenauer they want. Amid cries of "Konny, Konny," the West Berliners now embrace their chancellor, bestowing an American-sounding nickname upon him. (Reporters are left wondering whether it should be spelled "Konny" or "Conny.") This scene is a double triumph. Adenauer is being honored. He steps forward from the politicians lined up on the platform and waves. At the same time, West Berliners are also celebrating themselves as being American Berliners, which sets them apart from West Germans. By Americanizing the chancellor's name, West Berliners succeed in emotionally winning over the elderly chancellor.

What is wrong with Brandt? It is impossible to know precisely what he was thinking and feeling. Still, two explanations for his behavior seem plausible. First, Brandt does have a heavy burden to carry that day. Because he succeeded in getting Kennedy to come to Berlin, it is now Brandt's responsibility to ensure that not only the appearance at Schöneberg City Hall but the entire day runs smoothly. Therefore, Brandt is sensitive to any deviation from planned protocol and by the additional time required for the speeches. He is probably even more concerned about the level of emotion being demonstrated by the hundreds of thousands of people gathered in front of the city hall. In the days leading up to Kennedy's visit, Brandt had warned Berliners against expressing excessive emotion and called upon them to demonstrate restraint and discipline. Later, when Brandt himself recalled that day in Berlin, he expressed his reservations about the "seething masses" whose enthusiasm was "almost too unrestrained."[45]

Second, Brandt in particular is affected, politically speaking, by Kennedy's impromptu changes in the script of his speech. Since the erection of the Wall, the mayor had come a long way toward accepting the American policy of coexistence. He had fine-tuned his own concept of détente. This had been the purpose of the lectures he gave at Harvard University in October 1962. Two weeks before Kennedy's visit, Brandt was again at Harvard, this time to receive an honorary doctorate degree – a vindication of both the politician and his policies. Like Kennedy, Brandt seeks to achieve change despite the East-West conflict. He is prepared to acknowledge the existence of the opposing political bloc and pursue agreements with it that would positively alter the status quo.[46] Shortly after his second Harvard visit, Brandt publicly endorsed this approach at an event to commemorate the 1953 uprising in East Germany. On that occasion, Brandt had again emphatically expressed his hope that the Kennedy administration would support worldwide détente.[47]

As Brandt stands on the platform in front of the Schöneberg City Hall on June 26, he knows that he and his press secretary Egon Bahr will be attending a conference at the Evangelische Akademie Tutzing, a well-known meeting place for intellectuals and politicians, in exactly three weeks. At the conference, they plan to present in rough outline the policy that will become known as *Ostpolitik*. Brandt, taking a cautious tone, will focus on the long-term prospects for easing East-West tensions; Bahr, concentrating on the German question, will put forward the principle of "change through rapprochement." Both men will refer to Kennedy's "peace strategy" and apply it to the German situation.[48] However, there is no reference to rapprochement in Kennedy's remarks at Schöneberg City Hall. Still preoccupied with what he has experienced at the Berlin Wall, the president evokes images of an irreconcilable confrontation between the two opposing blocs. His comments in the first part of the speech seem to support the view that cooperation with the communists is by definition impossible. Brandt, for whom the Wall had become a daily reality, has recognized that it is possible, even necessary, to cooperate with the East, and he had taken Kennedy's pronouncements over the past two years as confirmation of his views. Little more than two weeks earlier, after all, Kennedy had made his strongest argument to date for coming to terms with the Soviets in his speech at American University.

Is Brandt now confused, disappointed, or merely surprised by the speech the president has just delivered? Does he think that the idea of coexistence has been completely repudiated? The evidence suggests Brandt was experiencing a range of feelings. The contradiction between Kennedy's speech at Schöneberg City Hall and his statements in previous years is too obvious for Brandt not to notice immediately. He sees little reason to smile. His uneasiness can be sensed when, at the end of his own speech, he invites Kennedy, somewhat dramatically, to sign the city's official guest book, the Golden Book. The signing is given a theatrical touch. For the second and last time during the visit, silence prevails. Unlike at the Berlin Wall, it is explicitly requested. Brandt calls on everyone present to honor a moment of "ceremonial silence": only the tolling of the Freedom Bell is heard. Men take off their hats and do as they have been asked. The crowd is silent: for the first time since the president's arrival, the chant "Ken-Ne-Dy" is not to be heard. Kennedy bends over the podium, signs the Golden Book, and shakes Brandt's hand. He then steps back to rejoin the others on the platform and to listen to the tolling of the bell.

Only six days before, on June 20, a delegation from the Crusade for Freedom – headed by James B. Conant, the former American high commissioner and U.S. ambassador to the Federal Republic of Germany – had presented Willy Brandt with a large bronze plaque commemorating the dedication of the Freedom Bell in 1950.[49] Clay and the initiators of the Crusade would have been very happy to have Kennedy unveil the commemorative plaque today, but that could not be squeezed into the already tight schedule. After the final toll of the Freedom Bell, the square again erupts into applause, cheering, and "Ken-Ne-Dy" chants. No one should expect the public to remain quiet for long on a day like this. Once again, the president approaches the podium and waves to the crowd. Then the dignitaries leave the platform and enter the city hall, where a festive banquet awaits them. Kennedy finds it hard to turn his back on the crowd. Once inside the city hall, he goes to a window and surveys the square, which only gradually begins to empty.

"ICH BIN EIN BERLINER": FOUR WORDS, THEIR ORIGIN, AND THEIR IMPACT

Kennedy's famous declaration "*Ich bin ein Berliner*" comes as no less of a surprise to political observers in the West and East than it does to the public. The impact of these four words is amplified by the fact that the president says them twice in his speech. The interpreter repeats the sentence each time so that, all told, the people gathered at Rudolph Wilde Platz hear it four times.

Let us quickly address and then shelve the persistent legend of the puta-
tive grammatical error that supposedly rendered the president's declaration
nonsensical. According to many a German grammar book and by common
usage, Kennedy should have said *"Ich bin Berliner"* without the indefinite
article *ein*. This is justified by the rule in which a noun requires no article
when it immediately follows the verbs *sein* (to be), *bleiben* (to remain), and
werden (to become). What gives the grammatical error its comical touch, if
one follows this interpretation, is that the president was declaring himself
to be a jelly doughnut, a pastry some Germans call *Berliner*.

The supposed error is much commented upon in Germany and, especially, the United States. The *New York Times* and *Newsweek* helped keep the
story alive by claiming years after the event that the crowd at Schöneberg
City Hall giggled and laughed when they heard the statement *"Ich bin ein
Berliner."*[50] Kennedy's supposed gaffe has become nearly as famous as the
sentence itself, but it has nothing to do with the events of June 26, 1963.
It can neither be proved nor disproved that several people among the hundreds of thousands gathered in front of the city hall grinned at the somewhat
unusual sentence – on account of either the use of the indefinite article or
the multiple meanings of *Berliner*. It is, however, very clear from the audiovisual documentation available that the crowd did not regard Kennedy's
declaration as comical or as reason to laugh any of the four times they heard
it. Nor did the German or American press accounts at the time say anything
about a grammatical mistake or the spectators finding the sentence amusing.
Aside from the moving moments such as the ringing of the Freedom Bell
when silence prevailed, the atmosphere was dominated by enthusiasm for
Kennedy.

Moreover, the use of the indefinite article *ein* in *"Ich bin ein Berliner"* is
neither incorrect nor entirely uncommon, as the linguistic scholar Jürgen
Eichhoff has demonstrated.[51] Although it might sound a bit unusual, comparable wordings are common in some German-speaking areas. Saying *ein
Berliner* is grammatically correct if it is used metaphorically. To take a more
common parallel example, the sentence *"Er ist Schauspieler"* (He is an actor)
is a statement of fact about a man's profession; the sentence *"Er ist ein Schauspieler"* means the man is putting on an act. Kennedy was not formally stating
his actual place of residence. He was, rather, metaphorically identifying with
the citizens of Berlin although not a citizen himself. Kennedy's declaration
was a symbolic expression of solidarity with West Berlin, with America's
Berlin. It was a rhetorical intensification of a symbolic common identity
linking Americans and Berliners. Indeed, his visit was to be the highpoint
of this special relationship.

Two further points argue against the claim that Kennedy made an amusing mistake. Shortly before the speech, several knowledgeable people, including Heinz Weber and other native speakers, had checked and approved the wording "*Ich bin ein Berliner.*"[52] Last but not least, scholarly research on local vernacular and everyday life in Berlin supplies additional evidence for dismissing the jelly doughnut joke. Berliners and most people living in the eastern regions of Germany do not call jelly doughnuts *Berliner* but rather *Pfannkuchen* (literally, "pancakes"). *Berliner* is the name used in much of western Germany.[53] In sum, it is safe to say that the jelly doughnut jokes can be relegated to the realm of legend.

A far more important issue is the origin of the declaration "*Ich bin ein Berliner.*" This has remained a puzzle, even though several explanations have been proposed. The origin of this sentence is as obscure as the statement itself is famous. This is all the more remarkable when we recall that these four words constitute one of the most famous examples of American polit- ical rhetoric in the twentieth century, if not the modern era as a whole. Surprisingly, the actual source behind Kennedy's memorable line has been entirely overlooked so far.

The few published references concerning the origin of this key sentence contradict one another and must be scrutinized closely. According to Willy Brandt, it was presidential advisor Theodore C. Sorensen who proposed the sentence and told the mayor about it the evening before in Bonn. In addition to an inaccuracy about when this conversation took place (the presidential entourage was in Wiesbaden on the evening in question, and Brandt was not there), something else speaks against this explanation. Sorensen was the last person to have the opportunity to revise the speech text drafted by Carl Kaysen before it was typed onto the index cards that the president would hold in his hands. Yet the sentence does not appear in the typed manuscript, and Sorensen himself never claimed authorship of the line.[54] Recently, Jay Lovestone, the head of the international department of the AFL-CIO, has been credited with suggesting the line to Kennedy in Berlin. However, no documentation has been offered to support this argument.[55]

A third version is found in the memoirs of the RIAS director Robert H. Lochner, who, as noted earlier, acted as Kennedy's interpreter during the trip to Germany. According to Lochner, Kennedy asked him to review his speech upon their arrival at the city hall. In Brandt's office, the president asked Lochner to write down the sentence "*Ich bin ein Berliner*" in German; together they then practiced Kennedy's pronunciation of it several times.[56] A fourth version comes from McGeorge Bundy, Kennedy's national security advisor, and was later backed by Kenneth O'Donnell, a colleague of Bundy's at the White House. According to Bundy, Kennedy asked his advisors during the flight to Berlin how the Latin sentence *"Civis Romanus sum"* could be best translated into German. Bundy says he came up with *"Ich bin ein Berliner"* and practiced the sentence with Kennedy later in Brandt's office.[57]

The actual course of events leading up to Kennedy's speech is more complicated than these accounts suggest. The story begins before the trip. On June 18, Kennedy summoned Lochner, who had been recommended by Lucius D. Clay as an interpreter, to the White House. Lochner had long worked for Voice of America, and he had often served as an interpreter for Clay and other American military officials in Germany.[58] He was also an American Berliner. His father, Louis P. Lochner, was bureau chief of the Associated Press in Berlin from 1928 to 1941. Also in attendance at the June 18 meeting were McGeorge Bundy and Margarete Plischke, a language instructor at the State Department's Foreign Service Institute. Although Lochner later did not remember her being there, Plischke's presence is documented in a report she wrote at the time.[59] According to her report, the president wanted to practice his pronunciation of several sentences in German that he was considering using upon his arrival in Berlin and in the speech at Schöneberg City Hall. A list of sentences and their phonetic spellings had been drawn up in the planning committees; it included lines such as *"Ich freue mich, in Berlin zu sein"* (I am glad to be in Berlin).

Lochner maintains that the president's pronunciation of German was miserable, whereas Plischke reports it was actually acceptable. However, both accounts agree that Kennedy was not particularly happy with the suggested sentences and found them meaningless. Plischke's account is the only record we have of the rest of the meeting. She reports that Kennedy and Bundy spent several minutes writing new lines. The group then considered the German wordings of several possibilities. On the lower half of the sheet with the list of phonetically spelled sentences, Kennedy wrote several lines in English, including the sentence "I am proud to be in this free city." These lines were translated into German, and Kennedy then practiced them. Here, in the lower right-hand corner of this sheet, we find the sentence written by Kennedy himself in blue ink on June 18: "I am a Berliner." Other documents make explicit reference to the sentences that Kennedy drafted on June 18, but this particular sheet is not among the voluminous materials pertaining to the Berlin visit now in the archives of the Kennedy Library in Boston, nor is it in the National Archives.[60]

Why is this sheet not in the Kennedy Library or the National Archives? The answer is simple: it is in Berlin. When the meeting on June 18 ended, the sheet of sentences with Kennedy's additions remained in the hands of

Margarete Plischke. She was called to the White House again the following day for another session of language training, but it was cancelled due to a lack of time.[61] In January 1978, Plischke put the annotated sheet up for sale at auction in New York; acting at the last minute, the West Berlin Senate acquired it for $8,000. That same year, it was placed on public display in an exhibit commemorating the fifteenth anniversary of Kennedy's speech at Schöneberg and is today in the possession of the Berlin city archives.[62]

The most important question still remains to be answered: How did Kennedy come up with the formulation "I am a Berliner"? There can be little doubt anymore that Kennedy himself was the author of this line in June 1963, that it was not suggested to him by someone while he was in Berlin, and that he sought help only with the German translation and pronunciation. The key to the puzzle of the origin of his famous sentence is Kennedy himself and the Latin phrase *Civis Romanus sum*.

In 1954, when signing West Berlin's Golden Book, former president Herbert Hoover wrote "I am a Berliner." His use of this sentence differed in many ways from Kennedy's nine years later. Hoover gave the sentence in English, not German. He did not present it as a personal, metaphorical declaration to the city as Kennedy did, but as a metaphorical analogy: the Berliners of today should be as proud of their city as the men of ancient Athens had been. Here lies another difference. Hoover erroneously associated the statement "I am a citizen of this city" with the Athenians when in fact the figure who most powerfully memorialized the line was the Roman politician, writer, and orator Marcus Tullius Cicero (106–43 BC).

For Cicero, *Civis Romanus sum* was a declaration of Roman citizenship and a claim to the rights, privileges, and protection that citizenship carried.[63] Men who made this declaration were not necessarily claiming residence in the city of Rome, but rather citizenship in the Roman republic or, later, empire. To identify oneself as a Roman citizen was particularly important outside Rome's borders and in dealing with local rulers because Roman citizens were ensured protection from bodily harm and persecution by foreign or local jurisdictions. Cicero used the claim *Civis Romanus sum* to criticize the Roman commander in Sicily, C. Verres, for his brutal treatment of Roman citizens. This interpretation of *Civis Romanus sum* is also found in the Acts of the Apostles in the New Testament. During his imprisonment in Philippi, Paul announces his Roman citizenship, to the horror of the local magistrates, in order to protest against the whipping he had been given.[64] In addition to the legal and political meaning of the statement, *Civis Romanus sum* was used even in antiquity in a more colloquial manner to express one's pride in communal membership.

Like his brother Robert, John F. Kennedy had been schooled in the classics and ancient history. In important speeches, the president liked to use quotations and indirect references to rhetorical expressions from antiquity or classical modern literature.[65] He was particularly eager to find appropriate quotes for his trip to Germany. On June 18 in Washington and nine days later in Berlin, Kennedy drew upon *Civis Romanus sum*. But he was not quoting Cicero directly or Hoover indirectly. Nor was he using a line supplied by one of his advisors. Kennedy was quoting himself. While searching for a sentence to express pride in a city, the solidarity of its citizens, and his own sense of solidarity with those citizens, Kennedy remembered an earlier speech he gave in a different context.

On May 4, 1962, Kennedy finds himself in New Orleans during a swing through the South. Very few presidents before him have visited the city. Kennedy is given an enthusiastic welcome by well over 200,000 people. He gives a policy speech on trade as part of his efforts to secure support for his proposal that the president be granted far-reaching powers to reduce tariffs. He also goes to Elgin Air Force Base and watches a simulated response to a combat alert. Less spectacular is the ceremony later in the day to make Kennedy an honorary citizen of New Orleans. Naturally, the president must express his thanks. He is obliged to couple gratitude and pride in New Orleans with a far-reaching political vision of the future. As he so often does, Kennedy sets the tone by invoking the idea of the New Frontier. Southern states like Louisiana, he assures his audience, are to be part of the drive for technological advance in the Space Age. Kennedy leaves no doubt that Americans are the engineers and architects of a better future. The bridge between the past and the future, between pride in past achievements and a mission for the future, is Cicero. At one point in his short address, the president says: "Two thousand years ago the proudest boast was to say, 'I am a citizen of Rome.' Today, I believe, in 1962 the proudest boast is to say, 'I am a citizen of the United States.'" On June 26, 1963, Kennedy uses the first part of that statement, word for word, in his speech to the West Berliners. He alters the second half to fit the situation in Berlin. Even the final passage of his New Orleans address is a precursor to Kennedy's statements thirteen months later: "I am proud . . . to come to this city."[66]

The solution to the mystery of the origin of Kennedy's declaration in Berlin lies in his words of thanks to the city of New Orleans a year earlier. As Kennedy plans his trip to Berlin, he struggles to find something memorable to say to the hundreds of thousands of people eagerly anticipating his speech. In searching for a usable quotation from the classics, he recalls the line from his New Orleans address. In that city, he quoted the Latin line *Civis Romanus sum* to emphasize membership in a nation, in much the same way that it had been understood in Cicero's time to signify membership in a political community that extended beyond the city of Rome itself. For Berlin, he gives the line a narrower meaning, using it as a metaphorical expression of his solidarity with the city. Following the June 18 meeting at the White House, a list of several sentences, including "I am a Berliner" and "I am proud to be in free Berlin," are again typed up in English and supplemented with phonetically rendered German translations. For example, the translation of "I am a Berliner" is given as "ish bin ine bear-LEAN-ar."[67] The next reference to this sentence is found, in Kennedy's handwriting, in the third revision of the speech, dated June 25. The key sentence is not included in the typed text but has been added by the president on the bottom of the first page in a slightly altered form ("I am a citizen of Berlin").[68]

In the hectic days preceding the trip to Berlin, communication is not working smoothly between the president, his office staff, and his speechwriters. There is little time for discussion of precise instructions. The line "I am a Berliner" is overlooked by the speechwriters, who continue to come up with new versions of the speech until June 26. Even in the June 25 version, Kennedy fails to indicate clearly whether and where his additions should be included in the text. This omission is part of the reason why the famous statement does not appear even in the final version of the speech, the one typed onto the index cards. As several observers later recalled, Kennedy looks through these cards again during the short break in Brandt's office. On the first index card, the president writes down the soon-to-be-famous sentence in a form he finds pronounceable ("Ish bin ein Bearleener"), its Latin origin ("kiwis Romanus sum"), and another German sentence that he will include in the speech moments later ("Lust z nach Bearleen comen") (Illustration 27). On the blank side of one of the index cards, he has again noted the pronounceable formulations of all three phrases in a column, starting on the top with "Ish bin ein Bearleener."[69]

Affected by the experience of seeing the Berlin Wall, Kennedy gives a speech that departs considerably from the prepared text. He falls back on the most memorable passage of his New Orleans speech given the year before, changing pride in being an American to pride in being a Berliner. Knowing that Kennedy was drawing on an earlier speech might make his *"Ich bin ein Berliner"* declaration seem like an empty rhetorical flourish. That view is, however, too simple. Kennedy's reuse of Cicero not only attests to his powerful memory but is also a very clever move. He could hardly have used the Cicero reference from the New Orleans speech for any city outside the United States except West Berlin. In New Orleans, he

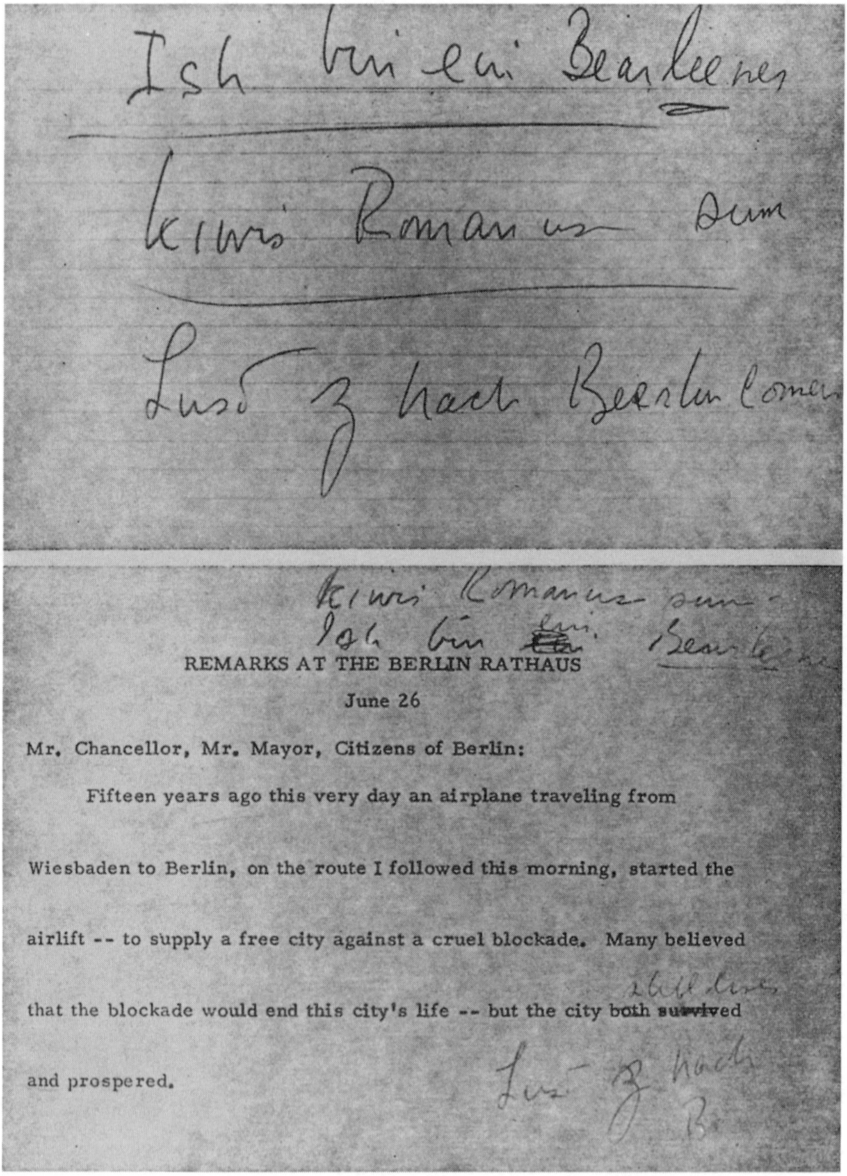

Ish bin ein Bearleener

kiwis Romanus sum

Lust z nach Bearlin comen

kiwis Romanus sum

Ish bin ein Bearleener

REMARKS AT THE BERLIN RATHAUS

June 26

Mr. Chancellor, Mr. Mayor, Citizens of Berlin:

Fifteen years ago this very day an airplane traveling from Wiesbaden to Berlin, on the route I followed this morning, started the airlift -- to supply a free city against a cruel blockade. Many believed that the blockade would end this city's life -- but the city ~~both survived~~ still lives and prospered.

Lust z nach B

Illustration 27. Four words that made history: Kennedy's stroke of genius – handwritten notes on how to pronounce the legendary sentence "*Ich bin ein Berliner*" and other foreign-language expressions for the speech at Schöneberg City Hall on June 26, 1963. Source: Landesarchiv Berlin.

had said that the only foreign stage where Americans were called upon to carry out their mission besides Vietnam was West Berlin. In his Schöneberg speech, Kennedy goes a step further and pays the West Berliners a double compliment. Theirs is the only city he metaphorically links to Rome, and he then places them on equal footing with the "Romans" of the new "Pax Americana," the Americans of the Cold War era. This makes sense politically because the people of West Berlin enjoy the special protection of the United States and have several times directly requested help from American leaders. The declaration "*Ich bin ein Berliner*" thus not only represents the rhetorical highpoint of America's Berlin but also provides a historical anchor for it.

The immediate political context notwithstanding, it would be too facile to characterize the Schöneberg speech as just another example of Cold War rhetoric. To be sure, Kennedy draws upon Cold War imagery and refers to the irreconcilable confrontation between communism and democratic societies. He is still moved by the experience of having seen the Wall, and he wants to speak more spontaneously, and more emotionally, than had been planned. So he improvises. The excitement generated by Kennedy's declaring himself a Berliner easily causes people, then and today, to over-look something. The president wants to employ the Johnson tactic – and he succeeds.[70] As his vice president had in Berlin two years earlier, Kennedy uses highly engaging rhetoric rich in historical references and emphatic formulations. With this rhetoric, the speaker demonstrates his empathy for the West Berliners. It turns empathy into a metaphoric merger of the speaker's identity and the West Berliners'. At the same time, like Johnson, Kennedy remains politically noncommittal. His speech contains no promises, no pledges of a specific military response in the event of Soviet aggression against West Berlin. He does not even mention the American "essentials" or defense commitments. Instead, Kennedy uses metaphors to integrate West Berlin once again into the master narrative of American history and its vision of an American-led march of democracy across the globe. But there is no trace of a concrete policy on Berlin in the speech. In this regard, Kennedy remains true to the policy his administration has pursued since 1961 despite the seemingly contradictory statements he has made during his visit to Germany.

At midday on June 26, however, the political problem of the Schöneberg speech is – as Daniel Schorr reports to his American viewers during the live broadcast – that the public appears to have been presented "another Kennedy," different from the "Kennedy of Washington."[71] The Kennedy of Berlin, still affected by his experience at the Wall, seems to have gotten the upper hand over the Kennedy of peaceful coexistence. The president's advisors are upset. The aggressive, anticommunist speech Kennedy has just given represents an enormous political risk. The administration is in danger of undermining its own policy of détente with the Soviet Union at a decisive moment in the negotiations on a nuclear test ban treaty. McGeorge Bundy pulls the president aside after the speech and warns him: "Mr. President, I believe you have gone too far."[72] Even Kennedy begins to feel a bit uneasy. He knows that the enthusiastic spectators would have marched to the Wall and torn it down had he called on them to do so.[73] Kennedy now needs to dampen the Cold War rhetoric, and he is given the opportunity almost immediately. The president has prepared a speech on foreign policy for his appearance at the Free University, a speech that is to rank alongside the one he gave at the Paulskirche the day before.

THE FINAL ACT: NO END TO THE CHEERING

Once the program at Rudolph Wilde Platz is over, the dignitaries and more than 150 guests sit down to a luncheon banquet in the city hall. The protocol planners have seen to it that representatives of the political, religious, and cultural circles in Bonn and West Berlin have been included. The already acclaimed young writer Günter Grass had been invited but does not attend. No expense has been spared in decorating the hall and the dining tables.

At the luncheon, Kennedy makes a toast in which he asks the guests to honor Berliners on both sides of the Wall. He also mentions the guests Clay, Conant, and Meany, describing them as great American friends of the city. At one point, the president notes somewhat wistfully that a person can be spoiled by a visit like his to Berlin. If a million people do not show up at his next speech in Massachusetts or Connecticut, he continues, the press will interpret it as a sign of American political apathy.[74] Once he has finished eating, Kennedy again appears with Brandt and Adenauer outside on the platform in front of the city hall to greet the remaining spectators, some of whom have turned up after hearing an announcement of this second, short appearance over radio or loudspeaker.

The presidential motorcade gets underway again around 3 p.m. and heads to the southwest section of the city. The weather has turned hot, and it rains – confetti, especially along Rheinstrasse. There is again an outpouring of enthusiasm from the crowds lining the streets. By the end of the day, the municipal street cleaners have swept up more than 4,300 cubic feet of the tiny scraps of paper that had showered down upon the motorcade.[75]

In the meantime, professors from both the Free University and the Technical University have gathered at the FU, in their faculty gowns, to sit in the hot sun together with 10,000 to 15,000 students to await the president.[76]

Because an audience of this size would exceed the seating capacity of any hall at the FU, the parking lot between the two wings of the Henry Ford Building has been converted into an outdoor auditorium. The FU decided against inviting additional guests or having musical accompaniment. The aim was to have as many students as possible attend the event. This is 1963, and the political atmosphere at West German universities is not yet as charged as it would become later in the decade, when FU students could no longer be counted upon to provide an American guest with a congenial audience.[77] On this day the mood among the students is relaxed and pleasant. The police call for quiet. It is important to make a good impression. The American president is going to be awarded the highest honor the FU has to give, honorary membership in the university (*Ehrenbürgerrecht*). Whereas honorary doctorates are awarded by a particular faculty of the university, it is the entire university that awards *Ehrenbürgerrecht*. Shortly before 4 p.m., almost a half hour behind schedule, the presidential motorcade finally arrives.

Just hours before, Kennedy had declared himself a "*Civis Romanus*" and "*ein Berliner.*" Now he becomes a "*Civis academicus*" of the German university most deeply influenced by the American model.[78] Without American support, the FU would not have been established, nor would it have developed into one of Germany's largest and most important universities. In 1963, 13,400 Germans and 800 foreigners are enrolled as students there.[79] There is a curious footnote concerning the Latin certificate presented to Kennedy during the ceremony. The political scientist Ernst Fraenkel, who had spent ten years in the United States after fleeing the Third Reich, prepared an English translation for the benefit of the American press. Fraenkel's rendering was, however, very stilted, so Gordon Craig, an American historian of Germany who was teaching at the FU as a visiting professor, stepped in at the last minute to polish the English text.[80]

The chairman of the FU foreign studies office, Horst Hartwich, had overseen the preparations for the Kennedy visit at the FU. A key figure in America's Berlin, he was an indispensable manager in German-American academic relations during the 1950s, 1960s, and beyond. Hartwich was one of the actors in the transnational relations between Germany and the United States, and he maintained close ties to the Berlin lobby in the United States. Hartwich began working for the university's foreign studies office in 1949 while still a student, and he quickly rose to the position of managing director. With unrelenting energy, he sought contact with American institutions and scholars. His ties to Harvard, Columbia, Princeton, and Stanford were particularly close. His efforts were decisive in securing the FU support from the Fulbright Commission and the Ford Foundation. In the early 1960s,

Hartwich was the person to call at the FU when it came to contacts abroad, especially with the United States.[81] Indirectly, he, too, is being honored on June 26, 1963, when he is invited to help the rector place a medallion around the president's neck during the ceremony.

At the FU, Kennedy again gives a speech in front of a symbolic architectural landmark linked to the traditions established and perpetuated by American Berliners. The construction of the Henry Ford Building had been funded by a grant from the Ford Foundation in 1951. The building, designed by Franz Heinrich Sobotka and Gustav Müller, houses the university's main auditorium and library along with numerous classrooms and lecture halls. The large glass windows in the building's foyer create a feeling of transparency. In 1954, the year that the Henry Ford Building was formally dedicated, four noted American citizens were awarded honorary doctorates: Frank L. Howley, the U.S. commander in Berlin during the blockade; Shepard Stone, director of the Ford Foundation and former member of the High Commission; Kendal Foss, a journalist and writer whose support for students excluded from East Berlin's Humboldt University in 1948 played an important part in the founding of the FU; and James B. Conant, the high commissioner and later American ambassador to Germany. Conant now sits on the platform watching Kennedy receive the honor that Shepard Stone had secured for him through his influence (Illustration 28).

In accepting the membership in the university, Kennedy goes far beyond a simple expression of gratitude. He uses this opportunity to make the last major speech of his trip to Germany. Since taking office two and a half years earlier, Kennedy has mentioned Berlin many times publicly. On June 25, 1961, for example, he delivered a televised speech to the nation on the crisis then coming to a head in Berlin.[82] The speech he gives today, however, will be his most important statement on Berlin and Germany because it directs attention beyond the divided country. For the first time, the German question – whether the two postwar German states will ever unite – is incorporated into Kennedy's concept of détente. This speech sets both issues in a broad context that looks beyond the particular issues of the moment. Kennedy moves far beyond the Cold War imagery of his Schöneberg speech and the emotions aroused by his experience of the Wall.

Very early in his speech, Kennedy presents his understanding of scholarship and the university. Both, he says, have a role to play in today's politics. They should help create free societies and not produce "merely corporation lawyers or skilled accountants."[83] Kennedy turns to early American history for examples: James Madison, Thomas Jefferson, and Benjamin Franklin

Illustration 28. *"Civis Romanus"* and honorary member of the university: Kennedy speaks at the Henry Ford Building of the Free University. Source: Landesarchiv Berlin.

were interested in scholarship and science, but they also were involved in working for the public good. We live in a time of change and a multitude of social and political challenges, Kennedy argues. "It is not enough to mark time, to adhere to a status quo, while awaiting a change for the better." The president is reiterating a theme he expressed in his speech at American University on June 10. He develops his ideas by expounding on the three

basic values – truth, justice, and liberty – found in both the motto and seal
of the FU ("*Veritas – Iustitia – Libertas*").

It is necessary "to face the facts as they are," he contends, and "not to
involve ourselves in self-deception." It is time "to refuse to think merely in
slogans" if we are to pursue creative policy. Germany will not be reunited in
the near future. It is necessary now to climb out of the trenches of the Cold
War and think globally. What counts is the trust placed on the strengths and
attractiveness of one's own system and to make its achievements available
to those who hold different opinions. Germans are not the only ones who
have the right of self-determination; it is a universal right. As important
as Germans are, it is crucial that the major powers decide to cooperate.
With this speech, Kennedy comes full circle back to the policy ideas he had
outlined early in his presidency. He subordinates the issues of both Berlin
and Germany under the greater context of global détente and the creation of
a just world order. The president leaves the FU an important legacy in both
foreign and German policy. He also leaves a symbolic outpost of American
culture somewhat better equipped: the America Institute, founded in 1953,
receives two Kodak slide projectors, 2,500 slides, and a book on American
art.[84]

For a moment, let us turn our attention away from this day in June 1963
and look ahead to 1968. Opposition to the United States has arisen that
could not have been predicted at the time of Kennedy's visit to the FU.
West Germans, especially students at the FU, are becoming increasingly
critical of the American government. Among some, criticism develops into
militant anti-Americanism. The factors behind this development are many
and varied; they neither can nor should be analyzed here, but we do want
to glance briefly at this chapter in German-American relations.

The criticism of the United States voiced at German universities is part of
a transatlantic protest movement.[85] At the same time, there is a specifically
German aspect to this criticism in the way that it invokes the recent German
past and builds upon theories of great power imperialism and decoloniza-
tion. These two lines of argument sometimes converge, as, for example, in
the charge that the United States is guilty of a second Auschwitz in Vietnam. Ironically, many students active in the protest movement have been
influenced considerably by American popular culture. Their criticism thus
centers on what they see as a fundamental contradiction. In the eyes of those
shaping student opinion, Kennedy's call for justice is being undermined
by America's own domestic and foreign policies. The Vietnam War is the
last straw. Student protests against American foreign policy are intertwined
with their critique of the institution of university, which they contend is

undemocratic and outdated. In the case of the FU, the students are challenging an organizational structure that only fifteen years earlier had been widely seen as a welcome "American" departure from the hierarchic classic German university.[86]

In the course of the 1960s, the FU and specifically the Henry Ford Building become centers of student protest against the Vietnam War and the United States. Late in the decade, the chant "Ho-Ho-Ho-Chi-Minh" resounds through the FU. The North Vietnamese leader has become a hero to many students. Still, many people much preferred when the students were chanting "Ken-Ne-Dy" back in 1963. Both chants symbolize much more than just support for these two men. They personify the divergent sociopolitical models that were increasingly the focus of conflict in the Federal Republic of the 1960s. The chants of 1963 and 1968 have an emotionally laden, plebiscitary tone in common, but the political views behind them are fundamentally different. The chant "Ken-Ne-Dy" is a spontaneous acclamation, an expression of a communal experience, a celebration of Kennedy and his charismatic leadership, an affirmation of German-American friendship and the promise of freedom it holds for the Federal Republic and West Berlin. "Ho-Ho-Ho-Chi-Minh" expresses an anti-imperialistic solidarity with the people of the Third World and a sympathy to – if not approval of – socialism. This preference is an indication that the United States no longer stands as the obligatory role model for West Germany. There are now clearly limits to the reach of America's figurative frontier. The chant of 1963 rings with the positive assumption that Germans and Americans share a common postwar history. The chant of 1968 reverberates with criticism of German and American history.

The contrast between "Ken-Ne-Dy" and "Ho-Ho-Ho-Chi-Minh" reflects one of the basic social rifts that became evident within West Germany in the 1960s. These chants convey opposing concepts of domestic social order and foreign policy, and they represent the poles of West German views on relations with the United States. The one chant is a declaration of allegiance to the transatlantic community of shared identity with the United States; the other, a critical rejection of self-identification with the United States and its government. The purpose of this book is not to explain how this polarization came about, but a history of Kennedy's visit to Berlin must acknowledge that the vision of German-American relations Kennedy personified would soon come under challenge. That said, let us return to the events of June 26, 1963. Following the visit to the Free University, the German and American delegations go their separate ways for the first time that day. The German contingent heads toward Tegel Airport. The Americans drive to the U.S. military headquarters in West Berlin. There, the president inspects an honor guard from his car and then takes time to exchange a few words with several of the assembled soldiers. Kennedy's address is short but very heartfelt. In the history of the United States, he says, there have been many "beleaguered garrisons."[87] Yet none have ever had to face the extremely difficult challenge of being located in the middle of the opponent's – Kennedy does not use the word *enemy* – territory. In keeping with his vision of the Atlantic community, the president makes a conspicuous effort during this stop to make reference to the British and French troops stationed in West Berlin.

From the U.S. garrison, the motorcade, moving faster than it had earlier in the day, travels northward in a slight curve toward Tegel Airport. The route takes Kennedy along the city's new freeway. The 88-foot-wide road is the first urban expressway in Germany, and the Berlin Senate is very proud of it. The president thus gets to see the automobile-friendly side of the city.[88] North of the Spree River and the park grounds of Charlottenburg Palace, the motorcade turns east and drives across Jakob Kaiser Platz and past a large new apartment complex. Once again, West Berlin presents itself as a modern, efficient city. The final stretch then leads to the side entrance of the airport. Along the route from the U.S. military headquarters to Tegel Airport, crowds once again line the streets and overpasses. They cheer the president and "shower their guest with a storm of enthusiasm" and flowers.[89]

Adenauer and Brandt are waiting for Kennedy at Tegel. Brandt brushes the last bits of confetti off his suit. Finally, the presidential motorcade arrives, escorted to the last by the press vehicle. Kennedy demonstratively chats with Adenauer on the runway. Then the president presents himself for the last time congenially at the side of the French commander, General Toulouse, as the band plays a march and a 21-gun salute is fired. According to the agreement between Bonn and Berlin, the honor of giving the farewell speech has been reserved for the chancellor. Adenauer keeps his remarks short. He is obviously moved and apparently somewhat tired after such an eventful day. As he did in his address at the banquet in Bonn, Adenauer dwells on the unusual display of emotion on the part of the Germans during this trip and turns it into political capital. The feelings expressed for Kennedy by the Germans were sincere; they came truly from the heart. The president, in turn, thanks his hosts for the "warmth of welcome" he received. Such a reception, he says, will disperse any doubts that Americans might have about the legitimacy of the country's involvement in the world. Kennedy again mentions the anecdote he told the previous evening in Wiesbaden about leaving his successor a small note that was only to be opened when things were going badly. He then adds that perhaps he himself will open that envelope one day for the advice "Go to Germany!"[90]

Three days earlier, Kennedy had arrived at the Cologne-Bonn Airport and descended the gangway with an air of unpretentious American civility. In Berlin, he bids farewell in similar manner. He shakes hands with the French commander of the honor guard, several journalists, and the members of his German motorcade escort, who have lined up in a final formation. There seems to be no end to the handshaking. Then Kennedy agilely ascends the gangway. At 5:45 p.m., more than eight hours after its arrival in West Berlin, Air Force One rolls down the runway. The noise from the jet engines drowns out the military band playing "*Berliner Luft.*" The plane takes off and the final curtain falls on Berlin. One of the most important, most carefully prepared, and most difficult-to-stage political performances of the twentieth century has come to an end.

Kennedy's European trip is far from over, however. The plane carrying the presidential entourage now heads toward Ireland, the home of Kennedy's ancestors. He is to spend three days in Ireland, and there, too, he receives a warm welcome. On June 29, he flies via Gatwick to Birch Grove in the English county of Sussex for a brief visit with Prime Minister Harold Macmillan. The next day he travels to Italy, where he meets President Antonio Segni as well as other high-ranking Italian politicians and NATO officials. A visit to NATO's southern headquarters in Naples is also included on the agenda, as is an audience with the new pope, Paul VI, who confers his blessing on the president. Kennedy leaves Europe on July 2. His plan to visit Europe had initially been quite controversial at home. The trip has now come off without a single faux pas and has not spurred any new political tensions. It is one of the most successful trips of Kennedy's presidency. This success can be attributed above all to the enormous demonstration of enthusiasm Kennedy experienced in Berlin, which will remain in the memory of generations thanks to his own declaration "*Ich bin ein Berliner.*"

4

After the Final Curtain

During Kennedy's tour through West Berlin, the public showered the presidential limousine with confetti and flowers – in blatant disregard of police warnings. These harmless, friendly projectiles were tolerated, however, and not only by the police. The West German politicians present in West Berlin watched the events unfold with smiles on their faces, proudly knowing that each piece of confetti and each bouquet of flowers increased the political capital to be gained from the trip to Berlin both for Kennedy and for German-American relations. Just as the chauffeur of Kennedy's limousine attempted to keep a clear view of the streets by using his hands and the car's windshield wipers to wipe away confetti and flowers, so, too, did political observers attempt to keep a clear view of the event, its political importance, and the road still to be traveled once the final curtain had fallen on this astounding performance.

WESTERNIZATION AS HAPPENING: STREET THEATER AND *EIGENSINN*

Kennedy's speech at the Paulskirche in Frankfurt, his stop to view the Berlin Wall, the moment of silence at Schöneberg City Hall as the Freedom Bell tolled – these moments helped give Kennedy's trip to Germany a festive yet serious character. These scenes symbolized German-American solidarity and the earnestness of the United States' commitment to Europe. They were, though, only part of the picture. There were other more popular, humorous and even carnivalesque moments. They too can be interpreted as evidence of West Germany's alignment with the West. At the same time, they can also be seen as part of the tradition of "street theater" as a medium for the expression of public opinion.[1]

Kennedy contributed to the popular tone of the visit with his smile and spontaneous words and gestures. It was, however, the active participation of the public that gave the visit its lively character and turned it into the biggest political happening in German postwar history until the fall of the Berlin Wall. The term *happening* evolved in the 1960s and was widely used throughout West Germany. It was originally used by artists at the time who took the Dada movement as a model. They attempted to abolish the distinction between artist, artwork, and audience – the distinction, more broadly, between the social contexts of creation and reception. The aim of artists such as Joseph Beuys, Allan Kaprow, and Wolf Vostell, was to turn the interaction between artist and audience into a creative process. The artistic process became an event and was often presented as a "performance."[2] In the course of the 1960s, the term *happening* was increasingly adopted outside the art world to describe certain forms of political action, such as demonstrations against the Vietnam War. *Happening* thus took on a somewhat subversive connotation that persists today. When we strip the term of this normative connotation – its suggestion of anti-American protest – happenings become more like theatrical performances in which the distinction between the audience and the actors is blurred. Such was the nature of Kennedy's visit to Germany. It was an interactive performance steeped in popular culture and difficult to control. This aspect of the event is, however, rarely alluded to in official accounts.

The public refused to remain passive during Kennedy's visit. Police measures, street politics, and the calls for restraint helped discipline the public but did not stop it from loudly registering its presence. Public pressure compelled planners to make changes to the itinerary, as in the case of the motorcade route, and to reposition the press platform facing the Schöneberg City Hall at the last minute. The public also had a direct influence on the politicians. The audience shaped the way Kennedy, Brandt, and Adenauer perceived the event; in turn, all three adjusted their speeches to address the audience directly. The main way the public influenced Kennedy's visit, however, was by using its freedom in the streets and testing the limits of control. They were not seeking to change the social order, but trying, rather, to influence the staging of politics. Individually and collectively, the members of the public refused to comply fully with the authorities' expectations even if they had no intention of actually disrupting or subverting the official program. During the course of the performance, the audience injected its own spontaneous meanings into the events. Its collective body language was not entirely in line with the authorities' ideas about mobilizing the public. At the same time, though, its behavior was by no means at odds with the authorities' goal of expressing solidarity with the president.

This phenomenon is best summarized, as noted at the close of Chapter 2, by the term *Eigensinn*.[3] Translated literally, *Eigensinn* means "one's own sense." As an analytical concept, it signifies the specific logic that individuals and groups bring to their social interactions. *Eigensinn* is not simply stubbornness or a refusal to obey rules; the term does not necessarily denote popular resistance to authority. It describes, rather, the desire to act independently of the claims or demands of others and to claim agency, even if only temporarily or in a circumscribed context.

Kennedy's visit provided West Germans and West Berliners a limited opportunity to violate the usual rules of public conduct and to exercise their *Eigensinn*. This attitude was first seen in Cologne. Following the president's short address outside the city hall, the jubilant crowd could hardly be contained. Far from trying to threaten Kennedy, the spectators wanted to get as close to him as possible, to bask in his aura. Police officers on horseback worked hard to hold the crowd in check. The American television correspondent Daniel Schorr reported: "The rules have been broken, the lines are down. The people of Cologne surge around." Only with a great deal of effort were police able to clear a path for the president to the Cologne cathedral. He did not escape the "flood of people" until the heavy bronze doors of the cathedral were closed behind him.[4]

Two days later in Wiesbaden, the situation was worse. By the time the reception started that evening in the Kurhaus, the city's spa, a crowd of 250,000 had gathered in front of the building. Hans Ulrich Kempski of the *Süddeutsche Zeitung* described the dramatic scene when the crowd pushed toward the Kurhaus and threatened to storm it: "The police on horseback dashed like Cossacks through the flower beds in order to keep the surging and irrational masses just barely in check. When Kennedy left the Kurhaus, his car rolled through an uninhibitedly excited crowd, over purses and hats that had been lost and over shoes that had been ripped off women's feet."[5] Kempski's vivid account is not mere journalistic hype. The German public had pushed the limits of acceptability in manifesting its enthusiasm.

Even in Berlin, where a plan for street politics had been worked out in great detail, the rules were repeatedly bent or broken. People in the crowd pushed, pressed, and swore at each other, especially when someone managed to reach the front row through some particularly clever trick. Traffic signs were bent out of shape as people attempted to climb them in the hope of getting a better view. The police were lenient. The only poster they removed, for example, was one hung along a street in Dahlem that read "Clay for President"; although it was apparently intended as an expression of admiration for the hero of the Airlift, police officials had the poster taken down to spare Kennedy potential embarrassment.[6] In all of the cities Kennedy visited, anticipation and excitement caused some of the people waiting for the president to collapse in exhaustion. The warm summer weather undoubtedly had an effect as well. As often happened at Beatles concerts at the time, the police had to carry women who had fainted to the first-aid tents. Red Cross workers and medical teams certainly had their hands full. At the Römerberg in Frankfurt, 250 people attending the rally were brought to the first-aid stations with bruises and contusions. During the Schöneberg rally in Berlin, 26 people required hospitalization.[7]

Something else is quite striking. The happening featured carnivalesque and anarchic aspects. Even Kennedy and Adenauer did their part to create a Carnival-like mood on June 23 by calling out "*Kölle Alaaf* " to the crowd in Cologne, a custom otherwise reserved for the pre-Lent Carnival season. There were other similarities to Carnival: the streets lined with jubilant spectators waiting for the motorcade, the procession through the crowded streets, the long line of vehicles led by a police escort, and, in Berlin, the rain of confetti. Some spectators at the Römerberg and other places dressed up as American Indians. They coupled German romantic views of North America and the Wild West, which were influenced by the immensely popular adventure stories of Karl May (1842–1912), with their enthusiasm for a president of what was now a nuclear-age superpower. These "Indians" signaled their respect for the official framework of the visit by displaying their enthusiasm for the president, just as the West German government wished. At the same time, they changed that framework and redefined it by taking the initiative in using popular culture for their display of enthusiasm.

The Berliners engaged in a distinctive form of carnivalesque celebration. They didn't simply toss confetti like Carnival spectators in Cologne: they let loose a storm of colored paper and balloons. Although not specifically planned by government officials, West Berliners and their confetti gave foreign observers who were familiar with tickertape parades in the United States the impression that the West Berliners were more American than the West Germans were. Confetti and balloons also helped create an atmosphere similar to that of an American election campaign. Indeed, the planners of Kennedy's trip employed what Theodore C. Sorensen described as "old Kennedy campaign techniques": preparatory public relations work in advance of the visit, a motorcycle escort, local color, humor, and as much television coverage as possible.[8] These elements gave the Kennedy trip the feeling of a show, as many visitors from the United States noticed – some skeptically, others approvingly. The Stanford University historian Gordon

Craig, a guest professor at the FU, pointed out the "elements of Hollywood and Madison Avenue in JFK's style" even before the president's arrival in Berlin. Craig felt that the concurrence of Kennedy's visit and the West Berlin film festival was characteristic. Some of his German colleagues also appeared to be irritated over the "frenetic excitement" of the jubilant crowd.[9]

It is important to understand the interaction between compliance and *Eigensinn* if we are to accurately perceive the full impact of the Kennedy trip with regard to the Americanization and Westernization of the Federal Republic.[10] This interaction reflects the West Germans' efforts to identify themselves politically with the West – to distance themselves from the Nazi past as well as from the conformity imposed by socialism in East Germany. Together, the police and the public maintained a balance between discipline and freedom, control and spontaneity; between public conformity to the government's aim of welcoming the president and public nonconformity in expressing that welcome. To observers in Germany and abroad, the fact that this balance was maintained demonstrated that democracy had gained a solid foothold in the Federal Republic. To have maintained this balance even as vast numbers of people turned out to see Kennedy is an amazing achievement that has yet to be fully acknowledged. The most spectacular breach of rules and expectations during Kennedy's visit was committed by the leading actor himself when he departed from the prepared script for his speech at Schöneberg City Hall and improvised much of what he said. It was this breach, this spontaneous act, that was applauded more than all else and by all sides. That, too, is part of the irony inherent in the Kennedy trip to Germany.

"KENNEDY FEVER": A SHOW OF EMOTION

Two days after Kennedy left Berlin, the American ambassador in Bonn, George McGhee, summarized the resonance of the president's visit in Germany: it simply dominated the mass media, and the Germans were speaking of little else. In particular, the "unexpected and overwhelming reception accorded the President at all stops, climaxing with jubilant enthusiasm and heartfelt response on the part of West Berliners, exceeded expectations of all experienced observers." The United States Information Service office in Bonn, a seismograph of public opinion, did not hesitate to use superlatives. The trip had a "record after-effect" and prompted "the largest spontaneous public response for a foreign visitor in German history."[11]

That observation points to the first concrete political gain achieved through the visit: Kennedy had won the popularity contest with Charles de

Gaulle. The consensus among political commentators was that the reception given Kennedy by the Germans surpassed the undeniably warm and enthusiastic welcome the French president had received in September 1962. The iconic image of Kennedy speaking to the crowds in front of Schöneberg City Hall proved as inspiring as that of de Gaulle and Adenauer in Reims and even came to overshadow it. In a radio and television address broadcasted to the American people on July 5, 1963, Kennedy himself deemed the trip a success and described it as "a moving experience."[12] Just as the success of the political talks held in Bonn and the impact of the key speeches Kennedy gave in Germany had been translated into political capital, so too was the reaction of the German people to the American president. Estimates of the size of the cheering crowds now carried great weight as political arguments among the Western allies. The performance had paid off.

The numbers alone were quite impressive. In West Germany, hundreds of thousands had celebrated Kennedy's visit. The crowds that turned out in West Berlin to see and cheer Kennedy were larger than in any other city on his European itinerary. Police put the number of spectators in Berlin at 1,412,000; lower estimates still put the number at more than 1.1 million, which translated to nearly 58 percent of the adults and young people of West Berlin.[13] According to a poll commissioned by the mayor's office, approximately 90 percent of the spectators who gathered in the streets of West Berlin to catch a glimpse of Kennedy returned home once the motorcade passed so that they could continue to follow Kennedy's visit on television. In fact, television was the most important multiplier of the event. At the time of Kennedy's visit, between 7.5 million and 8 million homes in the Federal Republic had televisions. On the third and fourth days of Kennedy's visit, more than 60 percent of West German televisions were on during the evening news brodcasts. Clusters of people gathered inside appliance shops and in front of store windows to watch – often with "hypnotic fascination" – the live broadcast of the visit. In response to continued interest in Kenendy's trip, the television station Freies Berlin produced a several-hour-long documentary about it three weeks later.[14]

Not only had many Germans watched the coverage of Kennedy's visit, an opinion poll found, but most were impressed by what they had seen, starting with the coverage of Kennedy's arrival at the Cologne-Bonn Airport. The ratings climbed as the trip progressed and peaked on June 26 with the broadcast from Berlin. On the whole, the viewer reaction was more favorable than it had been during de Gaulle's visit less than a year before.[15] Viewers described the Berlin broadcast as "exceptional," "spectacular," "breathtaking," and "moving." The day before Kennedy was in

West Berlin, one viewer succinctly summed up his impression by saying: "It's all so smashing, the whole event with Kennedy." Such quotes reveal a fascination with the medium that enabled electronically transmitted images to be experienced as immediate, tangible reality. Innumerable viewers stated expressly that television offered them the unique opportunity "to be able to experience everything so directly." Experiencing the event through the media could even seem to be more immediate than the live experience of being there on the streets. "You were always in the front row; better than if you had really stood there."[16] The television coverage of Vice President Johnson's visit two years earlier had had a similar effect. "All day I sat in front of the television screen and 'cheered' with the rest of them," one woman from West Berlin recalled shortly after Johnson's trip to Germany.[17]

Many viewers in June 1963 used another means to record for themselves and others what they were seeing and experiencing on television. They took photos of the television screen when Kennedy appeared; some people sent these photographs to the White House. This was another dimension of the politics of visibility. These photos of television images documented not only the objects on which the cameras had focused but the event of viewing as well. Reality as fabricated by the media provided the means to create miniature political icons.[18] Newspapers on both sides of the Atlantic favored photos of Kennedy on the viewing platform in front of the Berlin Wall and thereby popularized the most striking images of the trip.

The consensus in the German press was that the intensity of the warmth and enthusiasm expressed during the trip was unsurpassable. West Germans had an "exceptional, personal liking" for Kennedy, the *Frankfurter Rundschau* reported, that also signaled a broad-based acceptance of his administration's political goals. The *Bonner General-Anzeiger* went even further, claiming that the West Germans' response to Kennedy indicated their preference – should they have to choose – for American Atlanticism over the Gaullist vision of a more independent and self-confident Western Europe.[19] In his *Berlin Briefing* of July 6, Harold Hurwitz, a close associate of Willy Brandt, put his finger on the unique aspect of the West German willingness to support U.S. foreign policy: as a result of having experienced Kennedy, West Germans who had previously been skeptical now accepted his call for détente and a new realism in international relations.[20] Hurwitz's assessment shows how communal experience had become a means of affirming transnational relations with the United States during a period of political reorientation.

The American media took a similar tone. The trip received an enormous amount of attention from the print media and the television networks. The consensus in the media was that the trip was a success. Even the *New York*

Times and Walter Lippmann, who had been so critical of the trip initially, now found it hard to find anything to complain about. After all, the president had been able to warn "hot heads" in Germany to be cautious and realistic. Even Lippmann, as McGeorge Bundy observed in a friendly note to the columnist, could occasionally make a mistake.[21] Still, some within the Republican Party refused to applaud Kennedy or warned against misinterpreting his performance. Several major newspapers, including the *Chicago Tribune* and the *Wall Street Journal*, did not approve of Kennedy's "ventures in personal diplomacy." Others were relieved that the president had later used his speech at the FU to moderate the statements he made in his "supercharged speech" in Schöneberg.[22] Despite the scattered criticism, the German Consul General in New York was certain of one thing: "Millions would have been needed in order to achieve anything even close to this success with the means typically used in our political public relations work."[23]

The response among the other Western allies was less emotional and thus more predictable. From Rome to Paris, there was relief that Kennedy had downgraded the issue of German reunification. The official French reaction, understandably, was not enthusiastic, in light of the president's skeptical stance toward de Gaulle's European policies. Paris praised America's commitment to Europe but still questioned the long-term reliability of American military guarantees. The British press maintained that Britain, not the Federal Republic, was the true friend of the United States. The *Daily Express* was convinced that the Federal Republic only sought to support the transatlantic alliance until it got what it really wanted – nuclear weapons. Then the alliance would fall apart.[24]

As was to be expected, the greatest criticism was voiced in the Eastern bloc. The Soviet Union and East Germany condemned Kennedy's trip to West Germany in general and his visit to West Berlin in particular as concessions to West German revanchism that benefited the interests of American monopoly capitalism. What was worse, according to the Eastern press, was that Kennedy had backtracked on his pledge to pursue peaceful cooperation. At Schöneberg City Hall, Kennedy had let loose a tirade of "vile anticommunist attacks." The GDR pointed out the contradictions between Kennedy's address at American University on June 10 and the emotional speech on June 26 without, however, mentioning the "*Ich bin ein Berliner*" declaration. One particular detail seemed quite noteworthy to *Neues Deutschland*. Contrary to planned protocol, the president ended his visit to the Brandenburg Gate after only five minutes. In light of the "red flags of the working class, the national emblem of the GDR, the protective wall," and the posted slogans, the "otherwise so self-assured" president became "nervous."[25]

The spectacular Schöneberg speech was the only part of the trip that had troublesome consequences. How should supporters of détente in the United States and Berlin handle the fact that the president had declared cooperation with the communists impossible in light of what Berlin stood for? Why had he not drawn the opposite conclusion, much as he had in the June 10 speech? Damage control became a top priority and attention was to be redirected to Kennedy's statements in the FU speech. On June 28, Willy Brandt set out to do just that. The president was not categorically against negotiations between the Soviet Union and the United States, he maintained. Then Brandt rather rashly contended that Kennedy had actually been trying to argue in his speech at Schöneberg City Hall that France's communists should not be included in the country's new government.[26]

No other aspect of Kennedy's trip attracted as much attention as the level of emotion it produced. This provided Bonn, West Berlin, and Washington with political capital that each could draw upon, both in their dealings with one another and on the international stage. The German and American people defined their relations in terms of this emotionality. Earlier I named four dimensions that become apparent in connection with emotions in transnational relations, specifically when determining who is expressing them and what they are articulating. The first three dimensions – individuals, collective actors such as nation-states, and emotions as a factor in international relations – will be summarized here in light of the events described. The fourth dimension – the emotionality of large crowds – will be addressed in the following section.

Prior to the president's trip to Germany, three prominent American visitors to Berlin – Christian Herter (1959), Lyndon B. Johnson (1961), and Robert F. Kennedy (1962) – returned to the United States with extremely positive, emotionally laden impressions shaped by the strong expressions of feeling on the part of the West Berliners. All three consequently considered their trips to be political successes. Herter's trip was described by the U.S. ambassador to Germany as "a really touching spectacle." Upon his return to the States, Johnson reported to Kennedy that the trip had been "one of the most moving and satisfying experiences of my life." There was hardly a dry eye in the delegation. This was a surprising statement coming from such a hardened politician, who had come to the Berlin "front" with another "tough guy," Lucius D. Clay, as a colonel stationed in Berlin noted.[27] At the end of his visit, Bobby Kennedy thanked Willy Brandt for the "extraordinarily warm" hospitality. Later he wrote that he had never been "so moved" by crowds as he had in Berlin. He was convinced that Berliners were particularly "staunch friends of the United States and dedicated anti-Communists."[28]

The experience of the lead actors in 1963 was just as remarkable. Official comments and press accounts alike reiterated the idea that this trip was imbued with an extraordinary and unexpected cordiality. This same message carried over into the lead actors' political statements. The warm welcome given the president by the people of Berlin left Kennedy and Brandt feeling that their strategic interests were in harmony. "I have been impressed by the degree to which we see these great issues alike," Kennedy told the mayor. Close advisors to Kennedy confirmed through diplomatic channels that Kennedy himself was deeply impressed by the enthusiastic welcome he had experienced in Germany.[29] Adenauer used the "warmth of the welcome" extended to Kennedy to emphasize to his guest the strength of West Germany's solidarity with the United States and thereby to strengthen the country's position on the international stage. Personal contact did indeed engender greater trust between the elderly chancellor and the youthful president, Brandt's later claims to the contrary notwithstanding. This trust was not, however, to have lasting political effect. Adenauer told Kennedy rather matter-of-factly that he had received "useful impulses" for his policies.[30]

The chancellor was able, though, to take advantage of the emotional impressions Kennedy's visit had left in its wake. On July 4, 1963, Charles de Gaulle arrived in Bonn for a meeting with the chancellor. Adenauer cleverly emphasized that any doubts in the United States about Germans and Europeans had been dispelled by the "friendliness" of the welcome Kennedy had received in Germany and by the fact that Kennedy had been "extraordinarily impressed" at seeing the Berlin situation firsthand. After all, this experience had subsequently prompted Kennedy to depart from planned protocol and vehemently condemn communism.[31]

The most important foreign policy benefit resulting from Kennedy's trip was undoubtedly the favorable turn in German–American relations. The injection of such positive emotion lifted the relations out of crisis and mistrust. Less than a year after the controversy surrounding Ambassador Grewe and six months after the signing of the Franco-German treaty, relations between Bonn and Washington could once again be described as friendly. From the experience of community building arose a new degree of political loyalty and legitimacy on behalf of the transatlantic alliance. Neither would be permanent, nor did this turnround mean that existing problems had disappeared into thin air. However, the increase in loyalty and legitimacy represented an enormous political gain in light of the heavy toll on German-American relations that the seemingly unending Berlin crisis since 1958 and the conflicts over the Kennedy administration's new détente policy had taken. The West German embassy in Washington succinctly summed up the positive turn of developments by noting that the "atmosphere had improved" in German-American relations and that "an undertone of cordiality never before registered so clearly" had become apparent.[32]

The process of translating emotions into political arguments would not have occurred so smoothly without the help of the West German and American media. The media in both countries treated the German people as a collective actor when describing the public mood. The press portrayal of the Germans was limited to a few main features and relied on vivid metaphors. Three types of metaphors were usually used: temperature metaphors, weather metaphors, and body part metaphors. All three varieties of metaphor were used to describe the individual actors, the collective actor, and the relations between the Federal Republic and the United States. They became a vehicle of what could be called a politics of emotions.

Kennedy was initially the primary focus of attention. Though he was well liked, particularly in Germany, the president was considered to be the epitome of the cool, rational, Machiavellian politician before his European trip.[33] Marguerite Higgins, an American journalist and Berlin enthusiast, had high expectations of Kennedy as the trip approached. Kennedy needed to become emotionally involved in this trip, she argued, and to be exposed to the German people if he was to understand them. Writing in the newspaper *Die Welt* in late May, Higgins observed:

To date, Kennedy has no emotional attachment to the Germans....During the coming trip, however, the impersonal relations of expediency can be changed. If...President Kennedy comes into contact with masses of German people, he will have the opportunity to meet the common German as he truly is.

And this is important. To base a relationship to a people solely on intellect means to ignore not only the truly human components of a person's psychology, but those of the national character as well. Perhaps the president really needs to have stood at Ulbricht's wall himself in order to understand the psychological shock Berliners suffered because of American inaction in August 1961.[34]

Once Kennedy arrived in Germany, the recurring question in the press was whether the Germans' show of emotion would have a cathartic effect upon the usually even-tempered president. Each sign, gesture, and remark he made was interpreted in light of this question, particularly on the day he was in Berlin. The press portrayed the rise in temperature and in temperament as if tracking the course of a fever. The "cool, intellectual president"

(*Tagesspiegel*) was becoming more and more human, a man who stood in front of the cheering crowds in Schöneberg "almost as if [he felt] helpless and embarrassed" (*Süddeutsche Zeitung*) and delivered his "*Ich bin ein Berliner*" line "more or less humbly and modestly" (*Die Welt*).[35] For a few moments, the leader of the greatest superpower in the world appeared even to lose "control over his feelings." He expressed "his aroused feelings openly" to the world. In Berlin, in the shadow of the Wall, a "new Kennedy" was born, a man in whom "great passion suddenly broke through the existing cool veneer" he had maintained for so long. The Germans most responsible for this were the West Berliners, argued the *Berliner Morgenpost*. Their warmth had blazed a trail through the "cool and rational view of the world held by this man from Boston."[36]

"Kennedy fever" (*B.Z.*) proved highly infectious; even the president himself was not immune. It was able to melt the "ice that could be found here and there in German-American relations." America's Berlin had emerged during the Soviet blockade as the symbol of the postwar interests that tied Americans most closely to the Germans. This Berlin, consolidated through a dense network of ties, had become bound up with powerful associations and memories in both societies. Amid the excitement generated on both sides of the Atlantic by Kennedy's visit, America's Berlin radiated a warmth that brought a thaw to German-American relations. The city provided the emotional environment needed for the political transformation that turned the most powerful American alive into a warmhearted Berliner.

The Germans, too, were transformed, according to the press coverage during Kennedy's trip. Commentators frequently used weather metaphors to describe this transformation. The spectors who turned out to see Kennedy had been swept up in a "whirlwind of excitement," and their cheering resounded like a "storm." Other accounts spoke of the "mass intoxication" of the crowds and of spectators watching the proceedings in a "state of ecstasy."[37] The West Berliners, who lived at the "border to suffering" and had survived blockades and ultimatums, had been caught in a "surging wave of excitement." Whereas the celebration of Kennedy had been an "experience" in Cologne and a "rally" in Frankfurt, in Berlin it was – in the words of *Die Welt* – "one large roar of relief, of liberation."[38] In retrospect, the American commander in Berlin called it an "ovation" from the West Berliners that would never be matched in "warmth and sincerity."[39]

The images of emotional euphoria popularized by the media suggested a symbiotic emotional relationship: Kennedy the disciplined stategist was liberated by the crowds of excited Germans, just as he had helped them uncork their bottled-up emotions. The lead actor took his cue from the audience

Illustration 29. To touch the robe of salvation: West Berliners reach out for direct contact with the guest from America. Source: Süddeutscher Verlag, Munich (no. 00109931).

as the audience projected its hopes and feelings upon him. As one woman put it in late June 1963, she had been "Kennedied" (*"ge-Kennedy'd*).["40] Her words summed up the feelings of many. The idea of an emotional symbiosis inferred the ability on the part of the political leader to attract the masses and, in turn, the willingness on the part of the public to put their faith in this leader. It was, to cite Max Weber once again, a charismatic relationship between the politician and the people.[41] Another aspect of this relationship was the desire to be in the physical presence of the leader, which is characteristic of a political religion (Illustration 29).

As during the Berlin visits of Lyndon B. Johnson and Robert F. Kennedy, the people sought physical contact with the American guest in June 1963. They wanted to be near the president, to experience a moment of redemption and communion with him, even if this lasted no longer than the second or two it took to shake his hand. West Germans behaved, in the words of a contemporary observer, as if "they were dealing with a miracle-working relic" (*"Wunder spendende Reliquie"*). They attempted to "at least touch [Kennedy] with their fingertips."[42] Such behavior was prompted by a public longing for political salvation, much as had been the case during

Johnson's visit two years earlier. For most observers, it was both obvious and politically understandable that this hope for salvation was felt less intensely by those living in the relatively safe West German cities of Bonn, Cologne, Wiesbaden, and Frankfurt than in insular, dependent West Berlin.

In Berlin, the expectations placed on Kennedy grew into a fervent, religious-like hope of sustaining the moment of exhilaration and enthusiastic support: "Yet there is something else that was only occasionally apparent and never so intensely expressed during Kennedy's tours of Cologne, Bonn, Frankfurt, and Wiesbaden," *Die Welt* observed on June 27. "It is the hope, the anticipation, the devotion that moves Berliners so often to tears, the desire to hold onto this moment for themselves and for Berlin, and to let it become a decisive one for the fate of this city."[43] America's Berlin set its hopes on prolonging the present indefinitely, on continued American protection and charismatically conveyed transatlantic community.

The adoption of religious rites and expectation for secular public ritual was not limited to this longing for redemption through physical contact or the hope of everlasting protection. It was also expressed through direct appeals to God. This was not something new. The inauguration of the Freedom Bell back in 1950 was staged as an act of consecration, during which the people standing in Rudolph Wilde Platz listened in reverent silence as the bell tolled for the first time.[44] The planners of Kennedy's trip resorted to this tradition when arranging the ceremony in which Kennedy signed Berlin's Golden Book. Willy Brandt asked the hundreds of thousands of people in the square to "experience this truly significant moment in the history of this city . . . in ceremonial silence, in shared silence." In closing, Brandt translated into German the phrase engraved on the rim of the bell, a variation on a line from Abraham Lincoln's Gettysburg Address: "That This World Under God Shall Have a New Birth of Freedom." This line evoked a convergence, in the terminology of the philosopher Karl Löwith, of *Weltgeschichte* and *Heilsgeschehen* – of secular history and sacred history, of political history and the hope of salvation. Brandt later described the public's reaction at this point in the ceremony as the climax of a community-building experience: "The silence expressed the greatest measure of support and feeling of solidarity that Berlin could give. . . . Men bared their heads."[45]

This "greatest measure of support" was as much a voluntary act by the public as it was an orchestrated act of "political liturgy," a term historian George L. Mosse has used in describing the ideological and emotional foundations of modern nationalism. It is not merely a theoretical question to ask whether such liturgical elements, especially used in conjuction with symbolic politics and charismatic legitimacy, can and should be incorporated in a democratic system.[46] Observers at the time were ambivalent about the suggestive power of charismatic leadership and the emotional support it found among the public. During the visit of Charles de Gaulle in September 1962, the German press had described the French president as a "good judge of the soul of the masses" who had mastered the "technique of effectively dispensing" praise and support. He was, moreover, the "first man celebrated by the Germans as a hero since Germany's fall in 1945."[47] It was precisely the eagerness of the Germans to celebrate figures like de Gaulle and Kennedy that caused some observers, especially outside of Germany, to worry.

IN THE SHADOW OF HITLER

A large crowd cheers a political leader; men, women, and children stretch their arms out toward the powerful man in the hope of touching him; loud chanting echoes through the packed streets – such scenes were common during Kennedy's visit to West Germany and West Berlin. They were also laden with historical associations that could not be easily dismissed. Indeed, those associations were often explicitly noted, and description and prescription converged in the commentary on Kennedy's charisma and the behavior of the German crowds. Both in Germany and abroad, in short, the pictures of jubilant German crowds brought to mind all-too-familiar images of Hitler and the enraptured masses.

There is nothing uniquely German in scenes of masses of people mobilized to acclaim a leader or of participants in such events physically overcome by the emotional demands of the experience. Nor are such scenes a specifically twentieth-century phenomenon. They are, rather, aspects of a development that began with the "nationalization of the masses," to quote George L. Mosse again, at the end of the eighteenth century.[48] By the opening of the twentieth century, the idea of the nation had acquired enormous ideological power and could move vast numbers of people to action. Spectacular events such as rallies and commemorative ceremonies were staged to serve as a venue for plebiscitary acclamation of the nation and its leaders. Nation-states and patriotic organizations used these forms to conduct politics and exert pressure on established institutions of power. Groups from various ideological camps began to stage large gatherings, hold parades, and exploit the potential of modern media to create a mass audience for their messages. Often, the message was a call for war, imperial expansion, or violent seizure of power. The affective force of the nation and the nation-state played a central role in the efforts of self-styled leaders who, like Hitler, consciously attempted to exploit their charisma to serve their political ends.[49]

The authoritarian and totalitarian systems that arose in the first half of the twentieth century – state socialism, Fascism, and National Socialism – took mass mobilization to an extreme. Using parades, marches, party rallies, and violent street demonstrations, they imposed a sweeping conformity that extended beyond politics. They deployed the suggestive power of political liturgies and imposed their particular political aesthetics, which turned politics into a totalitarian spectacle.[50] Totalitarian regimes combined elements of sacred ritual in their secular mass mobilization and channeled human longing for salvation into support for their own political systems, each regime thereby creating its own political religion. A whole host of political symbols were integrated into these liturgies and at the same time influenced everyday life.[51]

No political system has been as closely associated with this style of mass mobilization as National Socialism. Swastikas and marching ranks of men clad in brown shirts; rhythmic anti-Semitic slogans and the staccato cry of *Sieg Heil!* reverberating in the streets; quasi-mythical celebrations of the solstice and seemingly endless rows of people participating in mass party rallies: such images shaped the way the Nazi dictatorship was viewed between 1933 and 1945 and later remained vivid in the memory of Germans and non-Germans alike.[52] After 1945, these images served as a warning against the reemergence of National Socialism and Nazi-inspired movements in Germany. Many of the people involved in planning Kennedy's trip to Germany and an even greater number of outside observers were aware of the negative connotations attached to any signs of mass mobilization and mass celebration. As mentioned earlier, this same awareness prompted the West Berlin Senate to decide against the large-scale use or distribution of flags. The "long shadow" of Germany's Nazi past fell upon Kennedy and his public in 1963.[53] Nowhere was this shadow as long and as dark as in Berlin, the city closely associated with Nazi rule from the Reichstag fire to Hitler's final days in the bunker below his Reich Chancellery.

No one in the West crudely equated the excitement Kennedy inspired with the frenzied adoration Hitler had prompted or simply accused the West Germans of demonstrating Nazi leanings. Hitler's shadow fell on Kennedy's visit in a variety of ways and, likewise, was perceived, forgotten, or repressed in a variety of ways. Those best at blinding themselves to the shadow were the West Germans themselves; many simply refused to see it. Some, though, saw it clearly. The West Berlin Senate, for example, took action to try to prevent public behavior that might bring unwanted historical and political associations to mind. Other observers considered the public response to Hitler a legitimate point of reference for gauging Kennedy's reception. One respondent to a survey suggested that even Hitler had never been as enthusiastically cheered and as warmly received as Kennedy had been. A small handful saw no difference between the clamorous greetings given Hitler and Kennedy: "Germans are just good at this," one person explained to a pollster.[54] Most West Germans, including many members of the press, dealt with Hitler's shadow by making only indirect reference to it when commenting on the conduct of the crowds. The *Frankfurter Allgemeine Zeitung*, for instance, noted in its front-page story on the Berlin visit that "no wrong overtones" had been heard and that the concern voiced before Kennedy's arrival about the "inflammability of the crowd" had proven to be unjustified.[55]

Foreign observers tended to take a more nuanced view, but they also tended to describe conformist mass excitement as something specifically German. RIAS director Robert H. Lochner, who had spent his youth in Berlin and, as the *Süddeutsche Zeitung* noted, did not hesitate to "speak about the tendency of the German people to succumb easily to mass elation," was quoted as saying: "This did not happen even during Hitler's best years!" The ever-cautious *Neue Züricher Zeitung* spoke evasively of the "proven ability" of the German people "to become enthusiastic under certain conditions," which they expressed "sometimes also in the familiar form of abruptly short choruses."[56] In particular, the chant "Ken-Ne-Dy" raised many a skeptical eyebrow. In the United States, several Republicans tried to corner the Democratic president by calling attention to the similarities between that rhythmic chant and the Nazi chorus *Sieg Heil*: Kennedy, they claimed, would have fit better in the atmosphere of the 1930s than that of his own times.[57] American television viewers learned from network correspondents that "misused enthusiasm" in Berlin had caused the "greatest error in German history" between 1933 and 1945. Although American journalists referred to Germany's "tragic error" – in retrospect, a rather apologetic and misleading formulation – there was no suggestion that Germans should stand condemned for all time. Since not a trace of Nazi symbolism was evident during Kennedy's trip, National Socialism appeared to be an exception and a deviation from the normal path of history.[58]

The memory of Hitler remained vivid among some of Kennedy's advisors. Arthur M. Schlesinger, the noted Harvard historian turned White House staffer, later used the word "hysteria" to describe the behavior of the crowd in Rudolph Wilde Platz during Kennedy's speech. "The crowd shook itself and rose and roared like an animal," he recalled. Schlesinger's account is the only one on record that paints such a picture. Others explicitly point out the absence of hysteria in Berlin, and they are supported by the television footage of the event, which likewise suggests that the comparison of the crowd to a crazed animal was a retrospective projection. The German press was particularly careful to emphasize that Kennedy was not trying to "fanaticize the masses" and that the enthusiasm expressed by the West Berliners was "genuine" and "not mass hysteria."[59] This observation was intended both to describe the event accurately and to make a clear distinction between the celebration of Kennedy and the fanatical adoration of Hitler.

Both the depiction of a supposedly hysterical crowd and the defensive reaction against such a depiction are prompted by two psychological concerns that are politically relevant. The first is the assumption that masses per se are irrational and unpredictable and therefore dangerous. History certainly offers some disturbing examples that might seem to support this view. The second concern is expressed in the opinion, derived from historical experience, that the masses in Germany are particularly susceptible to fanaticism – a sweeping but somehow understandable generalization. One thing was clear in June 1963: even John F. Kennedy did not escape the long, dark shadow cast by Hitler.

"NIKITA, NIKITA!": KHRUSHCHEV ON STAGE

When Kennedy departed from Tegel Airport in the late afternoon of June 26, the curtain appeared to have fallen on the Berlin stage. The platforms were dismantled, the confetti was swept off the streets, and the good reviews of the performance began to come in. But as the backstage celebration was kicking off in the West, preparations for a similar performance in the East were underway. On June 24, the GDR and the Soviet Union announced that the Soviet leader Nikita Khrushchev would visit East Berlin four days later. The official occasion for the visit was the seventieth birthday of Walter Ulbricht and the meeting of Eastern European leaders scheduled to take place during the celebration. Ulbricht had held the post of Secretary General of the Socialist Unity Party (SED) since 1950 (First Secretary since 1953), and in 1960, he became both the chairman of the National Defense Council and the chairman of the State Council. He was undoubtedly the most powerful man in East Germany, and therefore the celebration of his birthday was to be a major event. However, the central purpose of the Khrushchev trip was not to honor Ulbricht but to stage a performance to outshine the celebration of the American president in West Berlin. What had just taken place in the West was now to be outdone by the East.

The logic of the Cold War had dictated from the outset that a propaganda initiative by one side had to be offset by a countermeasure by the other. A public relations coup by one could not go unanswered. Each side kept a close watch on the other's staging of politics. Khrushchev's trip was thus undertaken to counter Kennedy's, providing another example of the continuous superpower competition in the realm of symbolic action. In this instance, the politics of visibility was supplemented by the politics of audibility. The chant "Ken-Ne-Dy" was to be drowned out by the cry "Nikita, Nikita!" coming from the East.[60]

The SED had already stepped up its public relations work in the days just prior to Kennedy's visit to Berlin. Political observers in East Berlin were well informed. *Neues Deutschland* and the *Berliner Zeitung* repeatedly ridiculed the Kennedy administration for domestic and foreign policy problems confronting it, the racial unrest in the Southern states and the country's growing military involvement in Vietnam. Conflicts within the Western alliance were also highlighted. In addition, there were broadside attacks against the Adenauer government's domestic policies. The familiar accusations about Bonn's revanchist agenda and the presence of former Nazis in important positions were repeated yet again. A political cartoon published in *Neues Deutschland* on June 25 shows Kennedy shaking the hand of Hans Globke, who was then undersecretary in the West German Chancellery; as a young lawyer during the Nazi era, Globke had helped draft the Nuremberg Laws. In the cartoon, blood drips from Globke's hand onto an oversized wanted poster on which his face appears next to an image of him in uniform giving the Nazi salute; the blood falls on the poster just above the words "*9,000,000 Tote*" – nine million dead.[61]

Like Bonn, East Berlin used television to set the tone for the visit by the American president, although with very different goals in mind. In a televised broadcast on June 15, Foreign Minister Lothar Bolz addressed Kennedy directly in demanding the recognition of both German states and the establishment of neutral status for West Berlin.[62] Another measure had a far greater impact. On June 21, the GDR issued new decrees subjecting the immediate border area to much stricter control. Only East Germans in possession of a special permit would be allowed in those areas.[63] The regime attempted to sweeten this bitter pill by distracting the attention of its people to the sky above them, where the bright future of the socialist German state seemed to be coming true on the eve of Khrushchev's arrival in East Berlin.

Following the *Sputnik* launch in 1957 and other developments in Soviet missile technology, space became an arena of technological competition and ideological struggle between East and West. The space race, the rivals seemed to agree, would be the true test to determine which political system was superior.[64] In the early 1960s, the Soviet Union was ahead of the United States in space travel. Therefore, Kennedy did not wait long after taking office to respond. On May 25, 1961, shortly before his summit meeting with Khrushchev in Vienna, Kennedy announced an ambitious space program with the goal of landing a man on the moon before the end of the decade.[65]

The Soviet Union nonetheless remained in the lead. While Kennedy was preparing for his trip to Europe, cosmonauts Valery Bykovski and Valentina Tereshkova, the first woman in space, circled the globe. They set a new record in the number of completed orbits, leaving the Americans trailing far behind. The GDR was thus able to frame its criticism of Kennedy's trip to the Federal Republic with upbeat reports of two other visits: the arrival of the two "cosmic siblings"[66] in Moscow on June 22 and Khrushchev's trip to East Berlin six days later.

Much like its West German counterpart, the East German media were determined to create a mass audience. East Germans were to be provided images of the populace expressing its elation, images of emotion that would also be politically useful. The day Kennedy landed in West Germany, readers of *Neues Deutschland* learned that "the storm of enthusiasm, the cheering, and the sea of flags, flowers, and waving hands [seemed] endless" – at the celebration of the cosmonauts' arrival in Moscow.[67]

It comes as no surprise that the East German media did not report on the positive reception given Kennedy by the West Germans and, especially, the West Berliners. Aside from ridiculing the security measures taken in West Berlin, the Eastern press focused on what *Neues Deutschland* called the "vile anticommunist attacks" Kennedy had made in his speech at Schöneberg City Hall. Somewhat unexpectedly, East German papers also took a shot at Bundestag president Eugen Gerstenmaier. His introduction of Kennedy in the Paulskirche in Frankfurt was described as an exercise in "repulsive, slavish bootlicking ideology," and Gerstenmeier was accused of having "thrown the ideals of the German nation–state overboard."[68] This attack illustrated how the polemics leveled against the hegemonic politics of the United States were being combined with an appeal by the left to nationalist sentiments.

Although the opposing sides pursued different aims, the techniques used to stage the competing visits of Kennedy and Khrushchev were astonishingly similar. East Germany copied the Western model in many details. It also put a premium on visibility. The press published the motorcade route of the Soviet leader through East Berlin before his arrival, complete with maps and street descriptions. Everyone was called upon to prepare a warm welcome

Illustration 30. Competing for visibility: Khrushchev visits East Berlin. Accompanied by Ulbricht, the Soviet leader waves to the crowds during his drive through Schöneweide on June 28, 1963. Source: Bundesarchiv Koblenz (no. 183/B 0628/15/26N).

for the prominent guest. Twenty television stations were commissioned to cover the live broadcast, and thirty cameras were used. Above all, the GDR organized what many in the West considered to be a Kennedy election campaign technique: Khrushchev and Ulbricht were seen standing in an open car as they drove through Berlin, escorted by a police motorcycle unit and followed by a long line of official limousines (Illustration 30). Unlike the populace in West Berlin, the people in the eastern portion of the city were expressly encouraged to display party and national flags and welcoming posters.

At exactly 2 p.m. on June 28, 1963, the Aeroflot plane carrying the Soviet guest from Moscow landed at Schönefeld Airport. A large reception committee made up of state and party dignitaries stood waiting. There had been no major problems to overcome in planning the protocol for the trip, in contrast to Kennedy's visit to West Berlin. It seemed quite natural to see Ulbricht and Khrushchev exchanging the fraternal kiss so customary among Socialists and to watch "these two men hug each other; the cabinetmaker and the locksmith; two communists, two close friends."[69] Accompanied by Khrushchev's wife, Nina, the delegation drove through southeastern Berlin to Alexanderplatz, the huge square at the center of East Berlin. There, Mayor

Friedrich Ebert and Khrushchev addressed the assembled crowd from the middle balcony of the Rotes Rathaus, the "Red City Hall" (the name had come from the red brick used for its exterior, not from the political views of the socialist municipal government then housed there).

Within the space of two days, the two most powerful men on earth had been in Berlin, but the ground they covered was completely different, both spatially and politically. Since Khrushchev had already visited East Berlin several times before, planners were in a bit of a spot. The parallelism of these events within such a short span of time reveals clearly just how greatly Cold War politics was dependent on the visibility of political presence and the staging of politics to secure approval from one's own camp and to demonstrate a feeling of superiority over the other. A comparison of the two visits is thus highly pertinent. Many aspects of the staging of the visits were similar, even though the Khrushchev visit lasted longer. Still, the differences between the two performances cannot be overlooked.

One of the most important differences lay in the political messages each leader sought to convey. Khrushchev announced his support for the Berlin Wall in a sentence quoted in the West German press as "I love the Wall."[70] In the most important policy speech he gave in Berlin, Khrushchev proposed on July 2 to link the nuclear test-ban treaty with a nonaggression pact between NATO and the Warsaw Pact. He offered generous economic aid to East Germany and expanded trade opportunities to West Germany; he held out the prospect of a Rapallo policy of Soviet-German bilateralism and sharply criticized the Adenauer government and Kennedy's Schöneberg speech. Reunification of the two German states, he insisted, would be possible only within a socialist system.[71] Khrushchev's speech suggested that the best the superpowers could hope for would be coexistence along the lines Kennedy had proposed.

Another difference between the two visits was the topography of the symbols. East Berlin did not offer Khrushchev any symbol encapsulating the failings of Western liberal democracy to counterbalance Kennedy's use of the Berlin Wall to criticize the Eastern bloc. Nor did East Berlin offer popular landmarks or locations that could serve as consensus-building focal points for the visit.

On both sides of the East–West divide, the visits by Kennedy and Khrushchev to Berlin were viewed from the Manichean perspective of the Cold War. The Eastern press described Khrushchev's drive through East Berlin on June 28 as a "triumphal procession," just as the Western press had Kennedy's drive through West Berlin two days earlier. The East German media used precisely the same metaphors for emotionality as the Western media. According to East German reports, Khrushchev was met with a "storm of enthusiasm" when he arrived at Schönefeld Airport, and at the Rotes Rathaus he experienced "unparalleled storms of applause." There was an atmosphere of "warmth and hospitality" for the "parade for peace" as the Soviet leader made his way through the East German capital. A jubilant crowd of 500,000 turned out to see him, and calls of "Nikita, Nikita" were intertwined with other welcoming cheers.[72] The West Berlin press described this same event as the "propagandistic counteract" to the Kennedy visit and observed it through a different lens. According to the Western media, only "thin, broken lines" of spectators and the "unemotional faces" of "tired, sad, numb, and resigned" people were to be seen on the streets of East Berlin. No more than a few thousand people were present at the Rotes Rathaus, Western reports contended, and most of them were members of the SED or party-related organizations.[73]

The available sources do reveal distinct differences between the two visits. In West Berlin, a balance was struck between the spontaneity of the crowd and the official efforts at supervision and control. The authorities imposed some restrictions, but they were not opposed to letting the positive reception they had encouraged develop into a happening. The people took advantage of the opportunity to express their emotion freely by chanting "Ken-Ne-Dy," by seeking to "touch the robe" of the long-awaited guest, and by showering his motorcade with confetti and flowers – in short, by demonstrating their *Eigensinn*.

In East Berlin, there was strong pressure on the spectators to conform, which did not necessarily exclude spontaneity. Kennedy's visit turned into an extraordinary shared experience of community. The Khrushchev trip met with popular approval, but it was too embedded in the existing rituals of friendship between the Soviet Union and the GDR to have the same symbolic impact. Kennedy departed from the script his planners had prepared. In improvising he came up with a unique, identity-forming sentence. In contrast to *"Ich bin ein Berliner,"* Khrushchev's "I love the Wall" was not well received despite the common touch the Soviet party chairman often demonstrated in his public appearances. His declaration failed to evoke enthusiastic acceptance among the masses in either a political or an emotional sense. The rousing power of *"Ich bin ein Berliner"* has proved to be enduring. Khrushchev's statement, on the other hand, did not remain part of the collective memory of Germans, not even of the East Germans.

THE DEATH OF THE HERO AND THE BIRTH OF THE MYTH

On November 22, 1963, almost five months after his trip to Europe, John F. Kennedy visited Dallas. As in Berlin, the president rode in an open car from the airport to the center of the city, accompanied this time by his wife, the governor of Texas, and the governor's wife. This time, however, the visibility proved fatal. At 12:30 p.m., 24-year-old Lee Harvey Oswald took aim at the presidential limousine from a window in a warehouse along the motorcade route. As the car passed, Oswald shot Kennedy. The news of the president's death circled the globe within minutes. Everywhere, even in the communist-ruled parts of the world, disbelief was soon followed by shock and grief. The German writer Ernst Jünger called this phenomenon an "eruptive explosion of worldwide sympathy."[74]

West Berlin, West Germany, and German-American relations were particularly hard-hit by the assassination of Kennedy. Only months before, the Germans gave the president the greatest show of support he had ever received in his career. The West Berliners in particular had experienced the charismatic Kennedy aura as a medium for creating political community, and they had celebrated his "*Ich bin ein Berliner*" declaration as proof that the president had become one of them. His successor was Lyndon B. Johnson, who had visited West Berlin during a crisis in German-American relations and received a remarkable welcome in 1961. The spontaneous reactions in Germany to Kennedy's assassination were linked to recollections of his and Johnson's visits, and those memories prompted a series of impressive events.

In many respects, the memorial services held in the wake of the Kennedy assassination represented more than just respectful expressions of mourning. They constituted the last major act in the drama of America's Berlin, a drama that in the preceding years had grown into a love story but now took a tragic turn. Media coverage was once again a central consideration in planning this final act. As during Johnson's and Kennedy's visits, it was the public that took center stage. The streets became the primary venue for public mourning. The memorial services and ceremonies adopted forms of speech, often with religious overtones, that had developed within the modern tradition of political commemoration and the modern cult of honoring the dead.[75] They embedded Kennedy in the literary and mythological tradition of the fallen hero. The memorial services for Kennedy were a medium to personify history and to glorify the political achievements of the dead hero as an *exemplum virtutis*, a model of virtue, for the present.[76]

With the death of the hero, the transatlantic community created by America's Berlin lost an important source of legitimation. Kennedy's charisma had enabled many people to experience the "extra-ordinary," to use Weberian terminology. Now the "disappearance of the personal charismatic leader" meant a "routinization" of social relations.[77] The shared experience of community spurred by Kennedy and Johnson took on historical value and was celebrated in commemorative rituals in the hope of preserving something of the experience for the future. People in West Germany and West Berlin gathered to mourn and pay their respects in the places in Cologne, Bonn, Frankfurt, and Berlin where Kennedy had been and had radiated his aura. The settings that had been carefully designed as stages for Kennedy's political performance during his visit, the places where people had come into direct contact with him, now became commemorative sites. The memorial services in Germany thus marked the beginning of ritualized memory and the construction of the Kennedy myth.[78]

Public mourning of the death of the hero in Germany was linked closely to the heady enthusiasm experienced during his visit five months earlier. Without that experience, the mourning would not have become one of the most moving mass events in the history of the Federal Republic. In Germany, it was half past six in the evening when the deadly shots were fired in Dallas. Even today, many Germans still remember the moment they learned of the assassination. Mass media coverage and word of mouth converged to spread the news. Six months before, a great deal of preparation had gone into setting the stage for Kennedy's visit to Germany long before the president touched German soil. Much effort had been made then to reach as wide an audience as possible. Now, within moments of his death, a new audience emerged spontaneously, without planning. People turned to television and radio again to experience this latest event, to see and hear and thereby become part of what was going on; indeed, they were shaping the event. One reporter used a vivid comparison to describe the scene in Frankfurt. The public reaction was a "wave of horror" and was reminiscent of the response to the news of a terrible natural catastrophe:

The news of the assassination of John F. Kennedy spreads...like an avalanche. People call out to one another that the American president has been murdered. They cannot grasp what they are hearing; some think the news bulletin is a bad joke. Others run to the nearest telephone in order to ask at home what is being reported on radio and television. Ghostly pale, they lay the telephone receiver back on the hook. Those standing around them want to know if it is true. Tears well up in women's eyes. Even men reach for handkerchiefs. When the initial shock has passed, the people hurry on. Pubs that have televisions soon become overcrowded. People crowd around a stopped car in which a radio is on. It is becoming increasingly quiet on the streets.[79]

Similar scenes occurred in towns and cities throughout the Federal Republic. Many Germans took part in spontaneous street gatherings or candlelight processions to pay their respects to the president within a few hours of his death. Throughout German history there have been occasions when the public has spontaneously congregated to form a "community of mourning."[80] Two prominent examples are the public reactions to the deaths of Emperor Wilhelm I in 1888 and President Friedrich Ebert in 1925. The reaction to Kennedy's assassination differed from those incidents in that the public show of emotion was not connected to feelings of national unity. The symbolism traditionally reserved for a national frame of reference was now applied to the leader of another country.

West Berliners took to the streets in especially large numbers.[81] On the evening of November 22, students and the Ring Politischer Jugend, an umbrella organization for political youth organizations, took part in a march that began near the Technical University and ended in front of Schöneberg City Hall. Calls to participate had been broadcast over the radio by student body representatives to all Berlin universities. Meanwhile, thousands of people were already gathering in Schöneberg.

Willy Brandt, just back from a trip to Africa, took it upon himself in a speech that night to place Kennedy's death in the historical context of America's Berlin. Brandt emphasized that he was "deeply upset and shaken" for he had just lost someone with whom he had been able to work "in trust and friendship." "We in Berlin" would especially grieve with the American people and all of "wounded humanity" over the death of the president. Kennedy, he said, had been the best friend Berliners had ever had; indeed, he had been one of them, and therefore they felt the loss suffered by Americans was also "our own loss." Once again, the history of Berlin was being integrated into the narrative of the American pursuit of liberty, particularly when Brandt referred to the 1865 assassination of Abraham Lincoln.[82]

Even before Brandt called on them to do so, West Berliners were placing candles in their windows. There is a long tradition of flame symbolism in religious rituals of sacrifice, mourning, and salvation, and that symbolism has been increasingly adopted for secularized political liturgy. The symbolic imagery associated with the flame is a particularly poignant example of what Reinhart Koselleck, Michael Jeismann, and Volker Ackermann describe as the convergence of politics and religion in the cult of death. This convergence has produced a repertoire of symbols, a mixture of Christian and secular symbols, that has changed remarkably little despite the political changes Germany has experienced since the late nineteenth century. One reason for the use of candles and metaphors of light lies in the close association of these symbols with the Christmas season.[83] Since the end of the Second World War, candles have often been used in Germany for public mourning and to express collective expectations for political salvation. Germans have lit candles spontaneously on political occasions, such as during the Berlin blockade and after the death of Ernst Reuter. At other times, the lighting of candles was deliberately planned, as, for example, in connection with events to protest Germany's division and to remember German POWs held in the Soviet Union after the Second World War.

Christian metaphors of light and flame played a significant role in the memorial events held for Kennedy. By the evening of November 23, many more people had heeded Brandt's call to place a lit candle in their windows. The same signs of mourning could even be found in the Eastern sector of the city, where the GDR media reported on Kennedy's assassination extensively. That night, guided by the light of torches, another symbolically significant mourning procession moved through streets in West Berlin. Following an appeal by representatives of West Berlin's vocational schools, approximately 50,000 people walked from the Platz der Lüftbrücke, the square where the Airlift Memorial stands, to Schöneberg City Hall. Once again, Willy Brandt addressed the crowd and referred to the death of Ernst Reuter a decade before.

One detail of the torchlight procession illuminates the degree to which national symbols, religious liturgy, and transnational community building merged on this occasion. At the head of the procession was a pine wreath that employees of a florist's shop in Schöneberg had decorated with carnations and bouquets of violets that would otherwise have been used to adorn graves on All Souls' Day the following Sunday. Gracing the wreath was a striped ribbon in black, red, and gold – the German national colors – reading: "You were our best friend; we will always remember you. Your Berliners."

In a memorial service in the Kaiser Wilhelm Memorial Church that same evening, the Lutheran Bishop Otto Dibelius repeated the metaphor of family identity and fraternal bonds used by Johnson in 1961 to describe the relationship between Berliners and Americans. People in Berlin were particularly grieved by the death of Kennedy, the bishop explained, because the president had proven himself in June to be their "brother."[84] The magazine *Illustrierte Berliner Zeitschrift* summarized the extraordinary aspect of this quasi-familiar bond by stating that the people were grieving "as if John F. Kennedy was one of their close relatives. When has this ever happened before in our rational and rationalized world!"[85]

As much as the West Berliners played up their special relationship with the United States, their tributes to Kennedy closely resembled those throughout West Germany. Tens of thousands of Germans signed the condolence books set out at city halls and U.S. government offices. All public buildings lowered their flags to half mast; the more than 2,600 ships of the German merchant marine followed suit. Radio and television stations changed their scheduled programming. In Bonn, a pontifical requiem was held for Kennedy; in Frankfurt, university students and school pupils marched solemnly by torchlight from the university to the Römerberg; in Hamburg, the city government passed a resolution to rename a new bridge after the assassinated president. As often as he had been criticized, Kennedy had also been celebrated, particularly in the Federal Republic of the late Adenauer years, as the promising young hope for the future and as a "shining light."[86] Many West German citizens had been counting on him to lead a new generation to new political shores.

That the West Germans made such a powerful show of sympathy, that this demonstration of sympathy became a shared experience of transatlantic community, and that this experience was initially expressed less in words than in symbols and cult signs, emotional gestures, and a wailing "cry" – all of this was only possible because Kennedy's death was embedded in the temporal and semantic deep structure that makes up the "cultural memory" of the Occident.[87] To many observers, Kennedy's assassination seemed to be an extraordinary sacrifice that could best be understood by reference to European political mythology. This mythology now included the saga of the president from far-off America who, with the help of Cicero, had transformed West Berliners into Roman citizens. The assassination of the American president was understood as the demise of a leading actor in the West's oldest political drama: "It is as if we have witnessed the age-old myth of the death of a hero, which the ancient Greeks insightfully celebrated with religious veneration in their tragedies. Fate has struck out at the youth of the world by striking down this man. When such a calamity occurred, the pious elderly cried 'woe, oh woe,'" a commentator in the *Frankfurter Allgemeine Zeitung* wrote. In this lamentation, Kennedy became the "American Prometheus." The torch that he had carried to Europe had been "of unusual fire" and had warmed a "world grown cold."[88]

The analogy to Prometheus introduces again the notion of the politician as redeemer. Prometheus, the titan who gave humankind fire, moved between the realm of the gods and the world of mortals. Through him we find a link to the figure of the Christian savior. In this eclectic mix of references to mythical and historic heroes, Kennedy was also cast as a modern-day Scipione del Ferro,[89] a Renaissance man who could do most anything. The man from Massachusetts was described as having fulfilled the "ancient Roman ideal" of the republican politician and was praised for reaching "for the stars." Not long after his death, the Kennedy White House began to be referred to as Camelot, the legendary home of the mythical King

Arthur and his Knights of the Round Table, an association encouraged by Jacqueline Kennedy.

In Germany, Kennedy's image was given a distinctly European coloring. Comparing him to Prometheus or an ancient Roman highlighted the idea of the *translatio imperii*, the "transfer of rule," from the Old World to the New and underscored a certain cultural skepticism toward America. Kennedy was said to have been able to rejuvenate the United States only because he possessed a European spirit: "He had made it his job – or did the gods assign him the task? – to give wealthy, dollar-chasing America a new and great aim. The young continent was to finish what the old one would no longer master alone. This young demigod lived from intellectual impulses. While a student at Harvard, he became a European."[90]

The Kennedy myth was built on an eclectic mix of cultural references. The German public and media contributed to the myth by inventing rituals that reassured them of Kennedy's extraordinary qualities, both real and imagined.[91] Two days after the assassination, several movie theaters in West Germany and West Berlin began to show the documentary film *Kennedy grüßt Deutschland* (Kennedy Greets Germany) that had been made in June; admission was free (Illustration 31). In Berlin, the showings were completely booked within minutes. On November 25, 1963, the day Kennedy was laid to rest at Arlington National Cemetery, the official memorial service for the president in West Berlin was held in front of Schöneberg City Hall. This memorial service impressively linked the past with the present; combined political, military, and religious symbols; and interwove national tradition with transnational community building. As during those now legendary days in June, the rules and rhythm of daily life were suspended. Many businesses followed the call of the unions and closed early; taxi drivers did not charge passengers for the ride to the memorial service; florists handed out free bouquets of flowers; pictures of Kennedy were put on display in city buses.[92]

Two hundred and fifty thousand people gathered at the same spot where the president had been cheered only five months before. The façade of city hall was now covered by a gigantic photograph of Kennedy framed by a black mourning sash. Candles, flowers, wreaths, and drawings by schoolchildren covered the steps of the building (Illustration 32). The service began with military symbolism. A U.S. military honor guard took up position at the entrance to the city hall. A Berlin police band played "*Ich hatt' einen Kameraden*" (I Had a Comrade), a song well established in German commemorative tradition. The words were written by Ludwig Uhland during

Illustration 31. The once-in-a-lifetime experience becomes a repeat performance: Berliners wait in line on November 25, 1963, three days after Kennedy is assassinated, to see the film on his trip to Germany. Source: Landesarchiv Berlin.

Illustration 32. Tributes to Kennedy in front of the symbol of Germany's division. Source: Landesarchiv Berlin.

the Napoleonic Wars and later put to music by Friedrich Silcher. From the late 1820s on, it has been customary in Germany – the changes in its political systems notwithstanding – to play "*Ich hatt' einen Kameraden*" to pay tribute to fallen soldiers.

Representing Willy Brandt, who was in Arlington at Kennedy's funeral, was Heinrich Albertz, another member of the municipal executive. Albertz reiterated the claim that Berliners and the fallen president shared a common identity: "He was a Berliner."[93] With the last sentence of Albertz's speech, the lights in front of the city hall went out. In the dark of night, two American soldiers played taps. It was, according to the press, the most moving moment of the service. The U.S. commander in Berlin, General James H. Polk, described it as "one of the most moving" he ever attended.[94] Tears were still flowing when the lights in the square went back on. The Freedom Bell began to toll, and police uncovered the plaque renaming the square in memory of John F. Kennedy. The America Institute at the Free University was also renamed in his honor.

The series of memorial ceremonies that took place in West Germany immediately following Kennedy's death were to be the last great demonstration of transatlantic community during the Cold War. In hindsight, they marked the end of a unanimous and spontaneous pro-American solidarity in Berlin. The *New York Times* wrote that Kennedy's death brought the people of West Germany and West Berlin closer to the United States than they had ever been – and would ever be. The only event to produce anything like the spontaneous show of solidarity with the United States on the part of Berliners since Kennedy's death was the September 11, 2001, terror attacks on the World Trade Center and the Pentagon: in the days following the attacks, countless thousands of Berliners gathered outside the U.S. Embassy to pay their respects to the vicitims.

The mourning for Kennedy also marked one of the final highpoints in the special relationship between Berlin and America: without fear of contradiction, Heinrich Albertz could claim that "the bridge between Washington and Berlin is strong, stronger than ever before." The new American president agreed with this assessment. Johnson seemed impressed by the "dramatic way" in which the people of Berlin had expressed their sorrow at losing Kennedy.[95]

An opinion poll commissioned by the West Berlin Senate shortly after the memorial ceremonies asked citizens their opinion of the new Johnson administration and the current state of affairs with regard to the Berlin issue. Kennedy's death, the pollsters found, had not sparked a crisis of confidence in the United States. On the contrary, West Berliners voiced greater trust than ever before that the Western allies would defend the city. In his *Berlin Briefing*, Harold Hurwitz concluded from his analysis of the poll results that the people of West Berlin, in their sorrow, seemed to identify with their city more than ever before. The West Berliners trust in the United States was closely bound up with their admiration for Kennedy; it had benefited the Western alliance that the president had "identified personally with the fate of the city." In November 1963, this trust extended to Kennedy's successor as well. Ninety-one percent of those polled after the assassination remembered that Johnson had also come to Berlin in August 1961, and their impression of his trip was positive. This retroactive association of Johnson with Kennedy greatly facilitated the "transfer of trust" to the new U.S. administration.[96]

The tidal wave of sympathy for Kennedy offered Willy Brandt an opportunity to strengthen his political standing. Brandt knew that he had to attend Kennedy's funeral in Washington if he wanted to underscore West Berlin's special position and to emphasize his own position as America's best friend among the German Social Democrats. At first, the recently installed government of Chancellor Ludwig Erhard hesitated to include Brandt as a member of the delegation accompanying the new chancellor to Washington. A compromise was eventually reached whereby Brandt would be included but would not travel with the rest of the delegation. Both the American-Berlin network and his own charismatic aura were strong enough to ensure Brandt privileged status in Washington. He met with Johnson and Jacqueline Kennedy, and on his return to Berlin Brandt reported that Johnson had told him he planned to visit the city again. The trip never materialized.[97]

Soon after her husband had returned from his European trip that summer, Jacqueline Kennedy wrote Brandt that "the President has told me every detail of his trip to Germany and I know he shall never forget the tremendously warm reception accorded him throughout the country." Later, after the memorial services and seeing Brandt again, she placed even greater importance on the Berlin visit and likened Brandt to her husband in unusually direct terms. Jacqueline Kennedy described the famous statement made by her husband in Berlin not only as the symbolic focal point of U.S. relations with Germany, but as one of the president's greatest achievements:

In so many ways you are like my husband. Were not the two of you the only young men of your generation who were leaders in the West? Everywhere else old men who belong to the past [*sic*] ... How strange it is – sometimes I think that the words of my husband that will be remembered most – were words he did not even say in his own language "*Ich bin ein Berliner.*" And for once the Germans understood through him that the United States was committed to them. I am so proud and grateful that at least he had the chance to do that.[98]

5

The Show Goes On

History is always that which is remembered. We think of something – be it an event, a person, a mood, a social situation, an intellectual development – as being historical because we can remember it or because we are reminded of it. From this we create our images of the past. The act of remembering is itself a process that results from numerous moments: the deliberate effort to remember, the search or discovery of the unknown, the rediscovery of long-forgotten memories, and the effort to forget and repress. Collective memories and the invention of traditions are always selective and changeable.[1] They thus contribute to the ways in which we interpret our past and become part of a politics of memory that is often used to serve current interests and to influence contemporary imagination.[2]

The credibility of our notions of the past is liable to change. To become and remain public knowledge, these notions need to be presented and anchored in public media. Books, television, school instruction, and visual images, to name a few examples, are key in this process of communication. Consequently, intermediaries, both individuals and institutions, play an important role in the effort to keep certain historical images alive in the public's consciousness. Success is only possible if the public perceives these historical images and accepts them as cultural knowledge. Much like the process of shaping politics, the processes of remembering and commemorating often take on the character of a performance. Likewise, public commemoration is often theatrical.[3]

The public commemoration of the Berlin Airlift in West Germany during the 1950s and early 1960s provides a good example. Officials in Bonn and West Berlin were keenly interested in keeping the Airlift, and with it American support for Berlin, alive in people's minds. The public accepted this take on the past and considered the memory of the Airlift to have tremendous, even decisive, bearing on the present. Agents such as the members of the Berlin lobby kept this memory alive through a number of rituals that reiterated the heroic saga of West Berlin's desire for liberty and of German-American friendship.[4] This tale began, however, to lose its persuasive force in the early 1960s. The West Berliners' seemingly unshakable faith in the promise of American support began to waver with the erection of the Berlin Wall. The Vietnam War shook the categorical assumption that the United States was the guarantor of a free, democratic order worldwide. Moreover, the emerging policy of East-West détente, as implemented by Kennedy and Adenauer's successors, undermined two other fundamental assumptions in the West about the Cold War. Politicians and the public in the West slowly stopped thinking of communism as a form of totalitarianism (Ronald Reagan was a late exception). As communist rule became less of a moral outrage in Western eyes, the Eastern bloc no longer seemed to pose an immediate threat.

The ways the West Germans commemorated Kennedy's visit after his assassination reflected these broad changes in Western political assumptions. It was generally not the first days of his visit in the Rhineland or his speech at the Free University that figured most powerfully in people's memories. Rather, it was the president's speech in front of Schöneberg City Hall, when he departed from his manuscript and lashed out against communism, that they recalled. Despite his harsh Cold War rhetoric, Kennedy nonetheless symbolized a new political beginning. He was often quoted as insisting that the "winds of change" were blowing on the other side of the Iron Curtain as well as in the West.[5] The way Kennedy's visit was remembered varied with people's political views. But more important in the shaping of public memory was the decoupling of Kennedy's image from the immediate context of his visit to West Germany. The popular image of Kennedy was reduced to a few striking features and overlaid with myth.

In West Germany and the United States, the memory of Kennedy's visit was simplified significantly. The government and media in both countries blotted out the complicated background to his trip to Europe, in particular the initial criticism of Kennedy's travel plans in the United States, the rivalry between Adenauer and Brandt, and the controversy over including Berlin on the itinerary. The brewing crisis that prompted the trip and the problems that arose in planning it did not fit in the narrative needed at the time to promote the desired political message. The shapers of public memory chose to spotlight Kennedy's eight hours in Berlin and his emphatic avowal of solidarity with West Berlin. An appealing symbol was needed to foster trust and consensus in German-American relations, and what worked best was Kennedy's *"Ich bin ein Berliner,"* set against images of confetti raining down on the presidential limousine. The public eventually lost sight of or completely forgot the context in which the trip had occurred.

Kennedy's visit to Germany provides a textbook example of the creation of political myth.[6] As Herfried Münkler has demonstrated with the example of the *Nibelungenlied*, political myth-making rests on a loosening of narrative rigor. The sequence of events is broken up into individual scenes that are, in turn, carefully rewoven in another – perhaps preexisting, perhaps new – story. The reworked story then serves to legitimate a particular vision of politics.[7] The shapers of public opinion work to keep the select scenes and images alive in the public memory by reiterating them and turning the act of remembering into a ritual. This process includes recurring commemorative celebrations, the canonization of certain individual pictures, the erection of monuments, and the dissemination of popular historical literature.[8] Through the ritual of remembering, the select scenes, images, and phrases merge in a seemingly cohesive, meaningful whole. They become political myth, which in the case of the Kennedy trip was meant to symbolize continuity in the transatlantic community and American solidarity with Berlin.

Once Kennedy's visit had been removed in public memory from its historical context and fragmented into individual scenes, the way was open for the perpetuation of the Kennedy myth. The specific circumstances and details of the trip were reduced to a few repeatedly recalled incidents. They served as a sort of symbolic shorthand in which the charismatic Kennedy personified the history of postwar German-American relations. This shorthand was used to bolster support for the West German–American partnership in a period of increasing criticism of the United States. Kennedy's early death facilitated the perpetuation of these symbols by making it impossible to measure his political vision against actual policies. *"Ich bin ein Berliner"* gradually became a commonplace: Kennedy's heroic declaration became trite through repetition and parody. In this process, however, monumental history turned increasingly into antiquarian history, in the Nietzschean sense – history that, while attempting to perpetuate the "long-ago moment" as "still living, bright, and great" into the future, consigns itself to a "sense of veneration of the past" and thus undermines the meaningfulness of its narrative for the present.[9]

The process of selecting memories and popularizing *"Ich bin ein Berliner"* was already underway as Air Force One winged Kennedy away from Berlin. *"Ich bin ein Berliner"* became a favorite quotation of the Berlin press. West Berliners incorporated it in the devotional mementos they crafted and sent to the White House.[10] The West Berlin Senate wondered whether it could somehow convert the line into political capital. Egon Bahr was taken by the suggestion of one journalist to use the statement for a large-scale political campaign. He played with the idea of creating an honorary Berlin medal to be sent to "everyone in the Free World" who spoke out on behalf of the city. The Senate's working group on public relations did not favor the idea because it feared such a campaign would take away from the "remarkable" character of the Kennedy visit and the "voluntary nature of the support expressed on both sides." It also wanted to avoid creating a situation in which the public felt "morally coerced" to remember the visit.[11]

As it turned out, there was no need to worry about stimulating interest in Kennedy after he had returned home. Both commercial publishers and government agencies did a booming business in special publications about the visit. An eighty-page glossy souvenir magazine published by Springer Verlag sold out one million copies within ten days. Two record companies offered recordings of Kennedy's most important speeches. The broadcaster Freies Berlin and the Deutsche Wochenschau produced film documentaries. Pictures and photos of Kennedy were still found gracing store windows weeks after his visit. Several Kennedy coins minted in silver and gold sold well.[12]

The memorial services for Kennedy in November triggered a second wave of commemoration. An opinion poll conducted in 1964 asked West Berliners to name the most important events of the previous year: 36 percent of those surveyed named Kennedy's visit and another 18 percent, his death. Only 31 percent mentioned the new treaty permitting West Berliners to visit their East Berlin relatives on Christmas and New Year's Day, 3 percent the inauguration of a new chancellor, and 2 percent the Berlin elections.[13] Once the memorial celebrations were over, it fell to the government and the media to create occasions for ritual remembrance of Kennedy. The most obvious locations for such rituals were those Kennedy had visited, especially in West Berlin. A donation drive was launched, for example, to raise money for a plaque commemorating Kennedy's speech for Schöneberg City Hall.[14]

The unveiling of the plaque took place on June 26, 1964, the first anniversary of Kennedy's visit. West Berlin used this occasion to recall and celebrate its close ties to the fondly remembered visitor. Brandt succeeded in convincing Robert Kennedy to come to Berlin. The mayor explicitly expressed his wish that the visit not be limited to paying tribute to the late president. He wanted to present a new Berlin and therefore advised Robert Kennedy against visiting the Wall.[15] The president's brother, however, had been quite moved by his experience at the Wall two years before. He now insisted that at least his wife, Ethel, and the three of their children accompanying them on the trip, Kathleen, Joseph, and Robert Jr., drive to the Cold War's most prominent border. After all, the Wall represented the essence of the historical and moral lesson one learned from Berlin.[16] The final itinerary was not, however, merely a repeat of Robert Kennedy's earlier visit. Particular attention was given to West Berlin's position as a modern industrial center. Kennedy visited the Berlin AEG plant, the company's largest in Germany and the city's second largest private employer.

The second unmistakable focus of the visit was to celebrate once more the heroic narrative of America's Berlin. The spontaneity and enthusiasm of the West Berliners was again on display. About 300,000 people lined the streets to cheer Robert Kennedy as they drove by, and more than 70,000 gathered at Schöneberg City Hall to hear Kennedy speak. Once again, the press spoke of the warmth of the public reception. Yet many aspects of the trip seemed to be no more than a rerun of the earlier event: the open car, the rain of confetti, the chants of "Ken-Ne-Dy." The media referred extensively to the presidential trip a year before. One camera captured a woman at the city hall holding a framed photographic portrait of the assassinated president.[17] In preparing his speeches for this trip, Robert Kennedy had tried to avoid quoting his slain brother too often. He did not take his staff's suggestion to echo "*Ich bin ein Berliner*" with either *Ich bin noch ein Berliner* (I am still a Berliner) or *Wir sind alle Berliner* (We are all Berliners).[18] The speeches he gave on the steps of Schöneberg City Hall and, that evening, at the FU were nevertheless full of references to the late president and his policies.

Schöneberg and the Free University had become so firmly established as sites of memory that it became impossible to look toward the future without making some reference to the past. At the city hall, Brandt accompanied Robert Kennedy through a photo exhibition about his brother. The visit officially kicked off a fund-raising campaign for the planned John F. Kennedy library in Boston and a fellowship program aimed in large part at West German students.[19] At the FU, Kennedy was awarded an honorary doctorate. In accepting the honor, he echoed his brother's words and ideas: the educational duties of science and scholarship; the importance of courage, strength, and liberty; and the role of the "Atlantic partnership." Kennedy outlined the "kind of future" that his brother had sought.[20] Before leaving Berlin the following morning, Kennedy laid a wreath at the Airlift Memorial at Tempelhof Airport and thus ended his visit by invoking, once more, the history of America's Berlin.

FROM AMERICA'S BERLIN TO THE BERLIN REPUBLIC

Five American presidents and several vice presidents have visited Berlin since John F. Kennedy's 1963 visit.[21] In reviewing these trips, even if only in passing, we see how they reflect the changes in German-American relations and Berlin's role in those relations during the second half of the twentieth century.[22] After Kennedy's visit, Berlin moved out of the spotlight of global attention. The Wall stopped the massive stream of refugees from the East and stabilized the GDR; the opposing blocs began to pursue détente. The East-West conflict continued, but the situation became less fraught along the line dividing Berlin and the access routes to West Berlin.

West Berlin continued to be affected by its special legal and political status and, of course, by the presence of the Wall, but it also began to become more normal, less exceptional. The much-acclaimed outpost of liberty became increasingly vulnerable to the problems most modern cities were facing. The insular atmosphere fostered political inbreeding and a susceptibility to corruption. It also offered the New Left and critics of the United States more room for maneuver than anywhere else in West Germany. As early as 1966, the journalist Fritz René Allemann astutely analyzed the change West Berlin was undergoing: the myth of the frontline city had lost its allure and credibility. He argued that the city was now on its own and therefore needed to search for a new political role. In 1967, *U.S. News & World Report* called West Berlin a "sick city," shaken by student unrest and blinded by "surface prosperity." Berlin was but a "sickly shadow of its former self." Such comments in American publications would have been unimaginable a few years earlier. They made clear that the myth of Berlin and the reality of the city had begun to drift apart.[23]

The majority of West Germans and West Berliners continued to support the political and military alliance with the United States. Yet there were periods, particularly during the presidencies of Lyndon B. Johnson, Richard Nixon, Ronald Reagan, and George W. Bush, when even that majority followed the alliance and American hegemony critically. Most West Germans viewed the escalation of the Vietnam War with skepticism. A more radically critical minority emerged amid the student unrest of the mid-1960s. The student movement went beyond repudiating the heroic version of the history of German-American relations and put forward a counternarrative of American imperialism.

From that point on, West Berliners mounted two opposing stagings for the visits of American leaders. There was, first, the official performance. German and American dignitaries made the rounds of the famous historic sites, where they would reaffirm the solidarity between the United States and the modern, democratic West Berlin. Running parallel to the official program would be a counterprogram of protest demonstrations, which could take forms ranging from peaceful marches to furious street battles. On the streets of Berlin, a classic stage for popular political action, the divergence in West Germans' views of the United States became visible.[24] No longer did presidential motorcades drive through streets filled with unanimously enthusiastic spectators. The visiting leader might drive by cheering crowds one moment and demonstrators battling police the next. At the highpoint of protests in the 1980s, the president's public appearances in West Berlin had to be limited to spaces such as the enclosed grounds of the Charlottenburg Palace where the police could be certain they could maintain order. The official and unofficial programs mounted for presidential visits demonstrated the very different political currents that existed in West Berlin and reflected the waning pertinence of the heroic story of America's Berlin.

The balance between discipline and spontaneity, control and happening that had been maintained during Kennedy's visit began to tilt in the direction of greater discipline. In 1963, it had been necessary to protect the president from acts of excessive enthusiasm by the crowd, and his limousine had to be cleaned of confetti and flowers. Six years later, the Berlin officials feared the most powerful man on earth might come under violent attack when he visited, and his limousine was pelted with paint bombs and eggs. The fact that planners could no longer count on an enthusiastic welcome for high-ranking visitors from the United States was evident in the topography of the places selected for and, in particular, excluded from the visitors' itineraries. Kennedy was the last president to address the public in front of Schöneberg City Hall and to speak before an audience open to all. No longer did the Freedom Bell toll in the presence of an American president. A motorcade route of more than 30 miles in an open car became unthinkable. Until 1994, no president stayed longer than five hours in West Berlin. Presidential visits were no longer emotionally exuberant mass events that the Soviet Union and East Germany might see as political threats that they had to answer with countervisits in the East.

The first signs of change came during the visit of Vice President Hubert Humphrey on April 6, 1967. The so-called extraparliamentary opposition used the occasion to stage a militantly anti-American protest against the Vietnam War. Just a few days before, demonstrators had attacked the Amerika Haus near the Bahnhof Zoo. The police took several members of the West Berlin "Horror Commune," who had stockpiled projectiles to throw, into custody shortly before Humphrey arrived. During the drive to the evening reception in Charlottenburg, chants on the street of "Johnson – Murderer" and "Washington go home" could be heard.[25] These protest activities were, however, only half the story. Thousands of Berliners greeted Humphrey with friendly cheers in front of the city hall. Likewise, the Berlin parliament applauded him when he repeated Kennedy's argument that Berlin and Vietnam were two fronts in the same war. In June 1968, when West Berlin was mourning the assassination of Robert F. Kennedy in Los Angeles, student organizations in the city refused to participate in the memorial services, in marked contrast to their response to his brother's death five years earlier.[26]

West Berliners increasingly disagreed in their assessments of the United States and its role in the world. The growing polarization of views was clearly manifested during the visit of Richard Nixon on February 27, 1969. "Things will be really bad in Berlin," predicted a police officer in Bonn. The West Berlin police prohibited all demonstrations and disbanded a teach-in at the Technical University. Despite these measures, confrontations occurred between police and protesters, who were burning American flags at the Kaiser Wilhelm Memorial Church and in front of the Amerika Haus. Chants of "*Amis raus aus Berlin*" (Americans out of Berlin) and "USA – SA – SS" (the SA, Sturmabteilung, were the Nazi party's "storm troopers"; the SS, Schutzstaffel, was a notorious elite Nazi organization that had a special military branch, the Waffen-SS) echoed in the streets. Still, hundreds of thousands crowded the streets to cheer the president. As his motorcade made its way through the city, Nixon repeatedly left his limousine to shake hands with people in the crowd. While on Kurfürstendamm, he even convinced Chancellor Kurt Georg Kiesinger and Mayor Klaus Schütz to stand on the back of the car in order to better wave to the crowds.

The political situation in the Federal Republic at that time was extremely delicate. The GDR had protested vehemently against the upcoming gathering of the Federal Assembly in West Berlin for the purpose of electing a new West German president, which was scheduled a few days after Nixon's visit. In protest, the East German regime had been hindering travel between the Federal Republic and West Berlin. The Bonn government, meanwhile, was pursuing a policy of détente with the Soviet Union; it was worried that its interests might suffer if, as expected, Washington and Moscow opened bilateral talks. Given this background, Nixon decided to make only a few gestures that pointed to the past while in Berlin, such as laying a wreath at the Airlift Memorial. The Republican president echoed Kennedy's rhetoric and simultaneously downplayed the notion of a special tie between Berlin and the United States when he told workers at the Siemens plant that "all the people of the world are truly Berliners." Nixon felt it necessary to assure people explicitly that Berlin was not at all a "dying city." The one surprise of Nixon's visit occurred not in Berlin but in Bonn, where he paid an unexpected visit to the Bundestag and pledged the Atlantic alliance's support for the upcoming negotiations on Bonn's relations with the Eastern bloc.[27]

There were fewer public demonstrations in West Germany to protest American policies after the end of the Vietnam War, but relations between the two countries were not entirely free of problems. The government of Chancellor Helmut Schmidt feared the Federal Republic's interests would not be taken into consideration in the arms control talks between the United States and the Soviet Union. As the superpowers discussed reductions in strategic arms, President Jimmy Carter provoked outrage in West Germany by proposing the development of a new tactical nuclear weapon, the neutron bomb. Bonn and Washington also found themselves at odds on economic policy, each accusing the other of not doing enough to stimulate the international economy.

Against this backdrop, Carter refrained from making any spectacular gestures during his trip to Berlin on July 15, 1978. Instead, he put emphasis on direct contact with the city's residents, who appreciated the president's unpretentious manner more than the chancellor did. Carter's side trip to Berlin was described by the press as an obvious "triumph" and "folk festival," even if not on a scale comparable to Kennedy's visit.[28] At a town meeting with a handpicked audience in the Congress Hall, Carter tried to be candid, open, and accessible. The goal of the visit was to demonstrate transparency instead of American hegemony. America's Berlin of the blockade and of armed confrontation at Checkpoint Charlie was fading into history. But Carter did go to see the Berlin Wall. He maintained a stony silence at first, one observer noted, and then "pose[d]" for a "Wall photo." Carter's stop at the Wall had none of the immediacy, none of the sense of direct confrontation that Kennedy's had fifteen years earlier. During a speech at the Airlift Memorial, Carter proclaimed in German twice that "*Berlin bleibt frei*" (Berlin remains free). That declaration met with "not exactly what one would call frenzied cheering," the German press reported, and it sounded to many like a "public relations slogan."[29]

During the presidency of Ronald Reagan, relations between Western Europe and the United States were marked by a level of tension unprecedented in the postwar period. Most West Germans did not support Reagan's abandonment of détente and economic cooperation with the Soviet Union or his return to the polarizing "good-versus-evil" outlook of the early Cold War. Reagan's policies served to mobilize the West German peace movement, which sometimes adopted an unmistakably anti-American tone. The refusal of the United States Senate to ratify the SALT II treaty, American pressure on West Europe to curb trade with the Eastern bloc, the deployment of American Pershing II missiles in Western Europe, Reagan's plans for a space-based antimissile defense system, and American policy on Central America: all met with strong criticism in West Germany. Western European governments were often skeptical of or even firmly opposed to many of the Reagan administration's policies despite the efforts of Chancellor Helmut Kohl to emphasize the importance of preserving strong transatlantic ties. West German public opinions of the United States seemed more divided than ever. During the Reagan years, in contrast to the early 1960s, Bonn and Washington did not succeed in resolving their differences or in easing tensions in German–American relations by undertaking a show of political symbolism.

For an act of political symbolism to succeed, as the history of America's Berlin between 1948 and 1963 demonstrated, the symbolic gesture needed to be able to win wholehearted acceptance among both Germans and Americans. It would need to have the support of lobby groups on both sides of the Atlantic. The media in both countries would have to take part in building consensus by publicizing the symbols. Just the opposite happened during the Reagan years. In May 1985, an attempt by Bonn and Washington to give a symbolic demonstration of postwar German–American reconciliation failed spectacularly.[30] There was no consensus in either West Germany or the United States on the legitimacy of the selected symbolic gesture or the chosen venue for it – a handshake between the two countries' political leaders at a military cemetery in Bitburg, Germany. Among the soldiers buried there were a number of Waffen SS troops, and that became a point of controversy in the United States and West Germany alike. The meaning of the symbolic act remained contested.

The differences in the interpretation of political symbolism in this instance did not stem from a fundamental deterioration in German–American relations. The two countries were working together closely and successfully in many areas. The Cold War no longer seemed so urgent, however, and no longer bound West Germany and the United States as tightly as it once had. In addition, the charisma with which the Kennedy brothers and Johnson had charmed the people of Berlin was missing. Ronald Reagan's charisma seemed to work its magic only among Americans. He actually alienated most Germans because his political beliefs remained mired in the ideology of the early years of the Cold War. As a result, Reagan's visits to Berlin in 1982 and 1987 turned out to be divisive performances.

The visit of Secretary of State Alexander Haig in 1981, shortly after the new Republican administration took office, proved to be an ominous prologue. Schöneberg City Hall had to be hermetically sealed off when Haig appeared there to sign the Golden Book as many, including Kennedy, had done before him. His visit prompted peaceful demonstrations against American foreign policy as well as street battles between masked radicals and police. Writing in the weekly *Die Zeit*, Michael Naumann lamented the "tarnished image of Berlin." The "ugly pictures" of the scenes that accompanied Haig's visit, he maintained, had received a great deal of attention in the United States and, nearly overnight, changed Americans' positive image of Germany.[31]

When Ronald Reagan visited Berlin on June 11, 1982, security measures were stepped up accordingly. Nothing better symbolized the gap between the president and urban reality than the change in street politics since the time of Kennedy's visit. The route of the presidential motorcade was no longer publicized beforehand; it was kept secret until the last minute. Reagan only traveled two short stretches by car – from Tempelhof Airport to Checkpoint Charlie and back. There was no crowd of tens of thousands waiting to greet the president at either location; violence broke out at Nollendorfplatz. To guarantee that the program went smoothly, the organizers of the visit were forced to have Reagan fly by helicopter over the streets of Berlin to the main event in the well-guarded Charlottenburg Palace. The primacy of visibility had been replaced by the primacy of security.

More than any other president before or after him, Reagan cast the history of America's Berlin as a heroic saga. Reagan described Berlin to his public as a "meeting place of light and shadow, tyranny and freedom," as a "prosperous island . . . in the midst of a hostile sea." This was the same Manichaean vocabulary that had been used during the early Cold War. Nor did Reagan fail to refer to Kennedy. After stating in German that "*Berlin bleibt doch Berlin*" (Berlin still remains Berlin), Reagan added that "we in America and in the West are still Berliners, too, and always will be."[32] Reagan's words, unlike Kennedy's, failed to produce an enthusiastic, emotional response from the crowds. Their meaning was anchored in a historic context that did not reflect most West Berliners' major concerns. Nor did they address the very real problems facing the city: student unrest, corruption scandals, house squatters, and the emergence of a new political force, the Alternative Liste.

The scene was much the same when Reagan visited Berlin a second time five years later. June 12, 1987, the day of the visit, saw the largest

Illustration 33. "Mr. Gorbachev, tear down this wall": Ronald Reagan at the Brandenburg Gate on June 12, 1987. Source: Landesarchiv Berlin.

police deployment in West Berlin since 1945. More than ten thousand police officers, backed by reinforcements from West Germany, were sent to quell violent demonstrations in the neighborhoods of Schöneberg and Kreuzberg. Instead of a triumphal procession like Kennedy's, the media reported a "disgraceful scene."[33]

More than ever, it was becoming clear that America's Berlin could be staged only as a revival. At a reception held at Tempelhof Airport, replicas of the Congress Hall and Brandenburg Gate were used as backdrops. Reagan visited an exhibit in the Reichstag on the topic of the Marshall Plan. His major speech, delivered in front of the Brandenburg Gate, was studded with German quotations and references intended to flatter Berliners (Illustration 33).[34] Still, his speech was as lackluster as his political proposals were unoriginal: to make West Berlin a center of international air travel, to establish the headquarters of a United Nations institution there, and to have East and West Berlin co-host the Olympic Games. Reagan, in sum, echoed only half of Kennedy's message. He took up the anticommunism of Kennedy's Schöneberg speech, but he offered nothing comparable to the farsighted ideas and multilateral view of the world that Kennedy had articulated at the FU.

Reagan did, however, surprise the world with a rhetorical flourish that made almost as strong an impression on the international public as Kennedy's declaration "*Ich bin ein Berliner.*" With the challenge "Mr. Gorbachev, tear down this wall!" Reagan turned the existence of the Berlin Wall into a litmus test of credibility for the new Soviet policies of glasnost and perestroika.[35] Post–Cold War triumphalism in the West notwithstanding, Reagan could not have imagined at the time that the Wall would indeed fall only two and a half years later. And much as some derided it, Reagan's call proved to be visionary even though it was inspired by a political ideology that belonged to the past.

When the Wall did come down, President George H. W. Bush remained realistic and pragmatic. To avoid provoking the Soviet Union, he did not go to Berlin and "dance" on the Wall, as several Democrats in Congress urged him to do.[36] Bush did not visit Berlin during his term in office. In 1989, while in Mainz, Bush made his often quoted statement about Germany and the United States being "partners in leadership." Had he said this in Berlin against the symbolic backdrop of Schöneberg City Hall, where expectations would have been high, his remark would have had much greater political impact and would have attracted much more public attention. Ultimately, the statement proved inconsequential.[37]

It has been both easier and harder for Bush's successors to stage appearances in Berlin. On the one hand, presidents could celebrate the fall of the Berlin Wall and incorporate it in the heroic saga of the West's defense of freedom. On the other hand, the end of Germany's division and the Cold War meant that the Berlin American presidents now visited was once again German: legally, politically, and symbolically. The city even gave united Germany its metaphorical name, the Berlin Republic.[38] The debate on whether Bonn or Berlin should be united Germany's seat of government centered in large part, both at home and abroad, on historical arguments and the multiple, often opposing, symbolic meanings associated with Berlin.[39] When the Wall came down, the United States lost a screen onto which American values of freedom and democracy could be projected. The fall of the Wall, the unification of the divided city, the Bundestag's decision of June 20, 1991, to move itself and the federal government to Berlin, the departure of Allied troops in the summer of 1994, and the first meeting of the newly elected Bundestag in the Reichstag building in November 1994 were all steps in the transition from America's Berlin to Germany's Berlin.

Bill Clinton was the first American president to visit unified Berlin and walk through the Brandenburg Gate.[40] Germans found the multilateralist Clinton considerably more to their liking than Ronald Reagan. Like

Reagan, Clinton tried to adapt the Kennedy style for his own ends when he visited Berlin in 1994. He encouraged the Germans to show a "new civil courage" and to work from Berlin to create a democratic Europe with a free market economy. Nor was Clinton immune to the pressure to make his own memorable Berlin quote. With the Brandenburg Gate as a backdrop for the keynote address of his visit, Clinton spoke several sentences in German and concluded with "*Nichts wird uns aufhalten. Alles ist möglich. Berlin ist frei*" (Nothing will stop us. All things are possible. Berlin is free).[41] The audience applauded, but Clinton's German lines did not set off an outpouring of enthusiasm. Such rhetoric no longer stirred great passion, nor did anti-American demonstrations. The political atmosphere in Berlin had changed considerably since Reagan's visit. It was now possible for the distinguished American guest to spend the night in Berlin undisturbed.

Clinton's second trip to Berlin, in May 1998, marked yet another step in relegating America's Berlin to history. The time when Berlin was seen as a frontline city was now long past. In the city that Reagan once called the "beacon of freedom," Clinton found himself "without a mission."[42] For this reason, he celebrated the history of postwar Berlin and the Airlift all the more grandly at Tempelhof, where an American transport aircraft was christened *Spirit of Berlin* (Illustration 34). This name was a double historical reference; it alluded both to the legendary morale and steadfastness of the West Berliners in the face of Soviet pressure and to the equally legendary 1927 solo flight of Charles Lindbergh over the Atlantic in his plane *Spirit of St. Louis*. The visit was dominated by the historicization of America's Berlin and what the the *Süddeutsche Zeitung* called "routine of symbolism." It was in this spirit that the president declared "*Berlin bleibt Berlin*" (Berlin remains Berlin).[43] Even the politics of visibility, which had played such a prominent role in American relations with Berlin since Ernst Reuter's call to "look upon this city" and the photos of the Airlift, became a matter of reiteration and historical quotation. A U.S. postage stamp issued in commemoration of the anniversary of the blockade featured a Berlin family watching an American transport plane approach for landing.[44]

One important act of symbolic politics during Clinton's 1998 visit was oriented toward the future even though it drew upon the past. At the insistence of Chancellor Helmut Kohl, the most spectacular event on Clinton's program was not staged within the city limits of Berlin, but in nearby Potsdam. Kohl chose Potsdam not for its association with the Potsdam Conference of 1945 but for its ties to an older Prussian tradition. The chancellor entertained Clinton in the eighteenth-century parks and palaces created for Prussian king Frederick II ("The Great"). The president was received with

Illustration 34. A commemorative ritual historicizing the Cold War: The celebration of the fiftieth anniversary of the Berlin Airlift. Left to right: Berlin mayor Eberhard Diepgen, U.S. Air Force general John P. Jumper, President Bill Clinton, German chancellor Helmut Kohl, and Gail Halverson, a former Airlift pilot (May 14, 1998). Source: Landesarchiv Berlin.

military honors at the enormous Neue Palais (New Palace) and given a luncheon across the park in Frederick's smaller, more elegant summer residence, Sanssouci. By putting the Prussia of the Enlightenment on display during Clinton's visit, Kohl was situating united Germany within what he saw as a positive national historical narrative. He wanted to present the Federal Republic as a normal, proud, and independent nation-state.[45] Frederick's Potsdam served the new identity of united Germany better than America's Berlin. Clinton's visit and Kohl's spotlighting of Prussian Potsdam thus marked a leave-taking from America's Berlin.

The most recent presidential visit to Berlin to date took place on May 22–23, 2002, and was again accompanied by protests. When George W. Bush flew into the German capital eight months after the terror attacks of September 11, 2001, the city's governmental district resembled a fortress. Many Germans were reminded of Reagan's visits in the 1980s.[46] Demonstrators voiced opposition to American Middle Eastern policy as well as to economic globalization. Some burned American flags and threw stones. However, the massive unrest that had been feared did not occur. Still, government officials made an effort to dispel any thought that Germany and the United States were drifting apart.[47] The Berlin where Kennedy and Reagan had spoken, the divided city of the Cold War, had finally faded into the shadows of history. Bush mentioned this Berlin only briefly in his speech to the Bundestag, and he did not attempt to make a memorable remark in German. Although Germany and the United States remained linked by an extensive network of connections, relations between the two countries had reached a point at which it was no longer possible to create public enthusiasm through emotional gestures.

Memory of Kennedy's declaration "*Ich bin ein Berliner*" remains vivid in Germany and the United States, but America's Berlin no longer exists. It has been replaced by the Berlin of united Germany. And in the era of the Berlin Republic, it is German history, not American, that informs the city's identity.

6

"A Comet of Promise Passing through Our Country"

In hindsight, John F. Kennedy's visit to Germany in June 1963 can be read as a microhistory of transatlantic politics and the Cold War as it played out in Germany – just as the history of America's Berlin mirrors the changing nature of German-American relations during the Cold War era. Kennedy's trip illustrates the international political scene of the early 1960s as well as the social changes then taking place and the cultural hopes associated with them. The prelude to and staging of the visit, its background, and its impact belong integrally and equally to German, European, and American history.[1] The history of Kennedy's visit to Berlin, as part of the history of Berlin's resonance in the United States, demonstrates that transnational ties impact political developments and have an effect on cultural identities within nation-states. The role West Berlin played in the American perspective on the Cold War and the role Kennedy played as the personification of the political hopes held by many in the Federal Republic attest to this transnational context, as the personal and emotional connections that linked West Berlin and the United States.

Kennedy's visit to Berlin also demonstrates that, in the era of mass media, politics can use the visibility of symbolic acts to enhance the impact and legitimacy of action. The dramatically staged presentation of politics therefore serves an important purpose both within nation-states and in international relations: it can become a powerful tool to achieve strategic aims and to create emotional ties. Politics as performance is, in the end, power politics on display.

Two and a half years after he entered the Oval Office, President Kennedy made his way to Europe, amid much criticism at home, in order to defuse the acute political crisis within the Atlantic alliance by demonstrating transatlantic solidarity and American commitment to Western Europe. This crisis had been building since the late 1950s. French unilateralism, American efforts to reduce the financial burden of maintaining a military presence in Germany, and Western European worries about the possible consequences of improved Soviet-American relations were sources of tension within the Western alliance. Washington's awareness of this crisis should not be underestimated. Only six days before Kennedy left for Germany, Undersecretary of State George W. Ball wrote to the president that Europe was in a "mess. . . . Never, at any time since the war, have European voices been so discordant"; nor, according to Ball, had Europe even been "in graver danger of backsliding into old destructive habits – the old fragmentation and national rivalries that have twice brought the world to disaster in the past."[2] Kennedy's trip was a deliberate staging of symbolic politics designed to counter the threat of erosion facing the transatlantic alliance and to maintain U.S. political dominance within the Western alliance.

For the Federal Republic of Germany and West Berlin, the Kennedy trip meant a great deal more. Adenauer's chancellorship was coming to a close, and West Germany found itself in a period of transition.[3] The Adenauer era had brought prosperity to many West Germans and saw the integration of the Federal Republic into the Western alliance. The international situation and social change now demanded a new generation of politicians, reform at home, and a broadening of perspective in foreign policy that looked beyond the static bipolarity of the Cold War. There were few promising political newcomers who seemed to have either the courage to propose change or the political skills to implement it. Even the youthful and ambitious Willy Brandt was not able to defeat the elderly Konrad Adenauer in the 1961 race for the chancellorship.

For many in West Germany, particularly younger people, John F. Kennedy personified the hope that outmoded habits of thought could be done away with and a new path blazed toward global détente. The democratic left in particular was very sympathetic to the Kennedy administration,[4] and not simply because Kennedy's age set him apart from the leading European politicians of the postwar years. He articulated an intellectually sophisticated understanding of politics. Bolstered by his wife's elegance, John F. Kennedy was uniquely appealing to Europeans. The West Germans most critical of the United States in the second half of the 1960s had in many cases been among those who cheered most loudly for Kennedy in 1963.

In welcoming Kennedy to Cologne, Mayor Theo Burauen pointed out the importance of the American president to West German society by using a simile that was as unusual as it was readily comprehensible to the audience: "If I may say so, Mr. President, you appear to us like a comet of promise passing through our country. We will see you only shortly, but we interpret this as a sign of good luck."[5] This image has its roots in the centuries-old tradition of interpreting heavenly bodies as heralds of change. Burauen's simile also shows that Kennedy, more than anyone else, personified political change in a time of transformation. The Federal Republic was becoming more affluent and, in the eyes of many, increasingly Americanized. West Germans did not simply welcome Kennedy the extraordinary figure who symbolized change: venerating him as if he were a "miracle-working . . . relic," they sought contact with him and looked to him for political salvation.[6]

From this perspective, George Meany was right when he later noted that Kennedy had been "greeted by these people [in Berlin] as if he were a God."[7] The encounter between a charismatic leader and a public who saw him as the personification of a new political future was more tangible in West Berlin than anywhere else. The people of West Berlin were particularly dependent on sustaining the trust of the most powerful man in the Western world; likewise, the United States needed the trust of West Berliners, as the trip by Vice President Johnson in August 1961 demonstrated. It was not simply coincidence that the *Tagesspiegel*, West Berlin's largest daily newspaper, drew upon the comet metaphor in reflecting on Kennedy on the first anniversary of his Berlin visit: "John F. Kennedy was like a brilliant comet rising out of the darkness of history, and it appeared not only to Berliners that he shone the brightest in their city, before his light was abruptly extinguished for reasons beyond all human understanding." The *Tagesspiegel* summarized the link between this individual and political history: "Certainly the friendship between America and Berlin is nothing new, but the new factor at work here was the charisma of a man who embodied all of the positive qualities Berliners so treasured about America: youthfulness and optimism, humanity and intelligence, energy and perseverance. . . . Here political history became an uplifting experience, which no one imagined would end so quickly and tragically thereafter."[8]

It has rarely been noted that two foreign leaders – Charles de Gaulle and John F. Kennedy – accomplished something no German political figure since Hitler had done: they inspired collective excitement among the West Germans and turned public political gatherings into highly emotional events. The acts of political symbolism staged during de Gaulle's and Kennedy's visits helped make the West Germans members of the Western community emotionally. The two most important points of orientation for West German foreign policy after 1949 – friendship with France and with the United States – provided a route for West Germans to experience a form of political community building with the West on a transnational level. Political community, as understood by Max Weber and Karl W. Deutsch, is the product of intensive social communication, dense societal networks, and reciprocal fulfillment of political expectations; it was more than a simple echoing of rhetoric about the Atlantic community. Herein lies the true meaning of the German term *Westbindung*, integration into and alignment with the West.

This understanding of community and *Westbindung* offers a new perspective on the subject of the Western orientation of the Federal Republic's political culture. Without a doubt, the Federal Republic's *Ankunft im Westen* (arrival in the West) was grounded in the West's efforts to democratize postwar Germany and was later facilitated by the Federal Republic's membership in the Western alliance and its openness to Western, in particular American, social and cultural influence.[9] It was, however, symbolic politics that enabled the public to identify with the West and to participate emotionally in a community with the country's Western partners. Symbolic politics became a key factor in this process, which began on a large scale with the media attention given to the Berlin Airlift of 1948–49, was sustained in the 1950s through staging acts of solidarity, and culminated with the visits of Charles de Gaulle to West Germany in 1962 and John F. Kennedy to West Berlin in 1963. Brilliantly scripted, these visits theatricalized West Germany's transnational integration in a way that made politics a sensory experience. These political performances brought the entire country together and transcended generational, gender, and social barriers. A German newspaper editorial looking back in 1964 on Kennedy's visit commented on this effect: "The feeling of belonging to the West, an otherwise abstract axiom of political strategy, so to speak, was revealed here as being something tangible for the whole world to see, namely as a tremendous wave of affection for a single human being."[10]

Last but not least, the forms of political theatricalization described here in connection with the trips by Lyndon B. Johnson, Robert F. Kennedy, Charles de Gaulle, and John F. Kennedy to Germany demonstrated that the Federal Republic had successfully asserted its identity and distanced itself from two other Germanys. West German officials were careful to avoid anything that might be reminiscent of the mobilizations that had contributed so much to creating the "alluring appearance of the Third Reich" and its blending of "seduction and force."[11] The political performances in West Germany also stood in marked contrast to the mass rallies staged in East Germany.

There were, to be sure, disputes over the staging of foreign leaders' visits. All parties involved had to compromise so that a balance between their often divergent interests could be found. Behind the scenes, there were battles over every detail of the programs. Many of the particulars – handshakes, seating arrangements, the order of speakers – became political statements.[12] The planners also implemented a street politics that encouraged a measure of self-discipline on the part of the public. It is precisely the give-and-take between spontaneity and control, between mass expression of emotion and government checks on those emotions that characterized these political performances. In addition, the program planners succeeded in using the protocol and political topography in Berlin to balance competing political interests. In the end, the protocol itself became a miniature version of the transatlantic community. All of the actors involved were willing to be innovative with regard to ceremonial tradition, to consult one another, and to trust that each party would comply with their agreements.

Everyone who participated in Kennedy's visit – the politicians on stage, the officials working behind the scenes, the public in the audience – was affected by emotion. This triggered a unique dynamic: Kennedy's visit became one of the greatest political happenings in Germany's postwar history. During this happening, ceremonial reverence, spirited jubilation, and carnivalesque fun merged into an expression of *Eigensinn*; refusing to conform fully to official expectations, the people in the streets behaved according to their own particular logic.[13] John F. Kennedy, Lyndon B. Johnson, and Robert F. Kennedy translated the emotionally laden, positive impressions they took home with them from Germany into arguments in favor of improving German-American relations. Emotions thus became a factor in shaping international relations.

John F. Kennedy's visit to Germany was staged as political theater, and the politics of visibility was the defining feature of the staging. In the age of mass media, the effectiveness of political authority is dependent to a large degree on its visibility. Seeing and being seen became the focal point in planning Kennedy's visit, which in turn meant the media would play a central role. The iconography of the images that resulted from the visit – Kennedy in front of the Brandenburg Gate and the Berlin Wall, for example – was created deliberately to serve as a weapon in the ideological competition with the Soviet bloc. Moreover, the act of seeing itself became a political argument. For that reason, Kennedy had to see postwar Berlin's multiple faces, which ranged from the brutality of the Berlin Wall to the consumer landscape of the Kurfürstendamm and the modern architecture of the Hansa Quarter. Likewise, the media was to publicize the intensity of emotion being expressed on the streets in the city.

Visual images alone did not account for the success of Kennedy's visit. The question whether the powerful images of Kennedy in Berlin might overshadow what he said there[14] was in effect answered by the president himself. The sentence *"Ich bin ein Berliner"* remains as vivid a part of the collective memory of Kennedy's visit as any of the images, if not more so. The effectiveness of combining emphatic rhetoric with an emotional appeal to the public had already been demonstrated by Lyndon Johnson in 1961. Kennedy not only duplicated the Johnson tactic, he enhanced it dramatically in his appearance at Schöneberg City Hall by departing from the prepared script and changing the tone of the rhetoric.

Following Kennedy's assassination in November 1963, West Germans of all ages and social backgrounds once again felt closely connected to America – so much so that West Berliners' trust in the security guarantees of the Western powers reached a new high.[15] Ordinary citizens commemorated Kennedy's visit in an endless variety of ways. Still, the ritualization of memory could not entirely overcome the lack of charismatic leadership after Kennedy's death. An unprecedented dissonance in West German–American relations became evident in the mid-1960s. Growing numbers of West Germans voiced criticism of the United States and, in particular, its foreign policy. That criticism often carried traces of the anti-Americanism harbored by a minority. In West Berlin above all, anti-Americanism found expression in radical forms of protest. This movement challenged the heroic narrative of German-American postwar cooperation and thereby called into question the West Germans' pro-American image. It thus became increasingly unlikely that any American president could ever again win broad public approval in West Berlin and the Federal Republic through symbolic action.

In no other place were both the heroic and ambiguous aspects of German-American relations after 1945 as clearly evident as in Berlin. Hitler had wanted to turn Berlin into the majestic capital of the empire he envisioned. By the end of the Nazi dictatorship, Berlin lay in ruins as the result of Allied air raids and the Soviet assault on the city in the spring of 1945. When the city fell to the Red Army, it appeared as if the many cultural and political connections between America and Berlin would be severed for a long time.[16] That did not happen, however. As the Americans marched into their assigned sector of Berlin in July 1945, many Berliners greeted them as liberators from Soviet occupation. When, amid rising political tension, the Soviet Union imposed its blockade of the Western sectors of Berlin in the summer of 1948, the United States renewed its relationship with Berlin and redefined the former Nazi capital as an American frontier city.

In the 1950s and early 1960s, the American lobby for Berlin repeatedly helped ensure that American support found tangible expression in financial assistance for rebuilding the city and reviving its cultural landscape. West

Berlin's role as the Cold War frontline city – as an island in a communist sea and an outpost of freedom, as two popular metaphors put it – made it an attractive example to those who wanted to cast U.S. history as the story of America's successful mission to spread freedom around the world. West Berlin became America's Berlin, a city the majority of Americans were ready to defend, and, in turn, the West Berliners became citizens of the Pax Americana.

America's Berlin, a symbolic place of transnational community, held a unique position in America's relations with Europe. The intense interaction between the superpower and the city led many to believe that they were linked by a special cultural, ideological, and emotional bond. Kennedy's declaration "*Ich bin ein Berliner*" marked the highpoint of this sense of connection, and the bond clearly began to weaken after 1963. The heroic self-portrayal inherent in America's Berlin came increasingly into conflict with protests in West Berlin against the Vietnam War and American foreign policy. At the same time, the Berlin lobby and the network of individuals and institutions that had worked to keep the city in the public eye began to lose sway in the United States.

The drama of West Berlin the outpost of freedom became less urgent and less compelling as the situation of East Germany became less precarious and as West Berlin was forced to turn its attention to its own municipal problems. As the Western Europeans came to feel less threatened by the Soviet Union and more confident in their dealings with the United States, West Germans were less inclined to support the United States and its policies unconditionally. This is not to say that West Berliners turned their backs on the United States: the majority certainly did not. But the heroic, community-building Berlin that had existed in the years between the Berlin Airlift and Kennedy's visit was becoming a historical relic preserved through ritualized commemoration. German unification in 1990 and the advent of the Berlin Republic marked the end of America's Berlin. The reunited city was a German city subject initially to critical scrutiny abroad.[17] What had once been America's city upon a hill during the Cold War was now the capital of a unified Germany.

Traces of America's Berlin nonetheless still survive today. America's Berlin has in effect migrated to the United States, where it has a firm place in the heroic master narrative of the nation's history. There are more remnants of the Berlin Wall on display as memorials in the United States than in any other country, Germany included. American interest in Berlin has by no means declined, even if attention has shifted to united, autonomous Germany as a whole. In the wake of unification, the withdrawal of the Allied troops from the city, and the relocation of the government and the Bundestag from Bonn, a new wave of Americans arrived in Berlin. The American Jewish Committee opened an office in the German capital, for example, and the American Academy has been bringing noted Americans from a variety of fields to Berlin since 1998. The Allied Museum, open since 1998, documents the influence exerted by the Allied powers in shaping the city from the end of the Second World War to the end of the Cold War.

Relations between the United States and the Federal Republic have undoubtedly become much more pragmatic since German unification and the removal of the last remaining limitations on German sovereignty. United Germany has sought to define its foreign policy and security interests for itself since 1990. In the process, it has underscored the interests it shares with the United States, but it has not backed away from calling attention to points of conflict as well. This is a normal part of international relations. Berlin is no longer the frontline city in need of American protection against a powerful enemy. Long gone is the pathos of the postwar period: West Berliners are no longer dependent on CARE packages or American tanks at Checkpoint Charlie.[18] This aspect of German–American relations, so important to the generation of transatlanticists personified by Lucius D. Clay, has disappeared.

At first glance, the transnational relations between the United States and Germany appear to be increasingly marked by asymmetries. In the face of many diverging political and economic interests, it is an open question whether a "new Atlanticism" or a "new Euro-Atlantic community" might be possible.[19] Simply dismissing the question, though, or prophesying an unhappy future for European–American relations would be unwise and historically naive. America's Berlin of the Cold War era is gone, but so, too, is the once seemingly permanent border that ran through Central Europe. Such transience is proof that societies and international relations are open to change. German–American interaction and cooperation in areas such as education and research, to say nothing of trade and investment, have actually expanded since the end of the Cold War.

Today's Berlin holds tremendous attraction for Americans, especially for students, young professionals, artists, and intellectuals. They see and experience a very different city from what their predecessors in John F. Kennedy's time did, but still they come. Berlin retains its hold on the American imagination. Its diversity and its often contradictory historical legacies continue to fascinate many Americans. Relations between America and Berlin, between the United States and Germany, are an ongoing and open-ended story.

Appendix

Ich bin ein Berliner: *John F. Kennedy's Speech at Schöneberg City Hall, June 26, 1963*

The following text records the exact wording used by Kennedy in his speech at Schöneberg City Hall and also the exact wording used by the head interpreter of the German Foreign Office, Heinz Weber, who stood next to Kennedy at the speaker's pulpit on the platform in front of the Schöneberg City Hall and translated into German, paragraph by paragraph, the words of the American president.

None of the German versions of the speech published to date give an accurate account of Weber's translation. Moreover, these versions differ in detail. Many versions do not include Kennedy's remark to Weber recorded here in the third paragraph. The spelling for the official name of the western half of Berlin often varies between "West-Berlin" and "Westberlin." The fact that repetitions made by the speaker have not been noted in earlier publications reflects common editorial practice. However, such repetitions have been included here. The published German versions closest to the verbatim record of the speech and its translation are found in *Ein Großer Tag in der Geschichte unserer Stadt*, edited by the Presse- und Informationsamt des Landes Berlin (Berlin: Presse- und Informationsamt des Landes Berlin, 1963), 6–27; and in *Ich bin ein Berliner: John F. Kennedy in der deutschen Hauptstadt am 26. Juni 1963* (Berlin: Arani, 1963), 28, 30.

The English version is based on the document found in *Public Papers of the Presidents of the United States. John F. Kennedy. Containing the Public Messages, Speeches, and Statements of the President. January 1 to November 22, 1963* (Washington, D.C.: U.S. Government Printing Office, 1964), no. 269, 524–25. In the following, repetitions of spoken words have been included, the term *Communism* has been capitalized throughout, and two small corrections have been made so that the text corresponds exactly to the originally spoken word ("it's" instead of "it is" and "Laßt" instead of "Lass'" in the fourth paragraph).

In the following versions, the public's reactions are noted in brackets. [A] stands for applause and cheering, which was usually interspersed with calls of "Ken-Ne-Dy"; [P] stands for those moments in which Kennedy paused to give Heinz Weber an opportunity to translate his sentences into German.

John F. Kennedy	Heinz Weber
	Meine Berliner und Berlinerinnen!
I am proud to come to this city as the guest of your distinguished Mayor, who has symbolized throughout the world the fighting spirit of West Berlin. And I am proud [A] – and I am proud to visit the Federal Republic with your distinguished Chancellor who for so many years has committed Germany to democracy and freedom and progress, and to come here in the company of my fellow American, General Clay [A], who [A] – who has been in this city during its great moments of crisis and will come again if ever needed. [A, P]	Ich bin stolz, heute in Ihre Stadt zu kommen als Gast Ihres hervorragenden Regierenden Bürgermeisters, der in allen Teilen der Welt als Symbol für den Kampf und Widerstandsgeist West-Berlins gilt. [A] Ich bin stolz, auf dieser Reise die Bundesrepublik Deutschland zusammen mit ihrem hervorragenden Herrn Bundeskanzler [A] besucht zu haben [A], der während so langer Jahre die Politik der Bundesregierung bestimmt hat nach den Richtlinien der Demokratie, der Freiheit und des Fortschrittes. [A] Ich bin stolz darauf, heute in Ihre Stadt in der Gesellschaft eines amerikanischen Mitbürgers gekommen zu sein, General Clay, [A] der hier tätig war in der Zeit der schwersten Krise, durch die diese Stadt gegangen ist, und der wieder nach Berlin kommen wird, wenn es notwendig werden sollte. [A]
Two thousand years – two thousand years ago the proudest boast was "civis Romanus sum." Today, in the world of freedom, the proudest boast is "Ich bin ein Berliner." [A, P]	Vor zweitausend Jahren war der stolzeste Satz, den ein Mensch sagen konnte, der: "Ich bin ein Bürger Roms!" Heute ist der stolzeste Satz, den jemand in der freien Welt sagen kann: "Ich bin ein Berliner!" [A]
I – [A] I – I appreciate – I appreciate my interpreter translating my German! [P]	Ich bin dem Dolmetscher dankbar, daß er mein Deutsch noch besser übersetzt hat.
There are many people in the world who really don't understand, or say they don't, what is the great issue between the free world and the Communist world. Let them come to Berlin. [A, P] There are some who say – there are some who say, that Communism is the wave of the future. Let them come to Berlin. [A, P] And there are some who say in Europe and elsewhere we can work with the Communists. Let them come to Berlin. [A, P]	Wenn es in der Welt Menschen geben sollte, die nicht verstehen oder die nicht zu verstehen vorgeben, worum es heute in der Auseinandersetzung zwischen der freien Welt und dem Kommunismus geht, dann können wir ihnen nur sagen, sie sollen nach Berlin kommen. [A] Es gibt Leute, die sagen, dem Kommunismus gehöre die Zukunft. Sie sollen nach Berlin kommen! [hissing, booing, A] Und es gibt wieder andere in Europa und in

John F. Kennedy	Heinz Weber

And there are even a few who say that it's true that Communism is an evil system, but it permits us to make economic progress. Laßt sie nach Berlin kommen. [A] Let them come to Berlin. [A, P]

anderen Teilen der Welt, die behaupten, man könne mit den Kommunisten zusammenarbeiten. Auch sie sollen nach Berlin kommen! [A] Und es gibt auch [A], und es gibt auch einige wenige, die sagen, es treffe zwar zu, daß der Kommunismus ein böses und ein schlechtes System sei; aber er gestatte es ihnen, wirtschaftlichen Fortschritt zu erreichen. [hissing, booing] Aber laßt auch sie nach Berlin kommen! [A]

Freedom has many difficulties and democracy is not perfect, but we have never had to put a wall up to keep our people in, to prevent them from leaving us. [P]

Ein Leben in Freiheit ist nicht leicht, und die Demokratie ist nicht vollkommen. Aber wir hatten es nie nötig, eine Mauer aufzubauen, um unsere Leute bei uns zu halten und sie daran zu hindern, [A] woanders hinzugehen. [A]

I want to say, on behalf of my countrymen, who live many miles away on the other side of the Atlantic, who are far distant from you, that they take the greatest pride that they have been able to share with you, even from a distance, the story of the last 18 years. I know of no town, no city, that has been besieged for 18 years that still lives with the vitality and the force, and the hope and the determination of the city of West Berlin. [A, P]

Ich möchte Ihnen im Namen der Bevölkerung der Vereinigten Staaten, die viele tausend Kilometer von Ihnen entfernt lebt auf der anderen Seite des Atlantiks, sagen, daß meine amerikanischen Mitbürger stolz, sehr stolz darauf sind, mit Ihnen zusammen selbst aus der Entfernung die Geschichte der letzten 18 Jahre teilen zu können. Denn ich weiß nicht, daß jemals eine Stadt 18 Jahre lang belagert wurde und dennoch lebt mit ungebrochener Vitalität, mit unerschütterlicher Hoffnung, mit der gleichen Stärke und mit der gleichen Entschlossenheit wie heute West-Berlin. [A]

While the wall is the most obvious and vivid demonstration of the failures of the Communist system, for all the world to see, we take no satisfaction in it, for it is, as your Mayor has said, an offense not only against history but an offense against humanity, separating families, dividing husbands and wives and brothers and sisters, and dividing a people who wish to be joined together. [A, P]

Die Mauer ist die abscheulichste und die stärkste Demonstration über das Versagen des kommunistischen Systems. [A] Die ganze Welt sieht dieses Eingeständnis des Versagens. Wir sind darüber keineswegs glücklich, denn, wie Ihr Regierender Bürgermeister gesagt hat, die Mauer schlägt nicht nur der Geschichte ins Gesicht, sie schlägt der Menschlichkeit ins Gesicht. [A] Durch die Mauer werden Familien getrennt, der Mann von der Frau, der Bruder von der Schwester, und Menschen werden mit Gewalt auseinander gehalten, die zusammen leben wollen. [hissing, booing]

(continued)

(continued)

John F. Kennedy	Heinz Weber
What is [hissing, booing] – what is true of this city is true of Germany – real, lasting peace in Europe can never be assured as long as one German out of four is denied the elementary right of free men, and that is to make a free choice. In 18 years of peace and good faith, this generation of Germans has earned the right to be free, including the right to unite their families and their nation in lasting peace, with good will to all people. [A, P]	Was von Berlin gilt, gilt von Deutschland: Ein echter Friede in Europa kann nicht gewährleistet werden, solange jedem vierten Deutschen das Grundrecht einer freien Wahl vorenthalten wird. [A] In 18 Jahren des Friedens und der erprobten Verläßlichkeit hat diese Generation der Deutschen sich das Recht verdient, frei zu sein, [A] einschließlich des Rechtes, die Familien und die Nation in dauerhaftem Frieden wieder vereint zu sehen, im guten Willen gegen jedermann. [A]
You live in a defended island of freedom, but your life is part of the main. So let me ask you as I close, to lift your eyes beyond the dangers of today, to the hopes of tomorrow, beyond the freedom merely of this city of Berlin, or your country of Germany, to the advance of freedom everywhere, beyond the wall to the day of peace with justice, beyond yourselves and ourselves to all mankind. Freedom is indivisible, and when one man is enslaved, all are not free. When all are free, then we can look forward to that day when this city will be joined as one and this country and this great Continent of Europe in a peaceful and hopeful globe. When that day finally comes, as it will, the people of West Berlin can take sober satisfaction in the fact that they were in the front lines for almost two decades. [A, P]	Sie leben auf einer verteidigten Insel der Freiheit. Aber Ihr Leben ist mit dem des Festlandes verbunden, und deshalb fordere ich Sie zum Schluß auf, den Blick über die Gefahren des Heute hinweg auf die Hoffnung des Morgen zu richten, über die Freiheit dieser Stadt Berlin, über die Freiheit Ihres Landes hinweg auf den Vormarsch der Freiheit überall in der Welt, über die Mauer hinweg auf den Tag des Friedens mit Gerechtigkeit. Die Freiheit ist unteilbar, und wenn auch nur einer versklavt ist, dann sind nicht alle frei. Aber wenn der Tag gekommen sein wird, an dem alle die Freiheit haben und Ihre Stadt und Ihr Land wiedervereint sind, wenn Europa geeint ist und Bestandteil eines friedvollen und zu höchsten Hoffnungen berechtigten Erdteiles, dann – wenn dieser Tag gekommen sein wird – können Sie mit Befriedigung von sich sagen, daß die Berliner und diese Stadt Berlin 20 Jahre lang die Front gehalten haben. [A]
All – all free men, wherever they may live, are citizens of Berlin, and, therefore, as a free man, I take pride in the words: "Ich bin ein Berliner." [A, P]	Alle [A] – alle freien Menschen, wo immer sie leben mögen, sind Bürger dieser Stadt West-Berlin, und deshalb bin ich als freier Mann stolz darauf, sagen zu können: "Ich bin ein Berliner!" [A]

Notes

PREFACE TO THE ENGLISH EDITION

1. Carlo Ginzburg, "Microhistory: Two or Three Things That I know about it," *Critical Inquiry*, 20, no. 1 (Autumn 1993), 27.

INTRODUCTION: AMERICA'S BERLIN AND JOHN F. KENNEDY

1. Hugh Sidey, "Present at the Creation," *Time*, 20 November 1989, 33. All German quotations have been translated into English by the translator unless specified otherwise; the original wordings are included in the notes.
2. It is amazing that the Kennedy trip has not been the subject of extensive study until now. For contemporary summaries of the speeches and impressions of the visit, see Presse- und Informationsamt des Landes Berlin 1963; *Ich bin ein Berliner* 1963; *Präsident Kennedy in Deutschland* 1963 (hereafter PK 1963); and Kennedy 1964. For some specific aspects regarding Kennedy's speech at the Schöneberg City Hall, see Prowe 1989 and Eichhoff 1993.
3. The traditional biblical reference to a "city on a hill" – found in Matthew 5:14 and introduced by John Winthrop in the seventeenth century in connection with the establishment of a new society on the North American continent – was applied to West Berlin as late as 1978 by President Jimmy Carter, who thereby drew a parallel to U.S. history; see *Public Papers of the Presidents of the United States* (hereafter PPP) 1978, 1295.
4. Daum 2000; see also May 1991, 1998; and Schwartz 1995.
5. See Bender 2002; Osterhammel 2001; and Conrad 2002.
6. For surveys of the postwar history of Germany, see Bark and Gress 1993 and Turner 1992.
7. See Ginzburg 1993 and Medick 2002, with recommended literature on microhistory; on the relationship between event and structure, see Koselleck 2004. For examples of the ways microhistory can be used to depict an epoch, see Blackbourn 1993 and Smith 2002.
8. See the list of printed sources and document collections in the bibliography at the end of this book. Essential for research on the history of international relations during the Cold War are the files on American and German foreign policy, see *Foreign Relations of the United States* (hereafter FRUS), 1961–1963, esp. vol. XIV: *Berlin Crisis 1961–1962* (1993) and vol. XV: *Berlin Crisis 1962–1963*; as well as *Akten zur Auswärtigen Politik*

227

der Bundesrepublik Deutschland (AAP), here vol. 1963, I–III; and pertaining to Berlin, *Dokumente zur Berlin-Frage* (1967 and 1987). However, the volumes include very little detailed information on the Kennedy trip of 1963; this topic requires archival research.

9. See, for example, Hunt 1984 and Wilentz 1985. For insights into the nature and direction of debates in cultural history, see Hunt 1989 and Bonnell and Hunt 1999.

10. For an important work in the German literature on this topic, see Loth and Osterhammel 2000. In the Anglo-Saxon discussion, which started earlier, see particularly Iriye 1979; Hogan and Paterson 1991; Leffler 1995; and Gienow-Hecht and Schumacher 2003. Important essays from a political science perspective can be found in Katzenstein 1996. For an overview of more recent work on the Cold War era, see Geppert 2002.

11. Risse 2002 and Risse-Kappen 1995. Two starting points of this approach were delineated by Karl Kaiser (1969) and Robert O. Keohane and Joseph S. Nye, Jr. (1971).

12. Lemert and Branaman 1997. The best review of relevant research, including Goffman's work, and numerous bibliographic references are found in Hare and Blumberg 1988. On the theatricality of modern political media, see *Die Inszenierung des Politischen* 2000, 45–77.

13. See Herzfeld 1973; Prowe 1973, 2004; and Daum 2000. On the history of Berlin in the twentieth century, see the overview given in Ribbe 1987 and Ribbe and Schmädecke 1990, as well as the well-known works by Alexandra Richie (1998) and David Clay Large (2000).

14. *New York Times*, 23 June 1963; Russell E. Singer, "Observations of an American traveler in West Berlin," Summer 1962, Lyndon B. Johnson Library (hereafter LBJL), Vice-Presidential Papers, 1961–1963, Subject Files, Box 136, folder: Foreign Relations – Germany (includes: Berlin).

15. Meier 1990, 1993. See also Münkler 1990.

16. Duindam 1994; Burke 1992; Hunt 1984; Lüsebrink and Reichardt 1990. The term *street theater* is borrowed from Davis 1986. The connection between public rituals, social worlds, and political culture was examined in the 1960s and 1970s particularly by E. P. Thompson and Raymond Williams.

17. Nipperdey 1976, 133–73; 1986, 156–71; Hardtwig 1994, 191–273. See also Behrenbeck and Nützenadel 2000.

18. Blackbourn 1987; Paulmann 2000; Wolfrum 1999.

19. Falasca-Zamponi 1997.

20. Reichel 1991.

21. Reichel 1991; Mosse 1991.

22. See Vondung 1971; Thamer 2000; as well as Thamer 1986; Hardtwig 2001; and Maier 2002. Thamer, Hardtwig, and Maier use the concept of political religion, which was introduced by Erick Voegelin and has enjoyed a renaissance in recent years. This concept has also been applied to the twentieth century by Sabine Behrenbeck (1996).

23. Recently, historians have rediscovered the research of the American political scientist Murray Edelman. Starting in the late 1950s, Edelman examined the meaning and importance of symbolic actions, public rituals, and performances in modern mass politics; see esp. Edelman 1964/1985. However, Edelman distinguished between symbolic performances and the sphere of political decision making, which he says is dominated by elitist networks. Edelman's dichotomy between symbolism and politics has now been criticized; see Dittmer 1977, 560–63; Dörner 1995; and Bizeul 2000. Dörner (1995) is

correct to emphasize the role symbols play in constituting politics and to protest against the common contention that symbols contribute no more than theatrical illusions. See Krotz 2002 on the constitutive role of symbolic actions for Franco-German relations after 1949. Two of the most influential works in recognizing and interpreting symbolic actions and, particularly, rituals as constitutive for social realities stem from Emile Durkheim and Clifford Geertz; see here Durkheim 2001 and Geertz 1971, 1980, 98–136.

24. Ronald Reagan, Remarks on the 750th Anniversary of the Founding of Berlin, 12 June 1987, in PPP 1987, book I, pp. 638–40, here 640.

25. This point is emphasized particularly by Hunt (1984, 14, 55–56) and Thamer (2000, 80). Symbolic activity is, in the words of Michael Walzer, a "creative process" and "perhaps our most important means of bringing things together, both intellectually and emotionally, thus overcoming isolation and even individuality" (1967, 198, 194). The theoretical groundwork is provided by the work of Peter L. Berger and Thomas Luckmann (1967) and John R. Searle (1995).

26. Historians working on symbolic practices, rites, and invented traditions have concentrated so far on the period from the eighteenth to the early twentieth centuries and studied primarily the formation of the modern concept of nation and the constitution of a bourgeois society; see Wilentz 1985; Anderson 1991; Hobsbawm and Ranger 1996; and Behrenbeck and Nützenadel 2000.

27. See Meyer 1992, 60–63, and the innovative study based on a close reading of anthropological literature, among other fields, by Jan Kubik (1994).

28. This elementary function of symbolic politics is concealed when symbolic politics is primarily viewed as a strategy to aestheticize politics and create illusions; it would thus be interpreted as the "expulsion of the political dimension"; see Meyer 1994, 143.

29. Paulmann 2005, 1.

30. Thamer 2000.

31. From the 'Briefing Book' for the Kennedy trip: President's European Trip. June 1963. Scope: Germany (14 June 1963), John F. Kennedy Library (hereafter JFKL), National Security Files (hereafter NSF), Trips & Conferences (hereafter T & C), Box 239, folder: President's Trip, Europe 6/63–7/63, Salinger Briefing Book, folder 1 of 4; also in National Archives II (hereafter NA), RG 59, Entry 3051 B: Executive Secretariat, Conference Files 1949–1963, Box 317, folder: CF 2274 – President's Trip to Europe 6/23–7/2/63, Briefing Book (1 of 2).

32. I would also consider the term *politics of seeing* as being an accurate alternative to *politics of visibility*.

33. Diers 1997, 7. The connection between the iconography of images and politics has been generating more and more interest in recent years in the fields of history, art history, and political science. As examples, see Münkler 1994 and Bredekamp 1999.

34. Bredekamp 1999, 7, 73, 83–91. Bredekamp is referring here specifically to the preoccupation of the political theorist Thomas Hobbes with the study of optics and optical instruments, which Hobbes and others understood as societal allegories.

35. Diers 1997, 43. See Hoffmann 1999.

36. Ries 1973, 1998, 2001. On earlier photos by Ries following the end of the Second World War, see Barnouw 1996, 158–61.

37. Reuter 1974, 479.

38. Vice President to the President, memorandum, 21 August 1961, LBJL, Vice-Presidential Security File, Box 2, folder: Berlin, Germany; Berlin Papers for the Vice President.

39. Several examples can also be cited to the contrary – trips in which the visitor expressed no true favor or liking for the party visited, such as the trip by British Prime Minisiter Arthur Neville Chamberlain to Bad Godesberg in September 1938 to meet Adolf Hitler and followed a couple of days later by his attendance at the Munich Conference.

40. Hans Ulrich Kempski, "Der Gast, der Deutsche im Ekstase bringt," *Süddeutsche Zeitung,* 28 June 1963.

41. *Frankfurter Allgemeine Zeitung,* 27 June 1963; *B.Z. Berlin,* 26 June 1963; Lohnbüro Standard Elektrik Lorenz AG to Kennedy, 5 July 1963, JFKL, White House (WH) Central Subject Files, Trips, Box 983: Trips folder: TR 56/CO92 7–10–63.

42. François, Siegrist, and Vogel 1995; Benthien, Fleig, and Kasten 2000; Frevert 2000; Kessel 2000.

43. See particularly Costigliola 1997a, 1997b, 1998, 2000. A review of the various definitions of emotionality and its role in explanations and theories of international relations is offered by Neta C. Crawford (2000).

44. This is the assumption of the so-called rational actor model, on which the realist and liberal schools of foreign policy analysis are based.

45. von Bredow 1996, 109.

46. See also Chapter 2, on the term *Straßenpolitik* (street politics), borrowed here from Thomas Lindenberger.

47. Memorandum of Conversation, 19 August 1961, LBJL, Vice-Presidential Security File, Papers for the Vice President, Box 2: Vice-Presidential Travel, folder: Berlin, Germany; Berlin.

48. Memorandum of Conversation, "President's European Trip, June 1963," 23 June 1963, NA, RG 59, Entry 5290, Lot File 70D4, Box 3, folder: Aviation (Civil). Routes & Schedules.

49. *New York Times,* 25 June 1963.

50. Weber 1978, vol. 1, 40–41. Weber then adds: "No matter how calculating and hard-headed the ruling considerations in such a social relationship – as that of a merchant to his customers – may be, it is quite possible for it to involve emotional values which transcend its utilitarian significance. Every social relationship which goes beyond the pursuit of immediate common ends, which hence lasts for long periods, . . . always [has] some tendency in this direction, although the degree, to be sure, varies enormously. Conversely, a social relationship which is normally considered primarily communal may involve action on the part of some or even all of the participants which is to an important degree oriented to considerations of expediency" (1978, vol. 1, 41). See Weber's thoughts on *Gemeinschaftshandeln* (social action) and *Gesellschaftshandeln* (rationally regulated action) in ibid., vol. 2, 1375–80 and in Weber 1988, 441–64.

51. For a general introduction, see Henrikson 1991. For more work specifically on the concepts of an Atlantic community and the Christian West, as well as their relation to one another, see Mausbach 2004; Schildt 1999b; and *The Atlantic Community* 1961.

52. Deutsch 1953; Deutsch et al. 1957; and modeled closely on Deutsch's work, Russet 1963. Within the context of the theoretical debate on political culture and political symbolism, see Dittmer 1977, 563–65. See also the important article by Thomas Risse-Kappen (1996), summarizing some of his earlier works.

53. Weber 1978, vol. 1, 243, 215.

54. Weber 1978, vol. 1, 215; see also Weber 1988, 481–88. Weber developed the concept of charisma in connection with his typology of legitimate forms of authority. He speaks of

a charismatic authority as the third type of authority in addition to legal and traditional authority. On the debate over Weber's concept of charisma and for references for further reading, see Joas 1996, 69–76; Kershaw 1987; Nippel 2000; and Daum 2004.

55. Schlesinger 1965, 885. See also O'Donnell and Powers 1972, 360–61, and Brandt 1964, 204.

56. Dörner 1995, 87–91; Thamer 2000, 81, 83; Maier 2002, 359; Nipperdey 1987.

57. "Rede des Bürgermeisters Heinrich Albertz auf der Trauerkundgebung vor dem Rathaus Schöneberg für den ermordeten Präsidenten John F. Kennedy," Pressedienst des Landes Berlin, no. 232, 25 November 1963, Landesarchiv Berlin (hereafter LAB), B Rep. 002, no. 3180.

58. Winkler 2006. See also Schildt 1999a.

59. Berghahn 1986, 1996; Volker R. Berghahn, "America and Social Change in Germany," in Junker, ed. 2004, vol. 1, 495–507; Doering-Manteuffel 1995, 1999; Kuisel 1993. For the current debate, see Ermarth 1993; Lüdke, Marßolek, and von Saldern 1996; Gassert 1999; Fehrenbach and Poiger 2000; and Schildt 2000.

60. Weber 1978, vol. 1, 27.

CHAPTER 1: THE STORY AND ITS PROTAGONISTS

1. For recent surveys on developments in American foreign policy, American-European relations, and international politics at the time, see Schulzinger 2002; Lundestad 2003; Hunt 2004; and Gaddis 2005.

2. See McDougall 1985.

3. Memorandum for the Record, "Meeting with President-elect Kennedy and Secretary of Treasury Anderson," 11 January 1961, Dwight D. Eisenhower Library (DDEL), Ann Whitman Files, Presidential Transition Series, Box 1, folder: Memos-Staff-re Change of Administration (1). See Zimmermann 2002.

4. For a general review of the foreign policy of the Federal Republic of Germany, see Hanrieder 1989 and Haftendorn 2006.

5. Hildebrand 1984, 229–40.

6. See Knapp 2004.

7. Lucius D. Clay in a conversation with Germany's President Lübke, in "Zusammenfassung des Gesprächs zwischen dem Bundespräsidenten und General Clay am 30.4.1962 im Schloss Bellevue," Archiv der sozialen Demokratie der Friedrich-Ebert-Stiftung (AFES), Willy-Brandt-Archiv im Archiv der sozialen Demokratie der Friedrich-Ebert-Stiftung (WBA), Berlin, Ordner 71/72, Mappe 72. Clay's remark is noted in this protocol in German: "nicht immer eine Atombombe schwenken [könne], wenn man die Durchfahrt der Autobahn erreichen wolle."

8. Cornides 1963, 428, 434.

9. Report of Senator Kennedy's National Security Policy Committee, Library of Congress (LoC), Paul H. Nitze Papers, Box 141, folder 8.

10. This is how Kennedy formulated the concept for a new transatlantic order, featuring the United States and Europe as its main pillars of support, on 4 July 1962 in Philadelphia, in PPP 1962, 537–39. About U.S. policy on the Berlin issue during the transition period from the Eisenhower to the Kennedy administrations, see Burr 1992, 21–24, 32; Arenth 1993; Bremen 1998; Smyser 1999; and Steininger 2001.

11. Costigliola 1989, 24–56; Schwartz 1994; Münger 1999; Daum 2007. An analysis of the government publications on American sources about the Berlin crisis can be found in Schwartz 1997.
12. See Schlesinger 1965, 380–94.
13. See Chapter 2 and Barclay 2000, 301–09.
14. Cornides 1963, 438.
15. Radio and Television Report to the American People on the Berlin Crisis, 25 July 1961, in PPP 1961, 533–40.
16. Schwarz 1983, 138.
17. *Bild*, 16 August 1963.
18. Brandt added these words to the sentence in which the mayor welcomed U.S. plans to take the demonstrative step of bolstering the American garrison in Berlin; see the draft letter by Egon Bahr, 15 August 1961, AFES, Depositum Egon Bahr, Ordner 324, Mappe 1. According to Diethelm Prowe (1985, 376), Brandt was also encouraged by the U.S. head of the Berlin mission, Allan E. Lightner, and the director of the U.S. Information Agency, Edward R. Murrow, who was in the city at the time, to approach Kennedy directly.
19. Summary of Confidential Discussion Between the Vice President and Mayor Brandt, 19 August 1961, LBJL, Vice-Presidential Security File, Box 2, folder: Berlin, Germany; Berlin Papers for the Vice President; John F. Kennedy to Willy Brandt, 18 August 1961, JFKL, NSF, Countries, Box 82, folder: Germany – Berlin, General: Vice President's Trip, 8/19/61–8/20/61; reprinted in FRUS, 1961–1963, vol. XIV, 352–3.
20. John F. Kennedy to Lyndon Johnson, 18 August 1961, JFKL, President's Office Files, Countries, Box 117, folder: Germany, Security 8/61–12/61. On the German domestic context of the events briefly summarized here, see Schwarz 1983, including page 151 on the Brandt letter to Kennedy.
21. Münger 2003, 129–31.
22. Clay to Dean Acheson, 22 December 1961, George C. Marshall Library (GML), Lucius D. Clay Papers, Box 5, folder 37.
23. Legere to Maxwell Taylor, memorandum, 12 December 1961, JFKL, NSF, Countries, Box 86, folder: Germany, Berlin, General Lucius D. Clay.
24. Clay to Rusk, Transcript of a handwritten letter dated 2 December 1961, JFKL, NSF, Countries, Box 86, folder: Germany, Berlin, General Lucius D. Clay. See also GML, Lucius D. Clay Papers, Box 7, folder 28.
25. Prowe 1976; Schmidt 2001.
26. Münger 2003, 159.
27. Schwarz 1983, 149.
28. JFKL, NSF, Countries, Box 84 A, folder: Germany, Berlin, General 8/62.
29. J.-J. Kausch, "Der Zorn der Berliner," *Die Welt*, 22 August 1962. See *Tagesspiegel*, 21 August 1962; Merseburger, 2002, 432–34; and FRUS 1961–1963, vol. XV, no. 95, 272–73.
30. Sebastian Haffner, "Gedulde Grausamkeit," *Die Welt*, 21 August 1962.
31. Jan Reifenberg, "Washington im Zwielicht der Berliner Krise," *Frankfurter Allgemeine Zeitung*, 24 August 1962.
32. Draft of letter by Brandt to John F. Kennedy, 30 August 1962 (not sent), AFES, WBA, Berlin, Ordner 126; Brandt to Clay, 31 August 1962 and 4 September 1962, GML, Lucius D. Clay Papers, Box 1, folder 40.

33. John F. Kennedy to Heinrich Lübke, 14 September 1962, JFKL, President's Office Files, Countries, Box 117, folder: Germany, General 9/62–12/62.

34. Kennedy 1969.

35. May and Zelikow 1997, 280.

36. Carl Kaysen, Record of Meeting with the President, 5 October 1962, JFKL, NSF, Countries, Box 76, folder 2; "Vermerk über das Gespräch, zu dem der Präsident der Vereinigten Staaten in Anwesenheit von Mr. Hillenbrand und Professor Kaysen den Regierenden Bürgermeister, begleitet von Botschafter Knappstein und Herrn Bahr, am 5. Oktober 1962 empfing," 8.10.1962, AFES, WBA, Berlin, Ordner 71/72, Mappe 72.

37. Ibid.

38. Brandt to John F. Kennedy, 29 October 1962, and Kennedy to Brandt, 14 November 1962, JFKL, NSF, Countries, Box 76, folder 4; FRUS 1961–1963, vol. XV, no. 155, 444.

39. Costigliola 1989, 34.

40. On Franco-German relations in the postwar period, see the comprehensive work by Lappenküper 2001 and Conze 1995a.

41. AAP 1963, vol. I. 1, no. 65, 229; John McCloy to Konrad Adenauer, 4 February 1963, JFKL, President's Office Files, Special Correspondence, Box 31. On Kennedy, see AAP 1963, vol. I. 1, no. 49, 162–65; on the transatlantic context, see Conze 1995b and Knapp 2004.

42. Münger 2003, 315.

43. *New York Herald Tribune*, 29 March 1959. The strong support for Berlin, even to the point of risking war, is clearly documented in the *Monthly Surveys of American Opinion on International Affairs* by the State Department. These surveys are based on opinion polls and a meticulous evaluation of the media and are available in NA, RG 59, Office of Public Opinion Studies (Schuyler Foster Files), 1943–65, here Box 13.

44. Key Questions and Answers in the Gallup Poll of July 1961, DDEL, C. D. Jackson Papers, Box 53, folder: Free Europe Committee, 1961 (1).

45. Gallup 1972, vol. 3 (1959–1971), 1734–35, 1738.

46. Robert C. Byrd to John F. Kennedy, 29 June 1961, JFKL, WH Central Files, Subject File, Countries, Box 55, folder: CO 92/LG/Berlin, Berlin Situation: June 1, 1961–Sept. 14, 1961; Roy W. Johnson to John F. Kennedy, 17 October 1961, ibid., Box 57, folder: CO 92/LG/Berlin, 10–26–61–1–31–62.

47. JFKL, WH Central Subject Files, Countries, folder: CO 92/LG/Berlin, Oct. 25, 1961.

48. May 1991, 79.

49. Willy Brandt to John F. Kennedy, 18 March 1963, AFES, WBA, Ordner 126; Willy Brandt to Robert F. Kennedy, 18 March 1963, JFKL, Robert F. Kennedy (RFK) Papers, Attorney General's Papers, General Correspondence, Box 6, folder: Willy Brandt.

50. Egon Bahr to Axel Springer, 13 May 1960, AFES, Depositum Egon Bahr, Ordner 48 A, Tageskopien 12.5.60–26.5.60.

51. See, from a historical perspective, Russet 1963; Reynolds 1995; and Dumbrell 2006. On Berlin's relationship to the United States, see also the panoramic volume by Tamara Domentat (1995).

52. Two advocates for a more differentiated view of Berlin's development as compared to the rest of Europe are Brunn 1993 and Briesen 1992.

53. See Jelavich 1996 and Fritzsche 1998.

54. Suhr 1990, 222, 224; Daum 2000, 60. See also Gordon A. Craig, "Die Entdeckung Berlins. Wie Amerikaner seit dem 19. Jahrhundert die deutsche Hauptstadt erkundeten und die Vereinigten Staaten später zur Schutzmacht des Westteils wurden," *Berliner Zeitung*, 2/3/4 October 1998 and Helbig 1987. On the changing perceptions and images of Berlin since the nineteenth century, see Daum and Mauch 2005.

55. Günter Gillessen, "Über die Dächer von Berlin. Die Luftbrücke brachte Kohle und machte Alliierte," *Frankfurter Allgemeine Zeitung*, 27 June 1998. See Shlaim 1983; Tusa and Tusa 1998; as well as two revisionist interpretations with references to additional literature, Koop 1998 and Stivers 1997.

56. See Daum 2000 and Schmundt-Thomas 1992.

57. Schwartz 1995, 556. See Risse 2002 and Berghahn, "America and Social Change" in Junker, ed. 2004, vol. 1; Feldman 2004; and Lutz 2004. Lutz's use of the term *transatlantic elite* is problematic and he does not fully explain it. A better explanation would seem to be that national elites existed in Germany and the United States who communicated across the Atlantic and, through this exchange, had a degree of political influence in certain areas.

58. Schröder 2001.

59. "Tale of Two Cities – The Story Khrushchev Didn't Tell," *U.S. News & World Report*, 14 June 1957, 34; Toni Howard, "The Squeeze is on Berlin," *Saturday Evening Post*, 28 February 1959, 75. See U.S. Information Service n.d. [ca. 1957] and Fehrenbach 1995, 234–53.

60. An important general study on the FU is Tent 1988; see also Schneider 1985. On Shepard Stone, see Berghahn 2001.

61. Hochgeschwender 1998.

62. Diefendorf 2004, 591. See Dulles 1967, 1980; on the architecture of the Congress Hall, see Lane 1984.

63. Ries 1973, 1998, 2001.

64. This is how the Irish politician and political thinker Edmund Burke (1729–1797) described a state as a social partnership: Burke 2001, 261.

65. Wetzlaugk 1988, 233.

66. *The Story of the World Freedom Bell* n.d. [ca. 1951], 36. See also Liebau and Daum 2000; Geppert 2001.

67. Egon Bahr, memorandum, 15 September 1960, AFES, Depositum Egon Bahr, Ordner 46 B, Tageskopien 1.9.-23.9.60.

68. Bürgermeister Franz Amrehm, "Thema: Freiheitsglocke," *Welt am Sonntag*, 30 October 1960, AFES, Depositum Egon Bahr, Ordner 46 A, Tageskopien 8.11.-30.11.60 1/ EBAA000147.

69. "General Clay ruft Mitbürger zum Salut für freies Berlin," *New Yorker Staats-Zeitung und Herald*, 11 August 1962.

70. Edward Murrow to Leo Cherne, 16 July 1962, Boston University, Department of Special Collections, Leo Cherne Collection, Box 4, folder: Berlin Wall, August 13 Observance 1962.

71. Joseph Kovago to John Richardson [August 1962], "Confidential Report on the Berlin Project," Hoover Institution Archives (HIA), Christopher Temple Emmet, Jr., Collection, Box 49, folder: Remember Berlin Day.

72. Barclay 2000, 278. See Angster 2002, 180–269.

73. Lichtenstein 1995, 344.

74. On the role of alliance managers, see Schwartz 1991, 1995.

75. "Spirit of the Front Line," *Time*, 29 January 1951, 32.
76. I thank Brad Bauer of the Hoover Presidential Library in West Branch for providing me the original English text. Neither the local Berlin *Tagesspiegel* nor the national press corps from Germany or the United States quoted this statement by Hoover. See *Tagesspiegel*, 27 November 1954, 2.
77. Willy Brandt, handwritten memorandum, 7 May 1962, AFES, WBA, Gruppe 6, Mappe 72.
78. Grabbe 1983; Kremp 1993.
79. H. Podeyn to Ernst Reuter, 16 August 1951, LAB, Ernst-Reuter-Archiv, E Rep. 200–21–01, no. 114
80. Brandt 1959; Kettlein 1959; Mümkel 2004.
81. Egon Bahr, memorandum, 15 September 1960, AFES, Depositum Egon Bahr, Ordner 46 B, Tageskopien 1.9.-23.9.60; Eleanor L. Dulles to Martin J. Hillenbrand, memorandum, 26 June 1959, NA, RG 59, Entry 3088, folder: 1957–61 Visits – U.S. to Germany (22.1).
82. Edward R. Murrow to McGeorge Bundy, memorandum, 28 July 1961; George C. Ball to the President, memorandum, 5 August 1961, JFKL, NSF, Countries, Box 82, folder: Germany – Berlin, General: 8/1/61–8/5/61; as well as McGeorge Bundy to Clark Clifford, 22 August 1961, JFKL, NSF, Countries, Box 82, folder: Germany – Berlin, General: 8/22/61.
83. The term *Straßenpolitik* (street politics) is discussed in Chapter 2.
84. David Kirkpatrick Ester Bruce Diaries, Virginia Historical Society, Richmond, Diaries Mss 5:1 B 8303:34, 1959 Jul 1–September 30, July 25, p. 33.
85. Memorandum to McGeorge Bundy, 17 August 1961, quote also here; Henry Owen to McGeorge Bundy, 17 August 1961, both in JFKL, NSF, Countries, Box 82, folder: Germany – Berlin, General: 8/17/61; John F. Kennedy to Lyndon Johnson, 18 August 1961, ibid., folder: Germany – Berlin, General: Vice President's Trip, 8/19/61–8/20/61; W. W. Rostow, to Foy D. Kohler, memorandum, 18 August 1961, LBJL, Vice-Presidential Security File, Box 2, folder: Berlin, Germany; Berlin Papers for the Vice President.
86. Clay to Taylor, 15 August 1961, GML, Lucius D. Clay Papers, Box 8, folder 1: Maxwell D. Taylor.
87. W. W. Rostow, Memorandum of Conversation with Dr. Josef Cohn . . . , [September 1961], LBJL, Vice-Presidential Security File, Box 9, folder: Germany and Berlin, 1961.
88. Lyndon B. Johnson to John F. Kennedy, memorandum, 21 August 1961, LBJL, Vice-Presidential Security File, Box 2, folder: Berlin, Germany; Berlin Papers for the Vice President.
89. As a result, the United States recommended reviewing the structures of command in Berlin as well as the use of economic sanctions against the East, modernizing military arms and equipment in the city, calling on its allies to step up their own defense efforts, communicating Kennedy's Europe policy better to the public, improving communication between the Western powers, and striving to establish a large cultural, academic, or educational center in West Berlin. See the Summary of Confidential Discussion Between the Vice President and Chancellor Adenauer, 19 August 1961; Memorandum of Conversation [with Adenauer], 19 August 1961; Memorandum of Conversation [with Brandt], 20 August 1961, all of which are found in LBJL, Vice-Presidential Security File, Box 2, folder: Berlin, Germany; Berlin Papers for the Vice President. See also *New York Times*, 21 August 1961.

90. *New York Times*, 20 August 1961; Lyndon B. Johnson to John F. Kennedy, memorandum, 21 August 1961, LBJL, Vice-Presidential Security File, Box 2, folder: Berlin, Germany; Berlin Papers for the Vice President.

91. Press release "Remarks by Vice President Lyndon B. Johnson On Arrival in Berlin," LBJL. On the Johnson visit, see also Brandt 1964, 75–94.

92. *New York Times*, 20 August 1961.

93. Walter C. Dowling to the Secretary of State, telegram, 20 August 1961, LBJL, Vice-Presidential Security File, Box 2, folder: Report and Related Papers re Vice President Johnson's Trip to Germany, August 19–20, 1961.

94. *New York Times*, 21 August 1961; *New York Herald Tribune*, 20 August 1961; *New York Times*, 20 August 1961; *New York Times*, 21 August 1961.

95. Brandt 1964, 90.

96. Ausland 1996, 24.

97. *New York Times*, 21 August 1961.

98. ibid.; Lawrence Westbrook to Lyndon B. Johnson, 19 August 1961, LBJL, Vice-Presidential Papers, 1961–1963, Subject Files, Box 109, folder: Public Activities – Travel – Foreign – Berlin (Pro) August, 2 of 2.

99. Interview with Robert Lochner, in http://www.gwu.edu/~nsarchiv/coldwar/ interviews/episode-4/lochner9.html (May 23, 2007); author's conversation with Robert Lochner on November 17, 2002.

100. Richard R. Salzmann to Lyndon B. Johnson, 21 August 1961, LBJL, Vice-Presidential Papers, 1961–1963, Subject Files, Box 109, folder: Public Activities – Travel – Foreign – Berlin (Pro) August, 2 of 2. On Johnson's role in the Senate, see Caro 2002.

101. Johnson's address to the Berlin parliament, *New York Times*, 20 August 1961.

102. As quoted in Biermann 1997, 137–38.

103. Johnson's address to the Berlin parliament, *New York Times*, 20 August 1961. See Schlesinger 1965, 396.

104. *Houston Chronicle*, 22 August 1961; see also *New York Times*, 22 August 1961.

105. *The Sunday Star* (Washington, D.C.), 20 August 1961.

106. William E. Griffith to Walt W. Rostow, 25 August 1961, JFKL, NSF, Countries, Box 82A, folder: Germany – Berlin, General: 8/25/61. On the response to the trip, see also LBJL, Vice-Presidential Security File, Box 2, folder: Report and Related Papers re Vice President Johnson's Trip to Germany, August 19–20, 1961.

107. Henry O. Hart, Director Audience Research Department, Radio Free Europe, Munich, to Lyndon B. Johnson, 23 October 1961, LBJL, Vice-Presidential Papers, 1961–1963, Subject Files, Box 79, folder: Foreign Relations – Berlin (1 of 3).

108. Attorney General to the President, memorandum, 17 August 1961; see also the memorandum to McGeorge Bundy August 17, 1961, both in JFKL, NSF, Countries, Box 82, folder: Germany – Berlin, General: 8/17/61.

109. Lightner to the Secretary of State, telegram, 19 February 1962, JFKL, RFK Papers, Attorney General's Papers, Series: Trips, 1961–1964, folder: Ed Gutham, Ring Binder 2, Miscellaneous; Berlin, 1/1962. On Kennedy's impressions of the Berlin Airlift, see the diary entry from July 1948, JFKL, RFK, Attorney General's Papers, Pre-Administration Personal Files, Box 24, folder: Travel Diary (1948, Mid-East & Europe), 51–57.

110. George Ball to the U.S. Embassy in Bonn and the U.S. Mission in Berlin, telegram, December 1962, JFKL, NSF, Countries, Box 86, folder: Germany, Berlin, General Lucius D. Clay.

111. Clay to the Secretary of State, 30 December 1961, JFKL, RFK Papers, Attorney General's Papers, Series: Trips, 1961–1964, Box 4, folder: Berlin 12/1961; Egon Bahr to director division II, memorandum, 27 November 1961, AFES, Depositum Egon Bahr, Ordner 44 B, Tageskopien, 29 November 1961–5 March 1962.

112. From the abundance of relevant documents, the following have been selected as a summary of events: Legere to General Taylor, memorandum, 12 December 1961; L. D. Battle to McGeorge Bundy, memorandum, 5 January 1962; McGeorge Bundy to the President, memorandum, 6 January 1962; Clay to Dean Rusk, 30 January 1962, all in JFKL, NSF, Countries, Box 86, folder: Germany, Berlin, General Lucius D. Clay. See Ausland 1996, 28–41, 203.

113. For an account of the trip, in addition to the contemporary press reports, see Kennedy 1962; Brandt 1964, 122–35; and the reports filed by the head of the U.S. Mission in Berlin, Allan E. Lightner, to the State Department, in JFKL, RFK Papers, Attorney General's Papers, Series: Trips, 1961–1964, Box 4.

114. Guthman and Allen 1993, 80–82; excerpts also in Kennedy 1962, 142–45; a German translation is included in Brandt 1964, 124–25.

115. Both the original text of the speech and its German translation are found in *John F. Kennedy – Robert F. Kennedy. Reden an der Freien Universität* 1996, 17–35; excerpts in Kennedy 1962, 153–61.

116. See Wolfrum 1999, 115–23.

117. Brandt 1964, 130.

118. Jay W. Gildner to McGeorge Bundy, memorandum, 10 January 1962; and Arthur R. Day, U.S. Mission Berlin, to the Department of State, telegram, 14 January 1964, both of which are found in JFKL, RFK Papers, Attorney General's Papers, Series: Trips, 1961–1964, Box 2, folder: Ed Gutham, Ring Binder 2, Miscellaneous; Berlin, 2/1962.

119. Lightner to the Secretary of State, telegram, 25 February 1962, JFKL, RFK Papers, Attorney General's Papers, Series: Trips, 1961–1964, Box 4, folder: Berlin 2/25/1962–2/28/1962.

120. An extensive look at the press coverage is found in Information Unit, United States Information Agency, U.S. Mission Berlin, "Berlin Press Commentaries," 23, 24, and 26 February 1962, JFKL, RFK Papers, Attorney General's Papers, Series: General Correspondence, Box 20, folder: Germany 1962.

121. JFKL, RFK Papers, Series: Trips, 1961–1964, Box 7, folder: Berlin 2/1962.

122. The trip to France that German president Lübke made before Adenauer's visits had been rather unspectacular. Unless noted otherwise, the following recapitulation is based on the comprehensive description of the Franco-German visits found in Lappenküper 2001, vol. 2, 1726–48 and Loth and Picht 1991, in particular, the contribution by Gerhard Kiersch (1991). See also Conze 1995a and Krotz 2002. Adenauer's account in his memoirs remains factual and sober, see Adenauer 1968, 158–84.

123. *Frankfurter Allgemeine Zeitung*, 7 September 1962; *Die Welt*, 6 September 1962.

124. On concepts of the Christian Occident, see Schildt 1999b.

125. Schwarz 1983, 259, with an illustration on 258 of the scene in Reims. Schwarz himself concedes that 1963 witnessed the public triumph of Atlanticism as was demonstrated by the Kennedy visit: 1983, 296.

126. *Frankfurter Allgemeine Zeitung*, 7 September 1962; *Frankfurter Allgemeine Zeitung*, 6 September 1962.

127. Lappenküper 2001, vol. 2, 1746; *Die Welt*, 7 September 1962.

128. *Frankfurter Allgemeine Zeitung*, 6 September 1962.
129. *Die Welt*, 10 September 1962, 4; *Frankfurter Allgemeine Zeitung*, 5 September 1962.
130. Memorandum of Conversation, 25 September 1962, JFKL, WH Central Files, Subject File, Box 85, folder: Germany, Berlin, General 9/62; Rostow, speech manuscript, "The Present Stage of the Cold War," NA, RG 59, Entry 5290, Lot File 70D4, Box 10, folder: Rostow Visit to Berlin 1962.
131. "Reasons Why President Should Visit Berlin," JFKL, NSF, T & C, Box 241, folder: President's Trip, Europe, 6/63–7/63, Germany, 1/17/63–6/19/63, folder 1 of 2.
132. See Hans-Peter Schwarz 1983, 104.
133. William H. Brubeck to McGeorge Bundy, memorandum, 14 March 1963, JFKL, NSF, T & C, Box 241, folder: President's Trip, Europe, 6/63–7/63, Germany, 1/17/63–6/19/63, folder 1 of 2.
134. See Granieri 2004.
135. The year of birth for each of these individuals: Adenauer, 1876; Brandt, 1913; Dulles, 1888; Eisenhower, 1890; Erhard, 1897; de Gaulle, 1890; John F. Kennedy, 1917; Robert F. Kennedy, 1925; Khrushchev, 1894; Macmillan, 1894; Monnet, 1888; Schumann, 1886; Ulbricht, 1893. On Kennedy see only the latest and comprehensive biography by Robert Dallek (2003).
136. A fundamental reference for this point is Schwarz 1995–97.
137. Kennedy 1940.
138. See the comprehensive biography by Peter Merseburger (2002).
139. Schwarz 1995–97, vol. 2, 514; Kennedy 1957, 49.
140. The copy of Kennedy's speech that Brandt read and highlighted is found in AFES, WBA, Ordner 126; see ibid., Ordner 92–93, Mappe 93.
141. Bussemer 2001, 477. See also Schütz 1995.
142. Charles W. Thayer, "Berlin's Willy Brandt. Calm Man in a Nervous Place," *Harper's Magazine*, February 1959, 56.
143. Reichstein 1986, 326–28.
144. Merseburger 2002, 338–40.
145. Flora Lewis, "The Fiery Brandt of Berlin," *Coronet*, May 1959, 101. See also Thayer, "Berlin's Willy Brandt" and Department of State, Biographic Information Division: Brandt Willy, March 1961, JFKL, President's Office Files, Countries, Box 117, folder: Germany, Security.
146. Charles E. Hulick, Jr., Memorandum of Conversation, 25 September 1962, JFKL, NSF, Countries, Box 85, folder: Germany, Berlin, General 9/62; conversation between the author and Carl Kaysen on 25 November 2002. An expanded version of the Harvard lectures were published both in English and German, see Brandt 1963 and Bahr 1996, 145–46.
147. Carl Kaysen, Record of the Meeting with the President, 5 October 1962, JFKL, NSF, Countries, Box 85, folder: Germany, Berlin, General 10/62; "Vermerk über das Gespräch, zu dem der Präsident der Vereinigten Staaten in Anwesenheit von Mr. Hillenbrand und Professor Kaysen den Regierenden Bürgermeister, begleitet von Botschafter Knappstein und Herrn Bahr, am 5. Oktober 1962 empfing, 8 October 1962," in AFES, WBA, Ordner 71/72, Mappe 72; Brandt 1964, 155–68.
148. See Brandt 1976, 71; Grabbe 1986; Schwabe 1994; Mayer 1994, 1996; Haftendorn 1999; and author's conversation with Carl Kaysen on 25 November 2002. On Adenauer's positon regarding the Federal Republic's alignment with the West, see Granieri 2003.

149. Brandt 1964, 176–79.
150. Henry A. Kissinger to the President, memorandum, 5 April 1961, JFKL, President's Office Files, Countries, Box 117, folder: Germany, Security 1/61–6/61.
151. Harold Hurwitz to Willy Brandt, 31 May 1961, AFES, WBA, Ordner 36–37, Mappe 36; Walter P. Reuther to Willy Brandt, 21 June 1961, ibid., Mappe 37.
152. Adenauer to John F. Kennedy, 18 January 1963, JFKL, President's Office Files, Countries, Box 117, folder: Germany, General 1/63–6/63. On 22 January 1963, Adenauer again contacted Kennedy from Paris in order to cushion the impact of the Franco-German friendship treaty and to assure the president that Germany would support efforts to allow Great Britain to join the EEC, see AAP 1963, vol. I. 1, 153–54.
153. John F. Kennedy to Adenauer, 19 January 1963, JFKL, President's Office Files, Countries, Box 117, folder: Germany, General 1/63–6/63; Department of State [Robert C. Creel] to the U.S. Mission, Berlin [Lightner], telegram, 18 January 1963, JFKL, NSF, T & C, Box 241, folder: President's Trip, Europe, 6/63–7/63, Germany, 1/17/63–6/19/63, folder 1 of 2.
154. AAP 1963, vol. I. 1, no. 83, p. 275.
155. FRUS 1961–1963, vol. XV, no. 169, p. 477; *New York Times*, 18 January 1963.
156. Schütz to John F. Kennedy, 28 January 1963, JFKL, NSF, Countries, Box 85, folder: Germany, Berlin, General 2/63–5/63; see Meyer 1997, 228.
157. Lightner, U.S. Mission Berlin, to the Secretary of State, telegram, 5 February 1963, and William H. Brubeck, Department of State, to McGeorge Bundy, memorandum, 13 February 1963, both in JFKL, NSF, Countries, folder: Germany, Berlin, General 2/63–5/63.
158. Lightner, U.S. Mission Berlin, to the Secretary of State, telegram 25 February 1962, JFKL, RFK Papers, Attorney General's Papers, Series: Trips, 1961–1964, Box 4, folder: Berlin 2/21/1962–2/24/1962; Kennedy 1962, 163.
159. Lightner, U.S. Mission Berlin, to the Secretary of State, telegram, 5 February 1963, JFKL, NSF, Countries, folder: Germany, Berlin, General 2/63–5/63.
160. Willy Brandt to John F. Kennedy, 8 February 1963, JFKL, President's Office Files, Countries, Box 117 a, folder: Germany, Security 1/63–3/63.
161. John F. Kennedy to Willy Brandt, 18 February 1963, JFKL, President's Office Files, Countries, Box 117, folder: Germany, General 1/63–6/63; Willy Brandt to John F. Kennedy, 12 March 1963, ibid., Box 117 a. On drafting this in German, see AFES, Depositum Egon Bahr, Ordner 324, Mappe 1.
162. Memorandum, 5 February 1963, AFES, Depositum Egon Bahr, Ordner 362, Mappe 2.

CHAPTER 2: THE SCRIPT AND THE STAGING

1. Before his June 1963 trip to Europe, Kennedy's most recent trips abroad had been to Mexico (29 June–1 July 1962) and the Bahamas (18–21 December 1962).
2. *New York Times*, 23 June 1963.
3. O'Donnell and Powers, 1972, 358–9; Theodore C. Sorensen to McGeorge Bundy, memorandum, 14 June 1963, JFKL, NSF, T & C, Box 239, folder: President's Trip, Europe 6/63–7/63, General, 2 of 4; Pierre Salinger, Background Briefing at the White House (European Trip), 19 June 1963, 2, JFKL, President's Office Files, Subjects, Box 108, folder: Trips: Germany.
4. *New York Times*, 5 June 1963; ibid., 20 June 1963; ibid., 23 June 1963.

5. *New York Times*, 17 June 1963.

6. Walt W. Rostow to the Acting Secretary, memorandum, 21 May 1963, JFKL, NSF, T & C, Box 239, folder: President's Trip, Europe 6/63–7/63, General, 1 of 4.

7. Theodore C. Sorensen to McGeorge Bundy, memorandum, 14 June 1963, JFKL, NSF, T & C, Box 239, folder: President's Trip, Europe 6/63–7/63, General, 1 of 4; Similarly, Pierre Salinger, Background Briefing at the White House (European Trip), 19 June 1963, p. 2, JFKL, President's Office Files, Subjects, Box 108, folder: Trips: Germany.

8. Walt W. Rostow to the President, memorandum, 19 June 1963, JFKL, NSF, T & C, Box 239, folder: President's Trip, Europe 6/63–7/63, General, 1 of 4.

9. *New York Times*, 23 June 1963.

10. *New York Times*, 25 June 1963.

11. Note, 1 February 1963, and memorandum, ref. II. 6, 14 March 1963, "Besuch des Präsidenten Kennedy in Bonn," Politisches Archiv des Auswärtigen Amtes (PAAA), B 8, vol. 497.

12. *New York Times*, 6 March 1963; *Die Welt*, 7 March 1963; Egon Bahr to the Mayor, memorandum, 6 March 1963, AFES, Depositum Egon Bahr, Ordner 362, Mappe 2.

13. Mappe "Amerika-Besuch Dr. Alex Möller – Juli 1963," in Alex Möller to Willy Brandt and others, 19 August 1963, AFES, WBA, Berlin, Ordner 44/45, Mappe 44; Willy Brandt to Walter P. Reuther, 20 March 1963, ibid., Mappe 45; Dean Rusk to U.S. Embassy Bonn and U.S. Mission Berlin, telegram, 6 May 1963, JFKL, NSF, T & C, Box 241, folder: President's Trip, Europe, 6/63–7/63, Germany, 1/17/63–6/19/63, folder 1 of 2.

14. Edward Murrow to McGeorge Bundy, memorandum, 13 February 1963, JFKL, NSF, T & C, Box 241, folder: President's Trip, Europe, 6/63–7/63, Germany, 1/17/63–6/19/63, folder 1 of 2; also without any explicit mention of Berlin, Murrow to Bundy, 26 February 1963, ibid.

15. William H. Brubeck to McGeorge Bundy, memorandum, JFKL, NSF, T & C, Box 241, folder: President's Trip, Europe, 6/63–7/63, Germany, 1/17/63–6/19/63, folder 1 of 2; L. J. Legere to Carl Kaysen, memorandum, 20 March 1963, ibid.; memorandum, "Reasons Why President Should Visit Berlin," no date, ibid. On Robert F. Kennedy, see AAP 1963, vol. I. 1, no. 129, 422.

16. *Frankfurter Allgemeine Zeitung*, 22 March 1963; *Frankfurter Allgemeine Zeitung*, 23 March 1963; U.S. Embassy Bonn to the State Department, telegram, 22 March 1963, JFKL, NSF, T & C, Box 241, folder: President's Trip, Europe, 6/63–7/63, Germany, 1/17/63–6/19/63, folder 1 of 2; memorandum, chief of protocol, 22 March 1963, PAAA, B 8, vol. 497. On Kennedy's reservations, see AAP 1963, vol. I. 1, no. 145, 479.

17. Hans-Jochen Vogel to John F. Kennedy, 21 March 1963, JFKL, NSF, T & C, Box 241, folder: President's Trip, Europe, 6/63–7/63, Germany, 1/17/63–6/19/63, folder 1 of 2; U.S. Representation Munich to the Secretary of State, telegram to Secretary of State, 3 April 1963, ibid.; Willy Brandt to Hans-Jochen Vogel, AFES, WBA, Berlin, Ordner 44/45, Mappe 44; *Süddeutsche Zeitung*, 22 April 1963.

18. David Klein to McGeorge Bundy, memorandum, 3 April 1963; Department of State, Memorandum of Conversation, 10 April 1963; Dowling to the Secretary of State, telegram, 16 April 1963; David Bruce to the Secretary of State, telegram, 4 March 1963; all in JFKL, NSF, T & C, Box 241, folder: President's Trip, Europe, 6/63–7/63, Germany, 1/17/63–6/19/63, folder 1 of 2.

19. "President's European Trip. June 1963," JFKL, NSF, T & C, Box 239, folder: President's Trip, Europe 6/63–7/63, Salinger Briefing Book, folder 1 of 4.

20. *Berliner Morgenpost*, 25 June 1963.

21. Commencement Address at American University in Washington, D.C., 10 June 1963, in PPP 1963, no. 232, 459–64.

22. PK 1963, 3, 25.

23. PK 1963, p. 5, and PPP 1963, p. 498. The official German translations published by the press and information office of West Germany shortly after the trip (PK 1963) offer an extensive documentary basis of this and other positions expressed by Kennedy during the trip. However, these publications do include translation mistakes and omissions. Equally unreliable are the texts in Kennedy 1964. The vigor, wit, and subtlety of Kennedy's rhetoric can only be captured in the original wording, which is documented in the *Public Papers of the President* (PPP 1963).

24. See PK 1963, 7–8, and PPP 1963, p. 499. For the events in Cologne, see *Kölner Stadt-Anzeiger*, 24 June 1963; *Kölnische Rundschau*, 24 June 1963; and *Express* (Köln), 23–23 June 1963.

25. PK 1963, 9, and PPP 1963, 499; *Berliner Morgenpost*, 25 June 1963.

26. *New York Times*, 24 June 1963; Interview with Robert Lochner, in http://www.gwu.edu/~nsarchiv/coldwar/interviews/episode-4/lochner9.html (28 May 2007).

27. PK 1963, 13, and PPP 1963, 500.

28. *Neues Deutschland*, 24 June 1963. See Mausbach 2003.

29. JFKL, WH Central Subject Files, Trips, Box 984, folder: TR 56/CO92, 6–24–63–7–9–63; Hillenbrand 1998, 215–18.

30. President's European Trip June 1963. President-Chancellor Adenauer (Talking Points), 12 June 1963, JFKL, NSF, T & C, Box 239, folder: President's Trip, Europe 6/63–7/63, Salinger Briefing Book, folder 1 of 4.

31. On the course and content of the conversation, see AAP 1963, vol. I. 2, no. 206, 661–70.

32. President's European Trip June 1963. Memorandum of Conversation, 24 June 1963, 10:15–11:30 a.m., Palais Schaumburg, JFKL, NSF, T & C, Box 240, folder: President's Trip, Europe, 6/63–7/63, Memoranda of Conversations, Extras; a summation of a report by Rusk is reprinted in FRUS, 1961–1963, no. 196, 528–30.

33. Memorandum of Conversation, 24 June 1963, NA, RG 59, Entry 3051 B: Executive Secretariat, Conference Files 1949–1963, Box 318, folder CF 2275. On the role of the Third World in the foreign policies of the two German states, see Gray 2003.

34. President's European Trip June 1963. Memorandum of Conversation, 24 June 1963, 3:00–4:15, Palais Schaumburg, JFKL, NSF, T & C, Box 240, folder: President's Trip, Europe, 6/63–7/63, Memoranda of Conversations.

35. Ibid.

36. PK 1963, 25, and PPP 1963, 506. See Thomas C. Sorensen, memorandum to Theodore C. Sorensen, 28 May 1963, JFKL, NSF, T & C, Box 240, folder: President's Trip, Europe, 6/63–7/63, Germany, 1/17/63–6/19/63, folder 2 of 2.

37. Brandt, 1964, 185; President's European Trip June 1963, Memorandum of Conversation, 23.6.1963, 6:00 Uhr, Bad Godesberg, JFKL, NSF, T & C, Box 240, folder: President's Trip, Europe, 6/63–7/63, Memoranda of Conversations; FRUS 1961–1963, vol. XV, no. 197, 530–35, quote on p. 532; Memorandum of Conversation, 24 June 1963, NA, RG 59, Entry 3051 B: Executive Secretariat, Conference Files 1949–1963, Box 318, folder CF 2275.

38. President's European Trip June 1963, President-Mayor Brandt (Talking Paper), 10 June 1963, JFKL, NSF, T & C, Box 239, folder: President's Trip, Europe 6/63–7/63, Salinger Briefing Book, folder 1 of 4; President's European Trip June 1963, Addendum to President – Mayor Brandt (Talking Paper), ibid., Box 241, folder: President's Trip, Europe, 6/63–7/63, Germany, 6/11/63–7/12/63, folder 2 of 4.
39. President's European Trip June 1963, Memorandum of Conversation, 23 June 1963, 6:00 p.m., Bad Godesberg, JFKL, NSF, T & C, Box 240, folder: President's Trip, Europe, 6/63–7/63, Memoranda of Conversations; printed in FRUS 1961–1963, vol. XV, no. 197, 534.
40. Adenauer in his dinner toasts on 23 and 24 June; PK 1963, 36–37, 14.
41. *New York Times*, 25 June 1963.
42. PK 1963, 35; PPP 1963, 511.
43. PK 1963, 15; PPP 1963, 502.
44. Willy Brandt, handwritten "Vermerk betr. Unterhaltung mit Präs. Kennedy am 25.6.63, 8.15," written on 27 June 1963, AFES, WBA, Ordner 74; Calhoun, U.S. Mission Berlin, to the Secretary of State, 3 July 1963, JFKL, NSF, T & C, 241 A, folder: President's Trip, Europe, 6/63–7/63, Germany, 6/11/63–7/12/63, folder 3 of 4; also in FRUS 1961–1963, vol. XV, no. 200, p. 538. See also Brandt 1976, 75–76.
45. George C. McGhee to the Secretary of State, telegram, 21 May 1963, JFKL, NSF, T & C, Box 241, folder: President's Trip, Europe, 6/63–7/63, Germany, 1/17/63–6/19/63, folder 1 of 2.
46. PK 1963, 42; PPP 1963, 515.
47. See Freitag 1998. The gifts that Kennedy received while in West Germany helped this trip find its permanent place in the history of German-American relations. In Cologne, Kennedy was given an original edition of an account, written in English, of a trip down the Rhine by the private collector and literary Frankfurter Baron Johann von Gerning, *A Picturesque Tour Along the Rhine, from Mentz to Cologne* (London, 1820). In Bonn, he received a set of recordings of Beethoven's symphonies; in Frankfurt, the German edition of the accreditation of the U.S. representative to the provisional government established in 1848 and an illustration of the Paulskirche framed in gold.
48. *New York Times*, 26 June 1963.
49. Edward R. Murrow to the Secretary of State, telegram, 15 May 1963, JFKL, NSF, T & C, Box 241, folder: President's Trip, Europe, 6/63–7/63, Germany, 1/17/63–6/19/63, folder 1 of 2; George C. McGhee to the Secretary of State, telegram, 21 May 1963, ibid. See also AAP 1963, vol. I. 1, no. 172, 558f., and McGhee 1989, 27.
50. PK 1963, 50, 54, 47, 55; PPP 1963, 518, 520, 516, 521.
51. George W. Ball to McGeorge Bundy, memorandum, 21 May 1963, JFKL, NSF, T & C, Box 241, folder: President's Trip, Europe, 6/63–7/63, Germany, 1/17/63–6/19/63, folder 1 of 2.
52. Milton Crane to David Klein, memorandum, 29 May 1963, JFKL, NSF, T & C, Box 241, folder: President's Trip, Europe, 6/63–7/63, Germany, 1/17/63–6/19/63, folder 2 of 2; memorandum "Three Themes for Germany," ibid., folder: President's Trip, Europe, 6/63–7/63, Germany, 6/11/63–7/12/63, folder 1 of 4.
53. Memorandum of Conversation, 25 June 1963, 6:00 p.m., JFKL, NSF, T & C, Box 240, folder: President's Trip, Europe, 6/63–7/63, Memoranda of Conversations, Extras.
54. PK 1963, p. 41 (the quote from this evening is not included in this edition); PPP 1963, 514, 522.

55. Brandt 1964, 191.
56. Presidential Visit Berlin – Protocol Aspects, JFKL, NSF, T & C, Box 241, folder: President's Trip, Europe, 6/63–7/63, Germany, 1/17/63–6/19/63, folder 2 of 2.
57. *New York Times*, 22 June 1963.
58. See Wetzlaugk 1988; Mahnke 1990; and on the issue of choosing a national capital, Dann 1983 and Süss 1999.
59. See Mai 1995.
60. Schwarz 1983, 74; see Meyer 1997, 137–43.
61. Presidential Visit Berlin. Protocol Aspects, JFKL, NSF, T & C, Box 241, folder: President's Trip, Europe, 6/63–7/63, Germany, 1/17/63–6/19/63, folder 2 of 2.
62. Paulmann 2000, 297, 304, 343.
63. Calhoun, U.S. Mission Berlin, to Secretary of State, 11 June 1963, JFKL, NSF, T & C, Box 241, folder: President's Trip, Europe, 6/63–7/63, Germany, 6/11/63–7/12/63, folder 1 of 4.
64. *New York Times*, 10 May 1963.
65. Presidential Visit Berlin, Protocol Aspects, JFKL, NSF, T & C, Box 241, folder: President's Trip, Europe, 6/63–7/63, Germany, 1/17/63–6/19/63, folder 2 of 2. See Wetzlaugk 1988, 164–66.
66. Hardtwig (1994, 221) has defined the term *political topography* as the arrangement of streets and squares in a tangible and conceptual relationship to the public buildings and monuments on city soil and the entirety of the political statements, which are vividly symbolized within the framework of this arrangement.
67. PK 1963, 33; PPP 1963, 510.
68. On the symbolic value of the Berlin Wall and how this had changed over time, see Bruner 1989 and Diers 1997, 121–41.
69. "'Mr. President' in Berlin" 1963.
70. Memorandum, "Besuch des Präsidenten Kennedy in Berlin," 9 May 1963, LAB, B Rep. 002, no. 7046.
71. See Bruner 1989.
72. Hulick, U.S. Mission Berlin, to the Secretary of State, telegram, pt. 1, 10 May 1963, JFKL, NSF, T & C, Box 241, folder: President's Trip, Europe, 6/63–7/63, Germany, 1/17/63–6/19/63, folder 1 of 2. Regarding Bernauer Straße, see the memorandum by Rudolf Kettlein, 20 May 1963, LAB, B Rep. 002, no. 4080.
73. JFKL, WH Central Subject Files, Trips, Box 984, folder: TR 56/CO 92 5–15–63–6–6–63 and folder: TR 56/CO 92 6–7–63–6–23–63.
74. State Department to U.S. Embassy Bonn, telegram, 1 May 1963, JFKL, NSF, T & C, Box 241, folder: President's Trip, Europe, 6/63–7/63, Germany, 1/17/63–6/19/63, folder 1 of 2; Georg Leber to George Meany, 25 April 1963, George Meany Memorial Archives (GMMA), RG 18–001, Box 2, folder: 002/12: Germany, 1963.
75. Willy Brandt to George Meany, 12 July 1961, AFES, Depositum Egon Bahr, Ordner 47 A, Mappe 1/EBAA000154.
76. JFKL, Oral History Interview, George Meany, 31.
77. Dean Rusk to U.S. Embassy Bonn and U.S. Mission Berlin, telegram, 6 May 1964, JFKL, NSF, T & C, Box 241, folder: President's Trip, Europe, 6/63–7/63, Germany, 1/17/63–6/19/63, folder 1 of 2; George McGhee to the Secretary of State, telegram, 21 May 1963, ibid.; memorandum, "Besuch Präsident Kennedy," 9 May 1963, LAB, B Rep. 002, no. 7046; McGhee 1989, 29.

78. See Berghahn 2001.
79. Shepard Stone to Horst Hartwich, telegram, 22 March 1963, and his letter to Rector Heinitz, 15 April 1963; E. Allan Lightner, Jr., to Eduard Neumann, 10 April 1963, "Protokoll der ausserordentlichen Senatssitzung vom 27. März 1963," all in Archiv der FU Berlin, Ordner: IV-2901/1, 27.3.1963–4.12.1963, Kennedy-Akte.
80. See Tent 1988.
81. Barth, "Vermerk über die Sitzung des Kennedy-Programm-Ausschusses am 10. April 1963," LAB, B Rep. 002, no. 7046.
82. Calhoun, U.S. Mission Berlin, to the Secretary of State, telegram, 7 June 1963, JFKL, NSF, T & C, Box 241, folder: President's Trip, Europe, 6/63–7/63, Germany, 1/17/63–6/19/63, folder 2 of 2; Broadcast transcript, *Berliner Abendschau*, 5 June 1963, LAB, B Rep. 002, no. 3657/II.
83. Broadcast transcript, *Berliner Abendschau*, 5 June 1963, LAB, B Rep. 002, no. 3657/II.
84. *Berliner Zeitung*, 14 May 1963.
85. Barth, "Vermerk über die Sitzung des Kennedy-Programm-Ausschusses am 10. April, 1963," LAB, B Rep. 002, no. 7046; Horst Schulze, "Vermerk, Besuch Präsident Kennedy," 9 May 1963, ibid.
86. *Tagesspiegel*, 9 May 1963; *Der Abend*, 10 May 1963; *Telegraf*, 11 May 1963.
87. Hulick, U.S. Mission Berlin, to the Secretary of State, 10 May 1963, JFKL, NSF, T & C, Box 241, folder: President's Trip, Europe, 6/63–7/63, Germany, 1/17/63–6/19/63, folder 1 of 2; Franke to the Leitenden Regierungsdirektor Schultze, memorandum "Berlin-Besuch Präsident Kennedy," 6 May 1963, LAB, B Rep. 002, no. 7046. On Adenauer's federalist argument, see Press Secretary Karl-Günther von Hase to Foreign Minister Gerhard Schröder, 17.5.1963, PAAA, B 8, Bd. 498.
88. Morris, U.S. Embassy Bonn, to the Secretary of State, telegram, 30 April 1963, JFKL, NSF, T & C, Box 241, folder: President's Trip, Europe, 6/63–7/63, Germany, 1/17/63–6/19/63, folder 1 of 2; Calhoun to the Secretary of State, 17 June 1963, ibid., folder: President's Trip, Europe, 6/63–7/63, Germany, 6/11/63–7/12/63, folder 1 of 4.
89. Hulick, U.S. Mission Berlin, to the Secretary of State, telegram, pt. 1, 10 May 1963, JFKL, NSF, T & C, Box 241, folder: President's Trip, Europe, 6/63–7/63, Germany, 1/17/63–6/19/63, folder 1 of 2; Calhoun to the Secretary of State, telegram, 29 May 1963, ibid., folder: President's Trip, Europe, 6/63–7/63, Germany, 6/11/63–7/12/63, folder 1 of 4; Holleben to Osterheld, 6 June 1963, PAAA, vol. 498.
90. Presidential Visit Berlin – Protocol Aspects, JFKL, NSF, T & C, Box 241, folder: President's Trip, Europe, 6/63–7/63, Germany, 1/17/63–6/19/63, folder 2 of 2.
91. Calhoun to the Secretary of State, telegram, 31 May 1963, JFKL, NSF, T & C, Box 241, folder: President's Trip, Europe, 6/63–7/63, Germany, 1/17/63–6/19/63, folder 2 of 2.
92. Diers 1997, 196.
93. Memorandum, "Besuch des Präsidenten Kennedy in Berlin," 9 May 1963, LAB, B Rep. 002, no. 7046; Spangenberg, memorandum, 13 May 1963, ibid.; Calhoun to the Secretary of State, telegram, 29 May 1963, JFKL, NSF, T & C, Box 241, folder: President's Trip, Europe, 6/63–7/63, Germany, 6/11/63–7/12/63, folder 1 of 4; Schütz to von Holleben, 30 May 1963, PAAA, vol. 498.
94. Barth, memorandum, 10 April 1963, LAB, B Rep. 002, no. 7046.

95. The Spangenberg quote is found in "Notizen über die Besprechung mit der Gruppe des Herrn von Holleben am 9. Mai 1963," LAB, B Rep. 002, no. 4080. See McGhee 1989, 29.

96. Barth, memorandum, 8 June 1963, and "Vermerk über die Sitzung des Kennedy-Programm-Ausschusses am 10. Juni 1963," LAB, B Rep. 002, no. 11163.

97. *Tagesspiegel*, 16 May 1963. On the offers made by private companies to the Senate, see LAB, B Rep. 002, no. 11163.

98. Rudolf Kettlein to Egon Bahr, memorandum, 6 May 1963, LAB, B Rep. 002, no. 4080; *Tagesspiegel*, 23 June 1963.

99. President's European Trip. June 1963. Scope: Germany (14.6.1963), JFKL, NSF, T & C, Box 239, folder: President's Trip, Europe 6/63–7/63, Salinger Briefing Book, folder 1 of 4; also in NA, RG 59, Entry 3051 B: Executive Secretariat, Conference Files 1949–1963, Box 317, folder: CF 2274 – President's Trip to Europe 6/23–7/2/63, Briefing Book (1 of 2).

100. *New York Times*, 23 June 1963.

101. Daily Press Review, United States Information Service (USIS), 24 June 1963, NA, RG 59, Entry 3051 B: Executive Secretariat, Conference Files 1949–1963, Box 318, folder CF 2276.

102. "'Mr. President' in Berlin" 1963, 232; Memorandum, 13 June 1963, LAB, B Rep. 002, no. 7046.

103. *Ich bin ein Berliner* 1963, 35f.; "Anweisung für den Ratskeller," LAB, B Rep. 002, no. 4080; memorandum "Kennedy-Besuch. Ratskeller," ibid., no. 3388.

104. On the importance of modern mass media in shaping public opinion on political issues, see Schildt 1995, 209–300; 1998, 477–92; and Dussel 2000, 673–94.

105. *Berliner Morgenpost*, 27 June 1963.

106. Charles E. Shutt to Pierre Salinger, 29 May 1963, JFKL, WH Central Subject Files, Trips, Box 983, folder TR 56 Europe – Italy – Germany "'Mr. President' in Berlin" 1963, 235.

107. *New York Times*, 23 June 1963.

108. *Neues Deutschland*, 27 June 1963.

109. Memorandum, dept. III B 1, 5 June 1963, LBA, B Rep. 002, no. 4080.

110. John A. Calhoun, memorandum, 30 April 1963, NA, RG 59, Entry 3051 B: Executive Secretariat, Conference Files 1949–1963, Box 319, folder CF 2280.

111. Memorandum of Conversation, Minister Calhoun's Call on Governing Mayor, 30 May 1963, JFKL, WH Central Files, Subject Files, Box 8.

112. *Berliner Morgenpost*, 25 June 1963.

113. Lindenberger 1995; Davis 2000.

114. Lindenberger 1995, 13.

115. On this point and for further details, see "'Mr. President' in Berlin" 1963.

116. *Die Welt*, 29 April 1963. Before Kennedy arrived, the chairmen of the three largest political parties in Berlin – SPD, CDU, and FDP – jointly appealed to the citizens of Berlin to give the president a warm welcome.

117. *Berliner Morgenpost*, 23 June 1963.

118. *Ich bin ein Berliner* 1963, 12.

119. *Tagesspiegel*, 19 June 1963; *Frankfurter Allgemeine Zeitung*, 19 June 1963.

120. "'Mr. President' in Berlin" 1963, 233.

121. Willy Brandt, "Wo uns der Schuh drückt," *Sender Freies Berlin*, 23 June 1963.
122. Memorandum Dietrich Spangenberg, 29 May 1963, LAB, B Rep. 002, no. 11163.
123. "Der Polizeipräsident in Berlin: Liebe Berliner Mitbürger!" in LAB, B Rep. 002, no. 4080.
124. For a short description and discussion of the term *Eigensinn*, introduced into historical debate primarily by Alf Lüdtke, see Lüdtke 2002.

CHAPTER 3: DRAMATIC CLIMAX

1. Depending on the source, the precise arrival time noted by contemporaries varies from that presented here by one to ten minutes.
2. *Tagesspiegel*, 27 June 1963.
3. I thank the late Robert H. Lochner for the information he provided me in a letter dated 18 September 2002 and a conversation on 17 November 2002 on his role as interpreter during the Kennedy trip.
4. PK 1963, 60; Presse- und Informationsamt des Landes Berlin 1963, 3; Brandt 1964, 192.
5. PK 1963, 60; PPP 1963, 522.
6. *Die Welt*, 27 June 1963.
7. Kennedy 1995, 59. See Hamilton 1992, 271–72.
8. *Die Welt*, 27 June 1963.
9. *Ich bin ein Berliner* 1963, 11.
10. One of the rare photos of this truck is reproduced in *Ich bin ein Berliner* 1963, 36; ARD-ZDF live broadcasts, JFKL, Audiovisual Archives, FON: 30, nos. 1 and 2.
11. See Dolff-Bonekämper and Schmidt 1999. American influence on the cityscapes and urban planning of West Germany and Berlin has been studied extensively and well summarized by Jeffrey M. Diefendorf in his chapter "America and the Rebuilding of Urban Germany" in Diefendorf, Frohn, and Rupieper 2004, 331–51, and in his summary in Diefendorf 2004. On the reconstruction of Berlin and the dealings with buildings dating back before 1945, see Ladd 1997.
12. Press folder: Zusätzliches Pressematerial für Berlin. Besuch des Präsidenten John F. Kennedy in Deutschland. Zusammengestellt von den Pressestellen des Senats von Berlin und der U.S. Mission Berlin. Juni 1963, LAB, B Rep. 002, Nr. 3657/I.
13. *Die Welt*, 27 June 1963.
14. Hochgeschwender 1998, 527–34.
15. Industriegewerkschaft Bau – Steine – Erden, *6. Ordentlicher Gewerkschaftstag Berlin 1963, Tagungsbericht: 3. Tag*, GMMA, RG 18–001, Box 2, folder: 002/12: Germany, 1963.
16. Calhoun to Secretary of State, 25 June 1963, JFKL, NSF, T & C, Box 241, folder: President's Trip, Europe, 6/63–7/63, Germany, 6/11/63–7/12/63, folder 2 of 4. The photo of Kennedy being presented the bouquet is reproduced on the inside cover of *Ich bin ein Berliner* 1963.
17. PK 1963, 63; PPP 1963, 523; *Neues Deutschland*, 27 June 1963, 2.
18. JFKL, President's Office Files, Speech Files, folder: Remarks to the German National Congress of the Industrial Trade Union of Construction Workers 6/26/63, including the note from Meany. The entire Franklin quote reads: "God grant that not only the love of liberty but a thorough knowledge of the rights of man may pervade all the nations

of the earth so that a philosopher may set his foot anywhere on its surface and say: 'This is my country.'" More on this episode from George Meany, Oral History Interview, JFKL, 34.

19. *New York Times*, 27 June 1963.
20. See Beevor 2002 and Naimark 1995.
21. Brandt 1976, 73.
22. Hans-Werner Graf von Finckenstein in *Die Welt*, 27 June 1963.
23. *Berliner Morgenpost*, 27 June 1963.
24. *Tagesspiegel*, 27 June 1963.
25. *Ich bin ein Berliner* 1963, 16.
26. Ibid, 18; Hans-Werner Graf von Finckenstein in *Die Welt*, 27 June 1963.
27. JFKL, Audiovisual Archives, NBC News Special Report "The President's Journey" 1963; Hans Ulrich Kempski, "Der Gast, der Deutsche in Ekstase bringt," *Süddeutsche Zeitung*, 28 June 1963.
28. ARD-ZDF live broadcasts, JFKL, Audiovisual Archives, FON: 30, no. 4.
29. Bahr 1996, 151. See Brandt 1964, 195–96.
30. Brandt 1964, 195.
31. *Ich bin ein Berliner* 1963, 23.
32. ARD-ZDF live broadcast, JFKL, Audiovisual Archives, FON: 30, no. 4.
33. *Tagesspiegel*, 27 June 1963.
34. PK 1963, 65; Presse- und Informationsamt des Landes Berlin 1963, 22.
35. PK 1963, 65–66; Presse- und Informationsamt des Landes Berlin 1963, 22.
36. Letter by Robert H. Lochners to the author dated 18 September 2002 and a conversation with the author on 17 November 2002; author's conversation with Heinz Weber on 11 November 2002.
37. JFKL, NSF, T & C, Box 241.
38. Diethelm Prowe has analyzed the speech from a historical and philological perspective and has also reprinted the prepared manuscript; see Prowe 1989.
39. Prowe 1989, 159. According to Hugh Sidey, "Present at the Creation," *Time*, 20 November 1989. Kennedy asked the American commander in Berlin, James H. Polk, who accompanied him on the flight to Berlin, what the commander thought of the president's prepared speech. Polk's answer is reported to have been: "I think it is terrible."
40. Today, excerpts of the speech can be listened to over the Internet; see www.jfklibrary.org/Historical+Resources/Archives/Reference+Desk/Speeches/JFK/003POF03BerlinWall06261963.htm (29 May 2007).
41. I thank Allan Goodrich and James Hill from the JFKL audiovisual department for their explanations of Kennedy's speaking skills and habits.
42. JFKL, President's Office Files, Speech Files, folder: Remarks at the Signing of the Golden Book at Rudolph-Wilde-Platz, Berlin, Germany 6/26/63.
43. PK 1963, 68–69; Presse- und Informationsamt des Landes Berlin 1963, 29–30; *Ich bin ein Berliner* 1963, 30, 32; Brandt 1964, 201–03.
44. See also Bahr 1996, 150.
45. Brandt 1976, 73, 72.
46. See Prowe 1976 and Schmidt 2001, who goes as far back as the 1950s in his analysis of Brandt.
47. *Die Welt*, 19 June 1963.

48. Brandt 1976, 77–78, 90–92; Bahr 1996, 152–61; Vogtmeier 1996, 59–72; Schmidt 2001, 497–503.

49. For a history of the Freedom Bell and the details presented here, see Liebau and Daum 2000; and JFKL, WH Central Subject Files, Box 984, folder: TR 56/CO 92 6–7–63– 6–23–63.

50. See, for example, *New York Times*, 30 April 1988; *Newsweek*, 18 January 1988, 15; *Newsweek*, 8 October 1990, 38.

51. Eichhoff 1993.

52. According to Heinz Weber and Robert H. Lochner in a conversation with the author on 17 November 2002, and 22 November 2002, respectively. On the way to the city hall platform, Kennedy also asked Karl Franke, one of Brandt's advisors, to help him once again practice saying "*Ich bin ein Berliner*" in German; see Eichhoff 1993, 75, 77, and Schorr 2001, 170.

53. Eichhoff 1993, 78.

54. Brandt, 1992, 70; Sorensen 1965, 600–01. See also Schlesinger 1965, 884–85.

55. Morgan 1999, 334 (regarding the revival of the popular jelly doughnut theory).

56. Interview with Robert Lochner, in www.gwu.edu/~nsarchiv/coldwar/interviews/ episode-4/lochner9.html (29 May 2007) and, in a shortened version, in www.cnn.com/ SPECIALS/cold.war/episodes/09/reflections (29 May 2007); Lochner in a letter to the author dated 18 September 2002.

57. Bundy 1998, 390; O'Donnell and Powers 1972, 360.

58. See Lochner 2002.

59. Report by Margarethe Plischke, LAB, B Rep. 002, Nr. 13591. I thank Dr. Christiane Schuchard from LAB for her help in locating this document and Margarete Plischke for sharing with me her personal recollections in a letter (9 August 2007) and a phone conversation (August 2007). See *Spandauer Volksblatt*, 27 June 1978; *Berliner Morgenpost*, 27 June 1978. See also, without any reference to Plischke, *Der Abend*, 25 June 1965. Margarethe Plischke had worked since 1957 at the language school of the State Department's Foreign Service Institute. Plischke's visit to the White House is also documented in Kennedy's Log Book, Tuesday, 18 June 1963, page 2, appointment from 5 to 6 p.m. I thank Vicki Futscher from the Office of the Historian, Bureau of Public Affairs, Department of State, who made copies of this entry available to me in August 2002. According to Robert Lochner, Margarete Plischke did not attend this meeting with Kennedy while Lochner was present; Lochner to the author in a letter dated 18 September 2002, and in a conversation on 17 November 2002.

60. Such as the reference found in "Arrival in Germany," JFKL, President's Office Files, Countries, Box 117 a, folder: JFK Visit, 6/1963 and [folio without a title, double-spaced with phonetic spelling on the left-hand side and an English version on the right] JFKL, NSF, T & C, Box 241, folder: President's Trip, Europe, 6/63–7/63, Germany, 6/11/63–7/12/63, folder 2 of 4.

61. The appointments Plischke had at the White House are also documented in Kennedy's Log Book for 18 and 19 June 1963.

62. See note 59 and *Berliner Morgenpost*, 9 February 1978.

63. See M. Tulli Ciceronis, *Orationes in Verrem Actionis in C. Verrem Secundae Liber Quintus*, 63.147: "Cervices in carcere frangebantur indignissime civium Romanorum, ut iam illa vox et imploratio, 'Civis Romanus sum,' quae saepe multis in ultimis terris opem inter barbaros et salutem tulit, ea mortem illis acerbiorum et supplicium maturius ferret." A similar reference made later in the text, ibid., section LXII, paragraph 162, reads:

"Caedebatur virgis in medio foro Messanae civis Romanus, iudices, cum interea nullus gemitus, nulla vox alia illius miseri inter dolorem crepitumque plagarum audiebatur nisi haec: 'Civis Romanus sum.'" These texts can be found at www.thelatinlibrary.com/ cicero/verres.2.5.shtml (29 May 2007). For an English translation see Cicero 1893, 528: "The necks of Roman citizens were broken in a most infamous manner in the prison; so that very expression and form of entreaty, 'I am a Roman citizen,' which has often brought to many, in the most distant countries, succor and assistance, even among the barbarians, only brought to these men a more bitter death and a more immediate execution." See also ibid., 534: "In the middle of the forum of Messana a Roman citizen, O judges, was beaten with rods; while in the mean time no groan was heard, no other expression was heard from that wretched man, amid all his pain, and between the sound of the blows, except these words, 'I am a citizen of Rome.'" I thank Georg Nicolaus Knauer and Elfriede R. Knauer for important information in connection with this source, in a letter to the author dated 10 August 2002.

64. Acts 16: 37–38 and Acts 22: 25–29. Paul refers here indirectly to the so-called provocation right that allows Roman citizens to call for a public meeting when handed a death sentence or threatened with a whipping.

65. On Kennedy's rhetoric, see Windt 1990, 17–87.

66. Remarks in New Orleans at a Civic Reception, May 4, 1962, in PPP 1962, 362. See JFKL, President's Office Files, Speech Files, Box 38, folder: Remarks in New Orleans at a Civic Reception 5/4/62. No drafts of this speech are found in the JFKL.

67. Folio without a title, double-spaced with phonetic spelling on the left-hand side and an English version on the right, beginning with "I am proud to be in free Berlin," JFKL, NSF, T & C, Box 241, folder: President's Trip, Europe, 6/63–7/63, Germany, 6/11/63–7/12/63, folder 2 of 4. On the bottom border of the folio is the explicit reference to the note that Kennedy wrote on 18 June, meaning specifically in the meeting with Lochner, Plischke, and Bundy.

68. "6/25/63 3rd draft rev," JFKL, Papers of President Kennedy, President's Office Files, Speech Files, Box 45, folder: Remarks at the Signing of the Golden Book at Rudolph-Wilde-Platz, Berlin, Germany 6/26/63.

69. The index cards and the text draft typed on them are found under "Remarks at the Berlin Rathaus – June 26" in ibid. See Illustration 27.

70. See Chapter 1.

71. Live CBS broadcast report, JFKL, Audiovisual Archives, vol. TNC 357–9.

72. As reported to the author by Robert H. Lochner in a conversation with the author on 17 November 2002.

73. Schlesinger 1965, 885. See also O'Donnell and Powers 1972, 360–61, and Brandt 1964, 204.

74. Toast at a Luncheon in the City Hall in Berlin, June 26, 1963, in PPP 1963, 525–26.

75. *Tagesspiegel*, 28 June 1963.

76. I thank Gerhard A. Ritter (Berlin) and Tom Johnson (Annandale, Virginia), who was an American student working at the FU foreign studies office in 1963, for information on Kennedy's appearance at the Free University.

77. Horst Hartwich to Senate Director Spangenberg, April 24, 1963, Universitätsarchiv der Freien Universität Berlin (FU Archiv), Ordner: IV-2901/1, 27.3.1963–4.12.1963, Kennedy-Akte, Mappe: President Kennedy; *Die Welt*, 27 June 1963.

78. See PK 1963, 69–70.

79. "Von Tegel nach Dahlem," in LAB, B Rep. 002, Nr. 3657/I. See Tent 1988.

80. Gordon A Craig Diaries, Stanford University Archives, vol. XIII: "Journal 1963," 39–51; Information from Georg Nicolaus Knauer and Elfriede R. Knauer to the author, August 2002. A German translation of the FU certificate of honorary citizenship is found in PK 1963, 76; versions in Latin, German, and English are found in the Free University Archives, Ordner: IV-2901/1, 27.3.1963–4.12.1963, Kennedy-Akte, Mappe: John F. Kennedy, Verleihung der Ehrenbürgerwürde der FUB am 26. Juni 1963.

81. FU Archiv, Ordner: IV-2095/4–1, 9. Jan. 1949–1. July 1954, Außenkommission, Sitzungsprotokolle; Ordner: IV-2095/4–1, 9. Aug. 1954–Feb. 1962, Außenkommission, Sitzungsprotokolle II; Ordner: Tätigkeitsberichte Ak, Statistik Außenkom. von 1951 bis 1963. In 1998, I was able to have a long talk with Horst Hartwich about his work in the FU foreign studies office and his contacts with America.

82. Radio and Television Report to the American People on the Berlin Crisis. July 25, 1961, in PPP 1962, 533–40.

83. This quote and the following ones taken from Kennedy's FU speech are found in PK 1963, 70–76, and PPP 1963, 526–29.

84. Ernst Heinitz, FU rector, to John F. Kennedy, Aug. 3, 1963, JFKL, NSF, T & C, Box 241 A, folder: President's Trip, Europe, 6/63–7/63, Germany, 6/11/63–7/12/63, folder 3 of 4.

85. See Leggewie 2004.

86. Mausbach 2003; on 1968 as a watershed year in the history of the post–World War II era, see Fink, Gassert, and Junker 1998.

87. Remarks at United States Military Headquarters in West Berlin, June 26, 1963, in PPP 1963, 530.

88. Von Tegel nach Dahlem, in LAB, B Rep. 002, Nr. 3657/I.

89. *Die Welt*, 27 June 1963.

90. PK 1963, 78; PPP 1963, 530.

CHAPTER 4: AFTER THE FINAL CURTAIN

1. For example, see Davis 1986.

2. Becker 1965; Vostell 1970; Buchloh and Rodenbeck 1999.

3. Lüdtke 1985, 1993, 2002; Lindenberger 1999.

4. Hans Ulrich Kempski, "Der Gast, der Deutsche in Ekstase bringt," *Süddeutsche Zeitung*, 28 June 1963.

5. Ibid.

6. LAB, B Rep. 002, no. 7046; *Die Welt*, 27 June 1963; *Ich bin ein Berliner* 1963, 21.

7. *Berliner Morgenpost*, 26 June 1963; *Die Welt*, 27 June 1963.

8. Sorensen 1965, 579. The *New York Times* (25 June 1963), too, was reminded of Kennedy's campaign style after the first day in Germany.

9. Gordon A.Craig Diaries, Stanford University Archives, vol. XIII. "Journal 1963," 41, 64. In the last quote, Craig was referring to the historian Walter Bußmann.

10. On this point, see the references to transatlantic community building in the Introduction.

11. George McGhee to the Secretary of State, 28 June 1963, JFKL, NSF, T & C, Box 241 A, folder: President's Trip, Europe, 6/63–7/63, Germany, 6/11/63–7/12/63, folder 3 of 4; quotes from James E. Hoofnagle, USIS Bonn, to USIS Washington, 9 Aug. 1963, ibid.

12. PPP 1963, 557.

13. *Die Welt*, 27 June 1963; Harold Hurwitz, *Berlin Briefing*, 6 July 1963, JFKL, NSF, T & C, Box 241 A, folder: President's Trip, Europe, 6/63–7/63, Germany, 6/11/63–7/12/63, folder 3 of 4.

14. Schildt 1995, 268; George McGhee to the Secretary of State, 28 June 1963, JFKL, NSF, T & C, Box 241 A, folder: President's Trip, Europe, 6/63–7/63, Germany, 6/11/63–7/12/63, folder 3 of 4 (including the quote "hypnotic fascination"); Infratest 1963, 2–3; James E. Hoofnagle, USIS Bonn, to USIS Washington, 9 Aug. 1963, JFKL, NSF, T & C, Box 241 A, folder: President's Trip, Europe, 6/63–7/63, Germany, 6/11/63–7/12/63, folder 3 of 4.

15. Infratest 1963, 4–6.

16. Ibid., 11, 17, 18.

17. Gertrud Schramm to Lyndon B. Johnson, 14 Sept. 1961, LBJL, Vice-Presidential Papers, 1961–1963, Subject Files, Box 110 (cont'd.), folder: Public Activities – Travel – Foreign – Berlin (Pro) September.

18. JFKL, WH Central Subject Files, Trips, Box 984, folder: TR 56/CO92 7–10–63.

19. George McGhee to the Secretary of State, 28 June 1963, JFKL, NSF, T & C, Box 241 A, folder: President's Trip, Europe, 6/63–7/63, Germany, 6/11/63–7/12/63, folder 3 of 4.

20. Harold Hurwitz, *Berlin Briefing*, 6 July 1963, JFKL, NSF, T & C, Box 241 A, folder: President's Trip, Europe, 6/63–7/63, Germany, 6/11/63–7/12/63, folder 3 of 4.

21. *New York Times*, 27 June 1963; McGeorge Bundy to Walter Lippmann, 13 Aug. 1963, JFKL, WH Central Subject File, Trips, Box 983, folder: TR 56 Europe – Italy – Germany.

22. James L. Greenfield to Carl Kaysen, memorandum, "Public Comment on President Kennedy's European Trip," 1 July 1963, JFKL, President's Office Files, Departments and Agencies, Box 88 A, folder: State 6/63–7/63.

23. Federer, General-Konsulat New York, to AA, 28 June 1963, PAAA, B 8, vol. 498.

24. *Tagesspiegel*, 28 June 1963; *Die Welt*, 27 June 1963.

25. *Neues Deutschland*, 28 June 1963; *Die Welt*, 28 June 1963.

26. PK 1963, 66; PPP 1963, 524; *Tagesspiegel*, 30 June 1963.

27. David Kirkpatrick Ester Bruce Diaries, Virginia Historical Society, Richmond, Diaries Mss 5:1 B 8303:34, 1959 July 1–September 30, p. 33; Lyndon B. Johnson to John F. Kennedy, memorandum, 21 Aug. 1961, LBJL, Vice-Presidential Security File, Box 2, folder: Berlin, Germany; Berlin Papers for the Vice President. Col. John R. Deane, Jr., 2nd Battle Group, 6th Infantry, was quoted as saying, "This is a real shot in the arm to the civilians. . . . Sending Clay with Johnson was a good thing. To Berliners, Clay was the original tough guy. Now he's back and another tough guy, Vice President Johnson, is out in front," in Charlie Boatner to the Vice President, memorandum, 21 Aug. 1961, LBJL, Vice-Presidential Papers, 1961–1963, Subject Files, Box 109, folder: Public Activities – Travel – Foreign – Berlin (Pro) August, 2 of 2.

28. Robert F. Kennedy to Willy Brandt, 16 April 1962, JFKL, RFK Papers, Attorney General's Papers, Series: Trips, 1961–1964, Box 7, folder: Berlin 4/1962; Kennedy 1962, 140, 164, 163.

29. John F. Kennedy to Willy Brandt, 23 July 1963, JFKL, President's Office Files, Countries, Box 117, folder: Germany, General 7/63–8/63; and in the same files, Brandt to Kennedy, 3 July 1963. See von Lilienfeld, Deutsche Botschaft Washington, to AA, 5 July 1963,

PAAA, B 8, vol. 499 with references to conversations with McGeorge Bundy, Maxwell Taylor, and Robert C. Creel.

30. Conversation on 24 June 1963, see AAP 1963, vol. I. 2, 661; as well as Adenauer to Kennedy, 8 July 1963, ibid., 728.

31. AAP 1963, vol. I. 2, 215–16. See also Adenauer 1968, 221–30.

32. Von Lilienfeld, Deutsche Botschaft Washington, to AA, 3 July 1963, PAAA, B 8, vol. 498.

33. *Berliner Morgenpost*, 23 June 1963.

34. *Die Welt*, 31 May 1963.

35. *Tagesspiegel*, 27 June 1963; *Süddeutsche Zeitung*, 27 June 1963; *Die Welt*, 27 June 1963.

36. Kempski, "Der Gast," *Süddeutsche Zeitung*, 26 June 1963; *Die Welt*, 27 May 1963; *Berliner Morgenpost*, 27 June 1963.

37. *Berliner Morgenpost*, 25 June 1963; *B.Z. Berlin*, 26 June 1963; Kempski, "Der Gast," *Süddeutsche Zeitung*, 26 June 1963.

38. *Tagesspiegel*, 27 June 1963; *Die Welt*, 27 June 1963.

39. John H. Polk to John F. Kennedy, 16 July 1963, JFKL, President's Office Files, Countries, Box 117, folder: Germany, General 7/63–8/63.

40. Gordon A. Craig Diaries, Stanford University Archives, vol. XIII. "Journal 1963," 77.

41. See Introduction.

42. Kempski, "Der Gast," *Süddeutsche Zeitung*, 26 June 1963.

43. *Die Welt*, 27 June 1963.

44. *The Story of the World Freedom Bell* n.d. [ca. 1951]; Liebau and Daum 2000.

45. PK 1963, 69 (verbatim); Brandt 1964, 203. Still very worthwhile to read on this subject is the work by Karl Löwith, *Weltgeschichte und Heilsgeschehen. Zur Kritik der Geschichtsphilosophie* (Stuttgart, 1983), which was first published in English as *Meaning in History: The Theological Implications of the Philosophy of History* (1949). In this American edition, page 225, note 1, Löwith explains the difficulties in translating the compound noun *Heilsgeschehen* into English: "'Salvation' does not convey the many connotations of the German word *Heil*, which indicates associated terms like 'heal' and 'health,' 'hail' and 'hale,' 'holy' and 'whole,' as contrasted with 'sick,' 'profane,' and 'imperfect.' *Heilsgeschichte* has, therefore, a wider range of meaning than 'history of salvation.' At the same time, it unites the concept of history more intimately with the idea of *Heil* or 'salvation.' *Weltgeschichte und Heilsgeschehen* both characterize the events as worldly and sacred, respectively."

46. See Joas 1996, 69–76; and Mosse, 1976, 1991.

47. *Die Welt*, 7 September 1962, 11 September 1962.

48. Mosse 1976; see also Mosse 1991.

49. Chickering 1984. See also Nipperdey 1987.

50. Falasca-Zamponi 1997.

51. Mosse 1991; Hunt 1984; Thamer 2000; Hardtwig 2001; Maier 2002.

52. Behrenbeck 1996.

53. Kielmansegg 1989. See also Chapter 2.

54. One of the answers in the public poll by Infratest on the fourth day of the Kennedy trip. Infratest 1963, 21. See O'Donnell and Powers 1972, 360; Kempski, "Der Gast," *Süddeutsche Zeitung*, 26 June 1963.

55. *Frankfurter Allgemeine Zeitung*, 27 June 1963.

56. Kempski, "Der Gast," *Süddeutsche Zeitung*, 26 June 1963; *Neue Zürcher Zeitung*, 2 July 1963.

57. Federer, General-Konsul New York, to AA, 28 June 1963, PAAA, B 8, vol. 498.

58. JFKL, Audiovisual Archives, FON 27: "Go to Germany: A Nation Welcomes President John F. Kennedy."

59. Schlesinger 1965, 885; a contrary account in Kempski, "Der Gast," *Süddeutsche Zeitung*, 26 June; the press excerpts were taken from George McGhee to the Secretary of State, 28 June 1963, JFKL, NSF, T & C, Box 241 A, folder: President's Trip, Europe, 6/63–7/63, Germany, 6/11/63–7/12/63, folder 3 of 4.

60. *Neues Deutschland*, 29 June 1963.

61. *Neues Deutschland*, 25 June 1963.

62. *Tagesspiegel*, 16 June 1963.

63. See *Berliner Zeitung*, 22 June 1963 and *Tagesspiegel*, 23 June 1963.

64. McDougall 1985.

65. PPP 1961, 396–406, here 403–04.

66. *Neues Deutschland*, 23 June 1963.

67. Ibid.

68. *Berliner Zeitung*, 26 June 1963; 29 June 1963.

69. Ibid., 29 June 1963.

70. *Tagesspiegel*, 30 June 1963; *Berliner Morgenpost*, 30 June 1963.

71. *Neues Deutschland*, 3 July 1963; *Tagesspiegel*, 3 July 1963.

72. *Neues Deutschland*, 29 June 1963; *Berliner Zeitung*, 29 June 1963.

73. *Tagesspiegel*, 29 June 1963; *Berliner Morgenpost*, 29 June 1963.

74. Quote taken from Ackermann 1995, 258.

75. Ackermann 1990; Koselleck and Jeismann 1994.

76. See Mai and Repp-Eckert 1988.

77. Weber 1978, vol. 1, 244, 246; see also Weber 1976, 141–43.

78. See François and Schulze 2001 and Chapter 5.

79. *Frankfurter Allgemeine Zeitung*, 25 November 1963.

80. Ackermann 1990, 97, see also 77–83, 270–80.

81. On the events described in the following, see *Berliner Morgenpost*, 24 November 1963; *Tagesspiegel*, 23 November 1963 and 24 November 1963; *Frankfurter Allgemeine Zeitung*, 25 November 1963; *Nacht-Depesche*, 26 November 1963.

82. Brandt's speech in *Pressedienst des Landes Berlin*, no. 231, 23 Nov. 1963, LAB B Rep. 002, no. 3180.

83. Kosellect and Jeismann 1994, 9–10, 25; Ackermann 1990, 259; Meyer 1997, 303–11; Wolfrum 1999, 182–83.

84. The speech texts in *Pressedienst des Landes Berlin*, Nov. 25, 1963, Anhang, LAB B Rep. 002, no. 3180; *Berliner Morgenpost*, 24 November 1963.

85. *Illustrierte Berliner Zeitschrift*, 49, 7 December 1963, 2.

86. *Frankfurter Allgemeine Zeitung*, 25 November 1963, see here page 5, and *Frankfurter Allgemeine Zeitung*, 26 November 1963, 4, 11, for details on the memorial ceremonies.

87. "Der Schrei," *Frankfurter Allgemeine Zeitung*, 25 November 1963; Assmann 1992.

88. *Frankfurter Allgemeine Zeitung*, 25 November 1963.

89. Scipione del Ferro (1465–1526) taught mathematics at the University of Bologna. He succeeded in solving an equation that Luca Pacioli had called impossible.

90. "Der Schrei," *Frankfurter Allgemeine Zeitung*, 25 November 1963.

91. For revisionists views on Kennedy and critiques of the Kennedy myth, see Chomsky 1993; Hersh 1997.
92. *Nacht-Depesche*, 26 November 1963; *Frankfurter Allgemeine Zeitung*, 26 November 1963.
93. Albertz speech in *Pressedienst des Landes Berlin*, no. 232, 25 Nov. 1963, LAB, B Rep. 002, no. 3180; film documentation in "Trauerfeier in Berlin–Kennedy," SFB, JFKL, Audiovisual Archives, FON 26.
94. James H. Polk to Heinrich Albertz, 26 Nov. 1963, LAB, B Rep. 002, no. 3180.
95. *New York Times*, 24 November 1963, 4E; Albertz's quote in *Pressedienst des Landes Berlin*, no. 232, 25 Nov. 1963, LAB, B Rep. 002, no. 3180; Johnson's quote in Lyndon B. Johnson to Willy Brandt, 30 Nov. 1963, delivered by Calhoun, U.S. Mission Berlin, to Brandt on 2 Dec. 1963, AFES, WBA, Gruppe 6, Ordner 126.
96. Harold Hurwitz, *Berlin Briefing*, 5 Dec. 1963, JFKL, RFK Papers, Attorney General's Papers, General Correspondence, Box 6, folder: Willy Brandt.
97. Memorandum "Betr.: Beteiligung des Regierenden Bürgermeisters an der Delegation der Bundesrepublik Deutschland zu den Trauerfeierlichkeiten in Washington," AFES, WBA, Gruppe 6, Ordner 126; Willy Brandt's speech at Tempelhof Airport, 28 Nov. 1963, ibid.; *New York Times*, 29 November 1963, 20.
98. Jacqueline Kennedy to Brandt, 3 Dec. 1964, AFES, WBA, Gruppe 6, Ordner 126.

CHAPTER 5: THE SHOW GOES ON

1. See Gillis 1994; Assmann 1992; Smith and Emrich 1996; Assmann and Frevert 1999.
2. Examples pertaining to the United States are Bodnar 1992; Kammen 1993; and Wallace 1996.
3. See Bodemann 1996, 83–84, and Samuel 1994.
4. See Chapter 1.
5. Kennedy's speech at the FU on 26 June 1963, PPP 1963, 528; for the German version see PK 1963, 74.
6. On the term and characteristics of the political myth, see the helpful references to the history of relevant research in Bizeul 2000; Dörner 1995, 76–97; and Behrenbeck 1996, 40–50.
7. Münkler 1995, 157–73.
8. I understand rituals, as defined anthropologically by Paulmann 2000, 17, to be "standardized, repetitive, and extraordinary actions, which possess symbolic meaning. In the forefront of the ritual is *active participation*, through which emotions are aroused, perceptions influenced, and frameworks for relationships created." See also Lemert and Branaman 1997, 109–27.
9. Nietzsche 1983, 68, 73. For the German original see Nietzsche 1984, 21, 29.
10. JFKL, WH Central Subject Files, Trips, Box 984, folder: TR 56/CO92 7–10–63.
11. Egon Bahr to Willy Brandt, 28 June 1963; memorandum to Egon Bahr, "Auswertung des Besuches des amerikanischen Präsidenten John F. Kennedy in Berlin," 28 June 1963, LAB, B Rep. 002, no. 7046.
12. PK 1963; Presse- und Informationsamt des Landes Berlin 1963; *Ich bin ein Berliner* 1963; USIS Bonn and USIA Washington, 9 Aug. 1963, JFKL, NSF, T&C, Box 241A, folder: President's Trip, Europe, 6/63–7/63, Germany, 6/11/63–7/12/63, folder 3 of 4.
13. *Spandauer Volksblatt*, 10 July 1964.

14. The artist commissioned to design the plaque was the sculptor Richard Scheibe, who had created the memorial in Berlin's Bendlerblock for the victims of the failed 20 July 1944 attempt to assassinate Hitler. Kurt Ihlenfeld drafted the text, incorporating a 1961 quote from Kennedy. See Chapter 1 and Chapter 3 on the commemorative plaque for the Freedom Bell, and Hübner 1997, 315. In 1988, on the occasion of the twenty-fifth anniversary of Kennedy's visit, another small commemorative plaque was added at the donation of the Ancient and Honorable Artillery Company of Massachusetts.
15. Donald M. Wilson to Robert F. Kennedy, memorandum, 2 June 1964, JFKL, RFK Papers, Attorney General's Papers, Series: Trips 1961–1964, Box 16, folder: Briefing Book Berlin.
16. Robert F. Kennedy to Willy Brandt, 27 July 1964, JFKL, RFK Papers, Attorney General's Papers, Series: General Correspondence, Box 6, folder: Willy Brandt.
17. *Die Welt*, 26 June 1964; *Nacht-Depesche*, 25 June 1964; *Bild*, 27 June 1964; *Der Abend*, 27 June 1964.
18. Elwood Williams III to Ed Guthman, memorandum "Attorney General's Speeches in Berlin, June 26, 1964," no date; Joseph Kraft "June 26 speech suggestions" (who translated the sentence "I am still a Berliner" into "*Ich bin jetzt ein Berliner*") no date, JFKL, RFK Papers, Attorney General's Papers, Series: Trips, 1961–1964, Box 16, folder: Berlin, Speech Suggestions.
19. *Die Welt*, 27 June 1964, including the text of the speech given at Schöneberg City Hall, also in LAB, B Rep. 002, Nr. 3180.
20. The text of the speech given by Robert F. Kennedy at the FU on 26 June 1964 is found in *John F. Kennedy – Robert F. Kennedy* 1996, 35–43, quotes on 40, 43, as well as in Matson 1967, 96–104.
21. Of Kennedy's successors, only Lyndon B. Johnson, Gerald Ford, and George H. W. Bush did not visit Berlin during their presidencies; Bush visited the city as vice president in 1983, as did vice presidents Hubert Humphrey (1967), Nelson Rockefeller (1976), and Walter Mondale (1977). Ronald Reagan, Bill Clinton, and George H. W. Bush also went back to Berlin once they were out of office.
22. For an general review, see Larres and Oppelland 1997 and Junker 2004.
23. Allemann 1966; "West Berlin: The Story of a City in Decline," *U.S. News & World Report*, 4 December 1967.
24. Daum 2000.
25. *Frankfurter Allgemeine Zeitung*, 7 April 1967. See also *New York Times*, 7 April 1967.
26. *Tagesspiegel*, 7 June 1968.
27. PPP 1969, 158, 155, 151–53. See *Süddeutsche Zeitung*, 26 February 1969 and 28 February 1969; *Frankfurter Allgemeine Zeitung*, 28 February 1969.
28. "Triumph" ("*Triumphzug*") was the description given in the *Süddeutsche Zeitung*, 17 July 1978; "festival" ("*Volksfest*") was term used by *Die Welt*, 17 July 1978.
29. *Frankfurter Allgemeine Zeitung*, 17 July 1978; *Süddeutsche Zeitung*, 17 July 1978.
30. See Hartman 1986.
31. *Die Zeit*, 18 September 1981.
32. PPP 1982, vol. I, 765, 768; German version in *Frankfurter Allgemeine Zeitung*, 12 June 1982.
33. *Frankfurt Allgemeine Zeitung*, 13 June 1987.
34. "Ich hab noch einen Koffer in Berlin," "Es gibt nur ein Berlin," "Berliner Herz, Berliner Humor, ja, und die Berliner Schnauze," in PPP 1987, vol. I, 634, 635.

35. Ibid., 635; German version in *Frankfurter Allgemeine Zeitung*, 13 June 1987.
36. Interview with George H. W. Bush, September and October 1997, in www.cnn.com/ SPECIALS/cold.war/episodes/23/interviews/bush (28 May 2007) and *New York Times*, 10 November 1999.
37. The speech given by George Bush, Sr., on 31 May 1989 in Mainz, in PPP 1989, vol. I, 650–54, here 651.
38. Hamilton 1994; Gross 1995; Habermas 1997.
39. Herles 1991; Hanf 1993; Daum and Mauch 2005.
40. Reagan also returned to Berlin in July 1990 and, in a symbolic act, chiseled out a piece of cement from the crumbling remains of the Berlin Wall.
41. Clinton also stated: "*Amerika steht an ihrer Seite, jetzt und für immer*" ("America stands by Berlin, now and forever"), in PPP 1994, vol. I, 1247–48. See also *Süddeutsche Zeitung*, 13 July 1994; and *Frankfurter Allgemeine Zeitung*, 13 July 1994.
42. Reagan 1987, in PPP 1987, vol. I, 640; Uwe Schmitt, "Missionslos. Bill Clinton in Berlin," *Frankfurter Allgemeine Zeitung*, 13 May 1998.
43. *Süddeutsche Zeitung*, 13 May 1998; PPP 1998, vol. I, 755.
44. *Berliner Zeitung*, 27–28 June 1998. On the anniversary of the Airlift, see also *Berliner Zeitung*, 29 June 1998; *Frankfurter Allgemeine Zeitung*, 29 June 1998; and "50 Jahre Luftbrücke," *Tagesspiegel* supplement, June 1998.
45. See *Süddeutsche Zeitung*, 14 May 1998; and *Frankfurter Allgemeine Zeitung*, 14 May 1998. Clinton visited Berlin again as president on 1 June 2000.
46. *Die Zeit*, 23 May 2002.
47. *Tagesspiegel*, 24 May 2002; see also *Tagesspiegel*, 23 May 2002, 9. Bush's address to the German Bundestag on 23 May 2002, in www.whitehouse.gov/news/releases/2002/05/ 20020523-2.html (28 May 2007). I thank Monika Hein and Anja Schüler for providing me with reactions of the Berlin press. On the transformations of German-American relations in recent years, especially after 9/11, see Szabo 2004.

CHAPTER 6: "A COMET OF PROMISE PASSING THROUGH OUR COUNTRY"

1. A brilliant and engaging history of Europe in the decades following World War II is provided by Judt 2005.
2. George W. Ball to the President, memorandum to the President, 20 June 1963, NA, RG 59, Entry 3051 B, box 319, folder CF 2280 – President's Trip to Europe 6/23–7/2/63, Substantive Misc. (2 of 2).
3. See Bark and Gress 1993, vol. 2, 3–52; Schwarz 1983, 323–82; Judt 2005, 324–53.
4. Interview with Antje Vollmer, *Stern*, 23 May 2002; Arthur M. Schlesinger to the President, memorandum, 10 April 1963, JFKL, Arthur M. Schlesinger Papers, Box WH-44, folder: President's Trip to Europe 1963.
5. Theo Buraunen, 23 June 1963, outside Cologne city hall, in PK 1963, 6. See also *Kölner Stadt-Anzeiger*, 24 June 1963.
6. Hans Ulrich Kempski, "Der Gast, der Deutsche in Ekstase bringt," *Süddeutsche Zeitung*, 28 June 1963 On how the two German states dealt with American popular culture see Poiger 2000.
7. George Meany, JFKL, Oral History Interview, 43.

8. *Tagesspiegel*, 26 June 1964.
9. See Schildt 1999a and Poiger 2000.
10. *Tagesspiegel*, 26 June 1964.
11. Reichel 1991; Thamer 1986.
12. See Paulmann 2000.
13. Lüdtke 2002.
14. As posed by the commentator during the live coverage of the Kennedy visit by German television from Berlin, in ARD-ZDF live transmissions, JFKL, Audiovisual Archives, FON: 30 R 1.
15. Egon Bahr to Willy Brandt, 9 Jan. 1964, AFES, Depositum Egon Bahr, Ordner 362, Mappe 2.
16. Daum 2000.
17. See, however, two thoughtful essays: Bertram 1998 and Craig 1998.
18. Weidenfeld 2000. Joffe 1987 is a prescient study written shortly before the end of the Cold War; for an astute analysis of German-American relations at the opening of the twenty-first century, see Szabo 2004.
19. Voigt 2000.

Bibliography

ARCHIVAL SOURCES

United States

Amherst College, Archives and Special Collections, Amherst, Massachusetts
John McCloy Papers

Boston University, Boston, Massachusetts
Leo Cherne Collection

Dwight D. Eisenhower Library, Abilene, Kansas (DDEL)
Dwight D. Eisenhower Papers as President of the United States, 1953–1961
White House Central Files
White House Office, Office of the Special Assistant for National Security Affairs,
   Records, 1952–1961

Eleanor Lansing Dulles Papers
C. D. Jackson Papers
Oral History Interviews

Ford Foundation Archives, New York, New York
Grant Files
Oral History Files

George C. Marshall Library, Lexington, Virginia (GML)
Lucius D. Clay Papers
James W. Riddleberger Papers

George Meany Memorial Archives, Silver Spring, Maryland (GMMA)
RG 18–001: International Affairs Department, Country Files, 1945–1971
RG 18–003: International Affairs Department, Jay Lovestone Files, 1939–1974
RG 18–004: International Affairs Department, Irving Brown Files, 1943–1989

Georgetown University Library, Special Collections Division, Washington, D.C.
Jean Edward Smith Papers

Harry S. Truman Library, Independence, Missouri
Harry S. Truman Papers, Presidential Papers

Dean Acheson Papers
J. Anthony Panuch Papers
Howland H. Sargeant Papers
Charles W. Thayer Papers
Oral History Interviews

Hoover Institution Archives, Stanford University, Stanford, California (HIA)
Christopher Temple Emmet, Jr., Collection
German Pictorial Collection
German Subject Collection
Howard Palfrey Jones Papers
International Rescue Committee Records
Jay Lovestone Papers
Kurt Richard Grossmann Papers
Robert D. Murphy Papers
Sidney Hook Papers
Walter H. Judd Papers

John F. Kennedy Library, Boston, Massachusetts (JFKL)
John Fitzgerald Kennedy Papers, Presidential Papers
    National Security Files
    President's Office Files
    White House Central Files

Robert F. Kennedy Papers
    Attorney General's Papers (RFK Papers)
Arthur M. Schlesinger Papers
Theodore C. Sorensen Papers
Oral History Interviews

Library of Congress, Manuscript Division, Washington, D.C. (LoC)
Joseph Alsop Papers
Charles E. Bohlen Papers
W. Averell Harriman Papers
Lincoln Sesquicentennial Commission Papers
Paul H. Nitze Papers

Lyndon B. Johnson Library, Austin, Texas (LBJL)
Lyndon Baines Johnson Archives, 1941–1968
National Security File
Pre-Presidential Daily Diary, April 1961–December 1962
Vice-Presidential Papers, 1961–1963

Vice-Presidential Security File
White House Central File
Willie Day Taylor Papers
Oral History Interviews

National Archives II, College Park, Maryland (NA)
RG 59: General Records of the Department of State
RG 84: Foreign Service Posts of the Department of State
RG 200: General Lucius D. Clay, Personal Papers, April 1945–May 1949
RG 260: Records of U.S. Occupation Headquarters, World War II, Office of
    Military Government for Germany (U.S. Zone)
RG 466: U.S. High Commission for Germany

Seeley G. Mudd Manuscript Library, Princeton University, Princeton, New Jersey
Allen W. Dulles Papers
John Foster Dulles Papers
George F. Kennan Papers

Stanford University Archives, Stanford, California
Gordon A. Craig Papers

Tufts University, University Archives and Special Collections, Somerville, Massachusetts
Edward R. Murrow Papers, 1927–1965

Virginia Historical Society, Richmond, Virginia
David K. E. Bruce Diaries
David K. E. Bruce Papers

Germany

Archiv der sozialen Demokratie der Friedrich-Ebert-Stiftung, Bonn (AFES)
Depositum Egon Bahr
Willy-Brandt-Archiv (WBA)
Nachlaß Paul Hertz [Mikrofilm-Ausgabe des Nachlasses im IISA Amsterdam]
Nachlaß Paul Hertz [Teilnachlaß aus Historischer Kommission, Berlin]
Nachlaß Richard Löwenthal
Bestand Kurt Schumacher

Auswärtiges Amt, Politisches Archiv, Berlin (PAAA)
B 8 [Protokollabteilung 1949–1976]
B 11 [USA, Vereinigte Staaten]
B 12, B 32, B 55

Bezirksamt Schöneberg/Berlin – Schöneberg Museum/Archiv, Berlin
Rathaus Schöneberg (Innen)
Text Archiv, Rathaus Schöneberg I

Freie Universität, Universitätsarchiv, Berlin (FU Archiv)
IV-2095/4–1, 9. Jan. 1949–1. Juli 1954, Außenkommission, Sitzungsprotokolle
IV-2095/4–1, 9. Aug. 1954–Febr. 1962, Außenkommission, Sitzungsprotokolle II
IV-2095/4–8n, Sonstige Kontakte Übersee
IV-2901/1, 27.3.1963–4.12.1963, Kennedy-Akte
Ford Foundation, Stone–Kimbler
Ford-Spende
Prof. Franz Neumann 1950–1955
Rektorat, Akte "Schriftwechsel i. Zus. mit der Gründung der FUB"
S. Neumann, Ford Foundation
Tätigkeitsberichte Ak, Statistik Außenkom. von 1951 bis 1963
Verabschiedung Dr. Hartwich 20.6.1989

Landesarchiv Berlin, Berlin (LAB)
B Rep. 002: Der Regierende Bürgermeister/Senatskanzlei
B Rep. 037: Amerikanische Behörden in Berlin
B Rep. 037: Oral History Interviews
E Rep. 200–18: Nachlaß Hans E. Hirschfeld
E Rep. 200–21: Ernst Reuter Nachlaß
E Rep. 200–21–01: Ernst-Reuter-Archiv

Sources of Illustrations, United States

Dwight D. Eisenhower Library, Abilene, Kansas (DDEL)
Audiovisual Archives

Harry S. Truman Library, Independence, Missouri
Audiovisual Materials Collection

John F. Kennedy Library, Boston, Massachusetts (JFKL)
Audio-Visual Archives, films:
    FON 26: SFB, "Berlin, den 25. November 1963" – "Trauerfeier in Berlin –
        Kennedy"
    FON 27: "Go to Germany: A Nation Welcomes President John F. Kennedy"
    FON: 30 R 1–8: ARD – ZDF Liveübertragung 26.6.1963
    One Day in Berlin
    TNC 266: CBS News Special: "The President in Germany," June 24, 1963
    TNC: 357–9: J.F.K. Speech in Berlin, No. 112427
    TNC 357:10: CBS
    TNN 280: NBC News Special Report: "The President's Journey," July 1963

Audiovisual Archives, White House Photograph Collection
    Album: Federal Republic of Germany 23.–26.6.1963
    Album: Visit of the President of the United States, John F. Kennedy, to the
        Federal Republic of Germany

Army Signal Corps
Cecil W. Stoughton Series
Robert Knudsen Series

Lyndon B. Johnson Library, Austin, Texas (LBJL)
Audiovisual Materials

National Archives II, College Park, Maryland
Motion Pictures, Sound and Video Branch (NNSM)
Universal Newsreels

Sources of Illustrations, Germany

Bezirksamt Schöneberg/Berlin – Schöneberg Museum/Archiv, Berlin
Sozialgeschichtliche Dokumente – Fotos, Nachkriegszeit 1945–1950

Landesarchiv Berlin, Fotostelle, Berlin (LAB)
1G: Johnson-Besuch
1 NK: Blockade – Luftbrücke
6PK: Kennedy, John F.
6pk: Kennedy, Robert F.
Freiheitsglocke

PRINTED SOURCES AND DOCUMENT COLLECTIONS

Akten zur Auswärtigen Politik der Bundesrepublik Deutschland. Commissioned by the Auwärtigen Amts and edited by the Institut für Zeitgeschichte. Munich: Oldenbourg, here for the years 1963–1965.

Bulletin des Presse- und Informationsamtes der Bundesregierung. Bonn: Deutscher Bundes-Verlag, here for the years 1951–1963.

Department of State Bulletin. Washington, D.C.: U.S. Government Printing Office, here for the years 1948–1963.

Dokumente zur Berlin-Frage, 1944–1966. Edited by Forschungsinstitut der Deutschen Gesellschaft für Auswärtige Politik e.V., Bonn in cooperation with the Berlin Senate. 3rd rev. and expanded ed. Munich: Oldenbourg, 1967.

Dokumente zur Berlin-Frage, 1967–1986. Edited by Hans Heinrich Mahnke for the Forschungsinstitut der Deutschen Gesellschaft für Auswärtige Politik e.V. in cooperation with the Berlin Senate. Munich: Oldenbourg, 1987.

Foreign Relations of the United States. Washington, D.C.: U.S. Government Printing Office, starting in 1945.

Präsident Kennedy in Deutschland. Sonderdruck aus dem Bulletin des Presse- und Informationsamt der Bundesregierung 108, 109, 110, 112, 113. Bonn: Deutscher Bundes-Verlag, 1963.

Public Papers of the Presidents of the United States. Washington, D.C.: U.S. Government Printing Office, for every president since Harry S. Truman.

NEWSPAPERS AND PERIODICALS

Der Abend (Berlin)
Berliner Morgenpost
Berliner Zeitung
Bild
Bonner General-Anzeiger
B.Z. Berlin
Express (Cologne)
Frankfurter Allgemeine Zeitung
Frankfurter Rundschau
Illustrierte Berliner Zeitschrift
Kölner Stadt-Anzeiger
Kölnische Rundschau
Nacht-Depesche (Berlin)
Neue Züricher Zeitung
Neues Deutschland
New York Herald Tribune
New York Times
Newsweek
Rheinische Post
Spandauer Volksblatt
Stern
Süddeutsche Zeitung
Sunday Star
Der Tagesspiegel
Telegraf
Time
Wall Street Journal
Washington Post
Die Welt
Die Zeit

INTERVIEWS

Gordon A. Craig
Horst Hartwich
Harold Hurwitz
Tom Johnson
Carl Kaysen
Melvin J. Lasky
Gerald D. Livingston
Robert H. Lochner
Karl Mautner
Martha Mautner
Margarete Plischke
Fritz Stern
Heinz Weber

SECONDARY SOURCES

Ackermann, Volker. 1990. *Nationale Totenfeiern in Deutschland: Von Wilhelm I. bis Franz Josef Strauß. Eine Studie zur politischen Semiotik.* Stuttgart: Klett-Cotta.

Ackermann, Volker. 1995. "Staatsbegräbnisse in Deutschland von Wilhelm I. bis Willy Brandt." In *Nation und Emotion,* edited by Etienne François, Hannes Siegrist, and Jakob Vogel, 252–73. Göttingen: Vandenhoeck & Ruprecht.

Adenauer, Konrad. 1968. *Erinnerungen 1959–1963. Fragmente.* Stuttgart: Deutsche Verlags-Anstalt.

Albertin, Lothar. 1998. "Politische Jugendarbeit und nationale Frage im geteilten Deutschland 1945–1961." In *Doppelte Zeitgeschichte: Deutsch-deutsche Beziehungen 1945–1990,* edited by Arnd Bauerkämper, Martin Sabrow, and Bernd Stöver, 32–43. Bonn: Dietz.

Allemann, Fritz René. 1966. "Berlin in Search of a Purpose." *Survey* 61: 129–38.

Anderson, Benedict. 1991. *Imagined Communities: Reflections on the Origin and Spread of Nationalism.* Rev. and extended ed. London and New York: Verso.

Angster, Julia. 2002. *Konsenskapitalismus und Sozialdemokratie: Die Westernisierung von SPD und DGB von 1940 bis 1965.* Munich: Oldenbourg.

Arenth, Joachim. 1993. *Der Westen tut nichts! Transatlantische Kooperation während der zweiten Berlin-Krise (1958–1962) im Spiegel neuer amerikanischer Quellen.* Frankfurt a. M.: Lang.

Assmann, Aleida and Ute Frevert. 1999. *Geschichtsvergessenheit – Geschichtsversessenheit: Vom Umgang mit deutschen Vergangenheiten nach 1945.* Stuttgart: DVA.

Assmann, Jan. 1992. *Das kulturelle Gedächtnis: Schrift, Erinnerung und politische Identität in frühen Hochkulturen.* Munich: Beck.

The Atlantic Community: An Introductory Bibliography. 1961. 2 vols. Leiden: A. W. Sythoff.

Ausland, John C. 1996. *Kennedy, Khrushchev, and the Berlin-Cuba Crisis, 1961–1964.* Oslo: Scandinavian University Press.

Bahr, Egon. 1996. *Zu meiner Zeit.* 3rd ed. Munich: Blessing.

Barclay, David E. 2000. *Schaut auf diese Stadt: Der unbekannte Ernst Reuter.* Berlin: Siedler.

Bark, Dennis L. and David R. Gress. 1993. *A History of West Germany.* 2 vols., 2nd ed. Oxford and Cambridge, Mass.: Blackwell.

Barnouw, Dagmar. 1996. *Germany 1945: Views of War and Violence.* Bloomington and Indianapolis: Indiana University Press.

Becker, Jürgen, ed. 1965. *Happenings: Fluxus: Pop Art.* Reinbek bei Hamburg: Rowohlt.

Beevor, Antony. 2002. *Berlin: The Downfall, 1945.* London and New York: Viking.

Behrenbeck, Sabine. 1996. *Der Kult um die toten Helden: Nationalsozialistische Mythen, Riten und Symbole 1923–1945.* Vierow bei Greifswald: SH-Verlag.

Behrenbeck, Sabine and Alexander Nützenadel, eds. 2000. *Inszenierungen des Nationalstaats: Politische Feiern in Italien und Deutschland seit 1860/71.* Cologne: SH-Verlag.

Bender, Thomas, ed. 2002. *Rethinking American History in a Global Age.* Berkeley: University of California Press.

Benthien, Claudia, Anne Fleig, and Ingrid Kasten, eds. 2000. *Emotionalität. Zur Geschichte der Gefühle.* Cologne: Böhlau.

Berg, Manfred and Philipp Gassert, eds. 2004. *Deutschland und die USA in der internationalen Geschichte des 20. Jahrhunderts.* Stuttgart: Steiner.

Berger, Peter L. and Thomas Luckmann. 1967. *The Social Construction of Reality: A Treatise in the Sociology of Knowledge.* Garden City, N.Y.: Anchor Books.

Berghahn, Volker R. 1986. *The Americanization of West German Industry, 1945–1973.* New York: Cambridge University Press.

Berghahn, Volker R. 1996. "Deutschland im 'American Century,' 1942–1992: Einige Argumente zur Amerikanisierungsfrage." In *Politische Zäsuren und gesellschaftlicher Wandel im 20. Jahrhundert. Regionale und vergleichende Perspektiven,* edited by Matthias Frese and Michael Prinz, 789–800. Paderborn: Schöningh.

Berghahn, Volker R. 2001. *America and the Intellectual Cold Wars in Europe: Shepard Stone between Philanthropy, Academy, and Diplomacy.* Princeton, N.J.: Princeton University Press.

Berghahn, Volker R. 2004. "America and Social Change in Germany." In *The United States and Germany in the Era of the Cold War, 1945–1968: A Handbook,* edited by Detlef Junker, vol. 1, 495–507. Cambridge and Washington, D.C.: Cambridge University Press.

Bertram, Christof. 1998. "Germany Moves On: Laying Angst to Rest." *Foreign Affairs* 77, 4 (July/August): 186–94.

Biermann, Harald. 1997. *John F. Kennedy und der Kalte Krieg. Die Außenpolitik der USA und die Grenzen der Glaubwürdigkeit.* Paderborn: Schöningh.

Bizeul, Yves. 2000. "Theorien der politischen Mythen und Rituale." In *Politische Mythen und Rituale in Deutschland, Frankreich und Polen,* edited by Yves Bizeul, 15–39. Berlin: Humblot.

Blackbourn, David. 1987. "Politics as Theatre: Metaphors of the Stage in German History, 1848–1933." In *Populists and Patricians: Essays in Modern German History,* 246–64. London: Allen & Unwin.

Blackbourn, David. 1993. *Marpingen: Apparitions of the Virgin Mary in Nineteenth-Century Germany.* Oxford: Oxford University Press.

Bodemann, Y. Michal. 1996. *Gedächtnistheater: Die jüdische Gemeinschaft und ihre deutsche Erfindung.* Hamburg: Rotbuch.

Bodnar, John E. 1992. *Remaking America: Public Memory, Commemoration, and Patriotism in the Twentieth Century.* Princeton, N.J.: Princeton University Press.

Bonnell, Victoria E. and Lynn Hunt, eds. 1999. *Beyond the Cultural Turn: New Directions in the Study of Society and Culture.* Berkeley: University of California Press.

Brandt, Willy. 1959. "Amerikanische und deutsche Einheit. Abraham Lincoln heute." *Aussenpolitik. Zeitschrift für internationale Fragen* 10, 4 (April): 209–13.

Brandt, Willy. 1963. *The Ordeal of Coexistence.* Cambridge, Mass.: Harvard University Press.

Brandt, Willy. 1964. *Begegnungen mit Kennedy.* Munich: Kindler.

Brandt, Willy. 1976. *Begegnungen und Einsichten: Die Jahre 1960–1975.* Hamburg: Hoffmann und Campe.

Brandt, Willy. 1992. *Erinnerungen.* Second, expanded ed. Berlin: Ullstein

Bredekamp, Horst. 1999. *Thomas Hobbes visuelle Strategien. Der Leviathan, Urbild des modernen Staates. Werkillustrationen und Portraits.* Berlin: Akademie.

Bredow, Wilfried von. 1996. "Bilaterale Beziehungen im Netzwerk regionaler und globaler Interdependenz." In *Deutschlands neue Außenpolitik*, edited by Karl Kaiser and Joachim Krause, vol. 3, 109–115. Munich: Oldenbourg.

Bremen, Christian. 1998. *Die Eisenhower-Administration und die zweite Berlinkrise 1958–1961.* Berlin and New York: de Gruyter.

Briesen, Detlef. 1992. *Berlin, die überschätzte Metropole: Über das System der deutschen Hauptstädte von 1850 bis 1940.* Bonn and Berlin: Bouvier.

Bruner, Michael S. 1989. "Symbolic Uses of the Berlin Wall, 1961–1989." *Communication Quarterly* 37, 4 (Fall): 319–28.

Brunn, Gerhard. 1993. "Berlin (1871–1939) – Megalopolis *Manqué?*" In *Megalopolis: The Giant City in History*, edited by Theo Barker and Anthony Sutcliffe, 96–115. New York: St. Martin's Press.

Buchloh, Benjamin H. D. and Judith F. Rodenbeck. 1999. *Experiments in the Everyday: Allan Kaprow and Robert Watts: Events, Objects, Documents.* New York: Columbia University Press/Miriam and Ira D. Wallach Art Gallery.

Bundy, McGeorge. 1998. *Danger and Surviva: Choices About the Bomb in the First Fifty Years.* New York: Random House.

Burke, Edmund. 2001. *Reflections on the Revolution in France*, edited by J. C. D. Clark. Stanford, Calif.: Stanford University Press.

Burke, Peter. 1992. *The Fabrication of Louis XIV.* New Haven, Conn.: Yale University Press.

Burr, William. 1992. "New Sources on the Berlin Crisis, 1958–1962." *Cold War International History Project Bulletin*, 2 (Fall): 21–24, 32.

Bussemer, Thymian. 2001. "Vor vierzig Jahren: Brandt-Wahlkampf als Kennedy-Kopie. Klaus Schütz erinnert sich." *Die Neue Gesellschaft – Frankfurter Hefte*, 48, 7/8 (July/August): 476–80.

Caro, Robert A. 2002. *Master of the Senate.* New York: Knopf.

Catudal, Honoré M. 1980. *Kennedy and the Berlin Wall Crisis: A Study in U.S. Decision Making.* Berlin: Berlin Verlag.

Chickering, Roger. 1984. *We Men Who Feel Most German: A Cultural Study of the Pan-German League, 1886–1914.* Boston: Allen & Unwin.

Chomsky, Noam. 1993. *Rethinking Camelot: JFK, the Vietnam War, and U.S. Political Culture.* Boston: South End Press.

Cicero, Marcus Tullius. 1893. *The Orations of Marcus Tullius Cicero*, translated by C. D. Yonge, vol. 1. London: G. Bell.

Conrad, Sebastian. 2002. "Doppelte Marginalisierung: Plädoyer für eine transnationale Perspektive auf die deutsche Geschichte." *Geschichte und Gesellschaft* 28: 145–69.

Conze, Eckart. 1995a. *Die gaullistische Herausforderung: Die deutsch-französische Beziehungen in der amerikanischen Europapolitik, 1958–1963.* Munich: Oldenbourg

Conze, Eckart. 1995b. "Hegemonie durch Integration? Die amerikanische Europapolitik und ihre Herausforderung durch de Gaulle." *Vierteljahreshefte für Zeitgeschichte* 43: 297–340.

Cornides, Wilhelm. 1963. "Präsident Kennedys Engagement in Berlin." *Europa-Archiv* 18: 427–44.

Costigliola, Frank. 1989. "The Pursuit of Atlantic Community: Nuclear Arms, Dollars, and Berlin." In *Kennedy's Quest for Victory*, edited by Thomas Paterson, 24–56. New York: Oxford University Press.

Costigliola, Frank. 1997a. "The Nuclear Family: Tropes of Gender and Pathology in the Western Alliance," *Diplomatic History* 21, 2 (Spring): 163–83.

Costigliola, Frank. 1997b. "'Unceasing Pressure for Penetration': Gender, Pathology, and Emotion in George Kennan's Formation of the Cold War," *The Journal of American History* 83, 4 (March): 1309–39.

Costigliola, Frank. 1998. "'Mixed Up' and 'Contact': Culture and Emotion among the Allies in the Second World War," *The International History Review* 20, 4 (December): 791–805.

Costigliola, Frank. 2000. "'I Had Come as a Friend': Emotion, Culture, and Ambiguity in the Formation of the Cold War," *Cold War History* 1, 1 (August): 103–28.

Craig, Gordon A. 1998. "Berlin, the Hauptstadt: Back Where It Belongs." *Foreign Affairs* 77, 4 (July/August): 161–70.

Crawford, Neta C. 2000. "The Passion of World Politics. Propositions on Emotion and Emotional Relationships." *International Security* 24, 4 (Spring): 116–56.

Dallek, Robert. 2003. *An Unfinished Life: John F. Kennedy 1917–1963*. New York: Back Bay Books.

Dann, Otto. 1983. "Die Hauptstadtfrage in Deutschland nach dem 2. Weltkrieg." In *Hauptstädte in europäischen Nationalstaaten*, edited by Theodor Schieder and Gerhard Brunn, 35–60. Munich and Vienna: Oldenbourg.

Daum, Andreas W. 2000. "America's Berlin, 1945–2000: Between Myths and Visions." In *Berlin: The New Capital in the East. A Transatlantic Appraisal*, edited by Frank Trommler, 49–73. Washington, D.C.: American Institute for Contemporary German Studies.

Daum, Andreas W. 2004. "Charisma und Vergemeinschaftung: Zur Westbindung der Deutschen im Kalten Krieg." In *Deutschland und die USA in der internationalen Geschichte des 20. Jahrhunderts*, edited by Manfred Berg and Philipp Gassert, 449–72. Stuttgart: Steiner.

Daum, Andreas W. 2007. "'Atlantic Partnership' or Simply 'A Mess'? Performative Politics and Social Communication in the Western Alliance During the Kennedy Presidency." In *John F. Kennedy and the 'Thousand Days': New Perspectives on the Foreign and Domestic Policies of the Kennedy Administration*, edited by Manfred Berg and Andreas Etges, 17–37. Heidelberg: Winter.

Daum, Andreas W., Lloyd C. Gardner, and Wilfried Mausbach, eds. 2003. *America, the Vietnam War, and the World: Comparative and International Perspectives*. New York: Cambridge University Press.

Daum, Andreas W. and Christof Mauch, eds. 2005. *Berlin – Washington, 1800–2000: Capital Cities, Cultural Representations, and National Identities*. New York: Cambridge University Press.

Davis, Belinda. 2000. *Home Fires Burning: Food, Politics, and Everyday Life in World War I Berlin*. Chapel Hill: University of North Carolina Press.

Davis, Susan G. 1986. *Parade and Power: Street Theatre in Nineteenth-Century Philadelphia*. Philadelphia: Temple University Press.

Deutsch, Karl W. 1953. *Nationalism and Social Communication: An Inquiry into the Foundations of Nationality*. New York and London: Technology Press of MIT/Wiley & Sons.

Deutsch, Karl W. et al. 1957. *Political Community and the North Atlantic Area: International Organization in the Light of Historical Experience.* New York: Greenwood Press.

Diefendorf, Jeffrey M. 2004. "American Influences on Urban Developments in West Germany." In *The United States and Germany in the Era of the Cold War, 1945–1968: A Handbook,* edited by Detlef Junker, vol. 1, 587–93. Cambridge: Cambridge University Press.

Diefendorf, Jeffrey M., Axel Frohn, and Hermann-Josef Rupieper, eds. 2004. *American Policy and the Reconstruction of West Germany, 1945–1955.* 1st pbk. ed. Cambridge and NewYork: Cambridge University Press.

Diers, Michael. 1997. *Schlagbilder: Zur politischen Ikonographie der Gegenwart.* Frankfurt a. M.: Fischer.

Dittmer, Lowell. 1977. "Political Culture and Political Symbolism: Toward a Theoretical Synthesis." *World Politics* 29, 4: 552–83.

Doering-Manteuffel, Anselm. 1995. "Dimensionen von Amerikanisierung in der deutschen Gesellschaft." *Archiv für Sozialgeschichte* 35: 1–34.

Doering-Manteuffel, Anselm. 1999. *Wie westlich sind die Deutschen? Amerikanisierung und Westernisierung im 20. Jahrhundert.* Göttingen: Vandenhoeck & Ruprecht.

Dolff-Bonekämper, Gabi and Franziska Schmidt. 1999. *Das Hansaviertel: Internationale Nachkriegsmoderne in Berlin.* Berlin: Bauwesen.

Domentat, Tamara, ed. 1995. *Coca-Cola, Jazz & AFN: Berlin und die Amerikaner.* Berlin: Schwarzkopf & Schwarzkopf.

Dörner, Andreas. 1995. *Politischer Mythos und symbolische Politik: Sinnstiftung durch symbolische Formen am Beispiel des Hermannsmythos.* Opladen: Westdeutscher Verlag.

Duindam, Jeroen Frans Jozef. 1994. *Myths of Power: Norbert Elias and the Early Modern European Court.* Amsterdam: Amsterdam University Press.

Dulles, Eleanor Lansing. 1967. *Berlin: The Wall Is Not Forever.* Chapel Hill: University of North Carolina Press.

Dulles, Eleanor Lansing. 1980. *Chances of a Lifetime: A Memoir.* Englewood Cliffs, N.J.: Prentice-Hall.

Dumbrell, John. 2006. *A Special Relationship: Anglo-American Relations from the Cold War to Iraq.* 2nd ed. Houndmills: Palgrave Macmillan.

Durkheim, Emil. 2001. *The Elementary Forms of Religious Life.* Translated by Carol Cosman; abridged with an introduction and notes by Mark S. Cladis. Oxford and New York: Oxford University Press.

Dussel, Konrad. 2000. "Vom Radio- zum Fernsehzeitalter: Medienumbrüche in sozialgeschichtlicher Perspektive." In *Dynamische Zeiten: Die 60er Jahre in den beiden deutschen Gesellschaften,* edited by Axel Schildt, Detlef Siegfried, and Karl Christian Lammers, 673–94. Hamburg: Christians.

Edelman, Murray. 1964/1985. *The Symbolic Uses of Politics.* Repr. Urbana: University of Illinois Press.

Eichhoff, Jürgen. 1993. "'Ich bin ein Berliner': A History and a Linguistic Clarification." *Monatshefte für den deutschen Unterricht, deutsche Sprache und Literatur* 85, 1: 71–80.

Ermarth, Michael, ed. 1993. *America and the Shaping of German Society, 1945–1955.* Providence, R.I.: Berg.

Falasca-Zamponi, Simonetta. 1997. *Fascist Spectacle: The Aesthetics of Power in Mussolini's Italy*. Berkeley, Los Angeles, and London: University of California Press.

Fehrenbach, Heide. 1995. *Cinema in Democratizing Germany: Reconstructing National Identity after Hitler*. Chapel Hill and London: University of North Carolina Press.

Fehrenbach, Heide and Uta G. Poiger, eds. 2000. *Transactions, Transgressions, Transformations: American Culture in Western Europe and Japan*. New York and Oxford: Berghahn.

Feldman, Lily Gardner. 2004. "German-American Societal Relations in Three Dimensions, 1968–1990." In *The United States and Germany in the Era of the Cold War, 1968–1990: A Handbook*, edited by Detlef Junker, vol. 2, 409–20. Cambridge: Cambridge University Press.

Fink, Carole, Philipp Gassert, and Detlef Junker, eds. 1998. *1968: The World Transformed*. Cambridge and New York: Cambridge University Press.

François, Etienne and Hagen Schulze, eds. 2001. *Deutsche Erinnerungsorte*. 3 vols. Munich: Beck.

François, Etienne, Hannes Siegrist, and Jakob Vogel, eds. 1995. *Nation und Emotion: Deutschland und Frankreich im Vergleich. 19. und 20. Jahrhundert*. Göttingen: Vandenhoeck & Ruprecht.

Freitag, Sabine. 1998. *Die Achtundvierziger. Lebensbilder aus der deutschen Revolution 1848/49*. Munich: Beck.

Frevert, Ute. 2000. "Angst vor Gefühlen? Die Geschichtsmächtigkeit von Emotionen im 20. Jahrhundert." In *Perspektiven der Gesellschaftsgeschichte*, edited by Paul Nolte et al., 95–111. Munich: Beck.

Frevert, Ute. 2002. "Vertrauen in historischer Perspektive." In *Politisches Vertrauen: Soziale Grundlagen reflexiver Kooperation*, edited by Rainer Schmalz-Bruns and Reinhard Zintl, 39–59. Baden-Baden: Nomos.

Fritzsche, Peter. 1998. *Reading Berlin 1900*. Cambridge, Mass.: Harvard University Press.

Gaddis, John Lewis. 2005. *The Cold War: A New History*. New York: Penguin Press.

Gallup, George H. 1972. *The Gallup Poll. Public Opinion 1935–1971*. 3 vols. New York: Random House.

Gassert, Philipp. 1999. "Amerikanismus, Antiamerikanismus, Amerikanisierung. Neue Literatur zur Sozial-, Wirtschafts- und Kulturgeschichte des amerikanischen Einflusses in Deutschland und Europa." *Archiv für Sozialgeschichte* 39: 531–61.

Geertz, Clifford. 1971. "Deep Play: Notes on the Balinese Cockfight." In *Myth, Symbol, and Culture*, edited by Clifford Geertz, 1–37. New York: Norton.

Geertz, Clifford. 1980. *Negara: The Theatre State in Nineteenth-Century Bali*. Princeton, N.J.: Princeton University Press.

Geppert, Dominik. 2001. "Die Freiheitsglocke." In *Deutsche Erinnerungsorte*, edited by Etienne François and Hagen Schulze, vol. 2, 238–52. Munich: Beck.

Geppert, Dominik. 2002. "Cultural Aspects of the Cold War." *Bulletin of the German Historical Institute London* 24, 2 (November): 50–71.

Gienow-Hecht, Jessica C. E., and Frank Schumacher, eds. 2003. *Culture and International History*. New York: Berghahn.

Gillis, John R., ed. 1994. *Commemorations. The Politics of National Identity*. Princeton, N.J.: Princeton University Press.

Ginzburg, Carlo. 1993. "Microhistory: Two or Three Things that I Know About It." *Critical Inquiry* 20, 1 (Fall): 10–35.

Grabbe, Hans-Jürgen. 1983. *Unionsparteien, Sozialdemokratie und Vereinigte Staaten von Amerika 1945–1966*. Düsseldorf: Droste.

Grabbe, Hans-Jürgen. 1986. "Das Amerikabild Konrad Adenauers." *Amerikastudien* 31, 3: 315–23.

Granieri, Ronald J. 2003. *The Ambivalent Alliance: Konrad Adenauer, the CDU/CSU, and the West, 1949–1966*. New York and Oxford: Berghahn Books.

Granieri, Ronald J. 2004. "Political Parties and German-American Relations: Politics Beyond the Water's Edge." In *The United States and Germany in the Era of the Cold War, 1945–1968: A Handbook*, edited by Detlef Junker, vol. 1, 141–48. Cambridge: Cambridge University Press.

Gray, William Glenn. 2003 *Germany's Cold War: The Global Campaign to Isolate East Germany, 1949–1969*. Chapel Hill: University of North Carolina Press.

Gross, Johannes. 1995. *Begründung der Berliner Republik: Deutschland am Ende des 20. Jahrhunderts*. 3rd ed. Stuttgart: DVA.

Guthman, Edwin O. and C. Richard Allen, eds. 1993. *RFK: Collected Speeches*. New York: Viking.

Habermas, Jürgen. 1997. *A Berlin Republic: Writings on Germany*. Lincoln: University of Nebraska Press.

Haftendorn, Helga. 1999. "Die einsame Eminenz: Adenauer im zeitgenössischen Urteil der USA." In *Macht und Zeitkritik. Festschrift für Hans-Peter Schwarz zum 65. Geburtstag*, edited by Peter R. Weilemann, Hanns Jürgen Küsters, and Günter Buchstab, 129–46. Paderborn: Schöningh.

Haftendorn, Helga. 2006. *Coming of Age: German Foreign Policy Since 1945*. Lanham, Md.: Rowman & Littlefield.

Hamilton, Daniel S. 1994. *Beyond Berlin: America & the Berlin Republic*. Washington, D.C.: Carnegie Endowment for International Peace.

Hamilton, Nigel. 1992. *JFK: Reckless Youth*. New York: Random House.

Hanf, Theodor. 1993. "Berlin or Bonn? The Dispute over Germany's Political Center." In *Capital Cities – Les Capitales: Perspectives Internationales – International Perspectives*, edited by John Taylor, Jean G. Lengellé, and Caroline Andrew, 295–316. Ottawa, ON: Carleton University Press.

Hanrieder, Wolfram F. 1989. *Germany, America, Europe: Forty Years of German Foreign Policy*. New Haven, Conn.: Yale University Press.

Hardtwig, Wolfgang. 1994. *Nationalismus und Bürgerkultur in Deutschland 1500–1914: Ausgewählte Aufsätze*. Göttingen: Vandenhoeck & Ruprecht.

Hardtwig, Wolfgang. 2001. "Political Religion in Modern Germany: Reflections on Nationalism, Socialism, and National Socialism." *Bulletin of the German Historical Institute Washington, D.C.* 28 (Spring): 3–27.

Hare, A. Paul and Herbert H. Blumberg. 1988. *Dramaturgical Analysis of Social Interaction*. New York; Westport, Conn.; and London: Praeger.

Hartman, Geoffrey H., ed. 1986. *Bitburg in Moral and Political Perspective*. Bloomington: Indiana University Press.

Helbig, Jörg, ed. 1987. *Welcome to Berlin: Das Image Berlins in der englischsprachigen Welt von 1700 bis heute*. Berlin: Stapp.

Henrikson, Alan K. 1991. "Mental Maps." In *Explaining the History of American Foreign Relations*, edited by Michael J. Hogan and Thomas G. Paterson, 177–92. Cambridge and New York: Cambridge University Press.

Herles, Helmut, ed. 1991. *Die Hauptstadtdebatte: Der Stenographische Bericht des Bundestages*. Bonn and Berlin: Bouvier.

Hersh, Seymor. 1997. *The Dark Side of Camelot*. Boston: Little, Brown.

Herzfeld, Hans. 1973. *Berlin in der Weltpolitik: 1945–1970*. Berlin: de Gruyter.

Hildebrand, Klaus. 1984. *Von Erhard zur großen Koalition, 1963–1969*. Stuttgart: DVA/F. A. Brockhaus.

Hillenbrand, Martin J. 1998. *Fragments of Our Time: Memoirs of a Diplomat*. Athens: University of Georgia Press.

Hixson, Walter L. 1998. *Parting the Curtain: Propaganda, Culture, and the Cold War, 1945–1961*. New York: St. Martin's Griffin.

Hobsbawm, Eric and Terence Ranger, eds. 1996. *The Invention of Tradition*. Cambridge: Cambridge University Press.

Hochgeschwender, Michael. 1998. *Freiheit in der Offensive? Der Kongreß für kulturelle Freiheit und die Deutschen*. Munich: Oldenbourg.

Hoffmann, Wilhelm, ed. 1999. *Die Sichtbarkeit der Macht: Theoretische und empirische Untersuchungen zur visuellen Politik*. Baden-Baden: Nomos.

Hogan, Michael J. and Thomas G. Paterson, eds. 1991. *Explaining the History of American Foreign Relations*. Cambridge and New York: Cambridge University Press.

Hübner, Holger. 1997. *Das Gedächtnis der Stadt: Gedenktafeln in Berlin*. Berlin: Argon.

Hunt, Lynn. 1984. *Politics, Culture, and Class in the French Revolution*. Berkeley, Los Angeles, and London: University of California Press.

Hunt, Lynn, ed. 1989. *The New Cultural History*. Berkeley: University of California Press.

Hunt, Michael H. 2004. *The World Transformed: 1945 to the Present*. Boston: Bedford/St. Martin's.

Ich bin ein Berliner: John F. Kennedy in der deutschen Hauptstadt am 26. Juni 1963. 1963. Berlin: Arani.

Infratest. 1963. *Die Reaktion der Fernsehzuschauer auf die Sonderberichte vom Deutschlandbesuch des amerikanischen Präsidenten J. F. Kennedy (So., 23.6.–Mi., 26.6.63)*. Munich: Infratest GmbH.

Die Inszenierung des Politischen: Zur Theatralität von Mediendiskursen. 2000. Opladen: Westdeutscher Verlag.

Iriye, Akira. 1979. "Culture and Power: International Relations as Intercultural Relations." *Diplomatic History* 3: 115–28.

Jeismann, Michael. 1992. *Das Vaterland der Feinde: Studien zum nationalen Feindbegriff und Selbstverständnis in Deutschland und Frankreich, 1792–1918*. Stuttgart: Klett-Cotta.

Jelavich, Peter. 1996. *Berlin Cabaret*. Cambridge, Mass., and London: Harvard University Press.

Joas, Hans. 1996. *Die Kreativität des Handelns*. Frankfurt a. M.: Suhrkamp.

Joffe, Josef. 1987. *The Limited Partnership: Europe, the United States and the Burdens of Alliance*. Cambridge, Mass.: Ballinger.

John F. Kennedy – Robert F. Kennedy. Reden an der Freien Universität. 1996. Berlin: Universitätsdruckerei.

Judt, Tony. 2005. *Postwar: A History of Europe Since 1945.* New York: Penguin Press.

Junker, Detlef, ed., in cooperation with Philipp Gassert, Wilfried Mausbach, and David B. Morris. 2004. *The United States and Germany in the Era of the Cold War, 1945–1990: A Handbook.* 2 vols. Cambridge: Cambridge University Press.

Kaiser, Karl. 1969. "Transnationale Politik. Zu einer Theorie multinationaler Politik." In *Die anachronistische Souveränität,* edited by Ernst-Otto Czempiel, 80–109. Special issue 1 of *Politische Vierteljahresschrift.* Cologne: Westdeutscher Verlag.

Kammen, Michael G. 1993. *The Mystic Chords of Memory: The Transformation of Tradition in American Culture.* New York: Vintage Books.

Katzenstein, Peter, ed. 1996. *The Culture of National Security: Norms and Identity in World Politics.* New York: Columbia University Press.

Kennedy, John F. 1940. *Why England Slept.* New York: W. Funk.

Kennedy, John F. 1957. "A Democrat Looks at Foreign Policy." *Foreign Affairs* 36, 1: 44–59.

Kennedy, John F. 1964. *Glanz und Bürde: Die Hoffnungen und Zielsetzungen des zweiten und dritten Jahres der Präsidentschaft Kennedys dargetan in seinen Botschaften und Reden mit dem vollen Texten aller öffentlichen Äußerungen während seiner Deutschland-Reise 1963,* edited by Allan Nevins, preface by President Lyndon B. Johnson. Düsseldorf and Vienna: Econ.

Kennedy, John F. 1995. *Prelude to Leadership: The European Diary of John F. Kennedy, Summer 1945,* introduction by Hugh Sidey. Washington, D.C.: Regnery.

Kennedy, Robert F. 1962. *"We must meet our duty and convince the world that we are just friends and brave enemies."* New York and Evanston: Harper & Row.

Kennedy, Robert F. 1969. *Thirteen Days: A Memoir of the Cuban Missile Crisis.* New York: W. W. Norton.

Keohane, Robert O. and Joseph S. Nye, Jr., eds. 1971. *Transnational Relations and World Politics.* Cambridge, Mass.: Harvard University Press.

Kershaw, Ian. 1987. *The "Hitler Myth": Image and Reality in the Third Reich.* Oxford: Oxford University Press.

Kessel, Martina. 2000. "Mentalitätengeschichte." In *Geschichtswissenschaften: Eine Einführung,* edited by Christoph Cornelissen, 235–246. Frankfurt a. M.: Fischer.

Kettlein, Rudolf. 1959. *Willy Brandt ruft die Welt: Ein dokumentarischer Bericht.* Berlin: Arani.

Kielmansegg, Peter Graf. 1989. *Lange Schatten: Vom Umgang der Deutschen mit der nationalsozialistischen Vergangenheit.* Berlin: Siedler.

Kiersch, Gerhard. 1991. "De Gaulle und die deutsche Identität." In *De Gaulle, Deutschland und Europa,* edited by Wilfried Loth and Robert Picht, 181–92. Opladen: Leske/Budrich.

Knapp, Manfred. 2004. "Divided Loyalties in Transatlantic Policy Toward Europe." In *The United States and Germany in the Era of the Cold War, 1945–1968: A Handbook,* edited by Detlef Junker, vol. 1, 125–32. Cambridge: Cambridge University Press.

Koop, Volker. 1998. *Kein Kampf um Berlin? Deutsche Politik zur Zeit der Berlin-Blockade 1948/49.* Bonn: Bouvier.

Koselleck, Reinhart. 2004. "Representation, Event, and Structure." In Reinhard Koselleck, *Futures Past: On the Semantics of Historical Time*. Translated with an introduction by Keith Tribe, 105–14. New York: Columbia University Press.

Koselleck, Reinhart and Michael Jeismann. 1994. *Der politische Totenkult: Kriegerdenkmäler in der Moderne*. Munich: Fink.

Kremp, Werner. 1993. *In Deutschland liegt unser Amerika: Das sozialdemokratische Amerikabild von den Anfängen der SPD bis zur Weimarer Republik*. Münster: Lit.

Krotz, Ulrich. 2002. "Social Content of the International Sphere: Symbols and Meaning in Franco-German Relations." Program for the Study of Germany and Europe, Working Paper No. 02.2. Cambridge, Mass.: Center for European Studies, Harvard University.

Kuisel, Richard. 1993. *Seducing the French: The Dilemma of Americanization*. Berkeley: University of California Press.

Ladd, Brian. 1997. *The Ghosts of Berlin: Confronting German History in the Urban Landscape*. Chicago: University of Chicago Press.

Lane, Barbara Miller. 1984. "The Berlin Congress Hall, 1955–57." *Perspectives in American History*: 131–85.

Lappenküper, Ulrich. 2001. *Die deutsch-französischen Beziehungen, 1949–1963: Von der "Erbfeindschaft" zur "Entente élémentaire."* 2 vols. Munich: Oldenbourg.

Large, David Clay. 2000. *Berlin*. New York: Basic Books.

Larres, Klaus and Torsten Oppelland, eds. 1997. *Deutschland und die USA im 20. Jahrhundert. Geschichte der politischen Beziehungen*. Darmstadt: Wissenschaftliche Buchgesellschaft.

Leffler, Melvyn P. 1995. "New Approaches, Old Interpretations, and Prospective Reconfigurations." *Diplomatic History* 19, 2 (Spring): 173–96.

Leggewie, Claus. 2004. "'1968': A Transatlantic Event and Its Consequences." In *The United States and Germany in the Era of the Cold War, 1968–1990: A Handbook*, edited by Detlef Junker, vol. 2, 421–29. Cambridge: Cambridge University Press.

Lemert, Charles C. and Ann Branaman, eds. 1997. *The Goffman Reader*. Malden, Mass., and Oxford: Blackwell.

Lewis, Flora. 1959. "The Fiery Brandt of Berlin." *Coronet* (May): 101.

Lichtenstein, Nelson. 1995. *The Most Dangerous Man in Detroit: Walter Reuther and the Fate of American Labor*. New York: Basic Books.

Liebau, Veronika and Andreas W. Daum. 2000. *Die Freiheitsglocke in Berlin – The Freedom Bell in Berlin*. Berlin: Jaron.

Lindenberger, Thomas. 1995. *Straßenpolitik: Zur Sozialgeschichte der öffentlichen Ordnung in Berlin 1900 bis 1914*. Bonn: Dietz.

Lindenberger, Thomas, ed. 1999. *Herrschaft und Eigen-Sinn in der Diktatur: Studien zur Gesellschaftsgeschichte der DDR*. Berlin: Böhlau.

Lochner, Robert H. 2002. *Ein Berliner unter dem Sternenbanner*. Berlin: Edition Goldbeck-Löwe.

Loth, Wilfired and Jürgen Osterhammel, eds. 2000. *Internationale Geschichte: Themen, Ergebnisse, Aussichten*. Munich: Oldenbourg.

Loth, Wilfried and Robert Picht, eds. 1991. *De Gaulle, Deutschland und Europa*. Opladen: Leske and Budrich.

Löwith, Karl. 1949. *Meaning in History: The Theological Implications of the Philosophy of History*. Chicago: University of Chicago Press.

Lüdtke, Alf. 1985. "Organizational Order or *Eigensinn?* Workers' Privacy and Workers' Politics in Imperial Germany." In *Rites of Power: Symbolism, Ritual, and Politics Since the Middle Ages*, edited by Sean Wilentz, 303–33. Philadelphia: University of Philadelphia Press.

Lüdtke, Alf. 1993. *Eigen-Sinn: Fabrikalltag, Arbeitererfahrungen und Politik vom Kaiserreich bis in den Faschismus*. Hamburg: Ergebnisse.

Lüdtke, Alf. 2002. "Eigensinn." In *Lexikon Geschichtswissenschaft: Hundert Grundbegriffe*, edited by Stefan Jordan, 64–67. Stuttgart: Reclam.

Lüdtke, Alf, Inge Marßolek, and Adelheid von Saldern, eds. 1996. *Amerikanisierung: Traum und Alptraum im Deutschland des 20. Jahrhunderts*. Stuttgart: Steiner.

Lüsebrink, Hans-Jürgen and Rolf Reichardt, eds. 1990. *Die Bastille: Zur Symbolgeschichte von Herrschaft und Freiheit*. Frankfurt a. M.: Fischer.

Lundestad, Geir. 2003. *The United States and Western Europe Since 1945: From "Empire" by Invitation to Transatlantic Drift*. Oxford and New York: Oxford University Press.

Lutz, Felix Philipp. 2004. "Transatlantic Networks: Elites in German-American Relations." In *The United States and Germany in the Era of the Cold War, 1968–1990: A Handbook*, edited by Detlef Junker, vol. 2, 445–51. Cambridge: Cambridge University Press.

Mahnke, Hans Heinrich. 1990. "Vom Londoner Potokoll zum Viermächte-Abkommen." In *Berlin: Vom Brennpunkt der Teilung zur Brücke der Einheit*, edited by Gerd Langguth, 88–106. Bonn: Bundeszentrale für politische Bildung.

Mai, Ekkehard and Anke Repp-Eckert, eds. 1988. *Triumph und Tod des Helden: Europäische Historienmalerei von Rubens bis Manet*. Mailand, Italy, and Zürich: Electa/Kunsthaus Zürich.

Mai, Gunther. 1995. *Der Alliierte Kontrollrat in Deutschland 1945–1948: Alliierte Einheit – deutsche Teilung?* Munich: Oldenbourg.

Maier, Charles S. 1989. "Alliance and Autonomy: European Identity and U.S. Foreign Policy Objectives in the Truman Years." In *The Truman Presidency*, edited by Michael J. Lacey, 273–98. Cambridge: Cambridge University Press.

Maier, Hans. 2002. "Deutungen totalitärer Herrschaft 1919–1989." *Vierteljahreshefte für Zeitgeschichte* 50: 349–66.

Matson, Floyd W., ed. 1967. *Voices of Crisis. Vital Speeches on Contemporary Issues*. New York: Odyssey Press.

Mausbach, Wilfried. 2003. "Auschwitz and Vietnam: The West German Protest Movement Against America's War in the 1960s." In *America, the Vietnam War, and the World: Comparative and International Perspectives*, edited by Andreas W. Daum, Lloyd C. Gardner, and Wilfried Mausbach, 279–98. New York: Cambridge University Press.

Mausbach, Wilfried. 2004. "Erdachte Welten: Deutschland und der Westen in den 1950er Jahren." In *Deutschland und die USA in der internationalen Geschichte des 20. Jahrhunderts*, edited by Manfred Berg and Philipp Gassert, 423–48. Stuttgart: Steiner.

May, Ernest R. 1991. "The American Commitment to Germany, 1949–1955." In *American Historians and the Atlantic Alliance*, edited by Lawrence S. Kaplan, 53–80. Kent, Ohio: Kent State University Press.

May, Ernest R. 1998. "America's Berlin: Heart of the Cold War." *Foreign Affairs* 77, 4 (July/August): 148–60.

May, Ernest R. and Philipp D. Zelikow, eds. 1997. *The Kennedy Tapes: Inside the White House During the Cuban Missile Crisis.* Cambridge, Mass., and London: Belknap.

Mayer, Frank A. 1994. "Adenauer and Kennedy: An Era of Distrust in German-American Relations?" *German Studies Review* 27, 1 (February): 83–104.

Mayer, Frank A. 1996. *Adenauer and Kennedy: A Study in German-American Relations, 1961–1963.* New York: St. Martin's Press.

McDougall, Walter A. 1985. *. . . the Heavens and the Earth: A Political History of the Space Age.* New York: Basic Books.

McGhee, George. 1989. *At the Creation of a New Germany: From Adenauer to Brandt. An Ambassador's Account.* New Haven, Conn.: Yale University Press.

Medick, Hans. 2002. "Mikrohistorie." In *Lexikon Geschichtswissenschaft: Hundert Grundbegriffe*, edited by Stefan Jordan, 215–18. Stuttgart: Reclam.

Meier, Christian. 1990. *The Greek Discovery of Politics*, translated by David McLintock. Cambridge, Mass.: Harvard University Press.

Meier, Christian. 1993. *The Political Art of Greek Tragedy*, translated by Andrew Webber. Baltimore, Md.: Johns Hopkins University Press.

Merseburger, Peter. 2002. *Willy Brandt 1913–1992: Die Biographie.* Stuttgart: DVA.

Meyer, Christoph. 1997. *Die deutschlandpolitische Doppelstrategie: Wilhelm Wolfgang Schütz und das Kuratorium Unteilbares Deutschland.* Landsberg am Lech: Olzog.

Meyer, Thomas. 1992. *Die Inszenierung des Scheins: Essay-Montage.* Frankfurt a. M.: Suhrkamp.

Meyer, Thomas. 1994. *Die Transformation des Politischen.* Frankfurt a. M.: Suhrkamp.

Morgan, Ted. 1999. *A Covert Life: Jay Lovestone: Communist, Anti-Communist, and Spymaster.* New York: Random House.

Mosse, George L. 1976. "Mass Politics and the Political Liturgy of Nationalism." In *Nationalism: The Nature and Evolution of an Idea*, edited by Eugene Kamenka, 38–54. New York: St. Martin's Press.

Mosse, George L. 1991. *The Nationalization of the Masses. Political Symbolism and Mass Movements in Germany from the Napoleonic Wars Through the Third Reich.* Ithaca, N.Y.: Cornell University Press.

"'Mr. President' in Berlin: Eine Darstellung d. schutzpolizeilichen Einsatzes am 26. Juni 1963." 1963. *Die Polizei* 54: 231–36.

Münger, Christof. 1999. *Ich bin ein West-Berliner: Der Wandel der amerikanischen Berlinpolitik während der Präsidentschaft John F. Kennedys.* Zürich: Forschungsstelle für Sicherheitspolitik und Konfliktanalyse, Eidgenössische Technische Hochschule.

Münger, Christof. 2003. *Kennedy, die Berliner Mauer und die Kubakrise: Die westliche Allianz in der Zerreissprobe, 1961–1963.* Paderborn: Schöningh.

Münkel, Daniela. 2004. "Als 'deutscher Kennedy' zum Sieg? Willy Brandt, die USA und die Medien." *Zeithistorische Forschungen/Studies in Contemporary History* 1 http://www.zeithistorischeforschungen.de/16126041-Muenkel-2-2004 (May 31, 2007).

Münkler, Herfried. 1990. *Odysseus und Kassandra: Politik im Mythos.* Frankfurt a. M.: Fischer.

Münkler, Herfried. 1994. *Politische Bilder, Politik der Metaphern.* Frankfurt a. M.: Fischer.

Münkler, Herfried. 1995. "Mythen-Politik. Die Nibelungen in der Weimarer Republik." In *Richard Wagner – "Der Ring des Nibelungen": Ansichten des Mythos,* edited by Udo Bermbach and Dieter Borchmeyer, 157–73. Stuttgart, Weimar: Metzler.

Naimark, Norman M. 1995. *The Russians in Germany: A History of the Soviet Zone of Occupation, 1945–1949.* Cambridge, Mass.: Belknap Press of Harvard University Press.

Nietzsche, Friedrich. 1983. "On the Uses and Disadvantages of History for Life." In *Untimely Meditations,* edited by Friedrich Nietzsche, translated by R. J. Hollingdale, 57–123. Cambridge: Cambridge University Press.

Nietzsche, Friedrich. 1984. *Vom Nutzen und Nachteil der Historie für das Leben,* edited by Michael Landmann. Zurich: Diogenes.

Nippel, Wilfried, ed. 2000. *Virtuosen der Macht. Herrschaft und Charisma von Perikles bis Mao.* Munich: Beck.

Nipperdey, Thomas. 1976. *Gesellschaft, Kultur, Theorie: Gesammelte Aufsätze zur neueren Geschichte.* Göttingen: Vandenhoeck & Ruprecht.

Nipperdey, Thomas. 1986. *Nachdenken über die deutsche Geschichte: Essays.* Munich: Beck.

Nipperdey, Thomas. 1987. "Mythos im Zeitalter der Revolution." *Geschichte in Wissenschaft und Unterricht* 38: 325–34.

Nye, Joseph S. 2004. *Soft Power: The Means to Success in World Politics.* New York: Public Affairs.

O'Donnell, Kenneth P. and David F. Powers, with Joe McCarthy. 1972. *"Johnny, We Hardly Knew Ye": Memories of John Fitzgerald Kennedy.* Boston and Toronto: Little, Brown and Co.

Osterhammel, Jürgen. 2001. "Transnationale Gesellschaftsgeschichte: Erweiterung oder Alternative." *Geschichte und Gesellschaft* 27: 464–79.

Paulmann, Johannes. 2000. *Pomp und Politik: Monarchenbegegnungen in Europa zwischen Ancien Régime und Erstem Weltkrieg.* Paderborn: Schöningh.

Paulmann, Johannes. 2002. "Peripatetische Herrschaft, Deutungskontrolle und Konsum: Zur Theatralität in der europäischen Politik vor 1914." *Geschichte und Wissenschaft im Unterricht* 53: 444–61.

Paulmann, Johannes. 2005. "Auswärtige Repräsentationen nach 1945. Zur Geschichte der deutsche Selbstdarstellung im Ausland," in *Auswärtige Repräsentationen. Deutsche Kulturdiplomatie nach 1945,* edited by Johannes Paulmann, 1–32. Cologne: Böhlau.

Poiger, Uta. 2000. *Jazz, Rock, and Rebels: Cold War Politics and American Culture in a Divided Germany.* Berkeley: University of California Press.

Presse- und Informationsamt des Landes Berlin, ed. 1963. *Ein großer Tag in der Geschichte unserer Stadt. 26. Juni 1963: John F. Kennedy in Berlin.* Berlin: Druckhaus Tempelhof.

Prowe, Diethelm. 1973. *Weltstadt in Krisen, Berlin 1949–1958.* Berlin: de Gruyter.

Prowe, Diethelm. 1976. "Die Anfänge der Brandtschen Ostpolitik in Berlin 1961–1963: Eine Untersuchung zur Endphase des Kalten Krieges." In *Aspekte deutscher Außenpolitik im 20. Jahrhundert: Aufsätze. Hans Rothfels zum Gedächtnis,* edited by Wolfgang Benz and Hermann Graml, 249–86. Stuttgart: DVA.

Prowe, Diethelm. 1985. "Der Brief Kennedys an Brandt vom 18. August 1961: Eine zentrale Quelle zur Berliner Mauer und der Entstehung der Brandtschen Ostpolitik." *Vierteljahreshefte für Zeitgeschichte* 33: 373–83.

Prowe, Diethelm. 1989. "'Ich bin ein Berliner': Kennedy, die Mauer und die 'verteidigte Insel' West-Berlin im ausgehenden Kalten Krieg im Spiegel amerikanischer Akten." In *Berlin in Geschichte und Gegenwart. Jahrbuch des Landesarchivs Berlin*, 143–67.

Prowe, Diethelm. 2004. "Berlin: Catalyst and Fault Line of German-American Relations in the Cold War." In *The United States and Germany in the Era of the Cold War, 1945–1968: A Handbook*, edited by Detlef Junker, vol. 1, 165–71. Cambridge: Cambridge University Press.

Reichel, Peter. 1991. *Der schöne Schein des Dritten Reiches: Faszination und Gewalt des Faschismus*. Munich: Hanser.

Reichstein, Andreas. 1986. "Das Bild John F. Kennedys in der westdeutschen Öffentlichkeit." *Amerikastudien* 31, 3: 325–34.

Reuter, Ernst. 1974. *Ernst Reuter: Schriften – Reden*, edited by Hans E. Hirschfeld and Hans J. Reichhardt. Vol. 3 of *Artikel – Briefe – Reden 1946 bis 1949*, compiled and edited by Hans J. Reichhardt. Berlin: Propyläen.

Reynolds, David. 1995. *Rich Relations: The American Occupation of Britain, 1942–1945*. New York: Random House.

Ribbe, Wolfgang. 1987. *Geschichte Berlins*. 2 vols. Munich: Beck.

Ribbe, Wolfgang and Jürgen Schmädecke, eds. 1990. *Berlin im Europa der Neuzeit: Ein Tagungsbericht*. Berlin and New York: de Gruyter.

Richie, Alexandra. 1998. *Faust's Metropolis: A History of Berlin*. New York: Carroll & Graf.

Ries, Henry. 1973. *Berlin vor 25 Jahren: Fotos aus der Zeit der Berliner Blockade. Ausstellung der Landesbildstelle Berlin vom 18. Mai bis 8. Juli 1973*. Berlin: Landesbildstelle.

Ries, Henry. 1998. *Berlin: Photographien 1946–1949*. Berlin: Nicolai.

Ries, Henry. 2001. *Ich war ein Berliner: Erinnerungen eines New Yorker Fotojournalisten*. Berlin: Parthas.

Risse, Thomas. 2002. "Transnational Actors and World Politics." In *Handbook of International Relations*, edited by Walter Carlsnaes, Thomas Risse, and Beth A. Simmons, 255–74. London: Sage.

Risse-Kappen, Thomas. 1995. *Cooperation Among Democracies: The European Influence on U.S. Foreign Policy*. Princeton, N.J.: Princeton University Press.

Risse-Kappen, Thomas, ed. 1995. *Bringing Transnational Relations Back In. Non-State Actors, Domestic Structures, and International Institutions*. Cambridge: Cambridge University Press.

Risse-Kappen, Thomas. 1996. "Collective Identity in a Democratic Community: The Case of NATO." In *The Culture of National Security: Norms and Identity in World Politics*, edited by Peter Katzenstein, 357–99. New York: Columbia University Press.

Russet, Bruce M. 1963. *Community and Contention: Britain and America in the Twentieth Century*. Westport, Conn.: Greenwood.

Salinger, Pierre. 1966. *With Kennedy*. Garden City, N.Y., and New York: Doubleday.

Samuel, Raphael. 1994. *Theatres of Memory*. London and New York: Verso.

Schildt, Axel. 1995. *Moderne Zeiten. Freizeit, Massenmedien und "Zeitgeist" in der Bundesrepublik der 50er Jahre.* Hamburg: Christians.

Schildt, Axel. 1998. "Der Beginn des Fernsehzeitalters: Ein neues Massenmedium setzt sich durch." In *Modernisierung im Wiederaufbau: Die westdeutsche Gesellschaft der 50er Jahre,* edited by Axel Schildt and Arnold Sywottek, 477–92. Unabridged, revised, and updated edition. Bonn: Dietz.

Schildt, Axel. 1999a. *Ankunft im Westen: Ein Essay zur Erfolgsgeschichte der Bundesrepublik.* Frankfurt a. M.: Fischer.

Schildt, Axel. 1999b. *Zwischen Abendland und Amerika. Studien zur westdeutschen Ideenlandschaft der 50er Jahre.* Munich: Oldenbourg.

Schildt, Axel. 2000. "Sind die Westdeutschen amerikanisiert worden? Zur zeitgeschichtlichen Erforschung kulturellen Transfers und seiner gesellschaftlichen Folgen nach dem Zweiten Weltkrieg." *Aus Politik und Zeitgeschichte* B 50: 3–10.

Schlesinger, Jr., Arthur M. 1965. *A Thousand Days. John F. Kennedy in the White House.* Boston: Houghton Mifflin.

Schmidt, Wolfgang. 2001. *Kalter Krieg, Koexistenz und kleine Schritte: Willy Brandt und die Deutschlandpolitik 1948–1963.* Opladen: Westdeutscher Verlag.

Schmundt-Thomas, Georg. 1992. "America's Germany: National Self and Cultural Other After World War II." PhD diss., Northwestern University.

Schneider, Ullrich. 1985. "Berlin, der Kalte Krieg und die Gründung der Freien Universität 1945–1949." *Jahrbuch für die Geschichte Mittel- und Ostdeutschlands* 34: 37–101.

Schorr, Daniel. 2001. *Staying Tuned: A Life in Journalism.* New York: Pocket Books.

Schröder, Hans-Jürgen. 2001. "Marshall-Plan-Propaganda in Berlin." In *Germany and America: Essays in Honor of Gerald R. Kleinfeld,* edited by Wolfgang-Uwe Friedrich, 146–64. New York: Berghahn.

Schulzinger, Robert D. 2002. *U.S. Diplomacy Since 1900.* 5th ed. Oxford and New York: Oxford University Press.

Schütz, Klaus. 1995. "Die Legende vom deutschen Kennedy: Willy Brandts Bundestagswahlkampf 1961." In *Westwind: Die Amerikanisierung Europas,* edited by Bernd Polster, 28–34. Cologne: DuMont.

Schwabe, Klaus, ed. 1994. *Adenauer und die USA.* Bonn: Bouvier.

Schwarz, Hans-Peter. 1983. *Die Ära Adenauer: Epochenwechsel 1957–1963.* Stuttgart and Wiesbaden: DVA/F. A. Brockhaus.

Schwarz, Hans-Peter. 1995–97. *Konrad Adenauer: A German Politician and Statesman in a Period of War, Revolution and Reconstruction.* 2 vols. Providence, R.I., and Oxford: Berghahn.

Schwartz, Thomas Alan. 1991. *America's Germany: John J. McCloy and the Federal Republic of Germany.* Cambridge, Mass., and London: Harvard University Press.

Schwartz, Thomas Alan. 1994. "Victories and Defeats in the Long Twilight Struggle: The United States and Western Europe in the 1960s." In *The Diplomacy of the Crucial Decade: American Foreign Relations during the 1960s,* edited by Diane B. Kuntz, 115–48. New York: Columbia University Press.

Schwartz, Thomas Alan. 1995. "The United States and Germany After 1945: Alliances, Transnational Relations, and the Legacy of the Cold War." *Diplomatic History* 19, 4 (Fall): 549–68.

Schwartz, Thomas Alan. 1997. "The Berlin Crisis and the Cold War." *Diplomatic History* 21, 1 (Winter): 139–48.

Searle, John R. 1995. *The Construction of Social Reality.* New York: Free Press.

Shlaim, Avi. 1983. *The United States and the Berlin Blockade 1948–1949: A Study in Crisis Decision-Making.* Berkeley: University of California Press.

Smith, Gary and Hinderk M. Emrich, eds. 1996. *Vom Nutzen des Vergessens.* Berlin: Akademie.

Smith, Helmut Walser. 2002. *The Butcher's Tale: Murder and Anti-Semitism in a German Town.* New York: W. W. Norton.

Smyser, W. R. 1999. *From Yalta to Berlin: The Cold War Struggle Over Germany.* New York: St. Martin's Griffin.

Sorensen, Theodore C. 1965. *Kennedy.* New York: Harper & Row.

Steininger, Rolf. 2001. *Der Mauerbau: Die Westmächte und Adenauer in der Berlinkrise 1958–1963.* Munich: Olzog.

Stern, Fritz. 1999. "Ernst Reuter: The Making of a Democratic Socialist." In *Dreams and Delusions: The Drama of German History*, edited by Fritz Stern, 77–96. New Haven, Conn., and London: Yale University Press.

Stivers, William. 1997. "The Incomplete Blockade: Soviet Zone Supply of West Berlin, 1948–49." *Diplomatic History* 21, 4 (Fall): 569–602.

The Story of the World Freedom Bell. n.d. [ca. 1951]. Grand Rapids, Minn.: The Herald Review.

Suhr, Heidrun. 1990. "*Fremde* in Berlin: The Outsiders' View from the Inside." In *Berlin: Culture and Metropolis*, edited by Charles Haxthausen and Heidrun Suhr, 219–42. Minneapolis: University of Minnesota Press.

Süss, Werner. 1999. "Die Bundesregierung und das Politikum der Hauptstadtfrage: Berlin – zwischen östlicher Lage und nationalem Symbol." In *Berlin. Die Hauptstadt. Vergangenheit und Zukunft einer europäischen Metropole*, edited by Werner Süss and Ralf Rytlewski, 194–234. Bonn: Bundeszentrale für politische Bildung.

Szabo, Stephen F. 2004. *Parting Ways: The Crisis in German-American Relations.* Washington, D.C.: Brookings Institute Press.

Tent, James F. 1988. *The Free University of Berlin: A Political History.* Bloomington and Indianapolis: Indiana University Press.

Thamer, Hans-Ulrich. 1986. *Verführung und Gewalt: Deutschland 1933–1945.* Berlin: Siedler.

Thamer, Hans-Ulrich. 2000. "Politische Rituale und politische Kultur im Europa des 20. Jahrhunderts." *Jahrbuch für Europäische Geschichte* 1: 79–98.

Thayer, Charles W. 1959. "Berlin's Willy Brandt: Calm Man in a Nervous Place." *Harper's Magazine* (February): 50–56.

Turner, Henry A. 1992. *Germany From Partition to Reunification.* New Haven, Conn.: Yale University Press.

Tusa, Ann and John Tusa. 1998. *The Berlin Airlift.* Staplehurst: Spellmount.

U.S. Information Service. n.d. [ca. 1957] *Deutsch-Amerikanische Zusammenarbeit in West-Berlin: Die amerikanische Wirtschaftshilfe in der Zeit von 1949 bis 1956.* Bad Godesberg: U.S. Information Service.

Vogtmeier, Andreas. 1996. *Egon Bahr und die deutsche Frage: Zur Entwicklung der sozialdemokratischen Ost- und Deutschlandpolitik vom Kriegsende bis zur Vereinigung.* Bonn: Dietz.

Voigt, Karsten. 2000. "Begründung eines neuen Atlantizismus: Von Partnerschaft zu euroatlantischer Gemeinschaft." *Internationale Politik* 3: 3–10.

Vondung, Klaus. 1971. *Magie und Manipulation: Ideologischer Kult und politische Religion des Nationalsozialismus*. Göttingen: Vandenhoeck & Ruprecht.

Vostell, Wolf. 1970. *Happening & Leben*. Neuwied: Luchterhand.

Wallace, Mike. 1996. *Mickey Mouse History and Other Essays on American Memory*. Philadelphia: Temple University Press.

Walzer, Michael. 1967. "On the Role of Symbolism in Political Thought." *Political Science Quarterly* 82, 2 (June): 191–204.

Weber, Max. 1976. *Wirtschaft und Gesellschaft: Grundriss der verstehenden Soziologie*, edited by Johannes Winckelmann. 5th rev. ed. Tübingen: Siebeck.

Weber, Max. 1978. *Economy and Society: An Outline of Interpretive Sociology*, edited by Guenther Roth and Claus Wittich. 2 vols. Berkeley and London: University of California Press.

Weber, Max. 1988. *Gesammelte Aufsätz zur Wissenschaftslehre*, edited by Johannes Winckelmann. 7th ed. Tübingen: UTB.

Weidenfeld, Werner. 2000. "Erneuerung der transatlantischen Beziehungen." *Internationale Politik* 3: 1.

Wetzlaugk, Udo. 1988. *Die Alliierten in Berlin*. Berlin: Arno Spitz.

Wilentz, Sean, ed. 1985. *Rites of Power: Symbolism, Ritual, and Politics Since the Middle Ages*. Philadelphia: University of Philadelphia Press.

Windt, Theodore Otto, Jr. 1990. *Presidents and Protesters: Political Rhetoric in the 1960s*. Tuscaloosa and London: University of Alabama Press.

Winkler, Heinrich August. 2006. *Germany, the Long Road West*. Translated by Alexander J. Sager. Oxford and New York: Oxford University Press.

Wolfrum, Edgar. 1999. *Geschichtspolitik in der Bundesrepublik Deutschland: Der Weg zur bundesrepublikanischen Erinnerung 1948–1990*. Darmstadt: Wissenschaftliche Buchgesellschaft.

Zimmermann, Hubert. 2002. *Money and Security: Troops, Monetary Policy and West Germany's Relations with the United States and Britain, 1950–1971*. Cambridge: Cambridge University Press.

Index